ROMANIA

Silistra

Ruse

Dobrich

Razgrad

Byala

Kavarna

Novi Pazar

Shumen

Devnya

Varna

Veliko Tûrnovo

Omurtag

BLACK
SEA COAST

Sliven

Aytos

Nesebûr

Yambol

Burgas

Stara Zagora

Sozopol

Galabovo

Elhovo

Tsarevo

Haskovo

Svilengrad

TURKEY

Black
Sea

0 kilometres   50

0 miles   50

D0413653

BU

EYEWITNESS TRAVEL

BULGARIA

Main Contributor **Jonathan Bousfield, Matt Willis**

LONDON, NEW YORK,
MELBOURNE, MUNICH AND DELHI
www.dk.com

Produced by Hachette Livre Polska Sp. z o.o.

Main Contributors Jonathan Bousfield, Matt Willis

Senior Graphic Designer Paweł Pasternak
Graphic Designer Paweł Kamiński
Senior Editor Agnieszka Trzebska-Cwalina
Editor Anetta Radziszewska
Photographers Dorota and Mariusz Jarymowicz,
Mirek Osip, Piotr Ostrowski
Illustrators Michał Burkiewicz, Dorota Jarymowicz,
Paweł Marczak, Joanna Sitarek
Cartographer Magda Polak

Dorling Kindersley Limited
List Managers Vivien Antwi, Christine Stroyan
Managing Art Editor Jane Ewart
Senior Editor Hugh Thompson
Designer Kate Leonard
Editor Lucilla Watson
Factchecker Petya Milkova
DTP Natasha Lu, Jamie McNeill
Production Linda Dare

Printed in Malaysia by Vivar Printing Sdn. Bhd.

First published in the UK in 2008 by Dorling Kindersley Limited
80 Strand, London WC2R 0RL

14 15 16 17 10 9 8 7 6 5 4 3 2 1

Reprinted with revisions 2011, 2014

Copyright 2008, 2014 © Dorling Kindersley Limited, London
A Penguin Random House Company

ISBN 978 1 40932 917 6

80 Strand, London, WC2R 0RL, UK, or email: travelguides@dk.com.

Front cover main image: Aerial view of the Black Sea coast

◀ Haramia peak at sunset, Rila National Park

Limestone cliffs near Kamen Briag, on the
Black Sea coast

Contents

Church of the Archangels Michael and
Gabriel at Arbanasi

Raikova Kŭshta, a 19th-century
house-museum in Tryavna

Houses on the cliffside at Veliko Tŭrnovo, on
the Yantra River

Sculpture of a lion at the Tomb of the
Unknown Soldier in Sofia

Aleksandŭr Nevski Memorial Church in Sofia, the
city's finest building

HOW TO USE THIS GUIDE

This travel guide helps you to get the most from your visit to Bulgaria, providing detailed practical information as well as expert recommendations. *Introducing Bulgaria* maps the whole country and sets it in its historical and cultural context. The first section, on *Sofia*, gives an overview of the capital's main attractions. Bulgaria's regions are charted in the *Area by Area* section,

which covers all the important towns, cities and places around the country, with photographs, maps and illustrations. Details of hotels, restaurants, shops and markets, entertainment and sports are found in *Travellers' Needs*, while the *Survival Guide* contains advice on everything from medical services and public transport to personal safety.

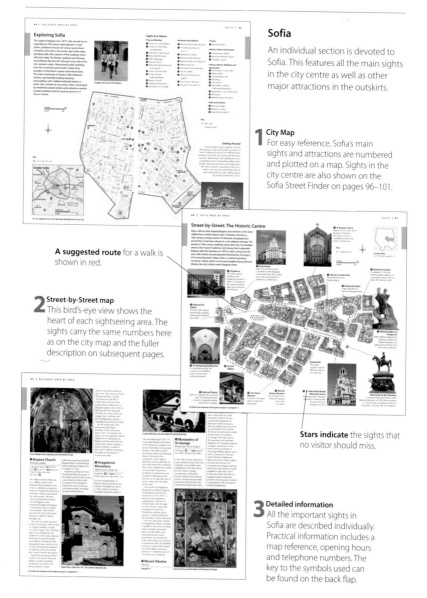

Sofia

An individual section is devoted to Sofia. This features all the main sights in the city centre as well as other major attractions in the outskirts.

1 City Map
For easy reference, Sofia's main sights and attractions are numbered and plotted on a map. Sights in the city centre are also shown on the Sofia Street Finder on pages 96–101.

A suggested route for a walk is shown in red.

2 Street-by-Street map
This bird's-eye view shows the heart of each sightseeing area. The sights carry the same numbers here as on the city map and the fuller description on subsequent pages.

Stars indicate the sights that no visitor should miss.

3 Detailed information
All the important sights in Sofia are described individually. Practical information includes a map reference, opening hours and telephone numbers. The key to the symbols used can be found on the back flap.

SOUTHERN BULGARIA

From December to April, most of this mountainous region is buried beneath thick snow. But the rest of the year it is an oasis of lush greenery and dense forests. The country's most spectacular scenery and most varied wildlife can be discovered here, and the architecture and folklore of this rugged landscape offer a fascinating insight into an intriguing and somewhat remote part of Bulgaria.

The highest peaks in the eastern Balkans rise in the Rila and Pirin mountain ranges. Both are national parks and both contain a great variety of flora and fauna, including wolves, bears, and many endemic plants. The Rhodopes, which cover a much greater area, are a largely undeveloped wilderness that, towards the east, tails off into the tobacco-growing Plains of Thrace. For centuries this area was inhabited by much of Bulgaria's Turkish community. In fact Panaʹeldhte, first roads discovered here show that human habitation of the region goes back 40,000 years. Thracians later settled in the area in large numbers. Smolyan's History Museum gives a superb overview of the region's past.

The Ottomans were largely tolerant of their Christian subjects, but there were

isolated campaigns to force Bulgarians to adopt the Islamic faith. A small number of Bulgarians found refuge in the Rhodope Mountains, where they established villages that remained free of Turkish influence. Their untainted medieval Bulgarian language, music, costumes and customs served as a model for the National Revival movement, which was so influential in the 19th century.

Two great monasteries, Rila and Bachkovo, were also established in the Rhodopes. The monks kept Bulgarian heritage alive by preserving and copying the ancient manuscripts for the plundered Bulgarian kingdoms. These monasteries became a focus of the National Revival movement.

Bulgaria Area by Area

The coloured areas shown on the map on the book's inside front cover show the five main sightseeing regions, into which Bulgaria has been divided. Each is covered in a full chapter in Bulgaria Area by Area *(see pp58–9)*. The most interesting towns and places to visit are numbered on Regional Maps throughout the book.

1 Introduction

The landscape, history and character of each region are portrayed here, with a description of how the area has developed over the centuries and what it offers to visitors today.

2 Regional Map

This shows the road network and gives an illustrated overview of the whole area. All interesting places to visit are numbered and there are also useful tips on getting around the region by road or train.

Each area of Bulgaria can be quickly identified by the colour coding on the inside front cover.

Sights at a Glance shows all sights that are covered in the chapter.

3 Major sights

Historic buildings are dissected to reveal their interiors; museums and galleries have colour-coded floorplans to help you find the most important exhibits.

The Visitors' Checklist gives all the practical information needed to plan your visit.

4 Detailed information to major towns

An introduction covers the history, character and geography of the town. The main sights are described individually and plotted on a Town Map.

A Town Map shows the location of all the sights described in the text.

INTRODUCING BULGARIA

DISCOVERING BULGARIA

The following itineraries have been designed to take in as many of Bulgaria's highlights as possible, while keeping cross-country travel as manageable as possible. First comes a two-day tour of the country's capital, Sofia; next are three regional tours, each lasting seven days. The first of the seven-day tours covers Northern and Central Bulgaria, a fascinating mix of old towns, archaeological treasures and unspoiled nature. Next comes Southern Bulgaria, with its heritage and dramatic mountain scenery. Finally, a seven-day tour of the Black Sea introduces a cavalcade of sandy beaches and vibrant Riviera-town resorts. Extra suggestions are provided for those who want to extend their trip to eight–nine days. Pick, combine and follow your choice of tour, or simply dip in and out and be inspired.

Rila National Park
One of the many lakes in the Rila National Park, where Bulgaria's highest peaks tower above glacial lakes and alpine meadows.

Key

— A Week in Southern Bulgaria

— A Week in Northern and Central Bulgaria

— A Week on the Black Sea

A Week in Southern Bulgaria

- Spend a day hiking in the **Rila National Park**.

- Enjoy the stunning frescoes and courtyards of the imposing **Rila Monastery**.

- Discover the historic town of **Bansko**, gateway to the imperious mountains of the **Pirin National Park**.

- Explore the ancient wine-producing village of **Melnik**, surrounded by strange sandstone pyramids.

- Admire the quaint villages of the **Rhodopes** region.

- Visit mountain-fringed **Smolyan** and the medieval monastery of **Bachkovo**.

- Revel in **Plovdiv**, home to a host of Roman, Ottoman and 19th-century Bulgarian architectural marvels.

0 kilometres 50

0 miles 50

◀ Early 19th-century illustration of a Bulgarian village on the Danube

A Week in Northern and Central Bulgaria

- Explore the mountain scenery of the **Iskûr Gorge** and the **Vratsata Gorge**.

- Visit the quaint, historic town of **Teteven**.

- Enjoy the war museums of **Pleven** before pressing on to the elegant Danubian port of **Ruse**.

- See the unique wetlands of **Lake Sreburna** before delving into the Thracian tombs at **Sveshtari**.

- Discover the impressive early-medieval ruins at **Shumen, Madara** and **Veliki Preslav**.

- Admire the medieval capital **Veliko Tûrnovo**, before strolling along the cobbled streets of **Arbanasi**.

- Marvel at the remnants of Thracian funerary culture in the **Valley of the Thracian Kings**.

Veliko Tûrnovo
Veliko Tûrnovo is Bulgaria's greatest medieval capitals.

A Week on the Black Sea

- Visit the buzzing resort town of **Varna**.

- See the eccentric rock formations of the **Stone Forest** and the sunken forests of **Kamchiya Nature Reserve**.

- Tour the cliffs, lighthouses and fishing villages of Bulgaria's northern coast.

- Discover the picturesque peninsula town of **Nesebûr**.

- Enjoy a day in **Burgas**, the laid-back capital of the southern coast.

- Explore the seaside town of **Sozopol** with its traditional architecture and sandy beach.

- Rove the golden beaches of Bulgaria's southern coast.

Varna
A stunning stretch of beach in the holiday town of Varna.

The Church of Sveta Petka Samardzhiiska, Sofia

Two Days in Sofia

Few capitals bear the imprint of history as clearly as Sofia.

- **Arriving** Sofia Airport is 10 km (6 miles) east of the city. It takes about 30 minutes to get to the centre by bus or taxi.
- **Transport** Tram and bus routes can be confusing. Taxis are cheap and the best way of getting around.

Day 1

Morning Central Sofia is a fascinating historical mishmash. Start the morning at the **Rotunda of Sveti Georgi** (p69), the late Roman/early Byzantine church hidden behind the Sheraton Hotel. From here it's a short walk to the glorious 16th-century **Banya Bashi Mosque** (p69), the **Art-Nouveau** Synagogue (p70) and the red-brick **Market Hall** (p70), together forming an eclectic architectural ensemble. Hidden in a pedestrian passageway near the Serdika metro station, the tiny **Church of Sveta Petka Samardzhiiska** (p68) provides another echo of Sofia's rich and complex past. An hour spent in the small but superbly presented **Archaeological Museum** (p72) will provide you

with a thorough grounding in ancient Thracian and medieval Bulgarian art and culture.

Afternoon The nearby **National Art Gallery** (p74) showcases the best of Bulgaria's 19th- and 20th-century painters. Walk in the fountain-splashed City Garden, overlooked by the Neo-Classical **National Theatre** (p85), before proceeding to admire the vibrantly decorated **Russian Church** (p75) and the golden-domed **Aleksandûr Nevski Memorial Church** (p76). The **Slaveykov Square** book market (p86) is one of the more dynamic downtown shopping areas. From here it's a short walk to the **NDK Arts Centre** (p87), fronted by a large park full of alfresco cafés. If you have the energy for more,

Banya Bashi Mosque in central Sofia, built in the 16th-century

head for **Borisova Gradina** (p84), a large park filled with meadows, flower beds and extensive woodland.

Day 2

Morning If the weather is good for hiking, base your day around **Mount Vitosha** (p92), the smooth topped mountain that looms above the city to the south. The winter skiing and summer hiking resort of Aleko, near the summit, is the perfect starting point for nature walks on the grassy plateau that crowns the mountain. Nearby Zlatni Mostove (Golden Bridges) with its boulder-strewn landscapes and deep forests, is a popular picnic spot. If the weather is not favourable for outdoor exploration, head for the **Military Museum** (p80) to the east of the city centre, with its captivating collection of 20th-century uniforms and Cold War-era military hardware.

Afternoon There are two major sights at the foot of Mount Vitosha, in Sofia's southern suburb of Boyana. The **Boyana Church** (p90), a medieval architectural jewel decked out in UNESCO-protected frescoes and the **National History Museum** (p88), whose array of exhibits covers prehistory, classical Greece and the golden treasures of ancient Thrace.

For practical information on travelling around Bulgaria, see pp262–9

A Week in Northern and Central Bulgaria

- **Arriving** Arrive and depart from Sofia Airport.

- **Transport** Trains and buses can be used to travel between the main towns and cities but a car is essential if you want to enjoy this region to the full.

Day 1: Iskûr and Vratsa gorges

Head north from Sofia through the **Iskûr Gorge** *(p188)*, a narrow valley edged by dramatic limestone cliffs. There are myriad places in the gorge where you can soak up the scenery. Arrive at the pleasant town of Vratsa and stroll into the nearby **Vratsata Gorge** *(pp186–7)*, edged by sheer rock formations.

> **To extend your trip...**
> Spend two days exploring the extreme northwestern corner of Bulgaria, home to the incredible rock pillars of the **Belogradchik** region *(p185)*, the prehistoric paintings of the mystical **Magura Cave** *(p184)*, and the Danube-hugging fortress town of **Vidin** *(p184)*.

Day 2: Teteven and monasteries

Continue east through the foothills of the Balkan Mountains towards the quaint market town of **Teteven** *(p152)*, starting point for a side-trip to the hilltop-hugging **Glozhene Monastery** *(p152)*. Proceed to the historic town of **Troyan** *(p153)*, known for its age-old ceramics industry, before taking the road to **Troyan Monastery** *(p153)*, home to some of Bulgaria's most beautifully decorated churches and cloisters.

Day 3: Pleven to Ruse

North of Troyan, the city of **Pleven** *(p189)* was the scene of a famous siege during the Russo-Turkish War of 1877, an event that forms the focus of several absorbing museums. Head northeast towards the valley of the **Rusenski Lom** *(p192)*, an unspoiled conservation area overlooked by spectacular medieval rock-carved monasteries. Spend the night in **Ruse** *(p190)*, an elegant town on the banks of the Danube.

Day 4: Silistra to Sveshtari

Head east along the Danube to the historical fortress town of **Silistra** *(p196)*, pausing en route to enjoy the reed-beds and birdlife of the marshy **Lake Sreburna** *(p196)*. Venture south across the Ludogorie plateau to **Sveshtari** *(p193)*, site of a world-famous Thracian tomb. East of Sveshtari, the city of **Shumen** *(p196)* is the best place to spend the night.

Day 5: Shumen

Shumen is a good base from which to visit the early medieval rock sculptures at **Madara** *(p197)* and the former royal capital of **Veliki Preslav** *(p197)*. Save some time for Shumen, which boasts of an enchanting hilltop fortress, a sublimely beautiful mosque and a café-filled pedestrianized centre.

Day 6: Veliko Tûrnovo

The greatest of Bulgaria's medieval capitals, **Veliko Tûrnovo** *(p160)*, deserves to be the main focus of at least one day of your tour. Tûrnovo's magnificient hilltop fortress, medieval churches and cobbled alleys can soak up a day's worth

Troyan Monastery in the historic town of Troyan

of sightseeing time. Located on a hill above the city is the perfectly-preserved 19th-century village of **Arbanasi** *(p166)*, with a wealth of traditional architecture. Get back to Veliko Tûrnovo in time for the evening *son-et-lumiere* show, in which the fortress is dramatically bathed in light.

Day 7: Valleys and highlands

South of Veliko Tûrnovo lies **Kazanlûk** *(p170)*, the main town of Bulgaria's Valley of the Roses. Just outside Kazanlûk, the **Valley of the Thracian Kings** *(p171)* is home to a compelling collection of ancient tombs. Heading east towards Sofia, the highland village of **Koprivshtitsa** *(p176)* has traditional 19th-century houses, and the provision of lovely B&B accommodation makes it a perfect place to spend the night.

Trapezitsa Hill as viewed from Tsarevets Hill, Veliko Tûrnovo

A Week in Southern Bulgaria

- **Airports** Arrive and depart from Sofia Airport.
- **Transport** Public transport between Sofia and Plovdiv is quick and cheap, although a private car is essential to access other places on this tour.

The ancient village of Melnik, surrounded by strange sandstone pyramids

Day 1: Rila National Park
Leave Sofia for the former royal mountain resort of **Borovets** (p111), the ideal base-camp from which to explore the well-marked hiking trails of **Rila National Park** (pp108–9), where Bulgaria's highest peaks tower above glacial lakes and alpine meadows.

Day 2: Struma Valley to Melnik
Head west through the Rila foothills to the Struma valley, and take the scenic mountain-fringed road to **Rila Monastery**

(pp112–113), a centre of arts and scholarship in the 19th-century. Pause in the university town of **Blagoevgrad** (p118), home to a charming old quarter and lively cafés, before pressing on south to the wine-producing village of Melnik and its cosy B&Bs.

Day 3: Melnik
Explore the narrow streets of **Melnik** (p120), a former trading town that has shrunk to the size of a tiny village. If it's not too hot, take a stroll among the pyramid-like rock formations surrounding the village, or take the 5 km (3 miles) trip to **Rozhen Monastery** (p119), another of Bulgaria's historic foundations.

Day 4: Rhodope region
Heading east from Melnik across the southern spur of the Pirin mountains brings you to the western foothills of the Rhodopes, a region studded with quaint villages. The stone-built highland settlement of **Kovachevitsa** (p129) is worth a detour, or press on eastward to the pine-covered central Rhodopes to visit the stalagtite-filled **Yagodina Cave** (p133) and the astounding **Trigrad Gorge** (p133). **Shiroka Lûka** (p131) is unarguably the prettiest of the traditional Rhodope villages and has plenty of atmospheric accommodation.

Day 5: Shirkoa Lûka to Plovdiv
East of Shiroka Lûka, **Smolyan** (p134) is the main town of the Rhodope range, starting point

Plovdiv, home to Roman and 19th-century Bulgarian monuments

of a scenic mountain road that heads north through the Pamporovo skiing region. Spend the afternoon looking around **Bachkovo Monastery** (p146) before heading to **Plovdiv** (p138).

Day 6: Plovdiv
A whole day can be spent in Plovdiv, where Roman, Ottoman and restored 19th-century Bulgarian monuments are crowded together in a tight maze of alleys. With restaurants and cafés dotting the streets, nightlife can be more enjoyable here than in Sofia.

Day 7: Rhodopes to Bansko
Take to the by-roads of the northern Rhodopes in a scenic drive northwest to **Bansko** (p122), a beautifully-preserved 19th-century town that serves both as a ski resort and gateway to the **Pirin National Park** (p126), where steep granite peaks overlook pine forests and meadows. Consider a side-trip to **Dobûrsko** (p124), site of a beautiful 17th-century church. After an overnight stay in one of Bansko's many family-run hotels, it's a short drive back to Sofia.

> **To extend your trip…**
> Use **Kûrdzhali** (p144) as a base to visit astounding rock formations such as the **Stone Wedding** and the **Stone Mushrooms** (both p145). Revel in the archaeological sites at **Perperikon** and **Tatul** (both p145).

Seven Lakes region in the Rila Mountains

For practical information on travelling around Bulgaria, see pp262–9

A Week on the Black Sea

- **Airports** Arrive at Varna airport and depart from Burgas airport.
- **Transport** In summer it is possible to travel between the main coastal resorts in public buses and minibuses, although a car can provide more flexibility and is recommended.

Day 1: Varna

Spend the day exploring **Varna** *(p202)*, the largest city on the Bulgarian coast and a vivacious holiday town in summers. An antiquity-packed archaeological museum and the remains of a Roman bath complex are among the many worthwhile sights. Follow the café-lined main street to the lush Sea Gardens, which overlook a lively stretch of beach.

Day 2: Stone Forest, Kamchiya Nature Reserve

Varna is a good base from which to explore the surrounding countryside. Head inland to admire the strange rock pillars known as the **Stone Forest** *(p209)*, before detouring southwards to take a boat trip in the coastal wetlands of the **Kamchiya Nature Reserve** *(p209)*. Just north of the city, relax on the beach at the resort complex of **Sveti Konstantin** *(p208)*.

Day 3: Villages north of Varna

Spend a day touring the rocky, cliff-scarred coast north of Varna, stopping at **Kaliakra** *(p207)*, a spectacular cape with a fortress at its tip. Of the many sleepy fishing villages further north, **Krapets** *(p206)* has a good beach, while **Durankulak** *(p206)* is famous for its nearby lake rich in fish and birdlife. You can stay overnight in **Krapets** *(p206)*, or return to Varna.

Day 4: Coast road to Nesebûr

Follow the coastal road south of Varna to reach **Obzor**

Strange rock formations at the Stone Forest near Varna

(p209), a developing seaside town with a white-sand beach. Continue southwards and pause at **Nesebûr** *(p212)*, a picturesque peninsula town that boasts a rich collection of medieval churches, pleasant seafood restaurants and some good accommodation options.

Day 5: Sozopol and around

Follow the road south round the Bay of Burgas to the former fishing village of **Sozopol** *(p215)*, and spend the day strolling its narrow streets lined with half-timbered houses. Savour Sozopol's town beach or head to Dyuni, a wonderful strip of beach just to the south. If you are not in beach-combing mood, consider a boat trip on the reed-fringed **Ropotamo** River *(p215)*.

View of the Black Sea as seen from a city park in Burgas

Day 6: Beaches near Sozopol

The coast south of Sozopol is characterized by a string of sandy bays, perfect for beach-hopping. **Lozenets** *(p216)* boasts a smooth stretch of sand, kite-surfing opportunities and a good selection of bars and restaurants. The most pristine beaches are at **Sinemorets** *(p216)*, right on the Bulgarian-Turkish border. Use Sozopol as a base for exploring this stretch of coast.

Day 7: Burgas

Head back north to Burgas for a final day, exploring the most relaxed and welcoming of Bulgarian cities. The flower-bedded city centre is perfect for extended strolling, while the beachside Sea Gardens are a wonderful place to unwind. Head for nearby **Lake Poda** *(p214)* for a spot of birdwatching, or enjoy the unsullied beaches at **Pomorie** just to the north *(p214)*.

To extend your trip...

Inland from Lozenets and Sinemorets, the forests and villages of **Strandzha Nature Park** *(p217)* merit a 1-2 day excursion. The small settlement of Brûshlyan features a well-preserved collection of traditional wooden houses, while the village of Bûlgari celebrates St Konstantin and St Elena's Day with displays of fire-dancing.

Putting Bulgaria on the Map

Located in the southeastern corner of Europe, Bulgaria covers an area of 110,550 sq km (42,685 sq miles). It is bordered by Turkey, Greece, Macedonia, Serbia and Romania, with the Black Sea on its eastern side and the Danube as much of its northern border. The rugged Stara Planina, or Balkan range, runs across central Bulgaria from west to east, with the higher Rila and Pirin massifs to the southwest, and the Rhodope mountains to the south. Sofia, the capital, is Bulgaria's largest city, and the hub of the country's political, economic and cultural life.

See inset map, right

Key

═══ Motorway

= = Motorway under construction

═══ Major road

─── Other road

─── Railway

═══ International border

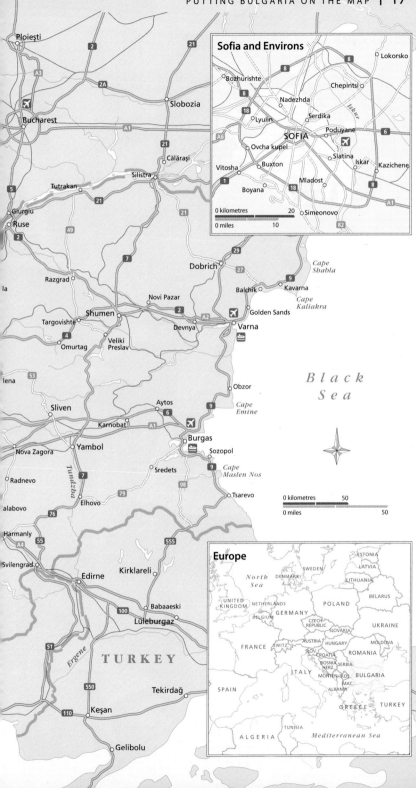

Sofia and Environs

Lokorsko
Bozhurishte
Chepintsi
Nadezhda
Lyulin
Serdika
SOFIA
Poduyane
Ovcha kupel
Slatina
Iskar
Kazichene
Vitosha
Buxton
Mladost
Boyana
Simeonovo

0 kilometres 20
0 miles 10

Ploieşti
Slobozia
Bucharest
Călăraşi
Silistra
Tutrakan
Giurgiu
Ruse
Razgrad
Dobrich
Cape Shabla
Novi Pazar
Balchik
Kavarna
Cape Kaliakra
Shumen
Targovishte
Devnya
Golden Sands
Varna
Omurtag
Veliki Preslav
B l a c k
S e a
Iena
Obzor
Sliven
Aytos
Cape Emine
Karnobat
Nova Zagora
Yambol
Burgas
Sozopol
Radnevo
Sredets
Tundzha
Cape Maslen Nos
alabovo
Elhovo
Tsarevo
Harmanly
Svilengrad
Edirne
Kirklareli
0 kilometres 50
0 miles 50
Babaaeski
Lüleburgaz
Ergene
T U R K E Y
Erigene
Tekirdağ
Keşan
Gelibulu

Europe

North Sea
ESTONIA
SWEDEN
LATVIA
DENMARK
LITHUANIA
UNITED KINGDOM
NETHERLANDS
BELARUS
POLAND
BELGIUM
GERMANY
CZECH REPUBLIC
UKRAINE
SLOVAKIA
FRANCE
SWITZ.
AUSTRIA
HUNGARY
MOLDOVA
SLOV.
CROATIA
ROMANIA
BOSNIA HERZ.
SERBIA
ITALY
MONTEN. KOS.
BULGARIA
MAC.
ALBANIA
SPAIN
GREECE
TURKEY
ALGERIA
TUNISIA
Mediterranean Sea

A PORTRAIT OF BULGARIA

A combination of stunning scenery and Mediterranean climate have made Bulgaria one of Europe's best-loved tourist destinations. Attention has focused on the Black Sea beaches and high-altitude winter resorts, but the sheer diversity of natural beauty spots, archaeological sites and picture-postcard villages ensures that there is much more here to stir the traveller's imagination.

Heritage plays a highly visible role in Bulgarian society, with medieval churches and monasteries drawing a steady stream of pilgrims, and folk festivals retaining an important position in rural life. Such traditions provide a contrast with contemporary Bulgaria's rapid transformation into a modern European society. Recent decades have witnessed the end of Communism, the birth of a market economy, and the country's integration into the European Union. This roller coaster of social change makes today's Bulgaria one of Europe's most vibrant and invigorating destinations.

Lined with long sandy beaches, Bulgaria's Black Sea coast is the country's most obviously captivating natural attribute – with purpose-built resorts such as Sunny Beach and Golden Sands alternating with historic ports such as Nesebûr and Sozopol.

Inland, some two-thirds of Bulgaria's territory is made up of hills and mountains. This vast area of wilderness provides plenty of scope for active holidays, whether hiking in summer or skiing in winter. The natural beauty and geographical isolation of the highland regions is one reason why so many monasteries were founded here in the Middle Ages. Rich in luminous icons and vibrant frescoes, monasteries such as Rila and Bachkovo shelter communities that preserve the spiritual heritage of the Bulgarian Orthodox Church. In many mountain villages, a traditional way of life, often based on sheep- or

Golden Sands, a popular purpose-built resort on the Black Sea coast

◀ Dancer wearing an elaborate colourful costume for a Kukeri procession

A glacial lake set in the extraordinary wild and remote Rila Mountains of southwestern Bulgaria

goat-farming, also survives. Settlements in the Pirin and Rhodope mountains still boast a wealth of 19th-century houses built in wood or stone. Some of these have opened their doors to tourists as rustic bed-and-breakfast establishments, giving these once-isolated- communities a new lease of life.

Bulgaria's Biggest Cities

Bulgaria's key cities have very different personalities. Sofia, the capital, grew out of virtually nothing in the late 19th century, its boulevards laid out in imitation of those of Paris and Vienna. Vastly expanded during the Communist period, when huge housing estates were constructed for a growing population, Sofia is currently undergoing an even more dramatic metamorphosis into a metropolis of shopping malls, multiplex cinemas and glass-and-steel business hotels. Plovdiv, Bulgaria's second city, could not be more different, with a historic centre of cobbled alleys and the Oriental-flavoured mansions of wealthy Balkan trading dynasties. Bulgaria's summer capital is Varna, a brash riviera town boasting a lively nightlife and a prestigious programme of major cultural festivals. The centrally located city of Veliko Tûrnovo, with its dramatic castle ruins set above a river gorge, is a lasting monument to the glories of Bulgaria's medieval tsars. Ruse is perhaps Bulgaria's most individual city, a Danube port that grew wealthy in the 19th century and is still full of Austrianate architecture. Blagoevgrad, south of Sofia, is a lively student town that offers a very different experience to the country's other major cities.

Sofia, Bulgaria's busy but beautiful capital

Meeting Point of Civilizations

Wherever you are in the country you will find the remnants of former civilizations. The Thracians ruled the country until they were conquered by the Romans in the 1st century BC. Thracian burial sites at Sveshtari, Kazanlûk and Starosel feature exquisite stone tombs, and deserve a place on every traveller's itinerary. Intricate Thracian jewellery also constitutes a major attraction of Bulgaria's museums.

The Thracians were superseded by the Romans, whose legacy is still visible in the ruined city of Nikopolis ad Istrum, the bathhouse complex in Varna, and in many other locations. The arrival of the Bulgars in the 7th century led to the construction of huge fortresses at Pliska and Preslav, whose ruins still make a dramatic impression. The medieval Bulgarian fortresses at Veliko Tûrnovo, Shumen and Cherven are more awe-inspiring still. Medieval Bulgaria was conquered by the Ottoman Turks, who in their turn left a significant cultural and architectural imprint on the country. Surviving mosques in towns and cities such as Sofia, Shumen and Plovdiv are among the most

Roman theatre in Plovdiv, built in the 2nd century AD

beautiful in the Balkans. During nearly five centuries of Ottoman rule, Bulgarian culture and traditions were preserved in the monasteries. A 19th-century upsurge in traditional values known as the National Revival led to the renovation of the great monasteries such as Rila, Troyan and Bachkovo, each of which was covered in glorious frescoes. Merchants in prosperous trading towns like Bansko, Koprivshtitsa and Tryavna built beautiful mansions using traditional crafts. Many of these mansions are open to visitors today.

Modernity and Tradition

One of Bulgaria's immediately visible peculiarities is that, unlike the rest of Europe, locals shake their heads when they say "yes", and nod when they mean "no". Such body language is symbolic of the way in which the country has remained remarkably resilient to outside influences and has preserved much of its folk culture. Although 21st-century Bulgaria is an urbanized, skilled society, modernity coexists with much that is traditional. Goatherds graze flocks beside highways; donkeys are a viable, efficient alternative to tractors; and traditional foodstuffs play an important part in the Bulgarian lifestyle. Many people still buy their fruit and vegetables from open-air markets, preserving a taste for fresh, local

Traditional country house in Melnik

Priest at a Bulgarian Orthodox Church service

produce. Knowledge of natural medicine is still widespread, and herbal pharmacies a feature of every high street. Folk festivals still mark the social calendar, ensuring that traditional songs, dances and costumes remain firmly rooted in the contemporary cultural mainstream. Even Bulgarian pop music is more in tune with the melodies and rhythms of the Orient than with anything from the West.

People and Society

Bulgaria has a population of around 7.5 million. The majority of its inhabitants are Christian Orthodox Bulgarians, descended from the Slav tribes who settled in the eastern Balkans in the 6th century. They speak a language related to Serbian, Croatian and Slovene, and more distantly to Czech, Polish and Russian. Like some other Orthodox Slav nations, they use the Cyrillic alphabet – although plenty of young Bulgarians use Latin script for text messages or emails.

Just below 10 per cent of the population are Muslim descendants of Turks who settled here in the late Middle Ages, or ethnic Bulgarians who converted to Islam under the Ottoman occupation. Bulgaria's Turks were persecuted in the 1980s, but now enjoy equal rights and representation in parliament.

Bulgaria is also home to between 300,000 and 450,000 Roma, or gypsies, who are split roughly half-and-half between the Christian and Islamic faiths. The Roma have been largely excluded from the social mainstream, and the question of how to improve their social position is a recurring theme of Bulgarian politics.

A largely agricultural country, Bulgaria is a major producer of wine, tobacco,

Traditional mule carts among vineyards in the Gavrailovo district near Sliven, central Bulgaria

Visitors at a seafront restaurant on the Black Sea coast

fruit, vegetables and grain. It also supplies the world's cosmetics industry with rose oil, from plantations in the aptly-named Valley of Roses in central Bulgaria.

Recent decades have seen Bulgaria buffeted by social and economic change. Under the Communist regime, the Bulgarian people became accustomed to regular employment, low housing costs, free education and health care. The collapse of the Communist system in 1989 removed many of these certainties. Trade with Soviet Russia, the main export market, disappeared overnight. The conflicts in Yugoslavia disrupted transport routes to central Europe. Profitable industries were driven towards bankruptcy, and people lost their right to job security and adequate state pensions. Provincial towns suffered serious depopulation as young people left to find work in the cities. Between 1990 and 2005, an estimated 800,000 people, mostly young and well-qualified, went abroad in search of better jobs. These are people Bulgaria can ill afford to lose; its birth rate is among the lowest in Europe, and the population will decline further unless current demographic trends are reversed.

Young rose-petal picker dressed in traditional costume

Present-day Bulgaria

The last decade has witnessed dramatic changes in Bulgaria's political and economic fortunes. Bulgaria's accession to the European Union in January 2007 led to a huge increase in foreign investment. Government corruption, a major issue in the 1990s, was brought under a measure of control. Most importantly, the fruits of economic growth began to trickle down to ordinary Bulgarians, whose standards of living finally began to rise.

One of these success stories has been the tourist industry. The Bulgarian Black Sea coast was a big draw for Eastern European holidaymakers from the 1960s onwards, and the tourist industry has gone from strength to strength with Bulgaria's discovery by the rest of the world. Bulgaria's popularity as a holiday and second-home-owning destination has turned real estate into one of the fastest-growing sectors of the economy. While this has led to the construction of unattractive apartment blocks along the coast, it has also helped regenerate depopulated inland villages, where rustic houses are being restored and returned to life.

Bulgaria's Folk Heritage

The National Revival *(see pp52–3)* ensured that Bulgaria's folk traditions were kept alive and that local arts became part of a national movement. Further encouragement and organization on a national scale came during the Communist period, as folk arts were seen as suitable for the people. Today, as well as being a major feature of its museums, Bulgaria's folk heritage is very much a living tradition. Many women still practise handicrafts such as embroidery and weaving, and tablecloths, rugs and blouses decorated with traditional folk motifs are a regular feature of outdoor markets.

Agriculture is still very important to Bulgaria and the country's festivals are usually related to the annual cycles of nature.

Traditional Folk Costume

This differs greatly from one region to another in Bulgaria, with even the choice of colours varying from one village to the next. Men's costumes are less bright, although jackets and trousers can be decorated with fine braiding. The kalpak, a black sheepskin hat, has always been something of a national trademark, although it is rarely seen on the streets these days.

Traditional women's folk costumes often feature a *sukman* (linen dress), a *riza* or *koshulya* (blouse with abstract or floral motifs) and a *prestilka* (patterned apron). Traditionally, married women wore headscarves and unmarried girls went bare-headed, with flowers or strings of coins in their hair.

Pafti are large belt buckles, here of silver with finely wrought natural designs, that secured colourful woollen belts.

Embroidery and Weaving

Embroidery was used to add diversity, individuality and regional styles to folk costumes. Carpet weaving, which came from the East, flourished in the 18th to 19th centuries as Bulgaria supplied the Ottoman lands. The most famous carpet-weaving centres are Chiprovtsi and Kotel. Chiprovtsi carpets have geometric patterns based on birds and trees (right, top). Kilims from Kotel display a wider range of primary colours and more abstract designs (right, below).

Embroidery stitching involves repetitive, layered geometric and floral designs and usually the colour red. Gabrovo is famous for its embroidery using gold threads.

Handwoven rugs, or *kilims*, are still made in a handful of villages in Bulgaria. The women work on wooden hand looms to produce the brightly patterned kilims that are so popular in the West.

Bulgarian Folk Music

Bulgarian singing has a huge repertoire of ritual songs and powerful, haunting laments, usually performed by women without musical accompaniment. Rural merrymaking involves a circle dance (horo) accompanied by a four- or five-piece band that often includes instruments such as the gadulka, the tambura (a long-necked lute) and the tapan (a bass drum). Highland shepherds play the kaval (wooden flute) and gaida (goatskin bagpipes), while the zurna is a clarinet-type instrument of the south.

Bulgaria's gypsies traditionally have an important place in village music-making and provide entertainment at rural wedding parties. Gypsy brass bands are a feature of towns in the northwest.

The gadulka is a stringed instrument played with a bow, perhaps recalling the lyre of Orpheus?

Musician playing the gaida (bagpipes)

Folk Festivals

A busy calendar of festivals and religious celebrations ensures that age-old songs and dances remain part of contemporary life. Traditional costumes, while no longer forming part of everyday attire, are still donned on such festive occasions. Some of these folk festivals attract participants and spectators from countries all over the world. Probably the largest folk event is the summer Koprivshtitsa Folk Festival, held every five years (the next one is in 2015). Other important summer festivals include the Apollonia Arts Festival in Sozopol, and international folk fairs in Varna and Nesebûr, on the Black Sea coast.

Baba Marta is a tradition of giving red and white tassels on 1 March for good luck.

Festival of the Rose takes place in the Kazanlûk region from the end of May to mid-June and celebrates the rose-petal harvest. After the harvest has been completed, there is singing, dancing and celebration.

Other Folk Arts

Expressions of creativity, folk arts usually develop unaided by any formal education or training, before then becoming characteristic of the culture in which they evolved. In an illiterate Bulgarian society, folk arts were an important means of preserving native culture. This is why they received such a boost during the National Revival. The importance of keeping folk crafts and traditions alive is still highly appreciated in Bulgaria. Together with commercial reasons, this is why Bulgarian folk traditions still flourish.

Woodcarving flourished during the National Revival, when it was used for iconostases and grand ecclesiastical pieces. Today it embellishes more modest items, like this icon of the Madonna and Child.

Folk pottery is typically rustic and practical, with appliqué of floral or natural motifs and a simple glaze.

Bulgarian Orthodox Church

Under Khan Boris I, Bulgaria was one of the first Eastern European nations to adopt the Christian faith. The religion spread rapidly in the country after the development of the Cyrillic alphabet, and later both Christianity and the Cyrillic script were exported to other Slav countries such as Serbia and Russia. In 1054, the Great Schism split the Christian community into the Roman Catholic Church in Western Europe and the Orthodox Church in the East. During the Ottoman period, the Bulgarian Orthodox Church was crucial in nurturing Bulgarian language and culture and is still an important part of the country's social fabric today.

Khan Boris I was converted to Christianity by Kliment and Naum, the disciples of Cyril and Methodius, in AD 865.

Early History

Khan Boris I wanted an autonomous Church for Bulgaria. He negotiated with both seats of Christian power, Constantinople and Rome, until in AD 870 the former granted Bulgaria an autonomous bishopric. In 1054, after disagreements mainly over doctrinal issues and jurisdiction, these two centres of Christianity split into what would become the Orthodox and Catholic churches.

Cyril and Methodius were 9th-century Greek monks who tried to convert the Slavs. Cyrillic script is named after St Cyril, who laid the foundations of the Cyrillic alphabet.

Candles are symbolic of many things, including the faith of the worshippers and the light of knowledge.

Monasteries, like this one at Bachkovo (see pp146–7), were built in mountain valleys so as to be near God and far from worldly temptations. In the Ottoman period, the monasteries became important repositories of Bulgarian culture, language and faith.

Orthodox Worship

Orthodox services can be very atmospheric as the church is lit mainly by candles, and the air is heavy with incense. The whole service is sung, as the human voice is believed to be the best instrument for praising the Lord. The service is a sung dialogue between the clergy and the people. Traditionally there are no chairs as everyone, except the infirm, stands during the service as a sign of respect.

Under the Ottomans the Bulgarian Church was again subordinate to Constantinople. But when Ottoman power waned, the Church reasserted itself. By 1895 Christianity was the national religion and the Bulgarian Church won its independence in 1945. The seat of the patriarchate is the Aleksandŭr Nevski Memorial Church (right).

The Church struggled under Communism and did not elect a patriarch until 1953. Maxim of Lovech (right) was elected in 1971. The 1991 Constitution recognizes Eastern Orthodoxy as the national religion.

The cross is an important symbol of the Church and has been described as the joining of the heavenly and the earthly. The three-barred cross, popular in Slavic countries, has an upper bar that represents the inscription over Christ's head, while the lower slanting bar represents the foot rest.

Parts of a Church

Orthodox churches are usually oriented on an east–west axis. Worshippers enter the church from the west (associated with Sin) and head up the aisle towards the light of Truth (in the east). The plan of a church is often either rectangular, like a ship (or Ark), or cruciform (like the Cross). Inside, the main space is the nave, with walls usually decorated with icons and frescoes. The altar, in the sanctuary, is hidden from worshippers' sight behind the icon screen, or iconostasis, but is visible during services, when the Royal Doors are opened.

Icons of Christ and the saints play a major role in the Orthodox Church. Not a mere illustration, the icon is a sanctified object that helps the faithful sense the presence of God. Icons have therefore always been highly stylized, and are not intended to be realistic works of art. Icons were especially useful when literacy was very low.

The congregation is traditionally separated, with men standing on the right and women on the left.

Beautiful frescoes, like these 16th-century ones at Arbanasi, cover the walls of Bulgarian churches and monasteries. Fresco-painting was introduced from Byzantium in the Middle Ages, and Bulgarian artists developed their own style. A popular subject on west walls of churches is the Apocalypse, reminding the departing faithful of judgment for their actions.

Iconostasis

The iconostasis is a screen on which icons of saints are displayed. Dividing the faithful from the Sanctuary, it also symbolizes the division between Earth and Heaven. It is usually of dark wood delicately carved with natural motifs. Dragons, symbolizing sinful passions tamed by Christian faith, are a frequent motif in Bulgarian iconostases.

The order of icons on an iconostasis is not rigid but usually follows the plan on the right. Rows may not follow the same sequence, and all five are not always featured. An icon of one of the church's patron saints sometimes takes the place of the icon of Christ.

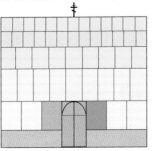

Key

- ☐ Icons of the Patriarchs
- ☐ Icons of the Prophets
- ☐ Icons of Liturgical Feasts
- ☐ Deesis (most important)
- ☐ The Sovereign Row
- ☐ Icon of the Virgin
- ☐ Icon of Christ or Church
- ☐ The Royal Doors

Bulgarian Architecture

From Thracian times to the present day, Bulgaria has been home to several remarkable civilizations. As a result, the country's architectural landscape is rich and varied. While the Thracians left impressive decorated tombs, the Romans, who made Bulgaria part of their Balkan empire, were great builders of theatres, temples and public baths. Their Byzantine and Bulgarian successors built sturdy fortresses and spectacular churches. The Ottomans also had a taste for grand civic projects, erecting mosques, bazaars and elegant stone bridges. The 19th-century National Revival led to a flowering of domestic architecture rich in ornamentation. By contrast, modern architecture is generally far less appealing.

Aleksandûr Nevski Memorial Church in Sofia, built in the Neo-Byzantine style

Ancient Architecture

Burial mounds built by ancient Thracian rulers are one of the trademarks of the Bulgarian landscape. Many have been excavated, revealing domed burial chambers richly decorated with finely executed paintings and sculpture. The graves were also filled with exquisite gold and silver treasure *(see pp44–5)*. The Thracians were conquered by the Romans, who built set-piece cities such as Nikopolis ad Istrum (now ruined), north of present-day Veliko Tûrnovo, and the first Christian churches, such as the beautifully proportioned Rotunda of Sveti Georgi *(see p69)*.

The Roman amphitheatre in Plovdiv was built in the 2nd century AD and is still used for concerts.

Thracian tomb built around the 4th century BC for a king or rich nobleman. The design of these tombs vary, being either barrel-vaulted, pyramidal or beehive-shaped (as here).

The interior of the tombs often features frescoes depicting burial rituals.

Medieval Architecture: 12th–14th Centuries

The medieval Bulgarian tsars were prolific fortress-builders. Ruins at Pliska, Preslav and Cherven reveal thick walls constructed from impressively sized blocks of stone. The hilltop stronghold of Veliko Tûrnovo has been largely reconstructed to show just how formidable a 14th-century fortress really was. The 13th and 14th centuries were a golden age for Orthodox Church architecture, when both Bulgarian and Byzantine architects experimented with ever more graceful forms. The coastal town of Nesebûr contains several spectacular examples of churches from this period.

Veliko Tûrnovo was the fortified capital of the 12th-century Second Bulgarian Kingdom. Despite walls 4 m (12 ft) thick, the fortress was captured by the Ottomans in 1393.

Zemen Monastery Church, built to a simple cruciform plan with a central cupola, is a wonderful example of 12th-century Bulgarian religious architecture. It is the only surviving building from the whole monastery complex.

Ottoman Architecture: 14th–19th Centuries

Hugely impressed by Balkan churches, Ottoman architects based the design of many of their mosques on the same basic principles. The 16th-century mosques in Sofia and Kyustendil feature graceful domes resting on cube-shaped buildings of brick and stone. The 18th-century Tombul Mosque in Shumen, with its arcaded courtyard and ornate fountain, marks the high point of Ottoman architecture in Bulgaria. Although the last 100 years have seen the loss of many Ottoman buildings, many fine examples still remain, including caravanserai at Shumen and Yambol, public drinking fountains in Samokov, and hump-backed bridges in the Rhodope Mountains.

The Devil's Bridge at Ardino is 56 m (185 ft) wide and was built on an ancient trade route to the northern Aegean coast.

Tombul Mosque (1744), the largest in Bulgaria, has an interesting structure. The base is square and the middle level octagonal, topped by a circular dome.

National Revival: 19th Century

As well as creating great monasteries, the National Revival brought about a distinct domestic architecture. In the 19th century, merchants built lavish houses, mixing ideas imported from Western Europe with home-grown arts and crafts. With ornately painted exteriors, these houses featured fine carpets and carved wooden ceilings displaying local craftsmanship. Bulgaria's most famous 19th-century architect was Nikola Fichev, who used Bulgarian folk motifs in projects such as the Turkish Governor's House in Veliko Tŭrnovo, the Church of Sveta Troitsa in Svishtov, and the Covered Bridge in Lovech.

Cantilevered upper storey makes best use of limited ground space.

National Revival houses mixed practicality with visual appeal. Originally the lower storey was made of stone, with few windows as it was a fortification.

Oslekov House (see p179), in the town of Koprivshtitsa, has a vivaciously painted façade held up by cedar pillars.

Modern Architecture

Modernist currents had little influence in Bulgaria, although the Bulgarian National Bank in Sofia (1938) was an attempt to combine functionalism with Bulgarian style. After World War II, the Communist regime built a handful of prestigious buildings, such as the Neo-Classical Party House in Sofia. To provide cheap housing, the Communists also built many concrete apartment blocks, which now look dull and neglected. Since the fall of Communism, sleek glass-walled office blocks have sprung up all over Bulgaria, although few of these are likely to stand the test of time. The Black Sea coast has also seen rapid building development.

National Palace of Culture (NDK), built in Sofia and opened in 1981, has a muscular functionality. It is the largest conference and arts centre in southeastern Europe.

Elenite, a resort on the Black Sea Coast, marks a gradual move away from the ugly developments of the 1970s and 80s. The design recalls Rila Monastery's arcaded interior.

Landscape and Wildlife of Bulgaria

The Bulgarian landscape offers enormous variety and biodiversity. Known for its long sandy beaches, the Black Sea coast also features dramatic cliffs and swampy river estuaries. Inland, fertile agricultural plains alternate with rugged mountain chains harbouring some of the most unspoiled wilderness areas in Europe. This pristine resource is inhabited by spectacular wildlife, such as wolves, bears, eagles and vultures. However, visitors are more likely to enjoy wildflower meadows flickering with clouds of colourful butterflies, and scenic rivers, lakes and marshes popular with native and migrant birds.

One of the beautiful high-altitude lakes of the Pirin Mountains

The Mountains

European lynx

Bulgaria is home to four main mountain ranges: the Rila and Pirin in the southwest, the Rhodopes in the south, and the Balkan range, which runs the length of the country from east to west. The highest peak is Musala Ridge (2,952 m/9,700 ft) in the Rila Mountains. Moufflon and lynx prowl among Rhodope pine forests, where raspberries, bilberries and mushrooms grow. Brown bears, even, can be found in the wilder regions of the Rila, Pirin and Balkan ranges. The area also harbours numerous birds of prey, alongside rare woodpeckers and elusive black storks.

Edelweiss flourishes at altitudes of more than 2,000m (6,560ft). A symbol of the Pirin Mountains, it is also a protected species.

The rare black stork can be found in spring, nesting in the limestone cliffs of the Rhodopes. From late summer, migrating populations can be seen along the Black Sea coast, heading south.

Rock Formations

Swallowtail butterfly

Spectacular rock formations dot the landscape – sheer-walled gorges, deep bat-filled caves, and bizarrely shaped stone columns. These are visitor attractions in their own right and home to many wildlife species. At Belogradchik, in northwestern Bulgaria, a huge area of red-brown rock pillars stands in stunning contrast to the woodland. The stone columns poking up from an arid landscape west of Varna are similarly dramatic, but the most famous rock formations are the so-called sand pyramids of Melnik. Here the brittle sandy hills have been eroded to form an other-worldly landscape of cones and pillars.

Egyptian vultures, an endangered species, like open, dry and rocky terrain. One of the smaller varieties of vultures, they feed mainly on carrion, especially roadkill.

The lesser horseshoe bat is one of many bat species found in Bulgaria. Large colonies roost in caves and emerge together at dusk to hunt for insects.

Valley of Roses

Really a lowland trough comprising three neighbouring valleys, the Valley of Roses is framed by the lofty Balkan mountains to the north and the thickly forested Sredna Gora hills to the south. The valley is named after the rose plantations which for centuries have supplied Bulgaria's rose-oil industry. Grown in villages around Karlovo and Kazanlŭk, the crop is harvested as soon as the blooms appear in late May – before the oil evaporates, so you won't see the pink flowers unless you're visiting then. The valley also features vineyards, luscious fruit orchards, and meadows covered in wild flowers every spring.

The damask rose, imported for cultivation by Ottoman merchants

The Danubian Plain

North of the Balkan mountains, the area of rolling hills and fertile farmland known as the Danubian Plain stretches towards the Danube. Thanks to a temperate climate, leafy vineyards thrive here, producing some of the country's best wines. Elsewhere, broad fields of sun-flowers provide glorious bursts of colour in summer. The easternmost part of the plain is Bulgaria's principal wheat-growing region. The vast Danube river system is home to many ducks, geese and herons, and in spring and autumn all of northern Bulgaria becomes a feeding ground for migrating birds, especially pelicans and white storks. The Danube island of Belene is also home to a colony of spoonbills in May.

Pelican

Spoonbills hunt for food by sieving water through their bill, and snapping it shut on insects, crustacea or small fish.

Sunflowers are a very important Bulgarian crop. Oil is extracted from the seeds.

The Coast

The Black Sea coast, especially in the south, offers any number of glorious white-sand beaches. The northern part, around the Kaliakra peninsula, features dramatic cliffs, and coastal steppe land covered in wild flowers. The estuaries of the Ropotamo and Kamchiya rivers are rich in sub-tropical vegetation and are a haven for watersnakes and other wildlife. In spring and autumn, the fish and insects of the coastal lagoons and lakes attract migrating birds such as lesser grey shrikes, pied wheateaters and all manner of terns.

Lesser grey shrike

Grass snakes are harmless to humans and feed mainly on amphibians. Fairly common, they are easily identified by their yellow collar.

Wild flowers are at their most colourful in the steppe between March and mid-July. You can see blue flax, peonies, adonises and every colour of iris. The meadows also attract many birds.

Wine Growing Areas of Bulgaria

Wine has been produced in Bulgaria since ancient Thracian times, when it played an important part in religious rituals. In the early 20th century, Western European grape varieties were introduced to the country, but it was not until the 1960s that Bulgaria started producing large quantities of quality wines and becoming one of the world's major wine exporters. Since then, Bulgarian wine has become a byword for high quality at a very affordable price.

Small oak casks are used to add beneficial phenolic compounds to Bulgarian wines. The result is "Reserve" quality wines – the highest category.

The Danubian Plain holds about 30 per cent of the country's vineyards. It is most famous for its red wine, especially Cabernet Sauvignon. The grapes are mostly still harvested by hand.

Struma Valley's favourable climate produces an excellent wine – Melnik Red – from a native varietal grape, Shiroka Melnishka, as well as good Merlots, and Cabernet Sauvignons.

Buying Wine

Well-known vineyards like Damianitza, near Melnik (see pp120–21), and Todoroff, near Plovdiv (see pp138–43), are open to tourists, who can sample the wines and buy a bottle or two to take home. Elsewhere in Bulgaria, wine is usually sold direct from wine cellars, or from roadside stalls, and is often decanted straight from the barrel into plastic bottles or other containers. This is a fun way to buy wine cheaply, but the quality can vary. It is often better to wait until you can buy a labelled bottle of wine from a reputable shop. Specialist wine shops include Loza in Sofia, and Bai Gencho, a chain with branches throughout the country.

Wine outlet attached to a local vineyard

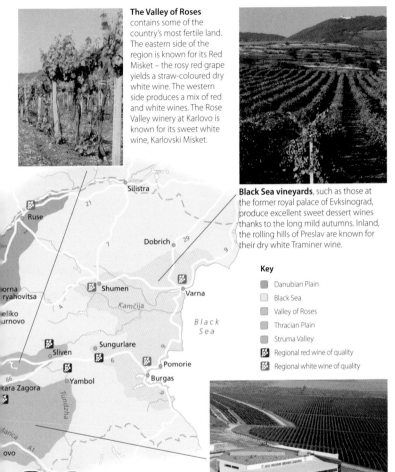

The Valley of Roses contains some of the country's most fertile land. The eastern side of the region is known for its Red Misket – the rosy red grape yields a straw-coloured dry white wine. The western side produces a mix of red and white wines. The Rose Valley winery at Karlovo is known for its sweet white wine, Karlovski Misket.

Black Sea vineyards, such as those at the former royal palace of Evksinograd, produce excellent sweet dessert wines thanks to the long mild autumns. Inland, the rolling hills of Preslav are known for their dry white Traminer wine.

Key

- ▨ Danubian Plain
- ▨ Black Sea
- ▨ Valley of Roses
- ▨ Thracian Plain
- ▨ Struma Valley
- 🏵 Regional red wine of quality
- 🏵 Regional white wine of quality

Thracian Plain enjoys long, dry summers and develops good, robust red wines – Mavrud from Asenovgrad and Merlot from around Haskovo.

Typical red wines include Merlot and Cabernet Sauvignon, but there are native varieties, notably Melnik, Mavrud and Gumza. Rkatziteli was the first grape used for white wine, but today Chardonnay is more popular.

Trifon Zarezan

One of the most important days in the vintner's calendar, St Tryphon's feast day marks the start of the pruning season. It is celebrated by ritually sprinkling the vineyard with a mix of holy water and last year's wine, ensuring healthy growth and a good harvest in the year to come. Celebrations take place on 1 or 15 February, depending on the area, and the feasting and merrymaking continue well into the night.

Local dignitary celebrating Trifon Zarezan

Ski Resorts in Bulgaria

Offering spectacular scenery, snow from December through to May and excellent value for money, Bulgaria's ski resorts have long attracted foreign visitors. Over the last decade, the resorts' facilities and standard of accommodation have been dramatically modernized. The "Big Three" ski resorts are Bansko, Borovets and Pamporovo, each of which has its own character, ski runs for all levels of skill, and lively après-ski culture. However, do also consider staying at one of the smaller satellite resorts for a quieter, more traditional holiday.

Skiers on a piste on the slopes of Mount Musala, near Borovets

Dragalevtsi has a chair lift, about 30 minutes' walk uphill from the centre, which takes skiers to Aleko.

Mount Musala has some of the best snow cover in Bulgaria. Peaking at 2,925 m (9,600 ft), it is also the highest mountain in the Balkans.

Vitosha
Although it is somewhat overshadowed by the Big Three resorts, Mt Vitosha (see pp92–3) has enough runs and is close enough to Sofia to be extremely attractive to many skiers in the capital – it can get very crowded at weekends. However, because of poor hotel facilities at Aleko, visitors are advised to find accommodation at Dragalevtsi or Simeonovo, further down the mountain.
Star attractions: Only 30 minutes from Sofia centre with fantastic city views from the runs

Borovets
The resort sits amid stunning scenery at the forested foot of Mount Musala. A combination of carpet lifts, gondolas and chair lifts whisk skiers to the mountain top. It caters for advanced skiers as well as beginners and there's even a ski-jump area. Long considered Bulgaria's top skiing destination, Borovets (see p111) has been eclipsed by Bansko's rampant growth. However, a €400 million "Super Borovets" project will vastly increase the resort's facilities and enhance its status.
Star attractions: Night skiing, great night life

Bansko
The newest of Bulgaria's "Big Three" resorts, Bansko (see pp122–4) has profited from massive investment. Hotels and apartment blocks have been built, and ski runs, lifts and cable cars cover the Pirin Mountains that tower majestically over the town. The ski runs are suitable for all abilities and for all types of skiing – boarders, cross-country, extreme and an area for tricks. However, despite intense development, Bansko is still a cozy town, with traditional taverns as well as modern bars and clubs.
Star attractions: Snowboard Park at 2,500 m (8,200 ft), uninterrupted 16-km (10-mile) ski run

The Pirin Mountains in winter, spectacular playground of skiers, snowboarders and snowshoers from Bulgaria and western Europe

Chepelare is a very small skiing resort with four fairly undemanding ski runs and a highest peak of 1,873 m (6,145 ft). However, it has a children's ski centre and would make a good place to stay for beginners. It is also a convenient and inexpensive base from which to ski at the much larger and more developed resort of Pamporovo.

Pamporovo
Bulgaria's southernmost and sunniest ski resort, Pamporovo is a purpose-built resort, with villas and hotels scattered around the base of pine-forested ski runs. Geared to catering for large groups, Pamporovo has long attracted Western European visitors on inexpensive package holidays.
Star attractions: Beautiful scenery Excellent for beginner/ intermediate skiers

Mount Snezhanka, which is just 1,926 m (6,321 ft) high, has gentle slopes, with short runs suitable for beginners and intermediate skiers.

Statistics

Bansko
Resort at 925 m (3,035 ft)
Highest skiing 2,600 m (8,500 ft)
65 km (40 miles) from Sofia
13 lifts, 14 runs
Longest run 7 km (4 miles)
Total skiing 65 km (40 miles)
Cross country 5 km (3 miles)
Snow December– April

Borovets
Resort at 1,350 m (4,430 ft)
Highest skiing 2,560 m (8,400 ft)
73 km (45 miles) from Sofia
14 lifts, 19 runs
Longest run 12 km (7½ miles)
Total skiing 58 km (36 miles)
Cross country 35 km (22 miles)
Snow December–April

Pamporovo
Resort at 1,650 m (5,410 ft)
Highest skiing 1,937 m (6,350 ft)
260 km (160 miles) from Sofia
18 lifts, 8 runs
Total skiing 25 km (16 miles)
Cross country 40 km (25 miles)
Snow December–April

Vitosha
Resort at 1,800 m (5,900 ft)
Highest skiing 2,290 m (7,500 ft)
10 km (6 miles) from Sofia
8 lifts, 6 runs
22 km of runs
Longest run 5 km (3 miles)
Total skiing 40 km (25 miles)
Cross country 10 km (6 miles)
Snow December–April

Snowshoeing

The sport developed from the necessity of having to get around in deep snow. Tribesmen used sticks and animal skins to create shoes with a large enough surface area to support the wearer's weight on the snow. These days, however, you use lightweight ski poles to help with balance and effective snowshoes, and once you work up a rhythm it comes quite naturally. It's easy but quite tiring. The joy of it is that you can get away into the silent, unspoilt wilderness of the mountains and really have a chance to take it in. And it's great exercise too. Snowshoeing trips can be organized for you by many tour operators (see p247).

Snowshoers enjoying the beautiful winter scenery of the mountains

Key

— Motorway
— Main road
— Other road
▲ Peak
≍ Pass

0 kilometres 25
0 miles 25

Bulgaria's Coastline

Bulgaria is deservedly famous for its golden sandy beaches. These make up 30 per cent of the country's Black Sea coastline, which stretches for 378 km (235 miles). At the major resorts of Sunny Beach, Golden Sands and Albena, the beaches have Blue Flag status and life-guards, and offer waterskiing, jet-skiing, para-skiing, and a multitude of other water-related activities. However, swimmers and sunbathers must pay to use these beaches, which also become uncomfortably crowded in the high season. Away from the major resorts, beaches are less crowded and access to them is free, although they may lack facilities and are unlikely to have lifeguards. The beaches further towards the south are windy enough to attract surfers, windsurfers and kite surfers.

Sunny Beach is an enormous resort that just keeps on growing and has everything the package tourist could ask for. A glut of bars, clubs, restaurants and shops cater for the thousands of European tourists that pass through every season.

Lozenets, once a quiet fishing village, is the current hotspot for well-to-do Bulgarians attracted by wind- and kite-surfing opportunities and some of the liveliest night-life outside the big resorts.

Dyuni is a wonderful windswept strip of beach that separates the sea from a marshy inland lake. A large hotel complex dominates the northern end, but the rest of the beach is free for the public to enjoy.

Obzor is a small seaside town that dates back to ancient times. While Greek and Roman remains ornament its pretty park, large hotels have sprung up along its superb beach.

Kamchiya
Dolni Chiflik
Staro Oryahov
Byala
Obzor
Vetren
Kableshkovo
Banya
Aheloy
Sunny Beach
Nesebur
Irakli
Burgas L.
Emine Cape
Burgas
Pomorie
Mandra L.
Sozopol
Dyuni
Malsen Nos Cape
Primorsko
Lozenets
Arapya
Tsarevo
Ahtopol
Rezovska R.
Sinemorets
Rezovo

Arapya, a hugely popular destination with Bulgarians, consists of a number of wooden beachfront restaurants and bars and a sprawling, partially shaded campsite.

Sinemorets boasts some of the area's best beaches and is overrun in summer. The main beach is dominated by package tourists, but there are plenty of quieter spots a little further afield.

Irakli's setting, bordered by forest, makes it one of the coast's wildest and most attractive beaches. Plans to build a luxury resort here caused uproar though, so the planned development now looks unlikely to go ahead.

For map symbols *see back flap*

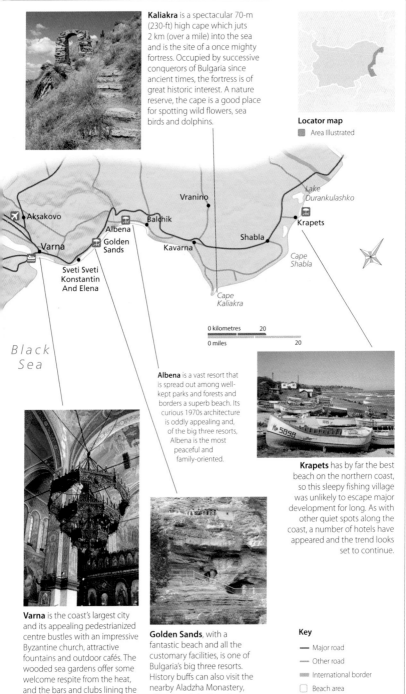

Kaliakra is a spectacular 70-m (230-ft) high cape which juts 2 km (over a mile) into the sea and is the site of a once mighty fortress. Occupied by successive conquerors of Bulgaria since ancient times, the fortress is of great historic interest. A nature reserve, the cape is a good place for spotting wild flowers, sea birds and dolphins.

Locator map

☐ Area Illustrated

Vranino

Lake Durankulashko

Aksakovo

Balchik

Albena

Krapets

Varna

Golden Sands

Shabla

Kavarna

Cape Shabla

Sveti Sveti Konstantin And Elena

Cape Kaliakra

Black Sea

0 kilometres 20

0 miles 20

Albena is a vast resort that is spread out among well-kept parks and forests and borders a superb beach. Its curious 1970s architecture is oddly appealing and, of the big three resorts, Albena is the most peaceful and family-oriented.

Krapets has by far the best beach on the northern coast, so this sleepy fishing village was unlikely to escape major development for long. As with other quiet spots along the coast, a number of hotels have appeared and the trend looks set to continue.

Varna is the coast's largest city and its appealing pedestrianized centre bustles with an impressive Byzantine church, attractive fountains and outdoor cafés. The wooded sea gardens offer some welcome respite from the heat, and the bars and clubs lining the beach have some of the Black Sea's best nightlife.

Golden Sands, with a fantastic beach and all the customary facilities, is one of Bulgaria's big three resorts. History buffs can also visit the nearby Aladzha Monastery, where monks' cells and chapels are cut into a cliff face.

Key

— Major road

— Other road

▬ International border

☐ Beach area

☐ Urban area

BULGARIA THROUGH THE YEAR

Bulgaria has four distinct seasons, with a warm spring, a long hot summer, a golden autumn and a crisp, cold winter. Religious holidays, saints' days and folk festivals form the backbone of Bulgaria's festive calendar. Although the Orthodox Church ties the dates of religious festivals to the Gregorian calendar, some rural communities still keep to the Julian calendar. The year is also punctuated by a wealth of arts festivals, ranging from film to jazz and classical music. Some of these events are of international importance. Lastly, Bulgaria fetes its bountiful produce, with festivals celebrating wine and the roses from which fragrant oil is extracted.

Spring

Spring presents Bulgaria at its most beautiful, with both open countryside and city parks bright with lush green grass and flowers in full bloom. Cultural activity is also at its height at this time. Concert seasons reach their climax in Sofia and Plovdiv. Easter, marked by religious processions as well as joyful family reunions and much feasting, is the high point of the church year.

Easter Sunday procession, with an icon of Christ

March

Baba Marta *(1 Mar)*. Red and white tassels are worn as bracelets or hung on trees in order to bring good fortune and prosperity in the coming year.

Shirokolushki peshyatsi *(1st weekend in Mar)*. Mummers parade through the village of Shiroka Lûka, in the Rhodope Mountains.

Masked mummers at Shirokolushki peshyatsi in Shiroka Lûka

St Theodore's Day *(Todorovden; 1st Saturday in Lent)*. Horse races in Koprivshtitsa, Dobrinishte and Momchilovtsi.

March Music Days *(late Mar)*, Ruse. Series of concerts of classical music.

April

St Lazar's Day *(Lazarovden; Saturday before Easter)*. In this important coming-of-age ritual, carried out in villages all over Bulgaria, girls perform songs and dances collectively known as *Lazaruvane* to mark their passage from childhood to puberty. *Lazaruvane* bring health, happiness, and the promise of a good marriage partner in the future.

Easter *(variable dates)*. Families celebrate Easter by decorating eggs with colourful designs and displaying them in the home. The main church service takes place late on Easter Saturday. At midnight, the priest emerges from behind the iconostasis, with a candle representing the Resurrection.

Easter Sunday Eleshnitsa and elsewhere in Bulgaria. Processions by *kukeri* (see p106).

May

St George's Day *(Gergyovden; 6 May)*. Military parades throughout Bulgaria. Open-air feasting at Ak Yazula Baba Tekke, near Obrochishte, and Demir Baba Tekke, near Sveshtari.

Festival of Humour and Satire *(mid-May)*, Gabrovo.

Sofia Music Weeks *(late May–early Jun)*. Concerts by Bulgaria's leading orchestras and chamber musicians.

Military parade of uniformed soldiers on St George's Day

Average daily hours of sunshine

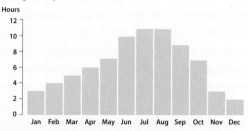

Sunshine Chart
Bulgaria's weather is very complex. It has two overlapping climate zones – Continental from the north and Mediterranean from the south. This brings plenty of sun from June to September, and reasonable levels of sunshine all year round.

Dancers in traditional costume at the Karlovo Rose Festival

Summer

Over the long, hot summer, mountain and coastal regions offer a welcome respite from the heat. While folk festivals take place all over the country, cultural activity centres on the Black Sea coast, where many arts festivals are held.

June

Fire Dancing (Nestinarstvo; 4 Jun or nearest weekend). Bŭlgari. A village event with dancing on hot coals.

Varna Summer (Varnensko lyato; early Jun). Bulgaria's foremost festival of international contemporary theatre.

Verdi Festival (first 2 weeks in Jun), Plovdiv. Opera in the ancient amphitheatre.

Karlovo Rose Festival (first Saturday in Jun). The rose harvest is celebrated with parades, music and dancing.

Kazanlŭk Rose Festival (first Sunday in Jun). Bulgaria's largest rose festival.

Festival of Chamber Music (mid-Jun, odd-numbered years),

Plovdiv. Prestigious international event.

St John's Day (Enyovden; 24 Jun). People go into the fields to gather medicinal herbs.

July

Varna International Music Festival (early–late Jul). Classical music.

Varna International Ballet Competition (mid–late Jul). Major event for young dancers.

St Elijah's Day (Ilinden; 20 Jul or 3 Aug, depending on region). Celebrations in towns and villages with a church dedicated to St Elijah.

International Folk Festival (late Jul), Plovdiv. Celebration of folk dance and music.

August

Varna Jazz Festival (early Aug). Major jazz event.

Pirin Sings (Pirin pee; even-numbered years), Predel Pass, near Bansko. Folk music.

St Elijah's Day Gathering (Ilindenski subor; early Aug), Gela. Folk festival. Popular with the students.

International Jazz Festival (early-mid-Aug), Bansko.

Rozhen Festival (early to mid-Aug, even-numbered years), in a meadow near Smolyan. Major Rhodopean folk festival.

Trigrad Festival (mid-Aug), Trigrad Gorge. Folk and pop music.

Feast of the Assumption (15 Aug). Parades of icons at Troyan Monastery and Bachkovo Monastery.

Koprivshtitsa Festival (mid-Aug, every five years, the next in 2015). Bulgaria's largest folk festival, featuring traditional performers from around the world. A smaller gathering, with local folk groups, is held annually.

Thracian Summer (Trakiisko lyato; mid–late Aug), Plovdiv. Chamber music concerts in old-town mansions.

White Brotherhood Gathering (late Aug), Seven Lakes, Rila Mountains. Dressed in white robes, followers of Petŭr Dunov gather to take part in mass callisthenics and nature-worship.

Performance at the International Jazz Festival in Bansko

Average monthly rainfall

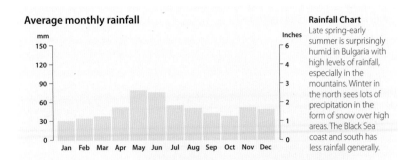

Rainfall Chart
Late spring-early summer is surprisingly humid in Bulgaria with high levels of rainfall, especially in the mountains. Winter in the north sees lots of precipitation in the form of snow over high areas. The Black Sea coast and south has less rainfall generally.

Autumn

Autumn is generally a very pleasant season in Bulgaria. The weather usually remains mild well into November with little rainfall, making this a good time for hiking and exploring rural areas. Besides many religious festivals, a wide spectrum of arts festivals fills the autumn months. The season starts with the great Apollonia Arts Festival in Sozopol, the largest event of its kind in Bulgaria.

Participants at celebrations to mark the Day of the National Enlighteners

September
Apollonia Arts Festival (early Sep), Sozopol. Music, theatre and dance of all kinds, at various venues in the town.
Birth of the Virgin (Malka Bogoroditsa; 6 Sep), Rozhen Monastery. Parade of icons.
Feast of the Cross (Krŭstovden; 14 Sep). Pilgrimages to Krŭstova Gora, in the Rhodope Mountains.

Feast of St Sofia (17 Sep). Sofia. Day of the city's saint.
Scene at the Crossroads (mid-Sep), Plovdiv. This is an international theatre festival.
Chamber Music Days (mid-Sep), Gabrovo.
International Puppet Theatre Festival (late Sep), Plovdiv. A feature of Plovdiv since 1977, this is one of Bulgaria's most prestigious cultural events.

October
Harvest Festivals (mid-Oct), Bansko, Blagoevgrad, Gotse Delchev and Melnik. Typical harvest celebrations.
Feast of St John of Rila (19 Oct), Rila Monastery. Festival in honour of the monastery's 9th-century founder.
St Demetrius's Day (Dimitrov den; 26 Oct). Celebrated where the churches are associated with St Demetrius.

November
Day of the National Enlighteners (1 Nov). Concerts and events all over the country.
Feast of the Archangel Michael (Arhangelovden; 8 Nov). Orthodox Bulgarians make offerings to St Michael, protector of the dead.
Kurban Bayram (variable; falls in Oct in 2014, and Sep in 2015 and 2016), Muslim areas. Feasting to commemorate the Sacrifice of Abraham.
Kinomania Film Festival (Nov). Bulgaria's biggest film festival runs throughout the month, and is held at Sofia's NDK building (www.kinomania.bg).

Band of musicians in concert at the Apollonia Arts Festival

Average monthly temperature

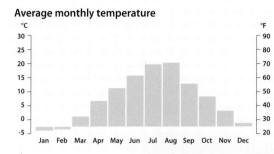

Temperature Chart
Thanks to the Black Sea, the coast avoids extremes of hot and cold. High areas are cooler all year round, but in valleys, such as along the Danube, it can be stifling in summer and icy in winter. For Sofia, mountains stop icy Russian winter winds and its elevation cools it in summer.

Winter

While the Black Sea coast enjoys mild winters, inland regions can be bitterly cold, and mountains are covered with a thick carpet of snow. This is welcomed by winter sports enthusiasts, with the skiing season starting in mid-December and lasting until March or April. Winter is particularly associated with *kukeri* rituals, when mummers wearing monstrous animal masks perform wild dances, shaking cowbells to drive away the evil spirits that are abroad during the long dark winter nights. Although traditionally associated with Cheese Shrovetide (the first Sunday before Lent), *kukeri* rituals take place at different times. They occur in January across much of southwestern Bulgaria, but are held in March in Shiroka Lûka, and as late as Easter in Eleshnitsa.

December

Young Red Wine Festival *(early Dec)*, Sandanski. The new season's wine is feted.
St Nicholas's Day *(Nikulden; 6 Dec)*.
Christmas *(Koleda; 25 Dec)*. *Koledari* (carol singers) tour villages, and are offered specially made bread in return.

January

New Year's Day Children tour their neighbourhood singing songs and bearing *survachki*, cornel twigs decorated with dried fruit, corn and ribbons. Today householders are beaten lightly with the twigs to bring them luck in the coming year; in the past the beatings were heavier.

Christmas lights, trees and decorations in a Sofia street

Kukeri processions *(1 Jan)*, Razlog.
Jordan Day *(Yordanovden; 6 Jan)*, Kalofer. People jump into an icy river to retrieve a wooden cross.
St John's Day *(Ivanovden; 7 Jan)*. The most important name-day of the year, and a celebration for everyone called Ivan or Ivana, or any of its derivatives.
Kukeri processions *(14 Jan)*, Pernik, Radomir and Breznik.

Costumed participants in Trifon Zarezan, the vine-pruning festival

February

Trifon Zarezan *(1 or 15 Feb, depending on region)*. Vine-pruning festival celebrated in all of Bulgaria's wine-growing areas. Vineyards are sprinkled with the previous season's wine to ensure an even better crop in the coming year. Freshly baked bread and roast chicken are the traditional food served.

Public Holidays

New Year's Day 1 January
Liberation Day 3 March
Easter Sunday & Easter Monday variable
Labour Day 1 May
St George's Day – Bulgarian Army Day 6 May
Day of Bulgarian Education and Culture 24 May
Unification Day 6 September
Independence Day 22 September
Christmas 25, 26 December

THE HISTORY OF BULGARIA

At the crossroads of Europe and the Orient, Bulgaria has come under the influence of many neighbouring cultures, from Greek and Roman to Byzantine and Bulgar. Part of the Ottoman Empire for nearly 500 years, Bulgaria gained independence in 1878, but became a Communist republic in 1946. Today, Bulgaria is a fully democratic state and a member of the European Union.

With a warm climate and fertile soil, the region that is now Bulgaria attracted human settlement from ancient times. Archaeological discoveries at Stara Zagora show that, as early as 5500 BC, Neolithic people were living in the region, where they grew crops, raised animals and made vividly decorated pottery. By 4000 BC, metalworking techniques in the region had developed to become one of the most advanced in Europe, as the exquisite gold jewellery found near Varna shows so vividly.

Thracians and Greeks

By 1000 BC, southeastern Europe was falling under the power of a people known as the Thracians. Across a territory consisting of present-day Bulgaria, Romania and northern Greece, the Thracians formed tribal states. These were ruled by warrior-kings who may also have played a priestly role.

It is thought that the Thracians performed ecstatic religious rituals similar to the wine-fuelled Dyonisiac revels of ancient Greece. The Thracians also believed in an afterlife, and it is likely that the cult of Orpheus, who journeyed to the Underworld in search of his wife Eurydice, originated in Thrace before it became established in Greece.

From the 7th century BC, Thracians and Greeks maintained close contact, with Greeks from Asia Minor establishing colonies on Thrace's Black Sea coast. Greek settlements such as Mesembria (present-day Nesebûr) and Apollonia (Sozopol) supplied Athens and other Greek cities with grain, honey and animal hides from the Thracian hinterland.

After the 4th century BC, several Thracian tribes, notably the Odrysae in central Bulgaria and the Getae in the northeast, established powerful states. But, being disunited, the Thracians were unable to resist their more powerful neighbours. Philip II of Macedon invaded southern Thrace in the 4th century BC, founding the city of Philippopolis (present-day Plovdiv). In 335 BC, his son Alexander the Great subdued Thracian tribes as far north as the Danube. As Macedonian influence grew, the Thracian tribes lost their independence, but this brought them into closer contact with Greek culture.

5500 BC Neolithic farmers in the Stara Zagora region produce richly patterned pottery

700 BC The Black Sea ports of Apollonia (Sozopol) and Mesembria (Nesebûr) are founded by Greek colonists from Asia Minor

342 BC Philip II of Macedon founds Philippopolis (Plovdiv)

6000 BC	4000 BC	2000 BC	AD 1

Neolithic marble fertility goddess

2500 BC Hunter-gatherers in north-western Bulgaria decorate Magura Cave with vibrant paintings

1000–800 BC The Thracians begin to form powerful tribal states in Bulgaria

148 BC Macedonia becomes part of the Roman Empire

73 BC The Thracian-born Spartacus leads a slave revolt against Rome

◀ Fresco of St George and the Dragon at an Orthodox church in Varna, on the Black Sea coast

The Ancient Thracians

The Thracians first emerged as a distinct tribal culture in the second millenium BC, but they never developed a written language, so we know relatively little about them. It is not until the 5th century BC that any information appears. According to Herodotus, the Thracians were the most numerous people in Europe. Politically divided, they often fought among themselves.

Archaeological evidence shows that in the 5th to 1st centuries BC, the Thracians established a thriving trading civilization in the Balkans, much influenced by the Greeks of Asia Minor. Despite brief periods of unity under individual warrior-chiefs, the constant warring left them open to the Roman conquest in the 1st century AD.

Locator Map
Thracian Tribal Lands c.500 BC

Religion, Myths and Legends

The Thracians' key religious beliefs involved fertility, birth and death. They held a strong belief in life after death, and it is likely that the cult of Orpheus began in Thrace before it won popularity in Greece. It is also thought that the Thracians practised ecstatic religious rites similar to the wine-fuelled Dionysiac revels of ancient Greece. Another important deity was the fierce Thracian Rider or Hero.

Servant offers wine, symbolic of Dionysus who died each winter to be reborn in spring.

The Thracian Rider, here on a 4th-century BC silver plaque from Letnitsa, was an archetypal hero. Very popular as a cult figure, his image appears in hundreds of tombs of the 3rd century BC. His cult lived on in the image of dragon-slaying Christian saints such as St George.

Two musicians play the trumpet. Music was linked to death and rebirth, as in the Orpheus myth.

The Great Mother Goddess was a central figure in Thracian religion. She guaranteed fertility in spring and the harvests in autumn, and presided over the mysteries of life and death. As on this pitcher, she is often depicted as a huntress, with power over the natural world, or as a charioteer, driving on the changing seasons.

Kazanlûk Fresco

Kazanlûk, in central Bulgaria (see pp170–71), is the site of this richly decorated chieftain's tomb. Dating from around the 4th century BC, it consists of a domed burial chamber covered by a large mound of earth. The frescoes that adorn the tomb depict a funeral feast, with the deceased accompanied by one of his wives. The Thracians appear to have had a positive view of the afterlife, and the transition from this world to the next was the cause for celebrations as well as mourning.

Royal death mask of a 4th-century BC Thracian ruler found near Kazanlûk, in the Valley of the Thracian Kings. It is likely that the king had some religious function as mediator between men and gods.

Thracian Tombs

To date, over 50 tomb complexes have been excavated in Bulgaria and many more are certain to be discovered. Believing in an afterlife, the Thracians built an eternal house for a dead king and filled it with weapons, jewellery and even horses or dogs. Animal sacrifice was an important part of the ritual, although whether this was for food or to accompany them is not known. These royal tombs became temples or sacred places.

Burial mounds such as Mogila Ostrusha, near Kazanlŭk, dot the Bulgarian countryside. Mogila Ostrusha dates from the 5th century BC and has five chambers. The ceiling is carved with reliefs of people, plants and animals.

The Great Mother Goddess is portrayed offering a tray of pomegranates, the fruit of death, to the deceased.

The deceased is shown seated, crowned with a ceremonial wreath and holding his wife's hand.

A wife would compete for the honour of being killed and buried with her lord, according to Greek historian Herodotus.

Thracian Art

Because of the lack of a writing system, most information about the Thracians has come from archaeological finds. It is clear that Thrace was greatly influenced by her neighbours. From Persia came the stylized depictions of mythical creatures that adorn Thracian gold and silver vessels. From Greece came more naturalistic portrayals, as in the frescoes in Thracian tombs.

Gold Amazon-head rhyton or wine-cup from Panagyurishte. The Amazon wears a veil over her neat hair and a necklace. At the top of the handle stands a Persian-style figure of a flying sphinx. The frequency of wine-cups in burials reveals the importance of wine in such rituals.

Heracles is shown on this 4th-century BC silver plate from Rogozen in a natural Greek style. A hero who came back from Hades, Heracles was a cult figure among the Thracians.

A Warrior Nation

Greek and Roman historians portrayed the Thracians as superior fighters – tough, mobile and with excellent cavalry. To the ancient Greeks, Thrace was a hostile and wild place, home of Ares, god of war. The Romans had a type of gladiator named after the Thracians – lightly armed with a curved sword and circular shield. Spartacus, the gladiator who started a revolt that nearly overthrew Rome (see p119), was Thracian.

Thracian helmet made of bronze and dating from around the end of the 3rd century BC. Examples of helmets have been found with leather inserts to ensure a firm fit to the skull. Other finds include breastplates, swords, spears and greaves, or shin guards.

Ruins of the Roman baths complex in Varna

The Romans

From the 2nd century BC, the Romans gradually replaced the Macedonians as the main power in southeastern Europe. By AD 50, they had taken control of the region, obliterating the old Thracian kingdoms and creating the provinces of Moesia and Thrace in their place. The Romans also built roads, founded new cities, and turned existing towns such as Philippopolis and Serdika (modern Sofia) into great metropolises.

In AD 330, Constantine the Great's establishment of a new imperial capital at Constantinople (Byzantium) boosted southeastern Europe's importance, bringing renewed vibrancy to the cities of Thrace.

Detail of a Roman mosaic, History Museum, Pleven

However, the Roman world's prosperity was increasingly threatened by barbarian invasions. The Visigoths ravaged the Danube region in 378, and the Huns sacked Serdika in about 450. In many cases the Byzantine authorities had no choice but to allow these migrating tribes to settle. The main beneficiaries of this policy were the Slavs, who came from northeastern Europe to the Balkans in the 6th century, and soon made up the majority of the rural population.

Birth of the Bulgar State

The Slavs lived peacefully under Byzantine rule until the arrival of the Bulgars, a warlike Turkic tribe whose origins lay in central Asia. In 681, a group of Bulgars under the leadership of Khan Asparuh crossed the Danube into what was to become Bulgaria. The Bulgars established a capital at Pliska, and gradually extended their rule over the Slavs already settled in the region. Unable to resist the Bulgars, Byzantium was forced to recognize their nascent state. Under Asparuh's successors, notably Khan Krum (803–14), Bulgaria's borders were extended southwards at Byzantium's expense.

The ruling Bulgar aristocracy adopted the language and culture of the Slavs, and the two communities merged to form the Bulgarian nation. This process was accelerated by Khan Boris's conversion to Christianity in 865. Boris invited the Slav-speaking monks Kliment and Naum to spread the faith, ensuring the primacy of the

Ancient pottery, Archaeological Museum, Sofia

Slav language. In order to translate the gospels into the Slav tongue, Kliment and Naum developed a new alphabet, which they named Cyrillic in honour of their mentor, St Cyril. With the new script, Bulgaria became a major centre of manuscript production, and the new spiritual and intellectual centre of the Balkans.

Ceramic icon of St Todor Stratilat, Archaeological Museum, Preslav

The First Bulgarian Kingdom

Bulgarian power reached its peak under Tsar Simeon (893–927), who pushed the Byzantines back to Constantinople, and extended the country's borders to the Black Sea in the east and to the Aegean in the west. However, Byzantine resurgence then halted further Bulgarian expansion. Bulgarian society was also weakened by a rift between the Church and a breakaway group of heretical preachers known as the Bogomils.

Squeezed by the Byzantines in the south and by Prince Svyatoslav of Kiev in the north, the Bulgarian kingdom fragmented in the late 10th century. A feeble Bulgarian state, under Tsar Samuil, survived in what is now Macedonia until 1014, when the Byzantine emperor Basil the Bulgar-Slayer destroyed Samuil's army at the Battle of Strumitsa. Four years later, Samuil's capital, Ohrid, fell to the Byzantines.

The Second Bulgarian Kingdom

Byzantine rule brought peace and stability to Bulgaria. However, heavy taxation, and the replacement of Bulgarian priests with Greek-speaking clergy, led to discontent. In 1185 Petur and Ivan Asen led local *boyars* (nobles) in a revolt against Byzantine rule. After a struggle for in-dependence, Ivan Asen was crowned tsar in 1187 and Veliko Tûrnovo became the capital of the reborn kingdom.

The fall of Byzantium to the Crusaders in 1204 gave the Bulgarian kingdom the opportunity to consolidate and grow. Under Ivan Asen II (1218–41), Bulgaria's territorial expansion resumed but in 1240 the Mongols swept through the Balkans, pillaging as they went. A group of Mongols (later known as the Tatars) settled on the northern Black Sea coast. With the revival of the Byzantine Empire after 1261, Bulgaria was once again at the mercy of its neighbours.

To stay in power, Bulgarian tsars often needed the support of either the Byzantines or the Tatars. The rebel and mystic Ivailo the Swineherd (1277–80) won the Bulgarian throne by promising to rid the country of Tatar influence, but in the end he fled to the Tatar court.

Medieval fortress in Shumen

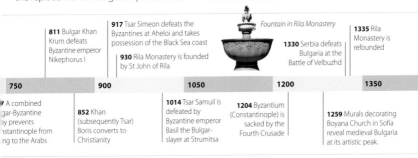

811 Bulgar Khan Krum defeats Byzantine emperor Nikephorus I

917 Tsar Simeon defeats the Byzantines at Aheloi and takes possession of the Black Sea coast

930 Rila Monastery is founded by St John of Rila

Fountain in Rila Monastery

1330 Serbia defeats Bulgaria at the Battle of Velbuzhd

1335 Rila Monastery is refounded

750 | **900** | **1050** | **1200** | **1350**

A combined Bulgar-Byzantine army prevents Constantinople from falling to the Arabs

852 Khan (subsequently Tsar) Boris converts to Christianity

1014 Tsar Samuil is defeated by Byzantine emperor Basil the Bulgar-slayer at Strumitsa

1204 Byzantium (Constantinople) is sacked by the Fourth Crusade

1259 Murals decorating Boyana Church in Sofia reveal medieval Bulgaria at its artistic peak.

Bulgaria's decline as a major Balkan power was sealed by the rise of Serbia. The Bulgarian emperor, Mihail Shishman, tried to take advantage of the Byzantine civil war and attacked Serbia, but was defeated in 1330. Under his nephew Ivan Aleksandŭr (1331–71) Macedonia was surrendered to the Serbs.

The Rise of the Ottoman Turks

Anatolia in the early 14th century was made up of a patchwork of Turkish tribal states, the most successful being the Ottoman Turk. Gradually absorbing Byzantine territory, they established a foothold in Europe in 1354. The effective light cavalry of the Ottomans soon made inroads into the Bulgarian kingdom.

Rather than outright conquest, the Ottomans made the Bulgarian tsars their vassals. Tsar Ivan Shishman's attempts to

Tombul Mosque and minaret in Shumen

throw off this vassal status provoked a brutal response. In 1393 Sultan Bayezid sacked Veliko Tŭrnovo, killed Ivan Shishman, and effectively wiped Bulgaria from the map.

In the anti-Ottoman crusade of 1396, King Sigismund of Hungary sought to liberate Bulgaria but was defeated by Bayezid at Nikopol.

Another crusade, led by King Wladyslaw Jagiello of Poland, met a similar fate at Varna in 1444. Nine years later, the fall of Constantinople, last outpost of the Byzantine Empire, left the Ottomans in control of the Balkans.

Bulgaria Under Ottoman Rule

The Ottomans initially used cruel measures to assert their control of Bulgaria. Nobles were imprisoned or executed, and their subjects deported or enslaved. The Orthodox Church was allowed to carry on its activities, but the Ottoman legal system gave precedence to Muslims over Christians.

Under the Ottomans, cities such as Sofia, Plovdiv, Shumen and Varna emerged as major trade and administrative centres, endowed with fine mosques, covered bazaars, drinking fountains and prestigious public buildings.

Interior of the Church of Nativity, Arbanasi, with 17th-century frescoes

With a population that included Bulgarian artisans, Greek traders, merchants from Armenia and Dubrovnik, and civil servants from all over the Ottoman Empire, these cities became highly cosmopolitan.

Some Bulgarian communities converted to Islam, perhaps to preserve their social status. Ottoman dervishes, who offered an accessible version of the Muslim faith, were key in making Islam attractive to potential converts. Those who adopted Islam were called Pomaks (Helpers) by their countrymen. Their descendants still inhabit the south of the country.

Ottoman bureaucracy was staffed almost entirely by slaves. These were usually collected under the *devshirme* system, by which the sultan's agents toured Christian villages, taking away an agreed proportion of boys aged between seven and 14. These were then forcibly converted to Islam, and educated in special schools before joining the army or the civil service. The brightest gained prestigious jobs. The Sultan's Grand Vezir (chief minister) was often a former *devshirme* boy. Cruel though it may have been, the *devshirme* system was broadly popular among Christian villagers because it offered their offspring an otherwise unimaginable degree of social mobility.

The Bulgarian nobility largely faded away, although a few rich land-owners who cooperated with the regime retained their wealth. The inhabitants of highland villages, such as Kotel,

Interior of the Ebu Bekir Mosque at Yambol

Decorated niche in the Bairakli Mosque, Samokov

Elena and Koprivshtitsa, also prospered. The Ottomans granted them privileges in return for keeping local mountain passes free of bandits and for supplying the Ottoman army with Balkan-reared sheep and wool.

By the late 18th century, central authority in the Ottoman Empire had started to weaken. Bandits known as *kurdzhali* roamed the Balkan region with impunity, attacking wealthy villages and sacking monasteries. By their failure to act, the authorities appeared to favour the bandits, and relations between Christian Bulgarians and their Muslim rulers deteriorated.

Long drawn-out wars with Austria and Russia had also weakened the Ottoman Empire. Educated Bulgarians began to look to the Russians, fellow Orthodox Christians who spoke a similar Slavic language, as their potential liberators from Ottoman rule. This coincided with a new interest in Bulgarian history and culture. In 1762 the monk Paisii of Hilendar wrote his *Slavo-Bulgarian History*, which opened Bulgarians' eyes

1650 The Church of the Nativity in Arbanasi is decorated with frescoes, showing that Bulgarian Christian art continues to flourish

1744 Construction of the Tombul Mosque in Shumen

Interior of the Tombul Mosque, Shumen

| 1600 | 1650 | 1700 | 1750 | 1800 |

1598 An anti-Ottoman uprising led by the merchant Pavel Dzordzic is crushed in Veliko Tŭrnovo

1688 Anti-Ottoman uprisings in Chiprovtsi and Veliko Tŭrnovo are put down.

1762 Paisii of Hilendar completes his *Slavo-Bulgarian History*, which is instrumental in awakening Bulgarian patriotism to their country's pre-Ottoman greatness. The authorities forbade the printing of Paisii's history, but it circulated in manuscript form and played a key role in awakening Bulgarian patriotism.

The National Revival

Bulgarian merchants who had grown rich from the wool trade began to fund patriotic cultural projects, such as the publication of books in the Bulgarian language, and to support schools where pupils were taught in Bulgarian. Funds were also raised for the refurbishment of historic monasteries such as Rila, Troyan and Bachkovo, and the best Bulgarian architects, icon painters and woodcarvers were commissioned to work on them.

This patriotic upsurge in education and the arts was later dubbed the National Revival. Many Bulgarian merchants built themselves lavish family houses that reflected the new taste for fine architecture and wood-carving. This gave rise to a National Revival style of domestic architecture.

Iconostasis detail, Museum of Icon Painting and Woodcarving, Tryavna

The patriotic spirit gradually spread from the cultural to the political sphere. From the earliest days of their rule, the Ottomans had placed the Orthodox Church in the hands of Greek-speaking priests and patriarchs. Bulgarian community leaders now pressed for the creation of a separate branch of the Church, a Bulgarian exarchate free of Greek control. The sultan conceded to these demands in 1872.

Frustrated by the slow pace of reform, Bulgarian intellectuals proposed more radical tactics. In 1871, patriots of the younger generation formed a pro-independence organization from the safety of the Romanian capital, Bucharest. The revolutionary leader Vasil Levski (1837–73) set about organizing an underground anti-Ottoman movement in Bulgaria itself, but was captured and executed in 1873. Meanwhile, young revolutionary ideologues like Lyuben Karavelov and Hristo Botev continued to pin their hopes on a mass uprising.

From Uprising to Liberation

This was the April Rising, which began in 1876 in Koprivshtitsa, a mountain village at a safe distance from the Ottoman-controlled lowland towns. The Ottomans easily quashed the rebellion, but used undisciplined auxiliaries known as *bashibazouks* to restore order. Outraged by the indiscriminate massacres carried out by the *bashibazouks*, public opinion in Russia and western Europe fell solidly behind the Bulgarian cause.

Rila Monastery, focus of restoration during the National Revival

1824 Petur Beron publishes his *Fish Dictionary*, the first widely available Bulgarian-language textbook for schoolchildren

1830 The National Revival gains momentum, as a flowering of the arts unfolds

Decorative detail at Lyutov House, Koprivshtitsa

| 1810 | 1820 | 1830 | 1840 | 1850 |

1810 As the Bulgarian economy grows, an urban middle class emerges

1835 The Velcho Conspiracy, a plot to overthrow Ottoman rule, is foiled in Veliko Tŭrnovo

1844 First periodical printed in the country in the Bulgarian language

Monument to martyrs of the April Rising, Koprivshtitsa

In April 1877 Russia declared war on the Ottoman Empire. Despite Ottoman resistance, Russian forces soon overran Bulgaria and forced the sultan to accept defeat. In March 1878, under the terms of the Treaty of San Stefano, an independent Bulgarian state was created. Besides core Bulgarian territory, it included large parts of Thrace and Macedonia.

Britain, France, Germany and other Western powers suspected that Russia would use the new Bulgarian state to increase its influence in the Balkans. In June 1878, at the hastily called Congress of Berlin, "Greater Bulgaria" was dismembered. A Principality of Bulgaria, still nominally subject to the Ottomans, was created north of the Balkans, with its capital at Sofia. Bulgaria south of the Balkans became a self-governing province of the Ottoman Empire, called Eastern Rumelia, with Plovdiv as its capital. Macedonia still remained a part of the Ottoman Empire, without self-governing status. For staunch Bulgarian patriots, the Congress of Berlin represented a major defeat, and their dream of reuniting the territories assigned to Bulgaria at the Treaty of San Stefano became the dominant theme of Bulgarian politics for the next 70 years.

Independent Bulgaria

Having played a key part in the Liberation, Russia expected to have a guiding role in the new Bulgaria. The Bulgarian army and civil service also desperately needed an influx of Russian bureaucrats to help the fledgling state get on its feet. Alexandûr Batenberg, a German aristocrat who had served as a volunteer in the Russian army, was chosen to become the principality's new ruler. A natural autocrat, Prince Alexandûr had difficulty in dealing with Bulgaria's radical politicians, many of whom had been republican revolutionaries before the Liberation. He also had problems with Bulgaria's Russian masters.

In 1886 Bulgarian nationalists took control of Eastern Rumelia and uni-laterally declared its union with the Principality of Bulgaria. The Russians, enraged that they had not been con-sulted, kidnapped Prince Alexandûr and tried to provoke a pro-Russian coup. Alexandûr was released, but was forced to abdicate. Another central European aristocrat, Ferdinand of Saxe-Coburg-Gotha, became the principality's new head, and Bulgaria's foreign policy was reoriented towards Germany and Austria-Hungary.

Evacuation of wounded from the Shipka Pass, 1877

1861 Bulgarian exiles form the Bulgarian Legion in Belgrade to fight alongside Serbs against the Ottoman Empire

1877–8 The Russo-Turkish War ends in defeat for the Ottomans

1878 The Congress of Berlin creates the autonomous Principality of Bulgaria

1893 Ivan Vazov publishes his masterpiece, the nationalist epic novel *Under the Yoke*

1860   1870   1880   1890   1900

Todor Kableshkov, a leader of the April Rising

1876 The April Rising breaks out in Koprivshtitsa

1885 Eastern Rumelia declares union with the Principality of Bulgaria

Ivan Vazov (1850–1921), author of Under the Yoke

Bulgarian National Revival

By the early 19th century, 400 years of Ottoman rule had forced Bulgarian culture into the background. Very few could read or write, and monasteries were the only places where scholarship lived on. However, a new generation of wealthy merchants wanted a Bulgarian-language education for their children, and raised money for teachers and schools. Before long, a cultural renaissance was under way, reawakening an interest in Bulgarian history and culture, and unleashing new energies in art and architecture. This was the National Revival, and by the mid-19th century its effect was felt in the political sphere, too, with radical young patriots demanding political change. Bulgarians dared to dream of a liberated future. A growing national consciousness swept through Europe. Greece gained independence from the Ottoman Empire in 1829, and Russia, long a friend to Bulgaria, was ready to take on the Turks and their allies.

The Beginning of the Revival

Spiritual godfather of the Bulgarian National Revival was Father Paisii of Hilendar (1722–73), a Bulgarian monk from Mount Athos. Dismayed by the Greek clergy's stranglehold on the Bulgarian Church, which used Greek as its official language, Paisii penned a patriotic manuscript entitled *Slavo-Bulgarian History*, which eulogized Bulgaria's medieval rulers in stirring fashion. It was, in essence, a manifesto of Bulgarian nationalism – a history of the Bulgarian state and Church. Although the Greek-controlled Church authorities forbade the printing of Paisii's book, it was widely circulated, and became required reading for subsequent generations of Bulgarian patriots.

The *Slavo-Bulgarian History* had three major chapters: On the Bulgarian Kingdom, On Bulgarian Saints and On Slav teachers.

Father Paisii of Hilendar distributed his pamphlet, urging people to study their own history and look after important national monuments. "The Lord has left only Rila Monastery to exist in our times…it is the duty of all Bulgarians to guard it, and to give alms to the sacred Rila Monastery."

Educational Reform

One of the main popularizers of Father Paisii's work was Neofit Rilski (1793–1881), a Bansko-born monk who devoted himself to the promotion of Bulgarian-language education. His *Bulgarian Grammar* (1835) was one of the first-ever text books in the language. He also translated a huge quantity of religious texts from Greek into Bulgarian, and spent decades working on a huge *Greek-Slavic Dictionary*. Most importantly, Neofit Rilski headed the first secondary school in Bulgaria, founded by Vassil Aprilov in Gabrovo in 1835. He went on to found a similar school two years later in Koprivshtitsa, introducing modern secular teaching methods later taken up across the whole of Bulgaria.

Aprilov High School, Gabrovo, built in 1835 to resemble the Rishelyov Lyceum in Odessa

The gravestone of Neofit Rilski at Rila Monastery, where he first worked as a teacher before becoming involved with schools. After teaching in Samokov, Gabrovo and Koprivshtitsa, Rilski returned to Rila for the last 29 years of his life, eventually becoming *Igumen*, or head monk.

Ecclesiastical Architecture

Zahari Zograf (1810–53), the artist, portrayed in the semi-Asiatic attire of a 19th-century Bulgarian gentleman.

Relatively unharmed by the Ottomans – and the only form of public construction permitted, churches acquired civic functions, becoming keepers of the national identity. As the only outlet for Bulgarian nationalism, a wave of church building activity swept the country during the 1830s and 1840s. The renovation of Rila Monastery was one of the great patriotic projects of the era, funded by contributions from Bulgarians keen to turn Rila into a national spiritual landmark. One of Neofit Rilski's most famous followers was Zahari Zograf, a Samokov-born painter whose work can be seen in churches and monasteries throughout the country. Among his best-known works are the icons inside Rila monastery church, and frescoes in the church's porch.

Rila Monastery's frescoes are a lively mix of Orthodox icon painting styles, European realism and traditional Bulgarian folk art.

Domestic Art and Architecture

The upsurge in Bulgarian culture was accompanied by changes in lifestyle. Wealthy merchants were travelling widely and building large family houses, often using traditional Bulgarian crafts in their design and construction. House painters used Bulgarian folk art as the inspiration for the colourful floral designs with which they covered outer façades and reception rooms. Wood carvers incorporated floral motifs, bird shapes and sunburst patterns into intricate fretted ceilings. This all maintained a link with the past and reinforced a national identity. This increasing demand for artists in turn led to the development of schools of art – at Tryavna, Samokov and Boyana for example. This artistic legacy remains and can still be seen in Plovdiv, Koprivshtitsa, Tryavna, Veliko Túrnovo and elsewhere.

Lyutov House, Koprivshtitsa, has ceilings with ornate flower motifs and paintings of exotic cities visited by the owner, a yoghurt merchant.

Oslekov House, Koprivshtitsa, is exquisitely decorated (see p179). The owner, Nincho Oslekov, took part in the April Uprising, and was later killed by the Ottomans.

The Will for Political Change

Bulgaria's newly literate population was unwilling to put up with the administration imposed by the Ottoman Empire. Radicals like Georgi Sava Rakovski (1821–67) established the country's first anti-Ottoman armed group, inspiring intellectuals and freedom fighters such as Lyuben Karavelov (1834–79), Vasil Levski (1837–73) and Hristo Botev (1848–76) to organize pockets of resistance. In April 1876 a large-scale uprising against the Ottomans was launched but was brutally put down (see p178). However, news of the massacres resulted in universal condemnation, the start of another Russo-Turkish War and ultimately independence for Bulgaria in 1878.

The Battle at Shipka Pass resulted in a Russian victory in the Russo-Turkish War of 1877–8. The ostensible cause for war was to help the Bulgarians but Russia had long been looking for a way of gaining access to the Mediterranean and ousting the Ottomans from the Balkans.

Vasil Levski, leader of the struggle for independence

Expulsion of occupying Bulgarian forces, perceived as invaders, by Macedonian civilians

Bulgarians and Macedonians

After the Congress of Berlin, many Macedonians, who saw Bulgaria as their main ally in the struggle against Ottoman rule, came to Sofia as exiles. Because of ethnic and linguistic similarities between Bulgarian and Macedonian Slavs, many people from both groups claimed that they were historically one nation. The Bulgarian court and the country's armed forces also sought closer links with Macedonian factions.

Prime minister Stefan Stambolov angered the court by trying to clamp down on the Macedonian lobby, and was dismissed by Prince Ferdinand in 1895. The following year Stambolov was murdered in Sofia by Macedonian revolutionaries. This was the first of many political assassinations linked to Macedonian émigré groups.

In 1903 the Macedonian Revolutionary Organization (IMRO) staged an uprising in Macedonia against Ottoman rule. The revolt was brutally put down, sending another wave of Macedonian exiles into Bulgaria. In 1908 the Ottoman Empire was again convulsed, this time by the Young Turks, a group of Western-oriented radicals who tried to introduce a modern liberal regime. Bulgaria took advantage of Ottoman weakness to declare itself an independent kingdom, with Ferdinand becoming Tsar Ferdinand I.

The Inter-War Years

Stambolyiski's policy of giving power to the peasants enraged the urban middle classes. He also lost the support of Bulgarian nationalists by failing to oppose Macedonia's becoming part of Yugoslavia. In 1923 Stambolyiski was murdered by embittered Macedonian exiles and their Bulgarian allies. An uprising by Bulgarian Communists was put down, leaving power in the hands of the authoritarian right.

Bulgarian soldiers in a trench during the Balkan Wars

1913 The Second Balkan War, in which Bulgaria is driven out of Macedonia by Greeks and Serbs

1912–13 The First Balkan War, in which Bulgaria defeats the Ottomans

1915–18 Bulgaria joins in World War I on the German side

1923 Stambolyiski is overthrown and murdered

| 1900 | 1905 | 1910 | 1915 | 1920 |

1903 The Ilinden Uprising in Macedonia ends in defeat, forcing many Macedonians into exile in Bulgaria

1919–23 Aleksandûr Stambolyiski's radical government tries to create a peasant-ruled state

Bulgarian irregular troops in World War I

Throughout the 1920s, Macedonian revolutionary factions continued to influence Bulgarian politics. They ran southwestern Bulgaria as a virtual gangster-state. Eager to bring the Macedonians under control, a group of intellectuals and Bulgarian army officers staged a coup in 1934. Tsar Boris III imposed a royal dictatorship the following year.

The Balkan Wars to World War I

Eager to force the Ottomans from their remaining European possessions in Macedonia and Thrace, Bulgaria was drawn into an anti-Ottoman alliance with Serbia and Greece. In the First Balkan War of 1912, these three Balkan states inflicted a crushing defeat on the Ottomans but disagreed on how to divide their conquests. The Greeks and Serbs occupied much of Macedonia, which Bulgaria regarded as rightly hers. Bulgaria responded by declaring war on her former allies, but was roundly defeated in the Second Balkan War of 1913.

Bulgaria's involvement in World War I was an even greater disaster. Once again lured by the chance to occupy Macedonia, Bulgaria joined the war on the German-Austrian side in 1915. Three years later a Greek-French-British army invaded Macedonia, sweeping the Bulgarian army aside. With the country in a state of collapse, Tsar Ferdinand abdicated in favour of his son Boris III, and Aleksandŭr Stambolyiski, radical leader of the Agrarian Party, became prime minister.

War and Revolution

In 1941, two years after the outbreak of World War II, Bulgaria joined the Axis,

Tsar Boris III of Bulgaria with his family

judging that an alliance with Germany would allow her to re-occupy Macedonia. By 1943, however, it was apparent that German victory was not assured, and Bulgarian politicians sought other options. In 1944 Bulgaria switched sides, hoping to head off an invasion by the Soviet Red Army. However, the Red Army invaded, providing the Bulgarian Communist Party with the opportunity to seize power.

The Communists' first priority was to banish all other political forces. Politicians sympathetic to the Communists were cajoled into joining the Fatherland Front, an umbrella organization controlled by the Communists. Anti-Communist politicians were denounced as traitors who were sabotaging the country's postwar reconstruction. Elections held in 1945 gave the Communists a landslide victory. A staged referendum in 1946 voted to abolish the monarchy, and Bulgaria became a republic. Persecution of the Communist

1925 Communist extremists bomb Sofia's cathedral, killing 150

Adolf Hitler and Tsar Boris III of Bulgaria

1935 Christo, the artist famous for wrapping up huge buildings, is born Hristo Yavachev in Bulgaria

March 1941 Bulgaria forms an alliance with Nazi Germany

September 1944 Bulgarian Communists, supported by the Soviet Red Army, seize power

| 1925 | 1930 | 1935 | 1940 | 1945 |

1934 Intellectuals and army officers involved in the secret organization Zveno ("Link") launch a bloodless coup

May 1943 Anti-government demonstrations save Bulgaria's Jewish community from deportation to the death camps

Liberation of Sofia, 1944

German forces on the streets of Sofia, after the Bulgarian government's alliance with the Axis powers

Party's opponents culminated in 1947 with the trial of Agrarian leader Nikola Petkov, who was executed for allegedly plotting with foreign intelligence services. Bulgaria was forced to accept the loss of Macedonia, which became a federal republic within Communist Yugoslavia. The BKP leader Georgi Dimitrov considered solving the Macedonian question by forming a Bulgarian-Yugoslav Confederation, of which Macedonia would be a constituent part. However, Stalin disapproved, and Dimitrov died in mysterious circumstances in 1949.

Celebrations marking the Russian Revolution in Sofia in 1947

Under his successor, Vulko Chervenkov, Bulgaria became a model Stalinist society in which political, economic and cultural life was tightly controlled. Agriculture was collectivized and the development of heavy industry fed economic growth. The death of Stalin in 1953 was followed by the fall of his close associates in Eastern Europe, and in 1956 Chervenkov stepped down in favour of Todor Zhivkov. Although he allowed greater cultural freedom, Zhivkov remained a hardline Communist loyal to the Soviet Union.

By the early 1980s, the Bulgarian economy was stagnating and Zhivkov could no longer rely on full employment and improving standards of living to ensure continuing support. He also launched a policy of bringing Bulgaria's Turks into the national fold. Turks were made to adopt Bulgarian surnames, and the use of the Turkish language in public places was discouraged. The policy was justified by the dubious theory that Bulgaria's Turks were ethnic Bulgarians, forcibly Turkicized during Ottoman rule.

The Collapse of Communism

By the 1980s, across Eastern Europe confidence in the Communist system was ebbing away. While the Soviet leader Mikhail Gorbachev addressed the problem through policies of *glasnost* (openness) and *perestroika* (restructuring), Zhivkov was unwilling to follow his lead. Instead, he opted to whip up nationalist passions by stepping up his anti-Turkish campaign. As a result, some 360,000 Bulgarian Turks fled to Turkey in 1989.

1946 Bulgaria becomes a republic and young Tsar Simeon II is forced to leave the country

1953 The death of Stalin in Moscow leads to a political thaw throughout Eastern Europe

1954–6 Chervenkov is removed from government, to be replaced by new party secretary Todor Zhivkov

1975 Todor Zhivkov's daughter Lyudmila becomes Minister of Culture

1945

1955

1965

1949 Communist Georgi Dimitrov is succeeded by the Stalinist Vulko Chervenkov

1965 Zhivkov survives coup by nationalist army officers

Georgi Dimitrov, Communist leader

1974 The Kozlodui nuclear power station in northern Bulgaria comes into operation

The exodus led to catastrophic labour shortages, and crops remained unharvested.

At the same time, Bulgarian dissidents became increasingly active, forming pressure groups such as the environmentally ethical Ecoglasnost, and the embryonic trade-union movement Podkrepa. The fall of the Berlin Wall in November 1989 suddenly changed Eastern Europe's political landscape. The Bulgarian Communist leadership forced Todor Zhivkov to resign, and embarked on a reformist path. Soon after, the anti-Communist opposition united to form the Union of Democratic Forces (UDF), led by the dissident intellectual Zhelyu Zhelev. Bulgaria's ethnic Turks, allowed political expression for the first time, founded the Movement for Rights and Freedoms (MRF).

Communist leader Todor Zhivkov

Contemporary Bulgaria

Under a new name, the Bulgarian Socialist Party (BSP), the Communists won the first free elections in Bulgaria in 1990. They were, however, greeted by a wave of protest, and were forced to accept the veteran anti-Communist Zhelyu Zhelev as president. Fresh elections in 1991 brought the UDF to power, but its radical programme of economic reform was halted when coalition partners, concerned by the social cost of free-market policies, deserted the government.

The BSP re-established itself as the dominant force in Bulgarian politics in 1994.

However, economic mismanagement led to runaway inflation and food shortages, provoking mass protests. The UDF was returned to power in April 1997, but it failed to stamp out government corruption, and in 2001 Bulgaria turned to a new, non-ideological party formed by Bulgaria's former Tsar, Simeon of Saxe-Coburg-Gotha.

Despite economic growth, prosperity failed to reach most of the populace, who returned the BSP to power in 2005. Boyko Borisov, former mayor of Sofia, was then elected prime minister in 2009, but he was ousted in 2013 after Bulgaria's largest public protests since the fall of Communism.

Despite these frequent changes in government, Bulgarian politics is relatively stable. Bulgaria joined NATO in 2004, and signed the European Union Accession Treaty in 2005. Bulgaria's entry into the EU in 2007 marked a significant new phase in the country's voyage from post-Communist chaos to political and economic stability.

Welcoming ceremony for Bulgaria and Romania to the EU, in 2007

1978 Bulgarian dissident Georgi Markov is assassinated with a poisoned umbrella in London	**1984–5** Bulgarian Turks are made to adopt Bulgarian names	**November 1989** Todor Zhivkov is forced to resign	**2001** Simeon of Saxe-Coburg-Gotha (Simeon II) is elected prime minister *Tsar Simeon II*	**2013** Borisov is forced out of office by massive public demonstrations **2005** Simeon of Saxe-Coburg-Gotha loses power to the Socialist Sergei Stanishev

1985	**1995**	**2005**

1981 An attempt on the life of Pope John Paul II is linked to the Bulgarian secret service	**1989** Mass exodus of Bulgarian Turks to Turkey, as anti-Turk campaign is stepped up	**December 1994** The Socialist Party returns to government, but is forced out after two years due to economic incompetence **2004** Bulgaria joins NATO	**2007** Bulgaria joins the EU **2009** Boyko Borisov becomes prime minister

BULGARIA
AREA BY AREA

Bulgaria at a Glance

Combining long sandy beaches with bustling cities, rich history and dramatic landscapes, Bulgaria is one of Europe's most varied destinations. Its two main cities, Sofia and Plovdiv, are urban centres rich in historical relics, contemporary cultural events and year-round nightlife. The mountains offer superb hiking opportunities, beautiful scenery and highland valleys, and are home to the traditional villages and monasteries that kept Bulgaria's culture alive during five centuries of Ottoman rule. The Black Sea coast has something for everyone, from beachside resorts pulsating with dusk-to-dawn night-life to stretches of wild coast with beautiful, unspoiled villages.

Svetlin Rusev Gallery in Pleven
is largely devoted to the work of Sveltin Rusev, a native of the town *(see p189)*. The building, in the Neo-Byzantine style, was originally a public baths complex.

Vidin

Oryahovo

Niko|

NORTHERN BULGARIA
(see pp180–97)

Montana

Berkovitsa

Vratsa

Lúkovit

Pleven

Lovech

Botevgrad

SOFIA
(see pp62–101)

Pridop

Russian Church in Sofia
was built for the community of Russians that settled in the city *(see p75)*. It is based on the design of 16th-century Muscovy churches and was consecrated in 1914.

Radomir

Karlovo

Kyustendil

Dupnitsa

Kostenets

Plovdi\

Blagoevgrad

Asenov\

SOUTHERN BULGARIA
(see pp102–47)

Smolyan

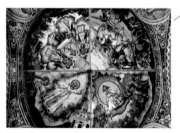

Petrich

Frescoes at Troyan Monastery
exemplify Bulgaria's 19th-century artistic renaissance. The monastery *(see p153)* is one the country's largest.

Plovdiv,
an important cultural and commercial metropolis, is Bulgaria's second-largest city *(see pp138–43)*. The historic centre is notable for its fine National Revival houses.

◀ Aerial view of the historic old town of Nesebûr, located on the Black Sea coast

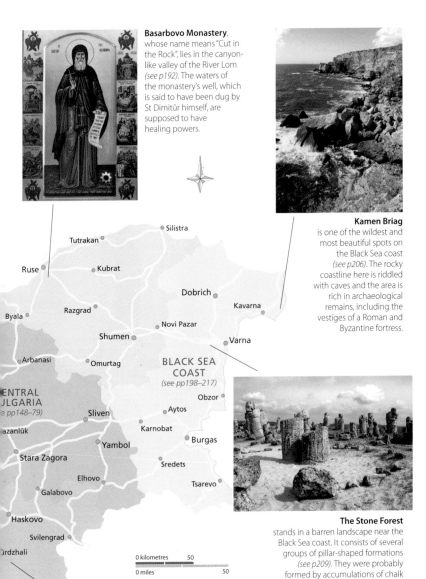

Basarbovo Monastery, whose name means "Cut in the Rock", lies in the canyon-like valley of the River Lom *(see p192)*. The waters of the monastery's well, which is said to have been dug by St Dimitŭr himself, are supposed to have healing powers.

Kamen Briag is one of the wildest and most beautiful spots on the Black Sea coast *(see p206)*. The rocky coastline here is riddled with caves and the area is rich in archaeological remains, including the vestiges of a Roman and Byzantine fortress.

The Stone Forest stands in a barren landscape near the Black Sea coast. It consists of several groups of pillar-shaped formations *(see p209)*. They were probably formed by accumulations of chalk and sand 50 million years ago.

Eastern Rhodope Mountains feature spectacular rock formations formed by the erosive action of wind and rain. Some of the more striking clusters are known by such names as the Stone Mushrooms and Stone Wedding *(see p145)*.

INTRODUCING SOFIA

Exploring Sofia

The capital of Bulgaria since 1879, Sofia was laid out on a grid plan by 19th-century urban planners. A royal palace, parliament house and various government ministries were built in the eastern part of the centre, providing Sofia with a quarter of fine buildings which still exists today. The Roman, medieval and Ottoman-era buildings that also dot Sofia give some idea of the city's ancient origins. Monumental public buildings from the Communist period add a melancholy grandeur to downtown squares and intersections. The main social artery of modern Sofia is Bulevard Vitosha, a permanently bustling shopping thoroughfare with cobbled residential streets on either side. Outside the city centre, Sofia is dominated by residential suburbs broken up by attractive swathes of green parkland and the looming presence of Mount Vitosha.

Changing of the Guard at the Presidency

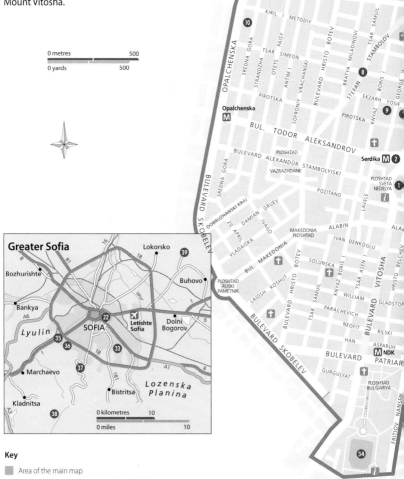

| 0 metres | 500 |
| 0 yards | 500 |

Greater Sofia

Key

Area of the main map

◀ The magnificent dome of the Aleksandŭr Nevski Memorial Church, Sofia

Sights at a Glance

Places of Worship
1 Church of Sveta Nedelya
3 Church of Sveta Petka Samardzhiiska
4 Rotunda of Sveti Georgi
6 Banya Bashi Mosque
9 Sofia Synagogue
16 Russian Church
17 *Aleksandûr Nevski Memorial Church pp76–7*
18 Church of Sveta Sofia
27 Church of Sveti Sedmochislenitsi
36 Boyana Church
37 Dragalevtsi Monastery
39 Monastery of St George

Museums and Galleries
10 National Polytechnic Museum
11 *Archaeological Museum pp72–3*
14 National Art Gallery
15 Natural History Museum
20 National Gallery of Foreign Art
22 Military Museum
28 Ivan Vazov House-Museum
30 City Art Gallery
35 *National History Museum pp88–9*
32 Peyu Yavorov Museum
33 Museum of Socialist Art

Theatre
29 National Theatre

Historic Streets and Squares
8 Zhenski Pazar Market
21 National Assembly Square
31 Slaveykov Square

Palaces, Historic Buildings and Monuments
2 Monument to Sveta Sofia
5 Mineral Baths
7 Central Market Hall
12 Presidency
13 Party House
23 Mausoleum of Prince Aleksandûr Batenberg
24 Monument to the Soviet Army
25 Red House
34 National Palace of Culture

Parks and Gardens
26 Borisova Gradina
19 Botanical Garden
38 *Mount Vitosha pp92–3*

Key
■ Major sight
— Pedestrian street

Getting Around
Central Sofia is easy to explore on foot, although you may need public transport to reach outlying museums. An efficient tram network covers the city centre and the inner suburbs, while buses and trolleybuses are a convenient means of reaching Sofia's outer fringes. Taxis are numerous and inexpensive. The metro system, consisting of two lines which cross the city centre from east to west and north to south, will be joined by a third sometime in 2015.

Aleksandûr Nevski Memorial Church

For hotels and restaurants in this region see pp222–3 and pp232–4

Street-by-Street: The Historic Centre

Many cultures have shaped Bulgaria, and nowhere is this more visible than in Sofia's historic heart. Orthodox churches, a 16th-century mosque and an Art Nouveau synagogue just around the corner bear witness to a rich religious heritage. The parade of 19th-century buildings along ulitsa Tsar Osvoboditel attest to the mood of optimism and energy that invigorated Bulgaria after the Liberation of 1878. In stark contrast are the stern office blocks around ploshtad Nezavisimost, the legacy of Communist power. Today, Sofia is a centre of growing consumer culture, which is at its most tangible along bulevard Vitosha, the city's vibrant main shopping street.

⑬ Party House
Built to house the Central Committee of the Bulgarian Communist Party, this is Sofia's most imposing example of Stalinist-era architecture.

⑫ Presidency
This 20th-century building is the Bulgarian president's office. A Changing of the Guard ceremony takes place hourly at the entrance.

⑭ National Art Gallery
This fine 19th-century former palace displays paintings by Bulgaria's best artists.

MOSKOVSKA

KNYAZ AL. BATENBERG SQUARE

SABORNA

KNYAZ AL. BATENBERG

DYAKON IGNATI

IVAN VAZOV

GEN. GURKO

⑪ ★ Archaeological Museum
A converted mosque, the museum has a dazzling array of ancient and medieval treasures.

㉚ City Art Gallery

㉙ National Theatre
Built in an opulent Neo-Classical style, the National Theatre is home to Bulgaria's leading state drama company.

㉘ Ivan Vazov Museum
It honours the great poet, novelist and playwright.

⑮ Natural History Museum
This museum has a collection ranging from rocks to snakes.

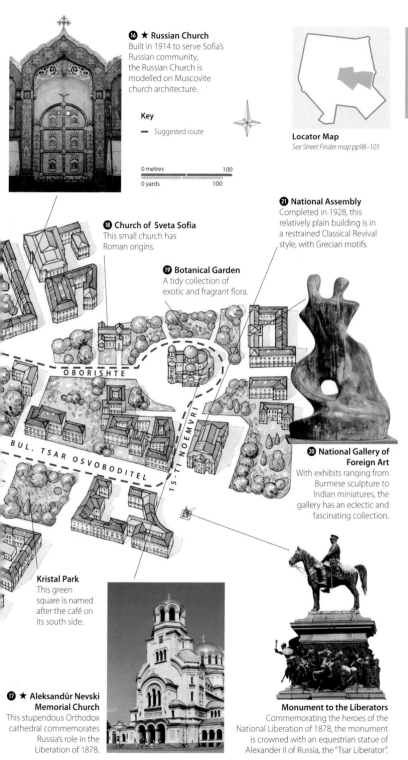

⑯ ★ Russian Church
Built in 1914 to serve Sofia's Russian community, the Russian Church is modelled on Muscovite church architecture.

Key

— Suggested route

Locator Map
See Street Finder map pp98–101

0 metres 100
0 yards 100

㉑ National Assembly
Completed in 1928, this relatively plain building is in a restrained Classical Revival style, with Grecian motifs.

⑱ Church of Sveta Sofia
This small church has Roman origins.

⑲ Botanical Garden
A tidy collection of exotic and fragrant flora.

OBORISHTE

15-TI NOEMVRI

BUL. TSAR OSVOBODITEL

⑳ National Gallery of Foreign Art
With exhibits ranging from Burmese sculpture to Indian miniatures, the gallery has an eclectic and fascinating collection.

Kristal Park
This green square is named after the café on its south side.

⑰ ★ Aleksandŭr Nevski Memorial Church
This stupendous Orthodox cathedral commemorates Russia's role in the Liberation of 1878.

Monument to the Liberators
Commemorating the heroes of the National Liberation of 1878, the monument is crowned with an equestrian statue of Alexander II of Russia, the "Tsar Liberator".

Church of Sveta Nedelya, built on the site of earlier churches and an important focus of Christian worship in Sofia

❶ Church of Sveta Nedelya

Църква "Света Неделя"

pl. Sveta Nedelya. **City Map** 1 B4.
Ⓜ Serdika. 🚃 1, 3, 5, 7, 8, 12, 18. **Open** 7am–6:30pm daily. ✝ 9am daily. ✉

Set on an island in central Sofia, the Church of Sveta Nedelya ("the Blessed Sunday") has long been one of the city's principal places of worship. It was built on the site of a 10th- century church. In Ottoman times it was known as the Church of Sveti Kral ("the Blessed King") because it held the relics of Stefan Urosh II Milutin, a 14th-century Serbian ruler who defeated the Bulgarian emperor, Mihail Shishman (see p48). The bones, believed to have miraculous healing powers, are kept in a casket beside the iconostasis.

The church was rebuilt in 1856–63 but was almost completely destroyed in 1925 when Communist extremists bombed it during a funeral service attended by Tsar Boris III and his family. The arcades on the north side and the gilt iconostasis survived. Frescoes executed in the 1970s and a marble floor added in the 1990s give the interior a contemporary look. The seat of the bishops of Sofia, the church has cathedral status.

❷ Monument to Sveta Sofia

Паметник "Света София"

pl. Nezavisimost. **City Map** 1 B4.
Ⓜ Serdika. 🚃 1, 3, 5, 7, 8, 12, 18, 20, 22, 23.

From a lofty pedestal, Georgi Chapkunov's statue of a golden-skinned, black-robed figure towers over Sofia's busiest crossroads. The Monument to Sveta Sofia ("Holy Wisdom"), erected in 2000 to stand as a millennial symbol of the city, was in-spired both by the Orthodox Church's concept of Holy Wisdom (typically symbolized by a saintly-looking woman), and Athena, Greek goddess of wisdom. The crowned figure holds a laurel wreath (symbol of blessing) and an owl (symbol of knowledge) perches on her shoulder. The statue stands on the spot once occupied by a sculpture of Lenin, removed in 1990.

❸ Church of Sveta Petka Samardzhiiska

Църква "Света Петка Самарджийска"

pl. Nezavisimost. **City Map** 1 B4.
Ⓜ Serdika. 🚃 1, 3, 5, 7, 8, 12, 18, 20, 22, 23. **Open** 7:30am–7:30pm daily. ✝ 8am daily. ✉

This tiny historic church, in an underground shopping mall just

The apse and high altar at the Church of Sveta Petka Samardzhiiska

below the Monument to Sveta Sofia, is dedicated to St Petka Paraskeva, a 3rd-century Christian girl from Asia Minor who was martyred during the reign of the emperor Diocletian. In the Ottoman period, the Guild of Saddlers financed the church's upkeep, and this accounts for its full name: Church of Sveta Petka of the Saddlemakers.

Entry to the church is via the crypt, which is thought to date from Roman times. A modern spiral staircase leads to the nave, built in the 11th century but strengthened with concrete in the 20th. Fragments of colourful 16th-century frescoes depicting scenes from the New Testament survive. The best-preserved are those on the north wall; they show a touching Deposition, and the resurrected Christ appearing to the disciples on Mount Tabor.

❹ Rotunda of Sveti Georgi
Ротонда "Свети Георги"

bul. Knyaz A. Dondukov 2. **City Map** 1 B4. Ⓜ Serdika. 🚊 1, 3, 5, 7, 8, 12, 18, 20, 22, 23. **Open** May–Aug: 7:30am–6:30pm; Sep–Apr: 8am–5:30pm. 🚹 8am, 9am & 5pm daily.

Set in a courtyard between the Sheraton Hotel and the Presidency (see p74), this graceful red-brick rotunda probably stands on the site of a pre-Christian temple. The building has been used as a church since the 6th century. The church was converted into a mosque in the 16th century, and briefly served as a mausoleum for Aleksandŭr Batenberg, independent Bulgaria's first prince.

The interior of the church is sumptuously decorated with medieval frescoes. A 14th-century depiction of Christ Pantokrator, accompanied by angels and symbols of the four evangelists, fills the cupola. Stretching round the drum that supports the cupola is a frieze containing 22 portraits of the prophets. A further tier has figures of 16 other prophets. Fragments of 10th-century

Rotunda of Sveti Georgi, with a plain exterior and colourful frescoes within

frescoes, including some beautiful angels' heads, also survive. Behind the Rotunda is a park where archaeological excavations have revealed the remains of 2nd-century Roman Serdica (see p46).

❺ Mineral Baths
Минерални Бани

City Map 1 C3. Ⓜ Serdika. 🚊 1, 3, 5, 7, 8, 12, 18, 20, 22, 23. **Open** only for temporary exhibitions.

Warm mineral springs rise in the centre of Sofia, and, to exploit them, both the Romans and the Ottomans built extensive public baths here. The present-day Mineral Baths (Mineralna banya) were built in 1913. The architects, Petko Momchilov and Friedrich Grünanger, drew inspiration from Byzantine church architecture. The result is a highly distinctive building crowned by three

The Mineral Baths, based on the design of an Oriental building

egg-shaped domes. The Art Nouveau tiles running on the façade provide a feast of colour. Due to the dilapidated state of the roof, the baths closed in 1986, and are currently undergoing renovation. While the south wing is planned to become a Museum of Sofia, at the moment the renovated part of the building hosts only temporary exhibitions.. Just north of the baths, on the opposite side of ulitsa Ekzarh Iosif, there are public taps, which people use to fill spa water.

❻ Banya Bashi Mosque
Джамия "Баня Баши"

bul. Knyaginya Mariya Luiza. **City Map** 1 B3. Ⓜ Serdika. 🚊 1, 3, 5, 7, 8, 12, 18, 20, 22, 23.

The Mosque of the Central Baths is the only Muslim place of worship in Sofia that still serves its original function. It was built in 1576, possibly by the Ottoman master-builder Sinan, architect of the Suleiman Mosque, Istanbul. It used to have the public bathhouse next door.

Constructed with large blocks of honey-coloured stone layered with terracotta bricks, this pretty building has a finely proportioned cubic design, topped with an octagonal drum that supports a graceful dome 15 m (50 ft) in diameter. The mosque's most attractive features are its slender reddish minaret, and the arcaded porch at the entrance, crowned by a trio of small cupolas.

❼ Central Market Hall

Централни Софийски Хали

bul. Knyaginya Mariya Luiza 25. **City Map** 1 B3. **Ⓜ** Serdika. 🚊 1, 7, 20, 22. **Open** 7:30am–9:30pm daily.

Boasting two huge floors of delicatessen stalls, food outlets, clothing shops and jewellery outlets, Central Market Hall (Tsentralni hali) is one of Sofia's busiest buildings. Built in 1909 and restored in the 1990s, it is also one of the most distinctive. The impressive Art Nouveau main portal bears Sofia's coat of arms and is topped by a dainty three-dial clocktower. The original mechanism, with shiny brass cogwheels and pendulum, is preserved in a glass case on the ground floor of the Hall. The Victorian-style iron pillars, balustrades and roofing beams of the cavernous interior convey a wonderful sense of period.

Central Market Hall, often simply called the Market Hall (Halite)

Colourful fresh produce at the popular Zhenski Pazar Market

❽ Zhenski Pazar Market

Женски Пазар

City Map 1 A2. 🚊 1, 7, 20, 22. **Open** 8am–7:30pm daily.

Five minutes' walk west of the synagogue, Zhenski pazar (Women's Market) is Sofia's biggest and most crowded open-air market, stretching for over 500 m (600 yards) along ulitsa Stefan Stambolov. Full of shoppers each day, it represents a lively and traditional alternative to the shopping malls springing up elsewhere in the city. Fruit, vegetables and other foodstuffs are the main attraction, although you can also pick up all manner of inexpensive clothes, crafts, and kitchenware. Flower sellers congregate around the northern end of the market. Zhenski pazar is enduringly popular with Sofia's pensioners, as prices here can be rather significantly lower than elsewhere in the city. Pickpockets also operate here, so visitors should exercise extreme caution.

❾ Sofia Synagogue

Софийска Синагога

ul. Ekzarh Iosif 16. **City Map** 1 B3. **Ⓜ** Serdika. 🚊 1, 7, 20, 22. **Open** 9am–4pm Mon–Fri, 10am–2pm Sun.

A spectacular Moorish design, one of the largest synagogues in Europe, this place of worship can hold as many as 1,300 people, although these days the numbers are far, far fewer. Designed by Austrian architect Friedrich Grünanger and completed in 1909, it is home

Detail of the ornate Moorish exterior of the Sofia Synagogue

to a magnificent and ornate brass chandelier weighing over 2,000 kg (4,400 lb). The interior also has some exquisite details in its Moorish mosaics, painted pillars and scalloped arches. It is not always possible to see inside the synagogue – knock at the door to see if a visit is possible – there is a Jewish Museum of History that tells the history of the Jews in Bulgaria.

❿ National Polytechnic Museum

Политехнически музей

ul. Opulchenska 66. **Tel** (02) 831 3004. **Ⓜ** Opulchenska. 🚊 1, 5, 22. **Open** 9am–5pm daily. 🅿 📷 **ⓦ** polytechnicmuseum.org

Located about a fifteen-minutes' walk west of the centre, the National Polytechnic Museum (Natsionalen politehnicheski muzei) is Bulgaria's principal science museum, with a large and eclectic collection of various machines, laboratory instruments and gadgets through the ages. Everything from telescopes to the history of television is covered in the display, which also includes a handful of elegant vintage cars, and a pair of motorbikes made by the famous Plovdiv-based "Balkan" factory in the 1960s. There's also a fine display of early 20th-century porcelain and tableware, most of it donated by Bulgaria's former royal family, the Saxe-Coburg-Gothas.

Sofia's Jewish Community

The majority of Bulgaria's Jews were descended from the Sephardic community, who were allowed to settle in the Ottoman Empire after their expulsion from Christian Spain at the end of the 15th century. Sofia's Jews were respected for their contribution to the life of the city. This was recognized by Tsar Ferdinand in 1909, when he presided over the opening of the Sofia Synagogue. By World War II, the Jews made up about one fifth of Sofia's population. However, Bulgaria's alliance in 1941 with Nazi Germany led to an increasing spiral of anti-Jewish legislation despite protests from the Orthodox Church. Matters came to a head in 1943 when German officials asked their Bulgarian counterparts to deport 50,000 Jews to German-occupied Poland.

The unsung hero – Dimitůr Peshev
Dimitůr Peshev, from Kyustendil, was the Minister of Justice for Bulgaria, interested in safeguarding the constitution. However, at first he was supportive of the alliance with Germany, thinking that Bulgaria would regain the lands taken unjustly away after the Balkan Wars 1912–13. However, on learning of the plans to deport Bulgaria's Jews he and his colleagues pressurized the deputy Prime Minister to cancel the deportation order at the last moment. He and many others then wrote a formal letter of protest to the Prime Minister and the Tsar.

Deportations from Thrace and Macedonia
However, the cancellation order did not reach Bulgaria's recently acquired territories of Thrace and Macedonia and over 11,000 Jews were rounded up and deported. The letter and threats of public demonstrations ensured that no more Jews from Bulgaria would be expelled. Two weeks later Prime Minister, Bogdan Filov sacked Peshev from his ministerial position. After the war Peshev was tried by the Communists and put in jail for being anti-Soviet as well as anti-Semite.

Tsar Boris III
There is still controversy over Tsar Boris's role during the war. He refused to hand over control to Germany on many matters, and in the end he did tell his ministers that somehow they must stop the deportation of Bulgarian Jews. However, some say he could have done more to prevent the Thracian and Macedonian deportations.

After the threat of Communism
After 1945, Bulgaria's atheist Communist rulers were profoundly hostile to traditional religions. Jewish community organizations were taken over by the state and synagogues were closed and left to fall into ruin. An increasing number of Jews chose instead to emigrate in the mid-1950s to the newly-established state of Israel rather than stay in Bulgaria. Today, probably fewer than 2,500 Jews still remain in Sofia, with an equal number spread throughout other major cities in the country.

⓫ Archaeological Museum

Археологически Музей

Many of Bulgaria's finest Thracian, Roman and medieval treasures are preserved in Sofia's Archaeological Museum (Arheologicheski muzei). The building itself was once the Buyuk Dzhamiya, or Grand Mosque, which was built in 1494 and converted into the present museum in 1892. The former prayer hall, a lofty cube-shaped space beneath nine graceful domes, provides the perfect ambience in which to admire an open-plan display of Greek, Roman and medieval sculpture. The side rooms are devoted to a stunning sequence of treasures dating from Bulgaria's prehistoric, Thracian and medieval periods.

Illyrian Helmet
This bronze helmet of the 6th century BC was found in the grave of an Illyrian warrior.

Laurel Wreath

Mezzanine III

★ Golden Burial Mask from Kran, near Shipka
Unearthed in 2004, this mesmerizing portrait of a Thracian king dates from the late 5th century BC. Found with a hoard of other items, it is finely crafted from 673 g (1 lb 8 oz) of solid gold.

Mezzanine II

Ground floor

★ Main Hall
Roman sculptures, tombstones and floor mosaics are arranged beneath a sequence of elegant arches.

Gallery Guide

This is an unusually inviting museum – it is located in an attractive building, the collection is not over-whelmingly large and the labelling is informative. After passing through the light and airy main hall, visitors can head up to the top mezzanine to see the Thracian gold, walk around the gallery and then, if time allows, simply explore at will.

Main entrance

Key to Floorplan

☐ Medieval Bulgarian Art
☐ Prehistoric Finds
☐ Iron Age Art
▨ Ancient Thracian Treasures
☐ Roman-era Art
▨ Non-exhibition space

Thracian Rider
Depictions of the hunter-god often adorn Thracian tombs. In this example, of the 3rd century BC, the rider is seated on a lion-skin saddle, as his horse tramples a wild beast.

Medieval Icons
This 17th-century Nativity scene from the Church of Sveta Petka in Krapets, southeast of Sofia, is just one of many valuable icons in the first-floor gallery.

Laurel Wreath
Discovered in a princely grave dating from the 4th century BC, in Rozovets near Plovdiv, this delicate wreath features 63 leaves of gold.

Upstairs gallery

Ceramic Icon of Sveti Todor
Found in the ruined Patleyna Monastery near Preslav, this tiled icon is one of the high points of 10th-century Bulgarian art.

Medieval Bulgarian Pottery
From the 12th to the 14th centuries, Bulgaria's ceramics workshops produced bowls and jugs lavishly decorated with animal, bird and floral designs, and glazed in vivid yellows and greens.

Roman-era Sarcophagus
This 2nd-century AD Roman sarcophagus from Ratiaria (Archar) on the Danube river is decorated with Eros and bulls' heads.

⑫ Presidency
Президенство

ul. Lege. **City Map** 1 B4. Ⓜ Serdika.
🚊 1, 3, 5, 7, 8, 12, 18, 20, 22, 23.
Closed to the public.

The Prezidentsvo, or office of
Bulgaria's president, is housed in
a 20th-century grey building that
it shares with the Sheraton Hotel
on the north side of ploshtad
Nezavisimost. The main entrance,
on ulitsa Lege, is guarded day
and night by soldiers dressed in
19th-century red-and-white
parade uniforms, complete with
braided jackets and feathered
hats. The Changing of the Guard,
in which one shift of soldiers
arrives and another departs in
ceremonial, high-stepped
marching style, takes place
every hour throughout the day.

Changing of the Guard ceremony outside
the Presidency

⑬ Party House
Партиен Дом

pl. Nezavisimost. **City Map** 1 C4.
Ⓜ Serdika. 🚊 1, 3, 5, 7, 8, 12, 18, 20,
22, 23. **Closed** to the public.

Diagonally opposite the
Presidency is Party House
(Partien Dom), built in 1954 to
serve as the headquarters of the
Bulgarian Communist Party.
Intended to symbolize political
power and prestige, it dominates
the wide open space of
ploshtad Nezavisimost, and is
an immediately visible landmark
to anyone approaching the
city centre from the west. The
building's monumental façade

Party House, once the headquarters of the Communist Central Committee

features a lower storey of grey
granite, a cream Neo-Classical
colonnade, and a soaring spire
that originally bore a huge
red star.

Following the political
changes of November 1989 *(see
p57)*, Bulgaria's Communists were
advised to take the red star
down so as to avoid provoking
anti-Communist sentiment. They
failed to do so, and in August
1990 an angry mob attacked
Party House, setting fire to the
lower floors. The building has
been renovated and it now
belongs to Bulgaria's Parliament,
whose MPs have offices here.

⑭ National Art Gallery
Национална Художествена
Галерия

pl. Knyaz Aleksandûr Batenberg 1.
City Map 2 D4. **Tel** (02) 980 0093.
Ⓜ Serdika. 🚊 1, 3, 5, 7, 8, 12, 18, 20,
22, 23. **Open** 10am–6pm Tue–Sun. 🖼
📷 🖥 nationalartgallerybg.org
Ethnographic Museum: ul.
Moskovskaga. **Tel** (02) 987 4191. **Open**
10am–6pm Tue–Sun. 🖼 📷 📷

The National Art Gallery
(Natsionalna hudozhestvena
galeriya) occupies the west wing
of the former royal palace. It was
built in 1873 for Sofia's Ottoman
rulers and after 1877 was adapted
for independent Bulgaria's
monarchs. The building's palatial
character persists. Many of the
exhibition halls have pre-World
War I parquet floors and intricate
stucco ceilings.

Bulgarian fine art grew out of
the icon-painting workshops
of the 19th century, and the
gallery's exhibition appropriately
begins with works by the
greatest of all Bulgarian religious
artists, Zahari Zograf, *(see p110)*.
Although he devoted most of
his life as an artist to painting
traditional frescoes for the
Orthodox Church, Zograf also
produced a series of realistic
portraits that show great
psychological insight. Through
these, he effectively launched
Bulgarian painting on a modern
European course. On display
here are Zograf's portraits of his
sister-in-law Kristina Zograf-ska,
the educationalist Neofit Rilski
(see p52), and a simple but
charismatic self-portrait.

The gallery's collection then
traces the development of
Bulgarian painting. Highlights
include a room devoted to the
work of local Impressionists,
which shows the impact of
Western artistic currents on
Bulgarian painting. Centrepiece
of the collection is the work of
Bulgarian painters of the
interwar generation, grouped
together in the Red Hall (the
former palace ballroom). These
paintings show how Bulgarian
painters fused modernist styles
of painting with traditional
native themes, creating a truly
national style. Foremost among
them was the mystically
inclined Vladimir Dimitrov-
Maistora (1882–1960), whose
paintings of Bulgarian peasant
girls surrounded by brightly

coloured fruit exude a quasi-religious aura. Zlatyu Boyadzhiev (1903–76) is represented by some empathic portrayals of the poverty-stricken Bulgarian peasantry, while the magic realism of paintings of 19th-century Plovdiv by Tsanko Lavrenov (1896–1978) conjure up a seductively nostalgic vision of the Bulgaria of the past. Exhibitions of contemporary art are often held on the ground floor.

The Ethnographic Museum (Etnografski muzei) in the east wing has a small but absorbing collection of traditional Bulgarian costumes. It also mounts temporary exhibitions devoted to Bulgarian folklore and the museum shop offers a wide range of traditional craft items.

🅕 Natural History Museum

Национален Исторически Музей

bul. Tsar Osvoboditel 1. **City Map** 2 D4. Ⓜ Serdika, Sveti Kliment Ohridski. 🚌 9, 84, 94, 280, 306. 🚊 1, 2, 4, 9, 11. 🚋 20, 22, 23. **Tel** (02) 987 4195. **Open** 10am–6pm daily. 🅿 🏠 Ⓦ nmnhs.com

East of the National Art Gallery, the Natural History Museum (Nationalen prirodonauchen muzei) is an enjoyable if rather old-fashioned museum, strong on geology and European fauna.

Entrance to the Natural History Museum on ulitsa Tsar Osvoboditel

Beginning with rocks and crystals on the ground floor, the display moves on to stuffed birds and mammals on the first and second floors, and an array of glass cabinets filled with butterflies and insects on the third. Walking up the staircase visitors pass glass tanks containing live snakes, lizards and rodents. The museum shop sells decorative stones and crystals.

🅰 Russian Church

Руска Църква

bul. Tsar Osvoboditel. **City Map** 2 D5, 4 D1. 🚌 9, 84, 94, 280, 306. 🚊 1, 2, 4, 9, 11. 🚋 20, 22, 23. **Open** 7:30am–6pm daily. 🚹

Standing beside the busy bulevard Tsar Osvoboditel, the Church of St Nicholas the Miracle-Worker (Tsurkva na Sveti Nikolai Chudotvorets), popularly known as the Russian

Church, is the most striking building in Sofia. It was built to serve Sofia's Russian community and was consecrated in 1914.

Modelled on 16th-century Muscovite churches, it boasts a cluster of shimmering gilt domes, one of which thrusts skywards at the tip of a pea-green spire. The porch, with a pitched roof covered in green tiles, exudes a fairytale charm.

The church's interior is covered with frescoes derived from 17th-century paintings in Moscow and Yaroslavl. Rich in swirling arabesques, they reveal the influence of exotic Eastern styles on Russian art.

A door on the west side of the church leads down to the crypt, last resting place of Archbishop Serafim, leader of the Russian Church in Bulgaria from 1921 to 1950. Serafim's congregation was largely composed of Russian exiles who had fled their homeland after the Bolshevik Revolution, and his reputation for anti-Communism, his kindness and his dignity made him enormously popular with Sofians at large.

Such is Serafim's enduring spiritual stature that his tomb is considered to be capable of working miracles. Because of this a regular stream of worshippers visit the tomb to place handwritten prayers of intercession in a box beside his sarcophagus.

Iconostasis in the Russian Church, with traditionally painted icons in elaborate gilt frames

⓱ Aleksandûr Nevski Memorial Church

Храм-паметник "Александър Невски"

Crowned with a cluster of gilt domes, the Aleksandûr Nevski Memorial Church (Hram-pametnik Aleksandûr Nevski) was built in stages between 1882 and 1924, to commemorate Russia's military contribution to the War of Liberation of 1877–8. It is named after one of Russia's most revered medieval rulers, Prince Aleksandûr Nevski of Novgorod, who defeated the Teutonic Knights on the frozen waters of Lake Peipsi in 1242. Modelled on Russian Neo-Byzantine churches, it is built in pale Bulgarian limestone. The solemn interior is bathed in amber light, which pours in from the windows, and the soft glow of hundreds of flickering candles.

View of the Church
The church's domes are its outstanding feature. While the central dome and belfry are gold-plated, the others are plated with copper, which has weathered to a green hue.

Entrance to the crypt

Clusters of Candles
Visitors to the church buy candles at the entrance, and light them as a symbol of prayer.

Main entrance

Mosaic of Christ
This mosaic of Christ, with arms outstretched, fills the tympanum over the portal's central arch.

KEY

① West window

② Gold-plated dome

For hotels and restaurants in this region see pp222–3 and pp232–4

Dome Fresco
God the Creator, with the Christ Child on his knee, looks down on the congregation. This church's frescoes were painted by Russian and Bulgarian artists.

VISITORS' CHECKLIST

Practical Information
pl. Aleksandûr Nevski. Main Church: **Tel** (02) 988 1704.
Open Nov–Feb: 7am–6pm daily; Mar–Oct: 7am– 7pm daily. Icon Gallery: **Tel** (02) 981 5775.
Open 10am–5:30pm Tue–Sun.
Liturgy 8am & 5pm daily. Evening vigil 6:30pm Sat. Service 9:30am Sun.

Transport
Sveti Kliment Ohridski. 9, 280, 306. 1, 2, 4, 9, 11.

★ Iconostasis
The marble, onyx and alabaster iconostasis features carvings of grapes, palms and peacocks. The icons include portraits of Christ and the Virgin.

Tsar's Throne
Built for Tsar Ferdinand (ruled 1887–1918), the throne is guarded by stone lions and crowned by a marble canopy. Behind is a portrait of the tsar and his wife.

★ Icon Gallery in Crypt
With icons dating from the 12th to the 19th centuries, and several delicately carved iconostases, the gallery contains the richest collection of religious art in Bulgaria.

Icons & Iconography

Icons play a major role in the Orthodox Church. Far from being mere depictions of Christ and the saints, icons are themselves sanctified objects that help the faithful to feel the presence of God. For this reason, icons are stylized, and are not intended to be realistic portraits. Icons displayed on an iconostasis are usually arranged according to a strict hierarchy. Those of Christ, the Virgin Mary and St John the Baptist occupy central positions, with those of saints of particular importance to the individual church hung on either side.

St George Among the most popular icons in Bulgaria are those of the dragon-slaying St George (Sveti Georgi), the demon-slaying St Demetrius, and other mounted warrior-saints of the late Roman era, such as St Eustace and St Menas. They symbolize the courage and perseverance that Christians must have to retain their faith in difficult times. Such icons were of great comfort to Orthodox Christians under Ottoman rule in Bulgaria.

St Nicholas (Sveti Nikola) is the patron saint of seafarers and icons of him are prominently displayed in churches on the Black Sea coast. He is invariably portrayed as a kindly old man with long white beard, often with a ship in the background.

St Constantine and St Elena Constantine the Great was the Roman emperor who, in the 4th century, made Christianity the official religion of the Western Roman Empire. His mother Elena was said to have discovered a fragment of the cross of Christ during a visit she made to Jerusalem. She preserved the fragment as a holy relic. In icons, St Constantine (Sveti Konstantin) and St Elena (Sveti Elena) are often portrayed together.

St John of Rila (Sveti Ivan Rilski), a 9th-century mystic and healer is Bulgaria's patron saint. After his death, possession of his remains became associated with the legitimacy of kingship.

St Cyril and St Methodius (SS Kiril i Metodii) were monks from Thessaloniki who set out to convert the Slavs of Moravia (now part of the Czech Republic) in the early 9th century. Their mission was only partially successful, but their work lived on through their disciples Kliment and Naum, who were responsible for converting Bulgaria's Khan Boris (later known as Tsar Boris) to Christianity in 865. The Cyrillic alphabet was named in honour of St Cyril, who did much preparatory work in developing the script.

Church of Sveta Sofia, with a lion at the Tomb of the Unknown Soldier

⑱ Church of Sveta Sofia

Църква "Света София"

pl. Aleksandŭr Nevski. **City Map** 2 E4. 🚌 9. 🚊 20, 22, 23. **Open** 9am–7pm. ✉

The origins of Sofia's oldest surviving Christian church go back to the 6th century. It was built on the site of two 4th-century churches, just outside the city walls. The spot was also the town graveyard of Serdika (as Sofia was known in ancient times), and the church remained Sofia's principal cemetery church well into the Middle Ages.

During the Second Bulgarian Kingdom (1185–1396), the church was probably the seat of the city's bishop, and the city itself (which was known in Bulgarian as Sredets) gradually took the church's name, which means "Holy Wisdom". After the Ottoman conquest, the church became a mosque, but was abandoned when an earthquake struck in 1858.

The church takes the form of a three-aisled Byzantine-style basilica. The interior is lofty, calm and peaceful, and the beautiful exposed brickwork of the walls and arches is completely devoid of ornamentation. Some fragments of mosaic from one of the 4th-century churches can be seen in the floor of the south aisle.

Outside the church, just beside the south wall, is the Tomb of the Unknown Soldier, which commemorates the thousands of Bulgarian soldiers who fell during World War I. The monument is guarded by a stately bronze lion.

⑲ Botanical Garden

Ботаническа Градина

ul. Moskovska 49. **City Map** 2 F4. **Tel** (02) 986 5043. 🚌 1, 2, 4, 9, 10, 11. 🚊 20, 22. **Open** Apr–Oct: 9am–5pm daily. ✉ 🔲 🌐 ubg-bg.com

Tucked away in a side street behind the Aleksandŭr Nevski Memorial Church, Sofia University's Botanical Garden (Botanicheska gradina) has a small but inviting collection of Mediterranean flora, and a fragrant rose garden. There is also a glasshouse where a humid atmosphere has been created for the cultivation of such exotic species as palms, banana trees and coffee bushes. The garden's shop has a range of seedlings for sale.

Main entrance to the National Gallery of Foreign Art

⑳ National Gallery of Foreign Art

Национална галерия за чуждестранно изкуство

pl. Aleksandŭr Nevski 1. **City Map** 2 F4. **Tel** (02) 986 5043. Ⓜ Sveti Kliment Ohridski. 🚌 1, 2, 4, 9, 11. 🚊 20, 22. **Closed** for renovation until late 2014. ✉ 📷 🌐 foreignartmuseum.bg

The pristine white building behind the Aleksandŭr Nevski Memorial Church houses the National Gallery of Foreign Art (Natsionalna galeriya za chuzhdestranno izkustvo). Opened in 1985, its collection comprises gifts made to the Bulgarian state, either by private individuals or by countries allied to the ruling Communist regime at that time.

On the ground floor are outstanding collections of African tribal sculpture and of Japanese woodblock prints. The display of 19th- and 20th-century painting upstairs seems mediocre in comparison. However, there are highlights, such as a pastel drawing by Renoir, a lithograph by Picasso, and some sketches by Eugène Delacroix. Thematic exhibitions are often held in the basement, which also houses a barrel-roofed late-Roman tomb.

The building itself is a modern reconstruction of the State Printing House (1883), one of post-Liberation Bulgaria's finest Neo-Classical buildings, which was destroyed by Allied bombing raids in 1944.

The Botanical Garden on a sunny autumn day

For hotels and restaurants in this region see pp222–3 and pp232–4

The National Assembly building, on National Assembly Square

㉑ National Assembly Square

Площад "Народно Събрание"

City Map 2 E5, 4 E1. M Sveti Kliment Ohridski. 9, 280, 306. 1, 2, 4, 5, 8–11. **Closed** to the public.

At the eastern extremity of bulevard Tsar Osvoboditel, National Assembly Square (ploshtad Narodno sûbranie) is a crescent-shaped space that takes its name from the National Assembly building on its northern side. Built in several stages from 1884 to 1928, the building is a plain, box-like structure, its decoration limited to a sparse row of Grecian-style urns atop the façade. Above the portal at the entrance are the words *Obedinenieto pravi silata* ("Unity is Strength"), a dictum attributed to the 9th-century Bulgarian ruler Khan Krum.

At the centre of the square stands the Monument to the Tsar Liberator (Pametnik na Tsar Osvoboditel), an equestrian statue of Tsar Alexander II of Russia, whose war with the Ottoman Empire (1877–8) led to the liberation of Bulgaria after centuries of Ottoman rule *(see p51)*. Designed by the Italian sculptor Arnaldo Zocchi (1862–1940), the bronze statue portrays the tsar on horseback, holding Russia's declaration of war on the Ottomans in his outstretched hands. Clustered round the pedestal are statues of Russian troops and Bulgarian volunteer fighters being resolutely led into battle by a winged figure of Nike, the Greek goddess of victory.

㉒ Military Museum

Военноисторически музей

ul. Cherkovna 92. **Tel** (02) 946 1805. 9, 72, 120, 313, 314. 20, 22. **Open** 10am–6pm Wed–Sun. 🖼 📷 🖥

Set in the grounds of Bulgaria's military academy, 2 km (over 1 mile) east of the city centre, the Military Museum (Voennoistoricheski muzei) houses a colourful display of the uniforms worn by the Bulgarian army through the ages. The display begins with the homemade tunics worn by anti-Ottoman insurgents during the April Rising of 1876 *(see p178)*, and ends with the combat fatigues worn by Bulgarian armed forces today.

The most impressive aspect of the museum is the extensive walk-around display of military hardware set out in the yard outside. Visitors can examine at close quarters various pieces of artillery, as well as armoured cars, tanks, and MiG fighter jets. But the presence of a pair of SS23 missiles, once fitted with nuclear warheads and stored in silos near Sofia, may send a shiver down the spine.

㉓ Mausoleum of Prince Aleksandûr Batenberg

Мавзолей на Княз Александър Батенберг

bul. Vasil Levski 81. **City Map** 4 E2. **Tel** (02) 983 1526. M Sveti Kliment Ohridski. 9, 84, 94, 280, 306. 1, 2, 5, 8. **Open** 9am–5pm Mon–Fri.

This charming domed pavilion with a Greek-style portico is the last resting place of Prince Aleksandûr Batenberg, the German-speaking aristocrat (1854–93) who served as a volunteer in the Russian army before being chosen as the Bulgarian principality's first monarch in 1879 *(see p51)*. Incapable of maintaining a balance between the pro- and anti-Russian factions in Bulgarian politics, he was forced to abdicate in 1886, and spent the rest of his life in the Austrian town of Graz.

Two uniforms from the historic display at the Military Museum

Mausoleum of Prince Aleksandûr Batenberg

Aleksandûr's wish to be buried in Bulgaria was honoured by the Bulgarian government, who initially displayed his sarcophagus in the Rotunda of Sveti Georgi (see p69), before moving it to its present purpose-built location.

The mausoleum is set in a tree-shaded park on the western side of bulevard Vasil Levski. The prince's tomb is carved from Carrara marble, and above the sarcophagus a portrait of the prince is held aloft by plump cherubs. On either side of the tomb are inscriptions referring to Aleksandûr's victories in the Serbo-Bulgarian war of 1885, when he was commander-in-chief of the Bulgarian army.

ⓤ Monument to the Soviet Army
Паметник на Съветската Армия

Orlov most. **City Map** 4 F3. 72, 76, 84, 204, 604. 1, 2, 5, 8.

Just five minutes' walk east of National Assembly Square, on the opposite side of bulevard Vasil Levski, is the Monument to the Soviet Army (Pametnik na Suvetskata armiya). It was unveiled in 1954, and is Sofia's finest Communist-era sculptural group. It consists of a granite pillar, 34 m (112 ft) high, on which stands an over-lifesize statue of a soldier of the Red Army, accompanied by a Bulgarian worker and a peasant woman

with a child in her arms. Reliefs at the base of the pillar show scenes from the Russian October Revolution of 1917 and from World War II. About 100 m (330 ft) northeast of the pillar stand a pair of oblong stone blocks that bear another set of reliefs. These portray Bulgarian workers, peasants and partisans greeting their Soviet colleagues as liberators. Despite the heavy-handed ideological message that they convey, the sculptures themselves are filled with an expressive vitality rare in the political art of the period. In recent years, skateboarding and rollerblading parks have been set up around the base of the monument, turning it into an unlikely meeting point for Sofia's youth.

Immediately east of the monument is Orlov most (Eagle Bridge), an important Sofia landmark. This is where Bulgarian prisoners held in Ottoman jails re-entered the city on their return from captivity in 1878. Nicknamed the Eagles in recognition of their fortitude, the prisoners are commemorated by a quartet of eagle sculptures mounted on pillars beside the bridge.

Figures on the Monument to the Soviet Army

ⓤ Red House
Червената къща

ul. Lyuben Karavelov 15. **City Map** 4 E4. **Tel** (02) 988 8188. Ⓜ Sveti Kliment Ohridski. 72, 76, 94, 204, 604. 1, 2, 5, 8. 2, 12. **Open** 10am–5pm Mon–Fri, check for temporary exhibitions. Ⓦ **redhouse-sofia.org**

The Red House (Chervenata kushta) is an independent cultural centre devoted to contemporary art, theatre and dance. It occupies one of Sofia's most famous modernist buildings, a flat-roofed, wine-red villa built in the 1930s for the sculptor Andrey Nikolov (1878–1959). Nikolov spent much of his professional life in Rome, and an Italian inscription *Voi ch'entrate qui, lasciate ogni cacattivo pensiero* ("Ye who enter here, leave all bad thoughts behind") stands above the main portal. Inside the house, the high-ceilinged rooms that Nikolov used as a studio now serve as an exhibition area for temporary exhibitions of modern art and photography. There is also a small permanent exhibition devoted to the life and work of Nikolov himself, featuring the portrait busts he made of prominent Bulgarians and a beautiful marble head of a woman entitled *Longing*. A life-size nude by Nikolov occupies a niche in the entrance hall.

Sculpture by Andrey Nikolov on display in a room of the Red House

Restored interior of the intricately designed Sofia Synagogue (see p70) ▶

A quiet corner of Borisova Gradina, the public park in southeastern Sofia

26 Borisova Gradina
Борисова градина

City Map 4 F4. Ⓜ Sveti Kliment Ohridski. 🚌 9, 72, 76, 84, 94, 206, 604. 🚎 4, 5, 8, 11. 🚃 10, 12, 18.

Beyond the elliptical grey form of the Vasil Levski sports stadium that marks the south-eastern fringes of the city centre, lies Borisova Gradina, Sofia's best-loved municipal park. It stretches out for some 2 km (just over 1 mile) beyond the stadium and was laid out by the Swiss garden designer Daniel Neff in 1884. It was later named Borisova Gradina (Boris's Garden) to mark the birth of Prince Boris (who became Tsar Boris III) in 1894.

Planted with elms, chestnuts, sycamores, limes and several species of conifers, and with large areas of oak forest at the far end, Boris's Garden has the atmosphere of semi-tamed woodland rather than that of a formal garden.

As well as the Vasil Levski stadium (the Bulgarian national football team's home ground) the park also has tennis courts, the CSKA football stadium, a velodrome and an open-air swimming pool.

Perhaps the most enjoyable part of the park is its north-eastern section, parallel to Tsarigradsko shose. Here there is a children's play-park with climbing frames, and long avenues of limes leading towards the Bratska Mogila (Mound of Brotherhood). This obelisk, 42 m (138 ft) high, was raised in 1956 to commemorate those who died in the cause of communism. It is a typical piece of pro-Soviet propaganda, with statues of anti-Fascist partisans at its base, and bronze reliefs on the pedestal showing the Red Army being enthusiastically greeted by Bulgarian civilians.

27 Church of Sveti Sedmochislenitsi
Църква "Свети Седмочислен ици"

ul. Graf Ignatiev 25. **City Map** 4 D3. 🚌 94. 🚎 1, 2, 5, 8, 9. 🚃 10, 12, 18. **Open** 7am–6pm daily. 🕐 8am daily. 📷

In a small park beside ulitsa Graf Ignatiev, the Church of Sveti Sedmochislenitsi ("the Holy Seven") honours the seven saints (Cyril, Methodius and their five disciples) who brought both Christianity and literacy to the Balkan Slavs in the 9th century.

It was built as a mosque in the 16th century, during Ottoman times, and it was known as the Black Mosque because of the dark-coloured marble that was originally used to build its minaret (which no longer exists). After the War of Liberation of 1877–8 (see p51), the Bulgarians used the mosque as a prison, and it was converted into a church in 1903. Using the famous 14th-century churches in the Black Sea town of Nesebûr (see pp212–13) as inspiration, the architects rebuilt the mosque's central dome and added many smaller cupolas and a bell tower.

Inside the church, ravishing frescoes blend medieval and modern styles. The north wall shows Tsar Boris being given copies of the

Mosaic of the Holy Seven, with the figure of Christ, above the entrance to the Church of Sveti Sedmochislenitsi

scriptures by St Kliment and St Naum, followers of the priests Cyril and Methodius who brought Christianity to the Bulgarian court.

Portrait of the writer Ivan Vazov at the Ivan Vazov House-Museum

㉘ Ivan Vazov House-Museum

Къща - музей на Иван Вазов

ul. Ivan Vazov 10. **City Map** 4 D2. **Tel** (02) 988 1270. 5, 8, 9. 1, 7, 10, 12, 14, 18. **Open** 1–5pm Tue–Thu, 11am–5pm Fri–Sat.

The life and work of Ivan Vazov (1850–1921), Bulgaria's best-loved novelist, poet and playwright, are honoured in this interesting and atmospheric museum. Most famous as the author of *Under the Yoke* (*Pod igoto*), the epic novel of Bulgarian resistance to Ottoman rule, Vazov personified the patriotic spirit of Bulgarian literature in the years immediately after the Liberation.

Vazov was born in the central Bulgarian town of Sopot *(see p172–3)*. He lived as an exile in Romania during the final years of Ottoman rule, returning to post-Liberation Bulgaria to serve as a magistrate in the provincial town of Berkovitsa. However, Vazov had an uneasy relation-ship with Bulgaria's political leaders, and he spent time in both Plovdiv (then the capital of Eastern Rumelia) and in the Russian port of Odessa before finally settling in Sofia.

The publication of *Under the Yoke* raised Vazov to the status of a national figure, and he served as Minister of Education in the late 1890s. His books still form an important part of today's school curriculum.

The museum occupies the house where Vazov lived from 1895 to 1921, and many of the rooms have been preserved intact. The upstairs bedrooms and sitting rooms, with Art Nouveau wallpaper and brightly coloured traditional carpets, are particularly seductive. Vazov's beloved dog Bobby, stuffed during the author's lifetime after an unfortunate incident with a tramcar, still enjoys pride of place in the study. In another room visitors can enjoy black-and-white photographs of places important to Vazov's life and career.

㉙ National Theatre

Народен театър Иван Вазов

ul. Dyakon Ignatii 5. **City Map** 1 C5, 3 C1. **Tel** (02) 811 9276 (museum); (02) 811 9227 (tickets). 9. 10, 12, 18. nationaltheatre.bg

Presiding over a leafy oblong of park known as the City Garden, the National Theatre (Naroden Teatur) has a Neo-Classical splendour that few other buildings in Sofia can match.

Sculpture at the National Theatre

Built in 1907 by the Viennese architects Hermann Helmer and Ferdinand Fellner, the theatre has a colonnaded façade topped by a pediment that contains a relief of Apollo surrounded by luxuriantly reclining muses. Even more sensuous are the sculptural groups that crown the towers on either side of the pediment. They consist of trumpeters borne along in grand chariots, each of which is drawn by a trio of fierce lions.

Home to Bulgaria's leading state drama company, the theatre concentrates on Bulgarian and international classics. It is worth buying a ticket even if only to enjoy the opulent balustraded foyer and plush auditorium.

The City Garden (Gradskata gradina) in front of the theatre is Sofia's oldest park. It was laid out during the Ottoman period, when it served as the governor of Sofia's private garden. Now with neat lawns, deciduous and evergreen trees and a modern fountain, it is popular for relaxed strolling year-round.

The elegant Neo-Classical façade of the National Theatre

Visitors at an exhibition in City Art Gallery

⓿ City Art Gallery

Градска художествена галерия

ul. Gûrko 1. **City Map** 1 C5, 3 C1.
Tel (02) 987 2181. Ⓜ Sveti Kliment Ohridski. 🚌 9. 🚊 10, 12, 18.
Open 10am–7pm Tue–Sat, 11am–6pm Sun. ⓦ **sghg.bg**

Standing at the southern end of the City Garden, the City Art Gallery (Gradska Hudozhestvena Galeriya) does not have a permanent collection, but hosts prestigious temporary exhibitions. These showcase the excellent work of contemporary Bulgarian painters and sculptors, although some challenging work by international artists is also shown here from time to time.

⓿ Slaveykov Square

Площад "Славейков"

City Map 3 C2. 🚌 9. 🚊 10, 12, 18.

The broad pedestrianized oblong of Slaveykov Square (ploshtad Slaveykov), just a short stroll southwards from the City Garden, is famous for hosting a large daily open-air book market. Although most of the books on sale here are in Bulgarian, visitors will also find a range of richly illustrated books in English on Bulgarian history and culture. A daily book market has been in the square since the early 1990s. At that time, many of Bulgaria's state-owned bookshops had gone bankrupt, and were replaced by the informal network of independent street stalls that began to spring up in Sofia. Most of these street stalls eventually gravitated towards Slaveykov Square.

The square is named in honour of the educationalist and patriotic activist Petko Slaveykov and his son, the modernist poet Pencho Slaveykov. The life-size bronze statue of father and son seated side by side on a bench at the western end of the square is a popular local landmark.

Life-size statue of Petko Slaveykov and his son Pencho in Slaveykov Square

㉜ Peyu Yavorov Museum

Музей на Пейо Яворов

ul. G.S. Rakovski 136. **City Map** 3 B3.
Tel (02) 987 3414. 🚌 9.
Open 10am–5pm Mon–Fri. 🖼

A short walk south of the book market on Slaveykov Square, this small but absorbing museum occupies the apartment where the poet Peyu Yavorov and his wife Lora Karavelova lived in 1913–14. Period furniture and original Art Nouveau wallpaper provide an intriguing insight into the tastes of the period.

Most Bulgarians associate this museum with the tragic suicides of both Lora and Peyu, and there are compelling references to both events in the display. One glass cabinet holds a glamorous black dress rent by a bullet, recalling the night of 29 November 1913 when a jealous Lora shot herself with Yavorov's pistol. In another room, a bloodstained cushion still rests on the couch where Yavorov committed suicide a year later.

A statue of Yavorov, showing the seated poet in an attitude of deep thought, occupies the front garden.

㉝ Museum of Socialist Art

Музей на Социалистическото Изкуство

ul. Luchezar Stanev 7. Ⓜ Joliot Curie & G.M. Dimitrov.
Open 10:30am–5:30pm Mon–Fri.
🖼 📷

This is Bulgaria's first-ever museum dedicated to its Communist past, a fascinating open-air display which brings together many of the country's Socialist-era statues and other works of state-commissioned art. The park has busts and figures of famous communist leaders and activists. Both the Lenin statue, that stood for more than 40 years in Sofia city centre, and the Red Star, which

The National Palace of Culture (NDK), a monolithic centre of the arts

topped the Communist Party Building (Party House) on pl. Nezavisimost, are here. A small exhibition hall hosts a collection of Socialist realist paintings. In all, the museum has 77 sculptures, 60 paintings and 25 smaller plastic artworks that were created between 1945 and 1989.

There are also regular screenings of socialist propaganda films, while the excellent museum shop stocks an interesting selection of quirky souvenirs.

❸ National Palace of Culture
Национален дворец на културата (НДК)

pl. Bûlgariya. **City Map** 3 A5. **Tel** (02) 916 6300. Ⓜ NDK. 🚌 72, 94, 204, 604. 🚃 1, 2, 5, 8, 9. 🚋 1, 7. 🖉 💻 📷
ⓦ ndk.bg

Marking the southern end of bulevard Vitosha, Sofia's main shopping street, the National Palace of Culture (Naroden Dvorets na Kulturata, or NDK) is one of the city's modern landmarks. Begun in 1978, it was completed in 1981, when it opened in celebration of the 1,300th anniversary of Bulgarian statehood (see pp46–7). This monumental eight-storey hexagon of concrete and glass dominates the flagstoned open spaces and neat flowerbeds of ploshtad Bûlgariya.

The building was originally named in honour of Lyudmila Zhivkova, daughter of the dictator Todor Zhivkov

(see pp56–7). She was Bulgaria's Minister of Culture from 1975 to 1981. Zhivkova died of a brain tumour in 1981, and was much missed by Bulgarian intellectuals, who felt that she had broadened the horizons of Bulgarian culture beyond the ideological constraints of the Communist party. She was also active in promoting Bulgarian culture abroad.

Inside the NDK, the principal space is a concert hall with seating for 5,000 and other smaller concert halls. Beneath the building is an arcade filled with stalls selling clothes.

A footbridge behind the NDK leads across bulevard Bûlgariya to the Hilton Hotel and Yuzhen Park (South Park), an expanse of lawns, flowerbeds and untended grassy areas that stretches out for 3 km (2 miles) towards dense wood- land. A conspicuous presence at the northern end of the park is the Thirteen Hundred Years Monument, an ugly, crumbling modernist sculpture. It stands as a reminder of 1,300 years of oppression, and bears the inscription "We are in time and time is in us", words attributed to Vasil Levski (see p173).

Peyu Yavorov (1878–1914)

Of all 20th-century Bulgarian poets, the one whose life and work most fascinates successive generations of readers is Peyu Yavorov. He began writing poetry while working at a provincial post office in the Black Sea town of Pomorie, and moved to Sofia when his work began to be published by the literary magazine *Misûl*. He is best known for the poems of obsessive love inspired by Mina Todorova, a teenage girl whose family considered Yavorov to be an unworthy suitor. Mina died of consumption in 1910, and Yavorov was immediately courted and captured by Lora Karavelova, an emancipated divorcée.

Yavorov was also a committed revolutionary, and his involvement in the guerrilla movement in Ottoman-occupied Macedonia made Lora feel abandoned and ignored. When in Sofia, Yavorov was constantly surrounded by female admirers, and Lora shot herself in a fit of jealous rage in 1913. Intending to commit suicide, Yavorov shot himself but survived. Lora's family accused Yavorov of her murder and pursued him through the courts. Abandoned by society, Yavorov finally committed suicide.

Statue of the poet at the Peyu Yavorov Museum

㉟ National History Museum
Национален исторически музей

Bulgaria's largest collection of historic artifacts is located 7 km (4 miles) from the centre of Sofia, but, despite the distance, most visitors will think the trip worthwhile. The museum has a delightful setting in the foothills outside the capital and contains some truly remarkable objects – the 4th-century BC Thracian gold treasures from Panagyurishte are the highlight. But there is plenty more to see in this slightly eclectic collection: icons and frescoes recall the Bulgarian Church under the Ottomans, while modern history is covered by military uniforms and hardware, and theatrical memorabilia. The building was once a Communist Party palace, so touring the vast opulent rooms adds extra interest.

★ Panagyurishte Gold
The 3rd-century BC Panagyurishte treasure consists of eight richly decorated gold rhytons or drinking vessels. Five rhytons are in the form of animal heads, while three depict Amazon warriors.

Second floor

First floor

Ceramics
The medieval cities of Pliska, Preslav and Veliko Tûrnovo were centres of ceramics manufacture, where vessels decorated with floral and animal motifs were made.

★ Earth Mother Statue
This clay figure was found near Targovishte, in north-eastern Bulgaria. It stands 14 cm (5½ in) high and is about 6,500 years old. The red and ochre spiral decorations indicate some sort of costume.

Ground floor

Key to Floorplan

- Prehistory
- Ancient Thracians Greeks and Romans
- Medieval Bulgaria
- Bulgaria under the Ottoman Empire
- Post-Liberation Bulgaria (post-1878)
- Folk Costumes and Craft
- Temporary exhibition
- Non-exhibition space

Main entrance

For hotels and restaurants in this region see pp222–3 and pp232–4

Cinema Props
Costumes worn and props used in some of Bulgaria's most famous films are displayed in the round hall on the second floor.

VISITORS' CHECKLIST

Practical Information
ul. Vitoshko Lale 16, Boyana.
Tel (02) 955 4280. **Open** Nov–Mar: 9am–5:30pm (last ticket 4:45pm); Apr–Oct: 9:30am– 6pm (last ticket 5:30pm). **Closed** 1 Jan, 3 Mar, 24 May, 24 & 25 Dec. (free last Mon in month). **w** historymuseum.org

Transport
63, 111. 2. M21.

Folk Costume
This collection features traditional dress from all over Bulgaria. Note the metal *pafti* or belt-buckles, frequently embossed with animals, figures of saints, or abstract designs.

Kilim of Teteven
This example of a 19th-century hand-woven woollen kilim bears the colourful starburst design favoured by weavers in the town of Teteven.

Gallery Guide
The halls work well chronologically, so start with Prehistory before moving on to the Thracians – the stars of the show, they are often on loan to other museums. The Medieval hall is a little disappointing, but there are items of interest in the other halls. It is also rewarding to explore the building just to see how the Communist leaders lived.

Wooden Icon Screen
The central doors of the icon screen, above, symbolize the divide between the material world and God's kingdom. The doors bear icons showing the Annunciation, framed by highly intricate woodcarving.

★ Last Judgment Fresco
The Last Judgment was a favourite subject for Bulgarian religious artists. This 17th-century example shows the grisly punishments awaiting sinners in hell.

Fresco in Boyana Church, depicting scenes from the life of Christ

Some of the finest paintings are in the 13th-century annexe. The ground floor contains 18 scenes from the life of St Nicholas, and one of the earliest known depictions of Bulgaria's patron saint, John of Rila (see p78). The portrayals of Christ, in scenes of the Last Supper, the Crucifixion and the Transfiguration, display a remarkable psychological depth.

On the south wall of the annexe are full-length portraits of Tsar Konstantin Asen (1257–77) and Irina, his queen. On the opposite wall are depictions of Sebastokrator Kaloyan and his wife Desislava, clad in fine clothes. Kaloyan is shown holding a model of the church, thereby indicating his status as the patron of its reconstruction.

36 Boyana Church
Боянска църква

ul. Boyansko ezero 3. **Tel** (02) 959 0939. 63, 64, 107. **Open** Apr–Oct: 9:30am–5:30pm; Nov–Mar: 9am–5pm.

The village suburb of Boyana, on a hillside south of the National History Museum (see p75), is a relatively prosperous district of modern family houses and villas. However, just above the main square is Boyana Church (Boyanskata tsurkva), one of Bulgaria's most renowned medieval buildings. Covered from floor to ceiling with beautiful 13th-century frescoes, the church has been declared a UNESCO World Heritage Site.

The church's origins go back to the 11th century, when it was a compact building, roughly 6 m (20 ft) square. Two centuries later, it was enlarged by the addition of a two-storey annexe built onto its western façade. According to inscriptions, this enlargement was carried out in 1259 by Sebastokrator Kaloyan, a nobleman who also funded the church's interior decoration.

Painted by anonymous local masters, the church's frescoes display a quality of realistic portraiture unusual for the period. Western artistic influences may have reached Bulgaria from Constantinople, which had been captured by Crusaders in 1204.

A glorious portrait of Christ Pantokrator fills the cupola, in the oldest section of the church. Lower down is a frieze with portraits of the Evangelists, followed by rows of armour-clad warrior-saints, including George and Demetrius.

37 Dragalevtsi Monastery
Драгалевски манастир

Dragalevtsi. 93. **Open** Apr–Oct: 8:30am–6pm; Nov–Mar: 8:30am–5pm.

On the wooded slopes of Mount Vitosha, just above the suburb of Dragalevtsi, stands a 14th-century monastery. Founded during the reign of

Boyana Church, built in the 11th–13th centuries in Byzantine style

Draglevtsi Monastery, one-time refuge of the patriot Vasil Levski

Tsar Ivan Alexandůr (1331–71), it was abandoned at the time of the Ottoman conquest, but was re-founded a century later thanks to the efforts of the local *boyar* (aristocrat) Radoslav Mavur. Frescoes in the monastery church depict Radoslav and his wife Vida, on the north wall of the vestibule. Also in the vestibule are scenes from the New Testament, including an impressive Last Judgment. Well-preserved frescoes of the apostles and of various saints line the walls of the nave.

The monks of Dragalevtsi frequently provided refuge to the Bulgarian patriot Vasil Levski *(see p173)* in 1871–2, when he was engaged in establishing a network of revolutionary cells through-out the country. Today, the monastery is home to a flourishing convent, and is used as a summer retreat by the Orthodox Church hierarchy.

From just above the suburb of Dragalevtsi, visitors can take a chairlift to the resort of Aleko, which provides panoramic views of Sofia. Aleko is an expanding winter sports destination. Its proximity to Sofia means that it can be busy at weekends, with city-dwellers coming to enjoy winter sports, and with walkers arriving in summer. It is therefore best to come here on a weekday.

❸ Mount Vitosha
Витоша

See pp92–3.

❹ Monastery of St George
Манастир "Свети Георги"

Kremikovtsi. 117. **Open** irregular hours. St George's Day (6 May).

In the 13th century Sofia was a major spiritual centre, and many monastic communities were established in the hills around the city. These outlying monasteries continued to flourish well into the Ottoman period, not least because they were some distance from the Turkish-dominated city centre.

The Monastery of St George, just above the village of Kremikovtsi, some 25 km (15 miles) east of Sofia, was one such focus of Bulgarian ecclesiastical life. In 1493 the local *boyar* Radivoy, grieving the loss of his children Todor and Dragana, funded the construction of a new monastery church. He also commissioned painters to decorate it with sumptuous frescoes. Radivoy and his family are portrayed in the narthex, the *boyar* presenting the model of the church to its patron, St George. The north wall of the nave bears an animated depiction of St George spearing a dragon. Elsewhere on the north wall are portraits of St George's fellow warrior-saints, such as Demetrius, Theodor Tyron, Theodor Stratilat and Mercurius, who is shown pulling an arrow from his eye. The monastery has irregular opening hours, but a key-holder is usually available to open the church. In the plain below Kremikovtsi, Bulgaria's largest steelworks presents an incongruous modern counterpoint to the monastery's medieval splendours.

Painting of St George and the Dragon at the Monastery of St George

③⑧ Mount Vitosha
Витоша

Rising above Sofia's southern suburbs, the granite massif of Mount Vitosha provides Bulgaria's capital with an easily accessible recreation area. The top of the mountain is relatively smooth, making it the ideal terrain for easy hikes. Acres of beech forest cover Vitosha's lower slopes, while spruce and pine predominate further up. The mountain's highest point, the 2,290-m (7,500-ft) Cherni Vruh (Black Peak), is surrounded by a plateau covered in grassland, juniper bushes and bogs. Protected as a nature park since 1934, Vitosha is a natural habitat for martens, deer, wild boar and, occasionally, brown bears.

Panorama of Sofia
For the best views of the city, which sprawls at the foot of Mount Vitosha, head for Kopitoto, or take a trip downhill on the Dragalevtsi chairlift.

★ Stone River
This compelling natural attraction consists of huge boulders deposited by a glacier in the last Ice Age and smoothed by seasonal meltwaters.

Mount Vitosha Plateau
West of the peak, this peat bog plateau supports rare wild flowers and insects. Much of it falls within the protected Torfeno branishte reserve, so hiking is discouraged.

KEY

① **Zlatni Mostove (Golden Bridges)**, directly below the Stone River, is an area of meadows and forest clearings popular with picnickers.

② **Kopitoto (The Hoof)** is a ridge topped by the slender television and radio mast that can be seen from all over the city, and a restaurant with terrific views.

③ **Simeonovo**, boasting fresh mountain air and plenty of green space, is one of Sofia's most affluent suburbs.

Meteorological Observatory
This weather station was built in 1935 and has been monitoring the weather conditions ever since. In winter, when Sofia is in cold fog, an interesting inversion takes place and Vitosha enjoys the winter sun.

Map labels: Boya Chu, 1348 m, 1087 m, ② Boyana Waterfall, 190(, Zlatni Mostove ①, 1969 m, Torfen Branish Reserv, 2041 m, 2108 m

★ Dragalevtsi Monastery

The Monastery of the Holy Virgin is set in deep forest just above the suburb of Dragalevtsi. Stunning 15th-century frescoes featuring warrior saints – St Demetrius of Thessaloniki, St George and St Mercurius – decorate the entrance hall of its church.

VISITORS' CHECKLIST

Practical Information
10 km S of Sofia. **i** ul. Antim I, 17, Sofia (02 988 5841).
w park-vitosha.org

Transport
93 to Dragalevtsi; 122 & 123 to Simeonovo; 61 to Zlatni Mostove: all from Hladilnika bus terminus, (on tram route 10).

Cable Car
The cable car runs from the pleasant suburb of Simeonovo to Aleko, and provides excellent views over the city.

```
0 kilometres        1
0 miles             1
```

Aleko Mountain Hut
First built in 1924, the Aleko mountain hut is a popular starting point for hikers in summer. In winter, Aleko becomes the centre of Mount Vitosha's busy ski scene.

★ Cherni Vruh
Vitosha's highest point is a popular destination for hikers. It is about an hour's walk up from Aleko, or a 30-minute walk above the last stop of the highest chairlifts, if they are running.

Key
— Major road
— Other road
-- Trail
△ Peak
•→• Cable car line
•→• Chairlift line
🚠 Chairlift station
⬜ Urban area

For additional map symbols *see back flap*

ENTERTAINMENT AND SHOPPING

In terms of opera, classical music and drama, Sofia offers a great deal for a relatively low price. The city's bar and club scene is vibrant and stylish, but also slightly unpredictable, with many venues swiftly coming into vogue and going out of fashion again. Many of Sofia's most culturally authentic clubs, where live musicians and belly dancers often perform, are those devoted to the Oriental-influenced Balkan pop music known as *chalga*. Live rock music, however, is less common in Sofia than in other European capitals, although there are plenty of piano bars where you can dance to jazz and blues. Sofia also has a lively retail culture, with shops and markets staying open late into the evening seven days a week.

Entertainment

The music, opera and dance seasons usually run from October through to June. Information and tickets for most cultural events in Sofia are available from the National Palace of Culture.

Opera, Dance and Classical Music

Sofia's elegant opera house is home to the **National Opera and Ballet** (Natsionalna opera i balet), a very prestigious organization that puts on quality performances three to four times a week during the concert season. The regular programme is firmly rooted in the classics, although international companies often perform modern works.

The Sofia Philharmonic Orchestra gives performances at the **Bulgaria Concert Hall** (Zala Bulgariya) at least once a week. The concert hall is also a venue for recitals by soloists and chamber music concerts given by Bulgarian and international musicians.

Major orchestral concerts featuring international performers also take place at the **National Palace of Culture (NDK)** (Natsionalen dvorets na kulturata), a modern concert and congress centre whose main hall has excellent acoustics and seating for 3,800.

Theatre

Sofia's leading theatre is the **Ivan Vazov National Theatre** (Naroden teatur Ivan Vazov), an opulent building that is the base of Bulgaria's best actors and directors. The programme is wide-ranging and includes Bulgarian classics as well as foreign contemporary drama. Modern plays are also put on by the **Sofia Drama Theatre** (Dramatichen teatur Sofia) and the **Aleko Konstantinov Satirical Theatre** (Satirichen teatur Aleko Konstantinov).

The leading venue for fringe and experimental drama is the interesting **Sfumato Theatre Workshop** (Teatralna rabotilnitsa Sfumato). Although performances are in Bulgarian, many are based on improvisation and movement rather than written text, so that they are accessible to non-Bulgarian speakers.

Clubs and Bars

Central Sofia is packed with clubs and bars, many of which have designer interiors and attract an equally dressed-up clientele. **Motto**, which serves cocktails and food in a stylish lounge-bar atmosphere, is typical of Sofia's contemporary bar scene. **Dada Cultural Bar** hosts regular performances, exhibitions and other events. There is also a growing number of pubs, which are popular with both Bulgarians and foreign visitors. Of these, **JJ Murphy's** is one of the longest-established.

Dance clubs are informal and inexpensive, with long-standing venues such as **Yalta** and **Chervilo** ("Lipstick") attracting international DJs and a youthful audience.

Shopping

Sofia's most glamorous shopping street is bulevard Vitosha, where brightly lit window displays feature clothing and accessories by modern international designers. Ulitsa Graf Ignatiev, just to the east, is also lined with shops, ranging from bakeries to bookstores.

Antiques, Crafts and Souvenirs

There is a daily antiques and bric-à-brac market on ploshtad Aleksandûr Nevski. A great range of items, from coins and old

A performance at the Ivan Vazov National Theatre, Sofia's main theatre

cameras to reproduction icons and folk costume, is on sale here.

For traditional woollen rugs, embroidered blouses and handmade jewellery, head for the **Ethnographic Museum Shop**. Crafts, pottery and textiles are also on offer at **Bulgarski Dyukyan**, which sells everything needed to recreate the Balkan look back home.

Markets

Central Sofia's liveliest market is **Zhenski pazar**, a vast open-air affair offering fresh fruit, vegetables and dairy produce, as well as clothes, textiles and kitchenware. Middle Eastern, Chinese and other exotic foodstuffs can be bought from shops in the narrow streets either side of the market.

The best place for indoor food shopping is **Tsentralni Hali** *(see p70)*, an Art Nouveau covered market with stalls selling olives, cheeses, pickled vegetables, smoked meats and other delicacies. This is also a good place to buy Bulgarian wines and spirits.

Antiques and collectables at the market on ploshtad Aleksandûr Nevski

Books and Music

Sofia's principal open-air book-browsing location is ploshtad Slaveykov *(see p86)*. An increasing number of high-street bookshops, such as **Booktrading** and **Helikon**, stock novels and guidebooks in English and other mainstream languages.

Orange stocks stationery, books and CDs of Bulgarian folk music. **Dyukyan Meloman** is another good place to seek out jazz and international music, including traditional Balkan sounds.

Shopping Malls

Sofia's most famous shopping mall is **Tzum**, with four floors of upmarket shops selling clothing, accessories and luxury goods. Tzum (Tsentralen universalen magazin, or Central Universal Store) was built in 1955, as Sofia's main department store, and the building is still a city landmark. Sofia's (and Bulgaria's) largest mall is **Paradise Center**, close to Sofia Zoo. Another good mall is near the city centre, **Mall of Sofia**, filled with shops selling a range of international fashions.

DIRECTORY

Opera, Dance & Classical Music

Bulgaria Concert Hall
ul. Aksakov 1.
Map 2 D5.
Tel (02) 987 7656.

National Opera and Ballet
ul. Vrabcha 1.
Map 2 D4.
Tel (02) 987 1366.
operasofia.bg

National Palace of Culture (NDK)
pl. Bulgariya 1.
Map 3 A5.
Tel (02) 916 6300, (02) 916 6400. ndk.bg

Theatre

Aleko Konstantinov Satirical Theatre
ul. Stefan Karadja 26.
Map 3 C2.
Tel (02) 988 1060.
satirata.bg

Ivan Vazov National Theatre
ul. Dyakon Ignatii 5. **Map** 1 C5. **Tel** (02) 811 9227.
nationaltheatre.bg

Sfumato Theatre Workshop
ul. Dimitar Grekov 2.
Tel (02) 944 0127.
sfumato.info

Sofia Drama Theatre
bl. Y. Sakuzov 23a.
Tel (02) 944 2485.

Clubs & Bars

Chervilo
bul. Tsar Osvoboditel 9.
Map 2 E5.
chervilo.com

Dada Cultural Bar
ul. Georgi Benkovski 10.
Map 2 D3. blog.
dadaculturalbar.eu

JJ Murphy's
ul. Kurnigradska 6. **Map** 1 A5. **Tel** (02) 980 2870.
jjmurphys.bg

Motto
ul. Aksakov 18. **Map** 2 E5.
Tel (02) 987 2723.
motto-bg.com

Yalta
bul. Tsar Osvoboditel 20.
Map 4 F2. **Tel** (02) 980 1299. yaltaclub.com

Antiques, Crafts & Souvenirs

Bulgarski Dyukyan
ul. Pirotska 11a. **Map** 1 A3.
Tel (02) 988 4139.

Ethnographic Museum Shop
pl. Aleksandûr Batenberg 1. **Map** 1 C4.

Markets

Bric-à-Brac Market
pl. Aleksandûr Nevski.
Map 2 E4.

Zhenski pazar
ul. Stefan Stambolov.
Map 1 A2.

Books & Music

Booktrading
Graf Ignatiev 50.
Map 4 D3.
Tel (02) 980 9699.

Dyukyan Meloman
ul. 6-ti septemvri 7a. **Map** 4 D1. **Tel** (02) 988 5862.
meloman-bg.com

Helikon
bul. Patriah Evtimii 68.
Map 3 A3.
Tel (02) 460 4060.

Orange
ul. Graf Ignatiev 2. **Map** 4 D3. **Tel** (02) 981 6594.

Shopping Malls

Mall Of Sofia
bul. Aleksandûr Stamboliiski 100.

Paradise Center
bul. Cherni Vrah 100.

Tzum
bul. Knyaginya Mariya Luiza 2. **Map** 1 B3.

SOFIA STREET FINDER

All the map references given for sights, hotels and restaurants in Sofia refer to this section of the book. The key map below shows the area of the city covered by the Street Finder. The first figure of the reference indicates which map to turn to, and the letter and number which follow are for the grid reference. Street signs in Sofia often use two scripts, Roman and Cyrillic, but spellings may not always be exactly the same. The most common words used in addresses that the visitor should recognise are *ploshtad* for "square", *ulitsa* for "street" and obviously *bulevard* for "boulevard" (abbreviated to *pl.*, *ul.* and *bul.* respectively).

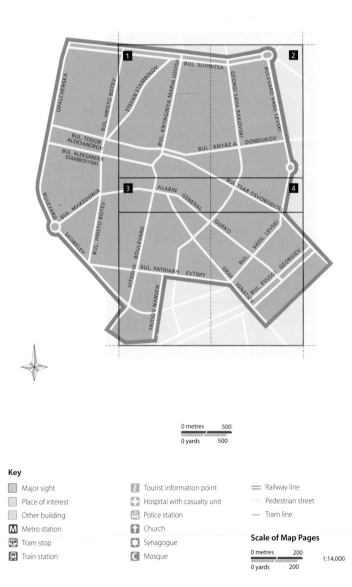

0 metres 500
0 yards 500

Key

- Major sight
- Place of interest
- Other building
- **M** Metro station
- Tram stop
- Train station
- *i* Tourist information point
- Hospital with casualty unit
- Police station
- Church
- Synagogue
- Mosque
- Railway line
- Pedestrian street
- Tram line

Scale of Map Pages

0 metres 200
0 yards 200

1:14,000

Street Finder Index

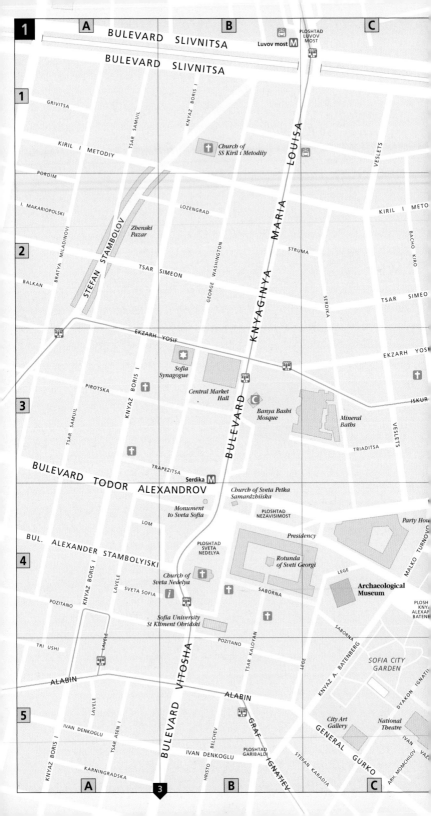

SOUTHERN BULGARIA

From December to April, most of this mountainous region is buried beneath thick snow, but the rest of the year it is an oasis of lush greenery and dense forests. The country's most spectacular scenery and most varied wildlife can be discovered here, and the architecture and folklore of this rugged landscape offer a fascinating insight into an intriguing and somewhat remote part of Bulgaria.

The highest peaks in the eastern Balkans rise in the Rila and Pirin mountain ranges. Both are national parks and both contain a great variety of flora and fauna, including wolves, bears, and many endemic plants. The Rhodopes, which cover a much greater area, are a largely undeveloped wilderness that, towards the east, tails off into the tobacco-growing Plains of Thrace. For centuries this area was inhabited by much of Bulgaria's Turkish community. In fact Palaeolithic flint tools discovered here show that human habitation of the region goes back 40,000 years. Thracians later settled in the area in large numbers. Smolyan's History Museum gives a superb overview of the region's past.

The Ottomans were largely tolerant of their Christian subjects, but there were isolated campaigns to force Bulgarians to adopt the Islamic faith. A small number of Bulgarians found refuge in the Rhodope Mountains, where they established villages that remained free of Turkish influence. Their untainted medieval Bulgarian language, music, costumes and customs served as a model for the National Revival movement, which was so influential in the 19th century.

Two great monasteries, Rila and Bachkovo, were also established in the Rhodopes. The monks kept Bulgarian heritage alive by preserving and copying the ancient manuscripts of the old Bulgarian kingdoms. These monasteries became a focus of the National Revival movement.

Glacial lake in the Pirin Mountains, one of three great massifs in southern Bulgaria

◀ Detail of the icon on the roof dome of the Rila Monastery

Exploring Southern Bulgaria

Southern Bulgaria's stunning mountain ranges offer plenty of opportunities for hiking, biking and skiing. The region has a wealth of historic buildings, the finest of which are Bulgaria's two UNESCO-listed monasteries, Rila and Bachkovo. Birdwatchers can see vultures at Madzharovo Nature Reserve and many other rare breeds throughout the mountains. Much of the region has piping hot mineral springs, and a well established spa industry offering high-tech treatments.

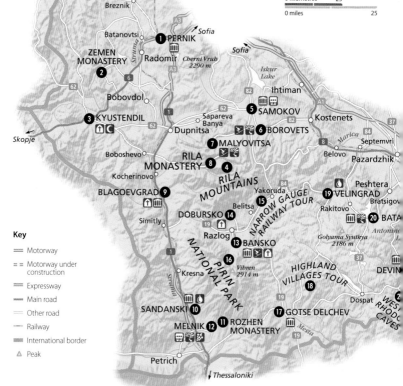

Key

═══ Motorway

═ ═ Motorway under construction

═══ Expressway

───── Main road

───── Other road

╍╍╍ Railway

▬▬▬ International border

△ Peak

Sights at a Glance

1. Pernik
2. Zemen Monastery
3. Kyustendil
4. *Rila National Park pp108–9*
5. Samokov
6. Borovets
7. Malyovitsa
8. *Rila Monastery pp112–15*
9. Blagoevgrad
10. Sandanski
11. Rozhen Monastery
12. Melnik
13. *Bansko pp122–4*
14. Dobûrsko
16. *Pirin National Park pp126–7*
17. Gotse Delchev
19. Velingrad
20. Batak
21. Devin
22. *Western Rhodopes Caves pp132–3*
23. Shiroka Lûka
24. Smolyan
25. Mogilitsa
26. Zlatograd
27. Momchilovtsi
28. Pamporovo
29. *Plovdiv pp138–43*
30. *Bachkovo Monastery pp146–7*
31. Haskovo
32. Kûrdzhali
33. Madzharovo Nature Reserve

Tours

15. Narrow-gauge Railway Tour
18. Highland Villages Tour
34. Eastern Rhodopes Tour

Church of Sveta Bogoroditsa at Bachkovo Monastery

Richly coloured fresco at the church of
Rila Monastery

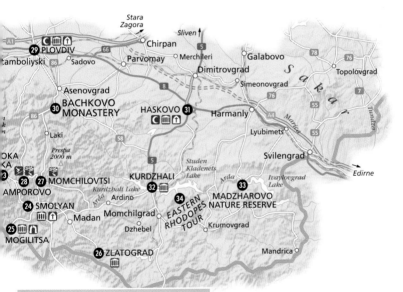

Madzharovo Nature Reserve, in the eastern Rhodopes

Getting Around

Winding roads mean that visitors should allow
plenty of time for journeys, especially if
travelling by public transport. Buses cover the
entire region, but services to remote villages
are often limited to one bus a day. To explore
the central and western Rhodope Mountains,
hiring a car is the best option. Regular train
services connect Sofia with Blagoevgrad and
Sandanski, and a narrow-gauge track branches
off the main Sofia–Plovdiv line, winding
through the mountains to Bansko. From
Plovdiv trains run to Haskovo and Kûrdzhali.

❶ Pernik
Перник

30 km (20 miles) SW of Sofia. **Map** B3.
🏔 81,200. 🚊 🚌 🚖 Kukeri and
Survakari Festival (end Jan, even
years). **W** surva.org

The history of Pernik, whose
name is derived from Perun, the
Slav god of thunder, dates back
to Thracian times. In the 9th
century AD, the now-ruined
fortress on Krakra Pernishki hill,
just outside the town, played a
key role in repelling Byzantine
attacks on the First Bulgarian
Kingdom. The hill is named after
Krakra, a local feudal leader.

After this turbulent period,
Pernik sank into obscurity and
was of little importance until
the 19th century, when huge
deposits of coal were discovered
nearby. It became Bulgaria's
largest coal mining centre, but by
the late 20th century economic
stagnation and dwindling coal
supplies led to its decline.

Today, Pernik's suburbs are
filled with crumbling tower
blocks and decaying Socialist-
era factories. The town centre

The Church of St Ivan the Theologian, focal point of Zemen Monastery

and the surrounding parks are
pleasant enough, but Pernik's
real attractions are the lively
biennial Kukeri and Survakari
festival *(see box)* and the **Mining
Museum**, in a shaft of the town's
first coal mine.

🏛 Mining Museum
pl. Sveti Ivan Rilski 1.
Tel (076) 602 911, ext. 262.
Open 10am–5pm Tue & Thu. 🖾 🎥

❷ Zemen Monastery
Земенски манастир

3 km (2 miles) SW of Zemen.
Map A3. **Tel** (077) 412 029.
Open May–Sep: 9:30am–6pm;
Oct–Apr: 9am–5:30pm. 🖾 🎥

In a sheltered hillside spot
above the town of Zemen
stands Zemen Monastery.
Founded in the 11th century,
it was occupied until the
advent of Ottoman rule, and
was restored in the late 19th
century. Modest single-storey
buildings sit around the small
12th-century Church of St Ivan
the Theologian, which contains
fine 14th-century frescoes.
Executed in the simple, bold
style of the Macedonian School
of early icon painters, they show
biblical scenes and portraits of
saints and of the monastery's
patron, Konstantin Deyan, and
his wife Doya.

Kukeri and Survakari

Pernik is the venue for the Balkans' largest gathering of Kukeri and
Survakari dancers. Held alternate years, it attracts over 5,000
participants from more than 90 national and international folk
groups. Survakari rites are winter dances that take place in western
Bulgaria on New Year's Eve and New Year's Day. Kukeri rites are pre-
spring dances performed during Lent in the rest of the country. The
dancers wear outlandish costumes and frightening masks, or cover
their faces in charcoal. The costumes also incorporate cow bells,
which are worn on belts. By adopting a loping gait, the dancers
rhythmically jangle the bells to protect themselves from the evil
spirits that they must drive away before celebrating the arrival of
the new year or of spring. The
rituals, which date back to
Thracian times, are acted out by
male dancers. Both Kukeri and
Survakari rituals involve
midnight visits by dancers
carrying flaming torches to
every home in a town or village
so as to drive out evil spirits. In
the associated fertility rituals,
Survakari dancers celebrate a
symbolic wedding. Kukeri
pre-spring rituals involve
symbolically impregnating the
earth with wooden ploughs and
sowing it with seed amid
a cacophony of jangling bells,
drums and joyful uproar.

Group of Kukeri dancers

Fresco in the Church of St Ivan the
Theologian at Zemen Monastery

❸ Kyustendil

Кюстендил

88 km (50 miles) SW of Sofia. **Map** A3.
🏔 44,500. 🚉 🚌 🚍

Thanks to its thermal springs, Kyustendil was known as the "town of baths" in Roman times. Later, the Turks built *hammams* here, and today Kyustendil is a popular spa resort. Although it no longer has a Muslim population, vestiges of its former Oriental culture remain.

The hefty Ahmed Bey Mosque houses the town's small **History Museum**, in which archaeological artifacts discovered in the region are displayed. The mosque is surrounded by the remains of the Pautalia Roman baths, Bulgaria's second-largest baths complex after that in Varna *(see p203)*. Built in the 2nd century AD it covered more than 1,000 sq m (11,000 sq ft) and had an unusual system of vaulted brick corridors to heat the building's floors.

Chifte Bathhouse is a 20th-century conversion of the Ottoman baths that were built over part of the Pautalia baths. It has separate pools for men and women, with a year-round water temperature of 36–40° C (98–104° F).

Beyond the mosque, on the corner of ploshtad Velbuzhd, is the pretty three-domed Church of Sveta Bogoroditsa. In obeisance to the Ottoman ruling that Christian churches should not cause offence to Muslims, it was set slightly below ground level.

Just off bulevard Bulgaria is a large **Art Gallery** devoted to the work of the local painter Vladimir Dimitrov-Maistora (1882–1960), who is known to Bulgarians as "Maistora" (the Master). His work is characterized by vivid colours and broad brushstrokes, and his bold portraits often feature peasant girls framed by the region's ripe fruits, echoing the Madonnas depicted by medieval icon painters. Several bearded self-portraits are on display, revealing a wild look in the eyes of a man who disdained city life in favour of a monastically simple village existence.

Immediately behind the gallery is the **Dimitûr Peshev House-Museum**. Dimitûr Peshev *(see p71)* was a prominent Kyustendil politician and vice-chairman of the Bulgarian parliament in the 1940s. When Nazi Germany put pressure on Bulgaria to deport its Jews, Peshev orchestrated a campaign to protect them. Although over 11,000 Jews from Bulgaria's newly occupied territories were sent to German concentration camps, a letter signed by 43 Bulgarian MPs, combined with the adamant support of the Orthodox Church, persuaded the Tsar and the government to defy Hitler by refusing to deport the country's 50,000 Jews.

Incredibly, following the Communist takeover in 1944, the signatories to the letter were

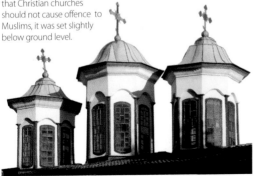
Dimitûr Peshev, national hero

Detail of Ahmed Bey Mosque in Kyustendil, built in the 16th century

arrested. Twenty were executed and the rest imprisoned. Peshev was sentenced to 15 years' hard labour; he only served one year but had his property confiscated and lived an ignominious existence until his death in 1973. However, his reputation was posthumously restored after the fall of Communism in 1989. The museum, in a building reconstructed in 2002 as a replica of his house, documents his story.

The wooded Hisarlûk hill that overlooks the town can be reached on foot along marked pathways, or by car following a road that snakes up the hillside. Close to the summit are the ruined walls of the once formidable Hisarlûk fortress. It was built in the 4th century and, with 14 towers and walls 2 m (6 ft) thick, it was a secure place of refuge during both the first and second Bulgarian kingdoms *(see p47)*. It was destroyed by the Ottomans in the 15th century.

🏛 **History Museum**
Ahmed Bey Mosque, ul. Stefan Karadzha, 2. **Tel** (078) 550 124. **Open** 9am–5pm Tue–Sat. 📷

🏛 **Art Gallery**
ul. Patriarch Evtmii, 20. **Tel** (078) 550 029. **Open** May–Oct: 10am–6pm; Nov–Apr: 9am–5pm Wed–Sun. 📷 📷

🏛 **Dimitûr Peshev House-Museum**
ul. Tsar Simeon I, 11. **Tel** (078) 551 811. **Open** 9am–5pm Wed–Sun. 📷 📷

Three hexagonal domes on the Church of Sveta Bogoroditsa, Kyustendil

❹ Rila National Park

Национален парк "Рила"

The source of several Balkan rivers, this massif, Bulgaria's largest national park, derives its name from the Thracian word *rula*, meaning "abundance of water". Its dense forests of spruce, fir, and Macedonian pine are home to wolves, bears, boar, Balkan chamois and *suslik* (ground squirrels) as well as the rare wallcreeper and the Alpine chough. No fewer than 57 endemic plant species, including the divine primrose, Rila pansy and Bulgarian avens, also thrive here. A network of hiking paths crisscrosses the park, reaching the imposing peaks of Musala and Malyovitsa and the Seven Lakes.

Wolf in the Rila Mountains

★ Seven Lakes
One of the Rila Mountains' most popular hiking trails follows this series of small glacial lakes, which are set amid spectacular scenery. The lakes, formed by melted glaciers, are set at ascending levels.

★ Mount Malyovitsa
At the head of a valley, the mountain rises to 2,729 m (8,957 ft). A cliff near Malyovitsa hikers' hut offers a tough challenge to rock climbers. A nearby rock is studded with memorials to those who failed.

Rila Monastery Forest Reserve
Created in 2000, the reserve covers more than 27,000 ha (67,000 acres) around Rila Monastery *(see pp112– 15)*. It includes a large beech forest.

0 kilometres 5
0 miles 5

Key

⎓ Main road
═ Other road
-- Trail
— Railway
△ Peak

Shtrashnoto Lake

Set at an altitude of 2,465 m (8,090 ft) the lake is ringed by the dark granite cliffs of the Kupenite peaks. A hikers' hut on the lakeside provides basic accommodation.

Musala Lakes are a set of pretty glacial pools set below the peak. The "Icy Lake" is the highest in the Balkans at 2,709 m (8,900 ft).

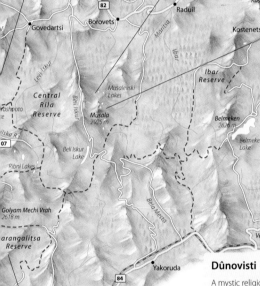

★ Mount Musala

At 2,925 m (9,600 ft) Mount Musala is the highest peak in the eastern Balkans. On a clear day, the arduous hike to the summit is rewarded by stunning views of the Pirin and Rhodope mountains to the south and of Mount Vitosha to the north.

Dûnovisti

A mystic religion based on the teachings of the priest-philosopher Petur Dûnov (1864–1944), Dûnovism caught on in 1900, when his book *The Seven Conversations* was published. Dûnov toured Bulgaria expounding his cosmic view of life. He advocated worship in the open air and daily meditation with a ritual of greeting the rising sun. Dûnov won international renown, but under Communism his message was suppressed. Since then Bulgarians have rediscovered his teachings and hundreds of his white-robed followers still gather at the Seven Lakes around 19 August to celebrate the Dûnovist new year's day.

Group of white-robed Dûnovists in a ritual

Parangalitsa Reserve

This reserve, on the southwestern slopes of the Rila Mountains, was established in 1933 to protect some of Europe's oldest spruce forests. It is now a UNESCO Biosphere Reserve.

❺ Samokov
Самоков

65 km (40 miles) south of Sofia.
Map B4. 🚂 28,150. 🚌

Although the town centre is an unattractive sprawl of drab concrete buildings, Samokov has a pleasant setting close to the Rila Mountains and the ski resort of Borovets. Established in the Middle Ages as a major centre of mining and manufacture, Samokov retained its industrial importance until the Liberation in the late 19th century. Today the town is the centre of Bulgaria's largest potato-producing region.

During the National Revival *(see p50)*, Samokov's thriving schools of icon painters and woodcarvers made a significant contribution to the decoration of religious and civic buildings throughout the country. They also left their mark in the town itself. Just off the main square stands **Bairakli Mosque**, a building constructed in a style typical of the National Revival period. The eaves of the mosque's red-tiled dome and roof are decorated with floral motifs, as are its interior walls. The entrance, fronted by wooden columns, is set into a delightful façade of trompe-l'oeil murals depicting theatrical stages. This decorative scheme is a fine example of Samokov artists applying their skills in a context other than that of traditional icon painting.

Icon Painters of Samokov

When he added floral motifs to a series of icons that he had painted for the consecration of Samokov's Metropolitan Church in 1793, Hristo Dimitrov unwittingly founded what became known as the Samokov School of icon painters. He subsequently trained his sons Dimitûr (1796–1860) and Zahari Zograf (1810–53) and, with Samokov's other icon-painting family, the Obrazopisovs, they produced a large number of icons and murals during the National Revival. During his short lifetime, Zahari Zograf attained legendary status as the creator of a new kind of secular art. Defying the rules of medieval icon painting, he introduced land-scapes and naturalistically rendered floral and animal motifs, and his grotesque scenes of Hell became a standard feature of church and monastery murals during the National Revival. The fact that he signed his works, and even added self-portraits to some of them, indicates that he considered his painting to be an art rather than a mere craft carried out by lowly and anonymous hands, as painting had been seen for centuries. His best works are on display at the monasteries of Rila, Troyan, Preobrazhenski and Bachkovo, and outside Bulgaria, in the western Balkans and Mount Athos, in Greece. His most famous self-portrait is in the National Art Gallery, Sofia *(see pp74–5)*.

Fresco by Zahari Zograf, Rila Monastery

The **History Museum** occupies a National Revival-style building set in a quiet garden. The highlights of its relatively small collection are two working replicas of Samokov's medieval forges. They were modelled on Saxon furnaces, and have water-powered bellows and huge hammers called *samokovi*, which gave the town its name. Enormous antique anvils stand beside the forges. Upstairs, a display of faded photographs documents Samokov's more recent past.

Five minutes' walk from the museum are the high stone walls that enclose **Sarafina House** (*Sarafska Kûshta*). In the 19th century it was the home of a wealthy Jewish family, and after restoration it was opened as a museum house. Its elaborate

Bairakli Mosque in Samokov, with floral decoration typical of the National Revival style of mural and icon painting

A room at Sarafina House in Samokov, once the home of a wealthy family

ceilings and floral wall paintings were executed by Samokov's woodcarvers and painters.

At the opposite end of the town, towards the Rila Mountains, is the Metropolitan Church (1793), a long stone building with a copper-clad bell tower. The church has a superbly detailed iconostasis by Samokov woodcarvers, and icons by Hristo Dimitrov, (*see box, opposite*).

C Bairakli Mosque
ul. Tûrgovska 49. **Tel** (072) 266 908. **Open** 9am–noon, 1–4pm Mon–Fri.

History Museum
ul. Profesor V. Zahariev 4. **Tel** (072) 266 712. **Open** 8:30am–12:30pm, 1:30–5:30pm daily.

Sarafina House
ul. Knyaz Dondukov 11. **Tel** (072) 260 301. **Open** 9am–5pm Mon–Fri.

❻ Borovets
Боровец

70 km (43 miles) south of Sofia. **Map** B4.

One of Bulgaria's three major ski resorts (*see pp34–5*), Borovets is located below the majestic peaks of the Rila Mountains. Its untidy centre is cluttered with large hotel blocks and lines of wooden huts that house nightclubs, bars, restaurants, ski shops and souvenir stalls.

During the winter season, visitors crowd the resort's network of ski runs and lifts and gather in its central bars and clubs for rowdy late-night partying. In summer the main

gondola lift whisks visitors up to Yastrebets, a peak that rises to 2,369 m (7,775 ft). From here hikers can follow a path to Musala refuge and the lofty summit of Musala (2,925 m/ 9,600 ft), the highest peak in the Balkans. The Sitnyakovo Express, a chairlift that operates at weekends only, takes visitors up to the highest point of the Sitnyakovo ski runs. A pleasant path leads back down to Borovets.

The resort also offers a range of summer activities, including pony trekking, motorized safaris, guided hiking, climbing and abseiling, most of which can be arranged through the large hotels here.

Apart from its attractions as a ski resort, Borovets's only feature of real interest is Bistritsa Palace. It was built as a hunting lodge for Prince Ferdinand in the late 19th century, making Borovets the country's oldest mountain resort. The palace's interior decor is a mix of luxurious Victorian fittings, elaborate Samokov woodcarving and hunting trophies.

Bistritsa Palace
15 minutes' walk from central Borovets. **Tel** (0750) 32710. **Open** 9am–4:30pm Tue–Sun.

❼ Malyovitsa
Мальовица

10 km (6 miles) W of Borovets. **Map** B4.

The small mountain resort of Malyovitsa consists of little more than a hotel, car park and mountain refuge. It has two drag lifts and a few pistes for beginners and intermediate skiers.

As such it offers a nice contrast to the bustle of Borovets in the winter sports season. In summer Malyovitsa is a convenient base for exploring the Rila Mountains (*see pp108–9*). From the resort a path leads up to Malyovitsa refuge and the looming peak of Malyovitsa mountain (2,729 m/8,957 ft). From the refuge hikers can continue along marked paths that lead westward to the Seven Lakes, or southward to Rila Monastery (*see pp112–15*).

Detail of Bistritsa Palace, Borovets

View into the valleys below Malyovitsa, in the Rila Mountains

❽ Rila Monastery
Рилски манастир

Established in the 10th century by St Ivan of Rila (Sveti Ivan Rilski), Rila Monastery is Bulgaria's most impressive example of National Revival architecture. Generously supported by successive kings, the monastery flourished until Ottoman raids destroyed it in the late 15th century. While the Russian Church sponsored its renovation, Rila's monks played a crucial role in preserving Bulgaria's language and history during the most repressive periods of Ottoman rule. Devastated by fire in 1833, the monastery was rebuilt with funding from wealthy Bulgarians intent on cultivating national pride at a time of great hope for liberation from the Ottomans.

Rila Monastery nestles in a valley at the foot of thickly forested mountains. It is protected by fortress-like walls 20 m (65 ft) high.

★ Murals
The murals in the arcade vividly depict sinners thrown into an apocalyptic vision of Hell. This contrasts with the arcades' graceful structure of arches, slender columns and blind cupolas.

Church of the Nativity

The exquisite Church of the Nativity, which stands proudly in the middle of Rila Monastery's courtyard, is the largest monastery church in Bulgaria. Its exterior is a busy but harmonious confection of layers of stripy colours and curved domes and arches set at different levels. Take some time to appreciate the outside thoroughly before entering the main part of the church.

Entrance to church

★ Murals
Magnificent murals adorn the church walls, illustrating characters and episodes from the Bible. Zahari Zograf (see p52), Bulgaria's greatest 19th-century painter, is the only one of the artists responsible to have signed his work.

★ Holy Relic of St Ivan
A silver casket holds the nation's holiest relic, St Ivan of Rila's preserved left hand. In the 16th century, the right hand was taken on a tour of Russia to raise funds for the monastery.

②

★ Iconostasis
This masterpiece was created by a team of Samokov woodcarvers working under Atanas Telador between 1839 and 1842. The 10-m (33-ft) wide iconostasis, covered in gold leaf, is elaborately decorated with complex carvings of stylized floral elements, symbolic human and animal images, biblical scenes and wild animals.

Grave of Tsar Boris
The heart of Tsar Boris III, who was allegedly poisoned by the Nazis in 1944 for saving Bulgarian Jews, is buried in this chapel.

St Ivan of Rila

The medieval hermit St Ivan of Rila (880–946), retreated into the Rila Mountains to escape what he saw as the moral decline of society. He was venerated for his wisdom and as a healer, and was persuaded by his followers to establish a monastery. After his death, pilgrims came to view his remains, which were believed to possess curative powers.

KEY

① **The arcades** are decorated with some of the finest murals.

② **The three main cupolas** contain murals of the Holy Trinity.

Exploring the Rila Monastery

Deep in the heart of a forest reserve, Rila Monastery has an imposing external presence. Enter by the west (Dupnitsa) gate, crossing over ancient stone slabs worn smooth by pilgrims' feet, then savour a first taste of the colourful treat to come. Several floors of wooden balconies enclose the courtyard and the central Church of the Nativity, with Hrelyo's Tower to one side. To the right of the west gate is the Treasury Museum, located in the south wing. The north wing, to the left of the west gate, contains the old kitchen and leads to the east (Samokov) gate, which conceals the entrance to the Monastery Farm Museum and leads out to a cluster of restaurants and souvenir shops.

One of over 100 intricately carved scenes on Raphael's Cross

Church of the Nativity

Construction of the Church of the Nativity began in 1835, two years after the monastery had been devastated by fire. The work directed by the master builder Pavel, from Krimin, who had previously worked on Mount Athos, in Greece.

The church's design was in-tended to be innovative and original, as befitted the National Revival period. For the interior, emphasis was placed on spatiality so as to draw worshippers into the centre of the building. The three large domes were positioned to allow maximum light to fall on the spectacular gilt iconostasis, while still keeping the rest of the interior in typically sombre darkness. The murals on the interior are also typical of the period and were executed by the country's best painters. The biblical scenes that cover the walls are brightly painted and show an attention to detail that was the hallmark of the National Revival movement. Among the many artists who painted these scenes were Zahari Zograf and his brother Dimitŭr, of the Samokov School *(see p110)*.

The walls are also busy with delightful displays of icons, some produced by 19th-century artists from Samokov and Bansko. Others date from much earlier times. On the left-hand side of the church as you enter, usually hidden away in a wooden drawer, is the serene 12th-century Icon of the Virgin.

A chapel on the right of the church contains a smaller iconostasis and the simple grave of Tsar Boris III, marked with a plain wooden cross.

Treasury Museum

Raphael's Cross is certainly the star of this fine collection. Just 81 cm (32 in) high, the cross bears a series of biblical scenes carved with needles, each one enclosed in silver-plated frames no larger than a fingernail. The work, completed in 1802, took 12 years and cost the monk Raphael his eyesight. The collection includes about 20 other miniature crosses, as well as jewelled silver boxes that contain ancient bibles, a ruby-encrusted communion cup and other church silver.

The lower floor has varied exhibits, including a 2-m (6-ft) musket and several swords and pistols. Nearby is a collection of books from the monastery library. The oldest dates back to the 10th century and is written on parchment in the Glagolitic script of the old Slavonic languages. Opposite is the Suchava Tetra, a large bible produced in 1529. Its embossed gold and enamel cover depicts Christ on the cross, with the four evangelists watching from each corner. Several other ancient Bibles are on show below some extravagantly jewelled icons.

A neighbouring glass case is filled with a selection of 19th-century gold church plate. At the far end of the room is a 14th-century ivory-inlaid bishop's throne that belonged to the original monastery church. Alongside are the skilfully carved original doors of Hrelyo's Tower and a pair of 14th-century icons of St Ivan of Rila *(see p113)*.

Church of the Nativity, dominant feature of the monastery's courtyard

Key

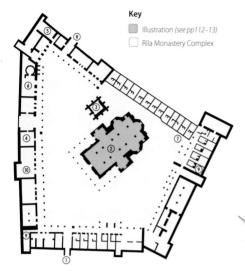

Illustration (see pp112–13)

Rila Monastery Complex

Rila Monastery Plan

① Western Entrance
  (Dupnista Gate)
② Church of the Nativity
③ Hrelyo's Tower
④ Monastery Kitchen
⑤ Farm Museum
⑥ Monastery Kitchen
  (Magernitsa)
⑦ Treasury Museum
⑧ Eastern Entrance
  (Samokov Gate)
⑨ Public Toilets
⑩ Ethnographic Museum

Monastery Complex

In contrast to the monastery's stern exterior, the courtyard is light and open; an elegant tracery of red, white, and black striped arches deftly frame more than 300 monks' cells and mirror the façade of the Church of the Nativity.

Hrelyo's Tower is the monastery's oldest surviving structure. It was built by Hrelyo Dragoval, a feudal lord, in 1334. A small chapel on the top floor, with 14th-century frescoes, is occasionally open to the public. Today, access to this mini-fortress is via wooden steps to the first floor, but was originally by a removable stepladder.

Hrelyo's Tower

An intriguing section of the north wing contains the **Monastery Farm Museum**. It is entered via the old guard house, off Samokov Gate. Here, muskets used by the guards are displayed, alongside their red and white uniforms with metal breastplates featuring a portrait of St Ivan of Rila and the monastery. Next door is a bare-walled room that houses the monastery's water-powered mill, and where hollow logs once used as sewage pipes are displayed. A 19th-century see-saw water pump used for fire-fighting embodies the precautions taken after the fire that devastated the monastery in 1833. The enormous domed brick oven that takes up most of the next room is an impressive sight. Like the huge pots and cauldrons of the old kitchen, and the giant wooden ladles in the adjoining room, the oven's great size was essential if food was to be provided for the hundreds of monks and pilgrims at the monastery. The kitchen's ceiling curves into a huge blackened chimney that tapers elegantly through the four floors of the north wing.

Around Rila Monastery

The **Chapel of St Ivan of Rila** and the dark cave where he spent the remainder of his life are an hour's walk north of the monastery and worth a visit just to get out into the surrounding countryside. Tourists can clamber through the narrow opening of the cave ceiling, a task once expected of visiting pilgrims: supposedly only the pure of heart will get through.

About 7 km (4 miles) northeast of the monastery, **Kiril Meadow** is an attractive leafy green picnic spot with cafés and a few places offering accommodation.

The Chapel of St Ivan of Rila, in countryside near the monastery

Deposition of Christ, Rila Monastery ▶

The Church of the Annunciation, built in 1841, in Blagoevgrad's old town

⑨ Blagoevgrad
Благоевград

97 km (60 miles) S of Sofia. **Map** B4.
🚠 71,000. 🚌 🚍 🚆

Studious youngsters clutching notepads and textbooks populate much of this bustling town, which is home to both the American University in Bulgaria (AUB) and Southwest Neofit Rilski University. It was the location's pleasant climate and hot mineral springs that attracted Thracian, then Roman, settlers here. Under Ottoman rule, when it was known as Gorna Dzhumaya, the town was predominantly Muslim but was integrated into the new Bulgarian state in 1912 (see p54). Later, Gorna Dzhumaya's Turkish inhabitants were replaced by Bulgarian refugees from Macedonia and the Aegean, and in 1950 the town was renamed Blagoevgrad after Dimitŭr Blagoev, founder of the Bulgarian Communist Party.

Ploshtad Georgi Izmirliev Makedonchero, the pedestrianized hub of the town centre, is a spacious square with pleasantly babbling fountains and an abundance of trees. On one side stands the huge AUB building, which served as the Communist Party's headquarters until 1989. To the east is ploshtad Bulgaria, a lively square lined with cafés and restaurants.

Fresco in the Church of the Annunciation, Blagoevgrad

Across the river is the cavernous **History Museum**, with thousands of artifacts exhibited on several floors. Minerals, stuffed animals and birds, ethnographic displays, and historic photographs fill the upper levels, but the most intriguing items are tucked away in the basement, where the museum's archaeological collection is laid out. Among the exhibits here is an array of votive figurines, dating from the 6th century BC and simply modelled in clay. They are thought to have been used in rituals connected with fertility, fruitfulness and the concept of Mother Earth. Also notable are a pair of Thracian bronze helmets of the 4th century BC, each with moulded beard and moustache, and a pair of bronze knee and shin protectors.

Behind the museum lies the Varosha quarter, Blagoevgrad's old town. Here, renovated National Revival buildings cluster around the boldly decorated **Church of the Annunciation**, with an eye-catching façade. The porch is decorated with biblical scenes, and inside is a stunning iconostasis with carvings of angels, birds, fruit and flowers by master-craftsmen from Bansko and Samokov (see p110).

🏛 **History Museum**
ul. Rila, 1.
Tel (073) 885 370. **Open** 9am–noon, 1–6pm Mon–Fri. 🎫 📷 📹

⛪ **Church of the Annunciation**
Varosha quarter. **Open** 7:30am–8pm daily. 🕆 8am daily.

⑩ Sandanski
Сандански

162 km (100 miles) south of Sofia.
Map B5. 🚠 26,500. 🚌 🚍 🚆
ℹ ul. Skopie 5 (0746 32403).

Sandanski is a pleasant town set in a sheltered, sunny valley with hot mineral springs. About 4,000 years ago, this favourable location attracted Thracian settlers of the Medi tribe, but it was much more intensively developed by the Romans, who arrived in the early centuries AD. The baths and residential complexes that they built have been discovered under the modern town.

Sandanski's residents make much of the possibility that Spartacus, the Thracian slave

Hot mineral pool at Sveti Vrach Park, in southeastern Sandanski

famed for leading a slave revolt against the Roman Empire in the 1st century BC, was born in the town, which in Roman times was known as Desudava. A statue of him stands just outside the town.

The centrepiece of the **Archaeological Museum**, built over an excavated Roman villa, is a mosaic floor with a swastika and other geometric motifs. Upstairs is a collection of marble reliefs that depict Thracian horsemen, as well as portraits, a child's tomb and brief information on archaeological sites discovered in the region. Next door to the museum are the ruins of a 4th-century Christian basilica and paving slabs from the town's original main street.

Running parallel to this street is Sandanski's present-day main thoroughfare, ulitsa Makedonia. Lined with clothes shops and cafés and set with fountains, it bisects the town centre. To the southeast it leads to Sveti Vrach Park, a vast wooded park with an outdoor spa pool filled with water heated to 31° C (88° F), and over 200 species of exotic trees. Nearby, steaming hot mineral water spouts from fountains, where local people queue to fill their bottles. The town's larger hotels also use this water in the various hydrotherapy treatments that they offer to guests.

Tomb, Archaeological Museum, Sandanski

🏛 Archaeological Museum
ul. Makedonia 55. **Tel** (0896) 713 202. **Open** Apr–Oct: 10:30am–noon, 1–5pm Mon–Sat; Nov–Mar: 10:30am–noon, 1–5pm Mon–Fri. 🖼.

⓫ Rozhen Monastery
Роженски манастир

Above Rozhen village, 7 km (4 miles) NE of Melnik. **Map** B5. **Tel** (073) 833 337. **Open** Apr–Oct: 8am–7pm, daily; Nov–Mar: 9am–6pm daily. 🕋 8am daily. 🖼 local fair (8 Sep).

Rozhen Monastery occupies a tranquil spot high in the hills with dramatic views of

Rozhen Monastery, sited on a plateau above the village of Rozhen

the region's sandstone cliffs. Established in 1220 by Aleksei Slav, a 13th-century overlord, it soon fell into disrepair, remaining neglected until it was restored in 1597. During the period of Ottoman rule, the Orthodox Church used the monastery as a convent until it passed back to Bulgaria in 1912, after the First Balkan War. Dispute over the monastery's ownership led the Macedonian revolutionary Yane Sandanski to begin the construction of the nearby Church of SS Kiril i Metodii (1914) for Bulgarian worshippers who were debarred from Rozhen by the Orthodox clergy. The church stands a short distance down the hill from the monastery, and behind it lies Sandanski's large marble grave.

The monastery's simple brick buildings form an irregular hexagon, fronted by rickety wooden balconies, around the 16th-century Church of the Birth of the Holy Virgin. A porch protects the church's exterior frescoes, which show believers ascending a ladder to Heaven with the help of angels, while devils endeavour to hurl them into the mouth of a fiery monster.

In a side chapel inside the church is a miracle-working icon of the Virgin, which is paraded around the monastery on 8 September, feast of the Birth of the Virgin. The church also contains well preserved frescoes of saints and a fantastic gilt iconostasis with bold icons and intricate woodwork that gleams in the semi-darkness. The refectory, with a long wooden dining table and vestiges of frescoes, is also open to the public.

Spartacus the Thracian

Leader of the Gladiatorial War of 73–71 BC against Rome, Spartacus and his army of runaway slaves and gladiators terrorized Italy for two years. Born in Thrace, Spartacus served in the Roman army but was disgraced and sold into slavery, where he trained as a gladiator. With other slaves, Spartacus escaped, and began a campaign of plunder and pillage. Joined by still others, the group grew into an army of some 120,000 men, who overcame successive Roman legions sent to destroy them. The rebels were eventually defeated and put to death.

Defeat of Spartacus by the Roman general Crassus, 71 BC

⑫ Melnik
Мелник

182 km (113 miles) south of Sofia.
🚗 385. 🚌 from Sandanski.

The enchanting small town of Melnik is tucked away in a valley formed by rocky, arid hills crowned with pyramidal sandstone formations. Once a thriving centre of winemaking and the capital of a principality, Melnik is now a quiet town with a much reduced population. However, it attracts coachloads of visitors, who come to admire the intriguing rock formations here, and to taste the famous Melnik wine, which is still produced by a few local families.

Wine has been Melnik's major export since the 13th century, when production was increased to take advantage of tax-free trade with Dubrovnik. During this period, the despot Aleksei Slav made Melnik the capital of his principality, funding the

Melnik and its square *konak*, the town hall during Ottoman rule

construction of churches and monasteries in the vicinity.

After the Ottoman conquest, Melnik fell into decline, but its fortunes revived in the 19th century, when the town's largely Greek population of 20,000 began to prosper from exporting tobacco and wine. Much of Melnik was destroyed during the Second Balkan War of 1913 and its remaining Greek

Melnik Wine Tour

Renowned throughout Bulgaria, Melnik wine is made from the dark blue grapes of the Melnik broad-leaved vine, an indigenous Bulgarian variety grown in the volcanic soil of the sunny Struma Valley, near Melnik. There once were 19 wine cellars (*izbi*) in Melnik, where pressed grapes were left to ferment and where wine was stored in wooden barrels. Today only four of these cellars are open to the public and only a handful of families still produce wine. The Damianitza winery, just outside Melnik, is now the only large producer of Melnik wine.

Traditional Bulgarian wine vessel

① Rodina Hotel
Though it advertises itself as a wine cellar, the Rodina Hotel does not have its own *izba*. It does, however, have a small *vinarna*, where visitors can sample the owner's Merlot wine.

Melnishka Rozhenski Dol

Town Hall
Pashovata Kŭshta
Vinarna Melnik ②
Konak
①
Rodina Hotel

SANDANSKI
🚌 Bus Stop
20 m (18 yards)

SS Petur and Pavel Church

② Vinarna Melnik
Although the Vinarna Melnik does not have an *izba*, it offers tastings of its Melnik, Merlot and Cabernet wines.

③ Lumparova Kŭshta
This pleasant family-run hotel has a rock-cut *izba* with a mineral spring and tables and chairs for visitors who come to taste Melnik wine.

residents left as a result of ensuing anti-Greek sentiment. Today, with a population of less than 250, Melnik is officially Bulgaria's smallest town.

Melnik's restored stone houses are clustered on either side of a dry river bed that rises eastwards into the mountains. Most of Melnik's attractions are at the top of the town. The **History Museum** occupies the upper floor of Pashovata Kûshta, the house from where Yane Sandanski *(see p119)* announced Melnik's liberation from Ottoman rule in 1912. The museum's exhibits include examples of locally made terracotta wine vessels and a small collection of regional costumes and photographs.

A little further on is **Kordopulova House** (1754), a wonderful example of early

Bottle of wine from Kordopulova House

National Revival architecture in which Western and Oriental motifs are combined on a grand scale. The decorative wooden façade sits atop high stone walls. While the lower windows are in the traditwional Bulgarian style, the stained-glass windows on the top floor show Oriental influences. The house's interior features a central salon with an intricately carved wooden ceiling and an Ottoman-style raised seating area. Doors lead off to a spacious sitting room lit by many windows, and to a dining room with a secret inner chamber concealed behind a bookcase. Downstairs is a small *mehana* connected to the house's labyrinthine wine cellar. Beyond Kordopulova House, a footpath leads to the remains of Bolyarskata Kûshta, Aleksei Slav's once formidable

Glazed terracotta wine vessels at Melnik's History Museum

fortress. On the opposite side of the valley, another footpath leads uphill from the 18th-century Church of Sveti Nikolai Chudotvorets to Nikolova Gora and the ruins of the Church of Sveti Nikola (1756).

🏛 **History Museum**
Pashovata Kûshta. **Open** 9am–noon, 1–5pm daily.

🏛 **Kordopulova House**
Open 9am–7:30pm daily.

---

④ **Pri Mitko Shestaka**
Carved deep into the rock, the wine cellars here were created over 250 years ago. The main cavity is used for storing and tasting wine. The Melnik wines stored here have been produced by the same family for over 150 years.

A taste of Melnik wine at one of the town's *izbi*.

Tips for Visitors

Tour length: approximately 1.5 km (1 mile).
Tips: There are no banks in Melnik so be sure to have some cash already with you. It is illegal to drive after drinking any alcohol.

⑤ **Kordopulova Kûshta**
This house overlies Melnik's oldest and largest *izba*. Labyrinthine passages snake into the hillside, and vast rock-cut wine cellars are filled with huge barrels.

⑥ **Litova Kûshta**
An 800-year-old *izba*, cut deep into the rock, lies beneath this hotel. Red Melnik wine, and white Keratzuda, Misket and Bouquet wines are stored in massive barrels here.

[Map labels: umparova ûshta, Rozhenski Dol, Sv. Antonii Church, Bolyarskata Kûshta, Zlatolistki Dol, Old Turkish Baths, Sv. Nikolai Chudotvorets Church, Pri Mitko Shestaka ④, Kordopulova Kûshta ⑤, Sv. Barbara Church, Litova Kûshta ⑥]

0 metres 100
0 yards 100

Key

— Suggested route

⓭ Bansko

Банско

The small mountain town of Bansko lies just below the jagged peaks of the Pirin Mountains. It was founded in the 9th century, but remained obscure until the 19th century, when its prospering merchants began to fund the building of churches here. As the birthplace of Neofit Rilski, the town is also closely associated with Bulgarian nationalism. Another of its famous sons is Father Paisii (1722–73), whose *Slavo-Bulgarian History* was to provide the impetus for the beginnings of the National Revival.

Bansko's historic centre consists of a labyrinth of cobbled streets running between high stone walls that conceal hefty 19th-century timber and stone houses. Its suburbs, which are mostly filled with new hotels and apartment complexes, reflect its more recent development into a prosperous ski resort and weekend retreat.

Painting and inscription in the Church of Sveta Troitsa

🔼 Church of Sveta Troitsa

pl. Vŭzhrazhdane. Open 8am–6pm daily. 🔼 9am Sun. 📷

Hidden by a stone wall 4 m (12 ft) high, the massive Church of Sveta Troitsa owes its existence to a bribe that local merchants offered Ottoman officials so as to secure their consent for its construction. A miracle-working icon, so the story went, had been found on the site, and this qualified it as a suitable place to build a Christian church. The wall that surrounds the church was built to conceal its eventual dimensions, which exceeded the limit set by the Ottomans.

Work on the church began in 1832. It was built in the

distinctive smooth, rounded stones characteristic of the region, each framed by red bricks to relieve the monotony of an otherwise featureless exterior. The bell tower was added in 1850.

The church's gloomy interior is lit by small windows, and a large gilt iconostasis shines in the flickering candlelight. Topped with dragons, fruit and birds of prey, the iconostasis was made by the master-craftsman Velyan Ognev, from

Debŭr, in Macedonia. Dimitŭr and Simeon Molerov created the icons. Hefty columns support the wood-panelled ceiling and a latticework screen at the rear of the nave hides a balcony where female worshippers were segregated from the male congregation.

Part of the stone- and timber-built Neofit Rilski House-Museum

🏛 Neofit Rilski House-Museum

ul. Pirin 17.**Tel** (0749) 88272.
Open 9am–1pm, 2–5:30pm daily. 📷

An attractive garden dotted with modern sculptures is the setting for the former home of Neofit Rilski, the 19th-century scholar who, through his promotion of the Bulgarian language and reform of the

Neofit Rilski (1793–1881)

The scholar Neofit Rilski is revered as the founder of modern education in Bulgaria and for his leading role in the National Revival movement. He was born Nikola Popetrov Benin in Bansko and studied teaching, icon painting and Greek at Rila Monastery. In 1835, he published the *Bulgarska Gramatika*, the first grammar of modern Bulgarian and an essential tool in the campaign to create a national, standardized Bulgarian education. That year he also became head of the first school to teach pupils in Bulgarian. It was opened in Gabrovo by Vasil Aprilov and followed the Bell-Lancaster system whereby pupils of all ages studied together, with older children helping to teach their younger classmates. By the time of the Liberation in 1878, there were some 2,000 such schools in Bulgaria. In 1852 Rilski returned to Rila Monastery, where he became abbot. He further contributed to the National Revival movement by translating the New Testament into Bulgarian and compiling the first Greek–Bulgarian dictionary.

Sculpture of Neofit Rilski, one of Bansko's famous sons

education system, became one of Bulgaria's national heroes. Now restored and opened as a museum, this beautiful National Revival house docu-ments Rilski's achievements, and illustrates aspects of daily life in the 19th century.

The building centres around a tree-shaded courtyard. The low ceilings of the kitchen rooms on the ground floor are blackened with soot from the bread oven. Next to the oven is a secret room where the family hid from the Ottoman authorities in times of trouble. Upstairs is a covered terrace that overlooks the courtyard, and rooms that illustrate 19th-century family life. In one of them, a small classroom, similar to those that Rilski would have taught in, has been re-created. The sand boxes here were for the use of younger pupils, who would learn to write by tracing words with their fingers or with wooden sticks. On the opposite side of the courtyard is a display of photographs, letters and texts relating to Rilski's life.

🏠 Velyanov House

ul. Velyan Ognev 5. **Tel** (0749) 88274. **Open** 9am–noon, 2–5:30pm Mon–Fri.

This fine stone house was reputedly built for Velyan Ognev, the craftsman from Debûr, in Macedonia, who came to Bansko to create the iconostasis for the Church of Sveta Troitsa, and who then settled in the town.

Built in local stone and surrounded by high walls, Velyanov House (Velyanova Kûshta) is typical of comfort-able 19th-century Bansko dwellings, and it is filled with furniture and carpets of the period. Of particular interest

VISITORS' CHECKLIST

Practical Information
160 km (100 miles) S of Sofia.
Map B4. 🚌 8,500. 🛈 pl. Nikola
Vaptsarov (0749 88580). 🎵 Pirin
Pee (folk music; Aug, even years).
🌐 **bansko.bg**

Transport
🚆 🚌 🚍

are the elaborate wood-carvings with which Ognev decorated the house, and the rich murals in the Blue Room, which he is thought to have painted for his wife, the daughter of a local priest.

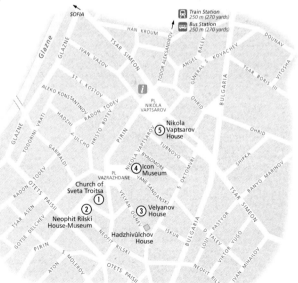

Velyanov House, a 19th-century family home, with a summer veranda

Bansko Town Centre

① Church of Sveta Troitsa
② Neofit Rilski House-Museum
③ Velyanov House
④ Icon Museum
⑤ Nikola Vaptsarov House

0 metres   100
0 yards   100

🏛 Icon Museum

ul. Yane Sandanski 3. **Tel** (0749) 88273. **Open** 9am–noon, 2–5:30pm Mon–Fri. 🅿

The glowing works of art in the Icon Museum's collection line the walls of the converted dormitories and barn of a former hostel for travelling nuns. The buildings, which date from 1749, are set round a peaceful courtyard, and the complex is enclosed by the sturdy walls that typify Bansko's old town architecture.

As visitors cross a wooden balcony to enter the museum's first room an audio tour introduces artists of the Bansko School of painting. The leading light of this school, which flourished in the 19th century, was Toma Vishanov-Molera (born c.1750). He studied in Vienna with Hristo Dimitrov, founder of the Samokov School (see p110). Like his son Dimitûr Molerov and his grandson Simeon Molerov after him, Toma Vishanov-Molera executed paintings for several churches in and around Bansko.

Nikola Vaptsarov House-Museum, childhood home of the anti-Fascist poet

A portrait of Christ in the Icon Museum

🏛 Nikola Vaptsarov House-Museum

pl. Nikola Vaptsarov. **Tel** (0749) 83132. **Open** 8am–noon, 2–5:30pm daily. 🅿

The home of the poet Nikola Vaptsarov (1909–42) honours the memory of a young man who died for his opposition to Fascism, and who was posthumously idolized by Bulgaria's Communist government. Vaptsarov grew up in Bansko, and after studying in Varna, he worked in Sofia. Here he wrote poems that enthused about the modern age. But his involvement with the Communists during World War II led to his arrest for anti-Fascist activities. While awaiting execution, he wrote this poem: *The fight is hard and pitiless/The fight is epic, as they say;/I fell. Another takes my place –/Why single out a name!/After the firing squad – the worms./Thus does the simple logic go./But in the storm we'll be with you/My people, for we loved you so.*

The museum contains family photographs, personal possessions and a re-creation of the room where Vaptsarov's mother read Bulgarian classics to him.

⑭ Doburско
Добърско

23km (14 miles) north of Bansko. **Map** B4. 🚗 450. 🚌

The road heading north from Bansko into the Rila Mountains leads to the sleepy village of Doburско. According to legend, this is where Tsar Samuil's army came in 1014. Its men had been blinded by the Byzantine emperor Basil the Bulgar Slayer, but they found a cure in the mineral springs here.

Today, Doburско is an increasingly popular centre of rural tourism. Besides this, its main attraction is the 17th-century Church of SS Teodor Tiron and Teodor Stratilat. Its well-preserved frescoes include a depiction of the Ascension with Christ framed by a curious triangular construction that has been likened to a space rocket.

🏛 Church of SS Teodor Tiron and Teodor Stratilat
Open 8am–5pm Mon–Fri. 🅿

The mountain village of Doburско, a centre of rural tourism with legendary mineral springs

⓯ Narrow-Gauge Railway Tour

Three trains a day make the scenic five-hour journey, following a stunning route through mountains. The line begins at Dobrinishte, but visitors are more likely to board at Bansko. From here the train leaves the Pirin Mountains and begins a gradual ascent of the Mesta River valley, set between the Rila Mountains and the western Rhodopes. After traversing a landscape of villages and meadows, it stops at Yakoruda. From there the route ascends into pine forests, then descends to Velingrad and follows a valley down to Septemvri.

Tips for Visitors

Map B4.
Tour length: 50 km (30 miles).
Departure points: Dobrinishte, Bansko or Septemvri. Mainline trains run between Septemvri and Plovdiv or Sofia.
Stopping-off places: There are hotels and restaurants at larger halts along the route.

⑥ Septemvri
This is the end station of the narrow-gauge line. From here, passengers can travel on the main line to Sofia or Plovdiv.

④ Yakoruda
A pleasant Pomak (Bulgarian Muslim) logging town. Its mosque and church come into view from a distance as the train rumbles past logs piled high for the saw mills.

Belovo
Sofia
Semchinovo
Varvara
Plovdiv
Milevi Skali
1592m
3704
Marista
8
8
84

③ Belitsa
From the station at Belitsa village, visitors can take a taxi to the Belitsa Dancing Bear Park, 10 km (6 miles) away. This is a refuge for bears rescued from a captive life as trained dancing bears, now illegal.

842
84
84
Yundola
84
⑤
Kostandovo
Rakitovo
8406
④
Ablanitsa
Yurukovo
③
Babyak
Mesta

⑤ Velingrad
With many hot mineral pools, the spa resort of Velingrad makes a welcome stop. Most of the pools are located within hotel complexes but are usually open to members of the public for a small fee.

②
Simitli
19
84
Banya
1903
Eleshnitsa
Bansko
19
①
19
Gotse Delchev

| 0 kilometres | 10 |
| 0 miles | 10 |

① Dobrinishte
The starting point of the narrow-gauge railway line is at this quiet town at the foot of the Pirin Mountains. Plans to merge it with the ski resort of Bansko will open it to tourism.

② Razlog
Razlog's golf course is its principal asset for visitors. The town comes alive when *kukeri* rites are performed on 1 January.

Key

- - Narrow-gauge Railway
— Railway
= Main road
= Other road
△ Peak

For additional map symbols *see back flap*

⑯ Pirin National Park
Национален парк "Пирин"

This rugged landscape of granite and limestone peaks, glacial lakes and steep-sided valleys makes up one of Bulgaria's wildest national parks. Its forested valleys offer plenty of scope for hiking but, with more than 80 peaks over 2,500 m (8,200 ft), this is also Bulgaria's most rugged terrain. The habitat of wolves, bears, foxes, wild cats and mountain goats, the park also shelters hundreds of rare plants, including Pirin thyme, the yellow Pirin poppy, and the Urumov milk vetch. Although it is a UNESCO World Heritage Site, the park is under threat from the expansion of the ski resort of Bansko.

★ Vihren
At 2,914 m (9,564 ft), Vihren is the Pirins' highest peak. From Vihren hut, the climb to the summit, on a marked path, takes three hours.

Bayuvi Dupki Dzhindzhiritsa Nature Reserve
The largest nature reserve in the Pirin Mountains was established in 1934 to preserve relict Balkan pine and Bosnian pine forests. It is also home to many rare plants, including the lake quillwort and the great yellow gentian.

★ Koncheto
This ridge connects a series of peaks, which rise up between steep valleys. The ridge is just 1 m (3 ft) wide in places and, despite the steel cable to assist hikers, walking it should only be attempted in good weather, and by experienced climbers.

Key

— Main road

— Other road

-- Trail

— Railway

△ Peak

Pirin
2592 m

Kamenishki Vrah
2522 m

• Betelevo

Bayuvi Dupki
Dzhindzhiritsa Nature
Reserve

Mochurishka R.

Koncheto

Vlahinska R.

Vihren
2914 m

Vlahins Lakes

Sinanitsa
2516 m

Mount Sinanitsa
The white limestone mass of Mount Sinanitsa, 2,516 m (8,257 ft) high, dominates the picturesque valley below.

★ Baikousheva Mura

Some 1,300 years old, this massive Bosnian pine (*Pinus heldreichii*) is believed to be Bulgaria's oldest tree. It is named after its discoverer, forest ranger Kostadin Baikushev, and is more than 26 m (85 ft) tall.

VISITORS' CHECKLIST

Practical Information
Bansko. **Map** B4.
Tel (0749) 88580.
🌐 pirin-np.com

Transport
🚌 from Blagoevgrad or Gotse Delchev. 🚉 narrow-gauge from Septemviri *(see p125)* linking to mainline.

Exploring the Park

With plenty of hotels and restaurants, With a good map, you can follow day-long trails into the park. For longer excursions, book a stay in a hizhi, or mountain hut. Bansko gets busy at weekends, but is quiet during the week.

In the Damyaritsa Valley, coniferous forests on the valley's lower slopes give way to picturesque alpine meadows and lakes at the foot of Mount Todorka, 2,746 m (9,000 ft) high.

Lake Popovo

Surrounded by towering peaks, Popovo is the largest and deepest of Pirin's 186 glacial lakes. It is a very popular spot for summer visitors.

The Brown Bear

The semi-open, mountainous terrain of the Pirin Mountains is an ideal habitat for brown bears. The animals once thrived here but, as elsewhere in Europe, their populations are now dangerously small. Until quite recently, dancing bears were a common sight on the streets of Bulgaria. This cruel practice was outlawed in 1998, and in 2000 the Belitsa Dancing Bear Park *(see p125)* began collecting the bears, paying their mainly Gypsy owners compensation. The 12-ha (30-acre) park, funded by Four Paws of Austria and the Brigitte Bardot Foundation, includes forest, pools and caves where the bears hibernate. Visitors can observe the bears from covered walkways, and there are regular guided tours.

Inhabitant of Belitsa Dancing Bear Park, refuge for maltreated bears

Map labels: Blagoevgrad, Bansko, Gotse Delchev, Gljorne, sheva, rka m, shki akes, Damyanitsa, Yulen Reserve, Polezhan 2890 m, Popovo Lake, Kremenski Lakes, Kamenitsa 2816 m, Kamenitsa, nska Bistritsa, Toufcha, Pirinska Bistritsa

0 kilometres 5
0 miles 5

⑰ Gotse Delchev
Гоце Делчев

48 km (30 miles) SE of Bansko. **Map** B5. 🏔 20,500. 🚌 🚉 pl. Makedonia 2 (0751 60125). **Open** 8am–5pm daily.

Thanks to crisp mountain air combined with warm winds blowing along the Mesta valley from the Aegean Sea, Gotse Delchev has a pleasant climate. It lies in the shadow of the Pirin but, despite this, the town is free of snow for most of the winter.

The area, known as Nestos in ancient times, was settled in about 5000 BC. Thracians arrived in 2000 BC and in the 2nd century AD Romans built Nikopolis ad Nestrum, which became the region's first major settlement. The poignant ruins, overgrown with vegetation, are 5 km (3 miles) from Gotse Delchev, on the main road to Kovachevitsa. After the decline of Nikopolis in the 6th century, a new settlement, named Nevrokop, was established nearby, on the banks of the Delchevska River. In 1950 the town was renamed Gotse Delchev in honour of the Macedonian revolutionary *(see box)*. The re-opened Greek border crossing into Greece, 20 km (12 miles) southeast of the town, has revived the

The History Museum, in Gotse Delchev

Bust of Vasil Levski in Gotse Delchev

trading route that was once a major link between Serdika (ancient Sofia) and the Aegean.

Gotse Delchev is a useful base for exploring the high-land villages of the northern Rhodopes *(see opposite)*. It is a quiet, pleasant town, with a pedestrianized centre. Its main attraction for visitors is the **History Museum**, in an impressive Ottoman Baroque house. The exhibits include early Thracian clay figurines dating from 1000 BC and the wheels and axles of a Roman chariot found nearby. The ethnographic collection features a display of 19th-century cow bells and a *kazan*, or still, for making the potent spirit *rakiya*, as well as local costumes, instruments and antique tools.

Also of interest is the **Church of St Archangel Michail**, the oldest church in the region, which was built in 1811. Inside is a rich collection of 17th-century painted icons.

🏛 **History Museum**
ul. Hristo Botev 26. **Tel** (0751) 60287. **Open** 8:30am–noon, 1:30–5:30pm Mon–Sat. 📷

⛪ **Church of St Archangel Michail**
ul. Ekzarch Antim I, 12.
Open 7:30am–6pm daily.
🕐 8am daily.

Macedonian Revolutionaries

The euphoria that swept Bulgaria after the Liberation of 1878 and the subsequent creation of a large Bulgarian state, which included most of Macedonia, was soon dashed when the Berlin Congress ordered the return of Macedonia to the Ottoman Empire. From this, two distinct groups emerged, both determined to free Macedonia from Turkish rule. One was the Internal Macedonian Revolutionary Organisation (IMRO), whose leader was Gotse Delchev (1872–1903). He believed in the creation of a separate Macedonian state. A group of influential Macedonian émigrés based in Sofia formed the Supreme Macedonian Committee (SMC), which argued for Macedonia's incorporation into Bulgaria. Both endeavours failed, but Delchev remains a hero. The towns of Gotse Delchev in Bulgaria and Delchevo in Macedonia were named after him.

Statue of Gotse Delchev, fighter for Macedonia's sovereignty

Room at the History Museum, Gotse Delchev, with ethnographic items

For hotels and restaurants in this region see pp223–4 and pp234–6

⑱ Highland Villages Tour

Over 300 years ago, Christian Bulgarians fleeing an aggressive Ottoman campaign to convert them to Islam sought refuge in the remote highlands. Here they established villages, using local materials to build fine stone houses. Almost deserted in the 1950s, these beautiful and still remote villages have become popular with city-dwellers in search of tranquillity. Both Kovachevitsa and Dolen are now protected as architectural reserves.

Tips for Walkers

Map B4. **Length:** about 40 km (25 miles).
Getting there: The easiest way is by car or taxi. There are limited bus services from Gotse Delchev.
Stopping-off points: There are B&Bs and inns at all villages.
Walks from Kovachevitsa: Various paths lead out of the village. One (2 km/1 mile) leads to the top of a hill within reach of the small Church of Sveti Georgi. Another (19 km/ 12 miles) crosses the mountains to Dolen.

① Kovachevitsa
Here, massive stone houses are set on the steep hillside. Their windowless ground floors sheltered animals and produce and served as defences against Ottoman raids.

0 kilometres 5
0 miles 5

③ Ognyanovo
The outdoor pools of Ognyanovo are popular in winter, when bathers can rub themselves with snow after a hot bath. A pleasant large indoor pool is filled with steaming warm spa water.

Key

▭▭ Tour route
═══ Main road
─── Other road
- - Trail

② Leshten
This tiny mountain hamlet, where visitors can stay, has been restored. The houses have original wooden floors, thick stone walls, and modern bathrooms and heating. The roofs are tiled with slabs of local stone.

④ Dolen
Unlike Kovachevitsa and Leshten, Dolen is still a working agricultural village. The inhabitants keep animals and work the land. Tobacco leaves are hung out on wooden frames and people can be seen sorting beans and corn on their doorsteps.

Map labels: Osikovo, Razlog, Gospodintsi, Skrebatno, Gorno Dryanovo, Baldevo, Banichan, Borovo, Marchevo, Garmen, Oreshe, Krushevo, Pletena, Satovcha, Dospat, Gotse Delchev, Debren, Dolno Dryanovo, Dabnitsa, Kribul, Drama, Kanina R., Rodopi Planina, Mesta, Bistritsa
Road numbers: 1905, 19, 1905, 197, 197, 1972

Swimming pool, filled with spring water, at one of Velingrad's spa hotels

⑲ Velingrad
Велинград

80 km (50 miles) SW of Plovdiv.
Map B4. 24,800.
i pl. Svoboda (0359-58401).
w velingrad.bg

This sprawling spa town owes its popularity to the springs that supply its many hotels, swimming pools and bathhouses with steaming hot mineral water. Wooded parks and a pleasant pedestrianized centre also contribute to making this one of Bulgaria's principal spa resorts. The most popular of Velingrad's many public baths are in the Chepino quarter, east of the town centre, where visitors can also hire rowing boats for excursions on a lake fed by the Kleptuza spring. Most of the town's larger hotels have their own mineral pools and offer hydrotherapy.

Besides this, the town's main point of interest is its **History Museum**, in the Kamenitsa quarter. It contains displays of black-and-white photographs, local costumes and jewellery, and painted Easter eggs.

Velingrad is also a station stop on the narrow-gauge railway from Septemvri to Dobrinishte *(see p125)*.

🏛 **History Museum**
ul. Vlado Chernozemski 2.
Tel (0359) 52591. **Open** 9am–5:30pm Mon–Sat.

⑳ Batak
Батак

45 km (30 miles) SW of Plovdiv.
Map C4. 3,500.

This unassuming Rhodopean logging town would have remained as anonymous as its neighbours were it not for the infamous events of April 1876, which inspired Ivan Vazov to write: "It goes without saying that without Batak there would not be a free Bulgaria." One of several towns that supported the revolutionary cause, Batak was punished with exceptional ferocity following the dismal failure of the April Rising *(see p178)*. Ottoman mercenaries known as *bashibazouks*, together with local Bulgarian Muslims, slaughtered 5,000 people in an indiscriminate attack. The local rebel Trendafil Kerelov was tied to a tree and set alight. Newspaper reports by

Bust of Trendafil Kerelov in Batak

English journalist J.A. MacGahan, who witnessed the aftermath, prompted international outrage, and ultimately led to pressure being put on Turkey to recognize Bulgaria's independence.

Much of Batak's **History Museum** is devoted to documenting the massacre. The names and ages of the victims cover a wall, while alongside are numerous photographs of skulls and bones piled next to elderly survivors. Muskets and woodsmen's axes used in the attack are on display, as are the crude cherry-tree cannons built by the revolutionaries.

Across the main square is the small **Church of Sveta Nedelya**, surrounded by a walled compound where Batak's inhabitants once sought refuge. In a report for *The Daily News* in August 1876 MacGahan described the scene as he entered the compound: "The whole churchyard for three feet [1 m] deep was festering with dead bodies… The church was still worse. The floor was covered with rotting bodies… I never imagined anything so fearful."

The church stands as a shrine to Batak's victims, with charred beams, signs pointing to bullet holes, and a pit dug by mothers desperate to find water for their children.

The nearby **Ethnographic Museum**, in a 19th-century farmhouse, makes no reference to the atrocities. Its covered courtyard contains displays of antique farming implements and logging equipment. The simple living quarters upstairs are laid out much as they would have been in the 19th century.

Batak Reservoir, the picturesque artificial lake near Batak

Environs

Picturesque **Batak Reservoir** lies 6 km (4 miles) north of Batak. The lake is surrounded by meadows, and only a small part of the lakeside has been developed for tourism.

🏛 **History Museum**
pl. Osvobozh Denie 3. **Tel** (03553) 2329. **Open** Apr–Sep: 9am–5pm Mon–Fri; Oct–Mar: 9am–noon, 1–5pm Mon–Fri. 🎫 Joint ticket for History Museum, Church of Sveta Nedelya and Ethnographic Museum. 📷

🏛 **Church of Sveta Nedelya**
pl. Osvobozh Denie 3. **Open** & 🎫 See History Museum (above). 📷

🏛 **Ethnographic Museum**
pl. Osvobozh Denie 3. **Open** & 🎫 See History Museum (above). 📷

㉑ Devin
Девин

80 km (50 miles) S of Plovdiv. **Map** C4. 🚌 7,050. 🚍

Besides the bottled mineral water for which Devin is well known, this small town's greatest merit is its thermal pools and baths. The Orpheus Hotel, in the town, has an outdoor thermal pool that is open to the public.

Devin also has a **History Museum**, with a collection of exhibits illustrating folklore of the western Rhodopes.

🏛 **History Museum**
ul. Orfei 1. **Tel** (03041) 2319. **Open** Mon–Sat, times vary so call ahead. 📷

㉒ Western Rhodopes Caves
Пещери в Западните Родопи

See pp132–3.

㉓ Shiroka Lûka
Широка Лъка

90 km (56 miles) S of Plovdiv. **Map** C4. 🚌 800. 🚍 🎪 🎫 Kukeri carnival (1st weekend in Mar); International Bagpipe Festival (Aug)

This quaint and atmospheric village is deservedly popular with visitors. It clings to the side of a steep valley washed

Gaida, Bulgarian Bagpipes

The Rhodope Mountains are thought to be the home of Bulgaria's oldest folk music tradition. Central to this is the *gaida*, or Bulgarian bagpipes. A *gaida* consists of a goatskin with a blowpipe attached to the neck hole and two other pipes – the drone and the melody chanter –attached to each of the front leg holes. Holding it under his arm, the player blows into the bag, forcing air out through the pipes. A feature of the *gaida* is the "flea hole", a smaller hole usually covered by the player's index finger. When uncovered, it raises any note by a semitone to create the unique ornamentation of Bulgarian folk music.

Folk singers are often accompanied by a *kaba gaida*, a large, low-pitched bagpipe. Bands of 60 to 100 pipers, known as *sto kaba gaidi*, produce a tremendous sound.

Gaida players at the International Bagpipe Festival in Shiroka Lûka

by a small river, and looks across to densely wooded slopes on the opposite side. Picturesque houses with bare stone foundations, timber and whitewashed walls, and roofs of roughly hewn stone slabs perch on terraces cut into the hillside. A network of cobbled streets threads through the town's haphazard layout.

The **Church of the Assumption** (1834), reached by crossing an ancient stone bridge on the western side of the village, is decorated with naive frescoes of a funeral and biblical scenes. Across the road from the church is the Sgurov Konak (Sgurov House), built by a wealthy local family in the late 19th century. Now the Town

Hall, the building houses the **Ethnographic Museum**, filled with original furnishings and other exhibits that illustrate the lives of the Sgurov family.

Shiroka Lûka has a strong association with folk culture. It is one of the best places to see a *kukeri* carnival *(see p106)*. The village is also the home of the National School of Folklore Arts, which organizes performances of folk music for tour groups, and it hosts the International Bagpipe Festival.

🏠 **Church of the Assumption**
Open rarely. Enquire in the village.

🏛 **Ethnographic Museum**
ul. Kapitan Petko Voivoda 26. **Tel** (0899) 465170. **Open** 8am–6pm daily. 📷

Houses at Shiroka Lûka, on a hillside above the Shirokolûshka river valley

❷ Western Rhodopes Caves
Пещери в Западните Родопи

The road southwest from Devin leads into the spectacular, pine-forested Rhodope Mountains, where it forks to either the spectacular Trigrad Gorge or the winding Buzhnov Gorge and Yagodina Cave. This remote border region is dotted with tiny villages dependent on small-scale farming. The locals are a mix of Christian Bulgarians and Muslim Bulgarians (pomaks) who have coexisted peacefully for many centuries; many villages here have both a church and a mosque. The area is excellent for hiking, mountain biking and bird watching, and pony-trekking tours can also be arranged from Trigrad. Although they are accessible by limited public transport, it is far easier to reach the villages and caves by car.

Western Rhodopes
This picturesque and diverse geography of mountains, caves, forests, rivers, lakes and valleys is home to a wide variety of flora and fauna.

Cave-dwelling Bats
Large colonies of bats – 28 out of the 35 bat species known in Europe – live in the Rhodope Mountains. All of them are under the protection of the law. In colder months they live deep in the caves but can roost in old buildings and trees in summer.

Haberlea Rhodopensis
This rare alpine flower is endemic to Bulgaria and enjoys the wet rocky climate of caves – so much so that it is also known as Orpheus's flower.

Orpheus in the Underworld

Orpheus, the mythological hero of Thrace, sang and played the lyre so beguilingly that his music charmed trees and animals. When his beloved wife Eurydice died, Orpheus descended into the Underworld to seek her. Moved by his music, Hades agreed to return Eurydice on condition that Orpheus did not set his eyes on her until they had reached the Overworld. But Orpheus looked back, and lost his wife forever. Heartbroken, Orpheus roamed the Rhodope Mountains, singing mournfully of his loss. He was killed by Thracian women and his head and lyre were thrown into a river. Lodged in a rock, his head became an oracle.

The death of Orpheus at the hands of a Thracian woman

Treecreeper
These are attractive little birds that hop around tree trunks, looking for insects, in steady little spirals working their way to the top, before flying off to the next tree flashing a golden wing bar.

★ Yagodina Cave

Stretching for 10 km (6 miles) over five levels, Yagodina Cave is the longest and deepest in the Rhodopes. Tunnels lead visitors through stunning galleries with interestingly shaped rock formations and evidence of prehistoric occupation.

VISITORS' CHECKLIST

Practical Information
Trigrad 30 km (20 miles) SW of Devin. **Map** C5. 🎵 Orphic Mysteries Folk Music Festival, Trigrad (Aug). Devil's Throat Cave: **Open** daily. 🕐 30 mins. 🎫
Yagodina Cave: **Open** daily.
🕐 45 mins. 🎫

Transport
🚌 from Devin

★ Trigrad Gorge

This gorge ascends gradually towards the Devil's Throat, where its steep walls narrow dramatically and the Trigradska River plunges into the cave.

★ Devil's Throat Cave

A long corridor leads into a vast cavern 110 m (360 ft) long and 35 m (115 ft) high traversed by walkways. A noisy 45-m (150-ft) waterfall reveals where the Trigradska River dives underground. Three hundred steep steps lead up to the cave mouth.

Buzhnov Gorge follows the winding Boinovska River. This gorge is less precipitous than Trigrad Gorge, but is still worth a visit..

Trigrad Village

This picturesque village is notable for the sight of a church and a mosque side by side. Birdwatchers should look out for the wallcreepers often spotted on rocks nearby.

0 kilometres 2

0 miles 2

Key

— Main road

— Other roads

-- Trail

For map symbols *see back flap*

The mountain town of Smolyan, one of the highest in Bulgaria

㉔ Smolyan

Смолян

103 km (64 miles) S of Plovdiv.
Map C5. 30,600. 📭 📻 *ℹ* bul.
Bulgaria 5, Mladezhki dom building
(0301-62530). **W** smolyan.bg

Smolyan is a narrow strip of a town strung out between densely forested mountains at an altitude of about 1,000 m (3,300 ft). The air here is crisp and fresh, and the climate pleasantly sunny.

Smolyan has a relatively short history. The original local settlement of Ezerovo, situated beside the lakes above the town, was destroyed by the Ottomans in the 17th century as a reprisal against those of its inhabitants who refused to adopt Islam. While they fled to the mountains, those that agreed to convert settled along the Cherna River, where they founded the villages of Smolyan, Ustovo and Raikovo. In 1960 the three settlements were amalgamated to form Smolyan, now the cultural and administrative capital of the central and western Rhodopes.

The town's modern centre was laid out in the 1980s. Its great central thoroughfare and enormous civic buildings, many of which appear to be underused, seem out of proportion to the relatively modest size of its population.

Icon of St John the Theologian, Smolyan

The **History Museum**, however, makes good use of its space. Its captivating exhibits begin with the earliest human presence in the central Rhodope Mountains. Flint tools from the Palaeolithic period are followed by objects from later prehistory, such as spindle weights and other stone implements. One room is devoted to the Thracians, who were most active in the region during the Iron Age. Objects in this section include ceramic vessels, bronze and iron clasps, swords and arrows, a bronze helmet with bearded cheek guards, and a a delightful bronze oil lamp in the shape of a doe.

Most of these objects were found in the many Thracian necropolises that have been discovered in the Rhodopes. Later exhibits relate to the Ottoman campaign to convert local villagers to Islam. Evidence of outward acceptance of Islam that concealed continued Christian belief is shown in such pieces as an Islamic gravestone with a cross carved on the underside. Upstairs, the museum's displays continue with beautiful fleecy rugs, woven in goat's wool coloured with vivid natural dyes.

The town's **Art Gallery**, opposite the museum, has an absorbing collection of paintings that includes romantic Rhodopean landscapes and modern works by local artists.

Further along bulevard Bulgariya is the modern Church of Sveti Vaserion Smolyanski, topped with eyecatchingly large copper-clad domes. Across the road are the somewhat smaller domes of the **Planetarium**, which has daily shows in several languages.

🏛 **History Museum**
ul. Dicho Petrov 3. **Tel** (0301) 62727.
Open 9am–5pm Tue–Sun. 🖼

🏛 **Art Gallery**
ul. Dicho Petrov 5. **Tel** (0301) 62328
Open May–Sep: 10am–noon,
1–6:30pm daily; Oct–Apr: 9am–noon,
1–5:30pm daily. 🖼

🏛 **Planetarium**
bul. Bulgariya 20. **Tel** (0301) 83074.
Shows in English at 3pm daily.
🖼 ♿ **W** planetarium-sm.org

Part of Agushev Konak, a fine fortified manor house in Mogilitsa

㉕ Mogilitsa

Могилица

20 km (12 miles) SW of Smolyan.
Map C5. 500. 📭

An easy day trip from Smolyan is the quiet village of Mogilitsa. It was once home to the wealthy Agushev family, who grew rich from sheep farming. The **Agushev Konak**, their winter residence, is one of the best surviving examples of a Rhodopean fortified manor house. It was begun in 1812 and completed in 1842 and, with a total of 221 windows, 86 doors and 26 chimneys, it is an imposing presence in the village. The complex is divided into three walled compounds, which were inhabited by Agushev's eldest sons and their families.

The Agushev Konak is no longer open to the public, but its exterior is of interest for its remarkable architecture. According to a local legend, Agushev cut off the architect's right hand to prevent him from designing such a beautiful building for anyone else.

Environs

About 3 km (2 miles) east of Mogilitsa is **Uhlovitza Cave**. The descent to the mouth of the cave, down steep steps, is rewarded by the dramatic sight of underground waterfalls and fascinating mineral formations. The cave can quite easily be reached by car, or on foot via a hiking trail.

🏛 **Agushev Konak**
Closed to the public.

🏠 **Uhlovitza Cave**
Open 9am–4pm Wed–Sun. 🖼

㉖ Zlatograd
Златоград

50 km (31 miles) SE of Smolyan. **Map** D5. 🏔 8,000. 🚌 🚏

Under Communism, Zlatograd (Gold Town) was a thriving mining centre. But by the late 1990s, rising costs and other factors had made its mines uneconomical and all were closed. More recently, however, Zlatograd has begun to recover, attracting visitors to its interesting **Ethnographic Museum Complex**.

This ensemble of restored National Revival buildings houses traditional workshops, an Ethnographic Museum, and an Education Museum. At the

A piste on the forested slopes above the ski resort of Pamporovo

Water Mill Museum, visitors can watch huge water-powered hammers processing woollen material. The complex also includes a guest house.

🏛 **Ethnographic Museum Complex**
bul. Bulgaria 123. **Tel** (03071) 4166.
Open 9am–6:30pm daily. 🖼 🖼 🖥
🖼 🖼 🖥 **eac-zlatograd.com**

㉗ Momchilovtsi
Момчиловци

90 km (56 miles) S of Plovdiv. **Map** C5. 🏔 450. 🚌 🚏 ℹ (03023) 2803.

This pretty Rhodopean mountain village lies at an altitude of 1,200 m (4,000 ft). With stunning views and great tranquillity, it has become popular as a weekend retreat for wealthy townspeople. Its nearby snowboard park also attracts winter visitors, and the area is used as a base by hunters visiting Kormisosh, Bulgaria's largest hunting reserve, 15 km (9 miles) away.

㉘ Pamporovo
Пампорово

85 km (53 miles) south of Plovdiv.
🚌 🚏

With Borovets and Bansko, Pamporovo forms part of the trio of major Bulgarian ski resorts. Second-largest of the three, it is also the southernmost and the sunniest. It was purpose-built under Communism, with large hotels set at the base of pine-forested pistes. While the resort covers a larger area than Borovets (see p111), it lacks the village atmosphere of Bansko (see pp122–4), and has fewer après-ski facilities.

As it is geared to catering for large groups, the resort has long attracted Western European tourists on cheap package holidays. With gentle slopes, Pamporovo is suitable for beginners and intermediate skiers, but offers little to challenge the more advanced.

With snow from December to mid-April, the resort is crowded during the winter season. In summer, by contrast, it is virtually deserted, despite the beauty of the landscape at that time of year and the efforts of tour operators to promote mountain biking and hiking here.

For spectacular views at any time of year, visitors can take the chairlift to Mount Snezhanka. The **Television Tower** on the summit, at a height of 1,926 m (6,320 ft), has an observation gallery.

📺 **Television Tower**
Mount Snezhanka. **Open** 9am–5pm daily. 🖥

Part of the Ethnographic Museum Complex in Zlatograd

Visitors having fun at a mountain lake in Pirin National Park ▶

㉙ Plovdiv
Пловдив

The three hills on which Plovdiv's Old Town stands were settled by Thracians in the 5th millennium BC. Philip II of Macedon captured the town in 342 BC and from the 1st to 4th centuries AD it was held by the Romans. It thrived, but was largely destroyed by Huns in 447. In the 6th century, Plovdiv was occupied by Slavs. It then passed back and forth between Byzantines and Bulgarians before the Ottomans took control of it in the 14th century. After the Liberation of 1878, Plovdiv was returned to the Ottomans as part of Eastern Rumelia but in 1885 it was reunified with Bulgaria. Now Bulgaria's second-largest city, Plovdiv is a pleasant town, with a pedestrianized centre, mosques, churches, Roman ruins and National Revival mansions.

🏛 Roman Stadium
pl. Dzhumaya.
Crumbling marble terraces and tumbled columns oddly incorporated into the concrete foundations of modern Plovdiv are almost all that remain of the town's once huge Roman stadium. It was built in the 2nd century AD, and could seat 30,000 spectators.

☪ Dzhumaya Mosque
pl. Dzhumaya.
Although the imposing nine-domed Friday Mosque is currently undergoing much needed structural repairs, it is still open to visitors. The central focus of its pale blue interior is a fountain surrounded by four massive pillars. It is thought to have been built as early as 1364, during the reign of Sultan Murad I. A café that abuts the

The diamond-patterned minaret of Dzhumaya Mosque

mosque's outer wall serves Turkish coffee and *baklava* (syrupy cake).

The Archaeological Museum, in a redundant revenue building

🏛 History Museum
pl. Suedinenie. **Tel** (032) 229 409.
Open 9am–noon, 12:30–5pm Mon–Fri, 9:30am–5pm Sat. 🏠 ♿
The History Museum is housed in what was intended to be Eastern Rumelia's parliament building. It was completed in 1885 but, with the unification of Bulgaria with Eastern Rumelia later that year, Sofia became the capital of Bulgaria. The building lost its purpose, and it has been a museum ever since. Consisting of declarations, weaponry, uniforms and photographs of soldiers and ragged rebels, its collection documents the unification of 1885 (see p51).

🏛 Archaeological Museum
pl. Suedinenie. **Tel** (032) 633 106.
Open 9:30am–5:30pm Tue–Sat. 🏠 ✉ 🖥 🅦 archaeologicalmuseum plovdiv.org

The archaeological museum has an excellent collection of antiquities from all periods. After a three-year long renovation, it is now one of the best in Bulgaria, boasting more than 100,000 exhibits.

☪ Imaret Mosque
ul. Han Kubrat.
Dating from 1445, this is one of more than 50 mosques built in Plovdiv during the Ottoman period. *Imaret* means "shelter for the homeless", and this was the mosque's original function. Its square walls support a central dome and a minaret with unusual zigzag brickwork.

Key

▪ Street-by-Street *pp140–41*

🏛 Natural History Museum
ul. Hristo Danov 34. **Tel** (032) 626 683.
Open 8:30am–noon, 1–5pm Tue–Sun.
🖼 🌐 rnhm.org

A stuffed deer at the museum entrance sets the scene for the remarkable collection of stuffed mammals, birds and reptiles that

Sights at a Glance

① Roman Stadium
② Dzhumaya Mosque
③ History Museum
④ Archaeological Museum
⑤ Imaret Mosque
⑥ Natural History Museum
⑦ City Art Gallery
⑧ Church of Sveta Marina
⑨ Hristo Danov House
⑩ Church of Sveta Bogoroditsa
⑪ Philippopolis Art Gallery
⑫ State Gallery of Fine Arts
⑬ Hipokrat Pharmacy
⑭ Georgi Bozhilov-Slona Gallery
⑮ Icon Museum
⑯ Nedkovich House
⑰ Hindliyan House
⑱ Nebet Tepe
⑲ Lamartine House
⑳ Roman Theatre
㉑ Trakart Cultural Centre

---

lie within. Among many notable exhibits are a camel and an anaconda. Downstairs is an aquarium where visitors can see live turtles and fish, including piranhas.

Other rooms contain displays of minerals and giant crystals, fossilized trees, mammoth tusks and teeth, and tiny fossils of organisms that lived millions of years ago.

🏛 City Art Gallery
ul. Knyaz Alexander Batemberg 15.
Tel (032) 624 221. **Open** 9:30am–12:30pm, 1–5:30pm Mon–Fri,
10am–12:30pm, 1–5:30pm Sat & Sun.
🖼 (free on Thu).

This gallery displays the work of Bulgarian and international artists in continually changing displays. It also has a permanent collection of 19th-century art. Another of Plovdiv's permanent art collections is kept at the State Gallery of Fine Arts (see p142).

Cloisters at the 18th-century Church of Sveta Marina

🕆 Church of Sveta Marina
ul. Dr Vulkovich 7. **Tel** (032) 623 276.
The present Church of Sveta Marina was built in 1783, on the site of a 16th-century church, which was destroyed by fire. It is renowned for its intricate iconostasis, which is decorated with tiny figures painted by artists including Zahari Zograf (see p110).

🏛 Hristo Danov House
ul. Mitropolit Paisii 2. **Tel** (032) 629 405.
Open 9am–noon, 2–5pm Mon–Fri. 🖼
Built on Taxim Tepe (Taxim Hill), Hristo Danov House overlooks Plovdiv. Steep steps lead up to it. Its arched gable is supported by four columns, and trompe-l'oeil pillars adorn the façade. The symmetrical interior is typical of National Revival

---

architecture, with rooms each side of the main drawing room.

Hristo Danov, founder of organized book publishing in Bulgaria, lived here from 1868 until his death in 1911. Danov was largely responsible for the first large-scale publication of school textbooks in Bulgarian. As well as Danov's study, the house contains a collection of books and a re-created 19th-century classroom.

🕆 Church of Sveta Bogoroditsa
ul. Saborna 6. **Tel** (032) 623 265.
Open 7am–7pm daily. 🕆 8am daily.
This imposing stone church has a distinctive pink and blue bell tower that was added with Russian assistance in 1880, after the Liberation. Its murals echo the mood of the late 19th century. They depict Bulgarian Orthodox saints alongside leaders of the Liberation movement. To the right are priests, intellectuals and peasants chained together under the whip of a cruel Turk. To the left are children being taught by a benign Bulgarian schoolmaster. The church's interior is lit by arched windows, and hefty columns lead towards a bright gilt iconostasis.

Murals with a political message, in the Church of Sveta Bogoroditsa

Street-by-Street: Plovdiv Old Town

One of the most picturesque of Bulgaria's historic urban centres, Plovdiv's Old Town consists of steep cobbled streets lined with fine National Revival houses, many of them built for wealthy merchants. Colourfully rendered exteriors protrude majestically over high walls, and within are breathtakingly opulent interiors. Mostly built in the mid-19th century, these houses gradually fell into decay as the cost of maintaining them outstripped their owners' means. However, state restoration projects in the 1970s did much to preserve these houses, several of which are now museums. Most of the Old Town is also under state protection as an architectural reserve.

★ Icon Museum
The beautiful icons on display here were painted in the 15th and 16th centuries, and come from churches in the vicinity of Plovdiv.

Zlatyu Boyadzhiev Gallery in Chomakov House
The rooms of this grand house are filled with paintings by Zlatyu Boyadzhiev (1903–76). These large-scale, colourful and impressionistic works were inspired by village life, and often depict peasants. The artist produced his most interesting works after 1951, when partial paralysis forced him to paint with his left hand.

ULITSA SABORNA

HISA
KAPI
PL

KNYAZ TSERETELEV

Apteka Hipokrat
This pharmacy museum gives a fascinating insight into the treatment of common ailments in the 19th century.

Georgi Bozhilov-Slona Gallery
The work of Bulgarian modernist painters fills the rooms of this gallery.

★ Church of SS Konstantin & Elena
Richly coloured frescoes decorate both the entrance to this church and its interior. There is also an iconostasis partly decorated by Zahari Zograf.

VISITORS' CHECKLIST

Practical Information
Map C4. 8,602. 🛈 pl. Tsentralen 1 (032-620 229). 🎭 Winter Festival of Symphonic Music (first 2 weeks of Jan); International Trade Fair (early May and last 2 weeks of Sep); International Folklore Festival (Aug); City Holiday (6 Sep). 🅦 eventsplovdiv.info

Transport
🚉 🚌

★ Kuyumdzhiogh House
This beautiful house is one of the Old Town's showpieces. Built in 1847, it is now an Ethnographic Museum, with regional costumes and a traditional rose-oil distiller.

ULITSA TSANKO LAVRENOV

ARH. PEEV HRISTA

P.R. SLAVEYKOV

Nedkovich House
Secluded behind a high wall, Nedkovich House was built for a textile merchant in 1863. The rooms contain many of the house's original furnishings, imported from East and West to create a blend of European and Oriental styles.

Georgiadi House
Built for a wealthy Greek merchant in 1846, this grand house has rooms with projecting box windows. Among objects on display here is the bell that tolled during the April Rising of 1876.

0 metres	20
0 yards	20

Key

— Suggested route

Exploring Plovdiv

With narrow cobbled streets leading off in all directions, Plovdiv's Old Town can be disorientating at first, but with the help of a good map visitors should be able to find their way around. The easiest approach is to enter from ulitsa Saborna, off ploshtad Dzhumaya. This street leads through the old town, passing many museum-houses and galleries, all the way up to Nebet Tepe, from where there are stunning views of Plovdiv. Ulitsa Tsanko Lavrenov passes both the History Museum and Nedkovich House, and joins ulitsa Kiril Nektariev, which leads to Lamartine House and on towards the Roman Theatre. From here there is a sweeping view of the city and the Rhodope Mountains beyond.

🏛 Philippopolis Art Gallery

ul. Saborna 29. **Tel** (032) 622 742.
Open 10am–6pm daily. 🌐 🌐 🌐

This appealing gallery occupies an elegant house with fine furnishings. Downstairs is a collection of late 19th- and early 20th-century Bulgarian portraits and landscapes, most of which are for sale.

The permanent collection fills the rooms upstairs. Many of the works have romantic themes. Ivan Trichkov's *The Sower* (1920) portrays a barefooted peasant sowing in an ochre landscape, while a large canvas by Dimitar Gyudzhenov (1975) depicts a gathering of revolutionaries bathed in the light of a setting sun.

🏛 State Gallery of Fine Arts

ul. Saborna 14a. **Tel** (032) 635 322.
Open 9:30am–12:30pm, 1–5:30pm Mon–Fri, 10am–12:30pm, 1–5:30pm Sat & Sun. 🌐 (free on Thu).

In a grand old building that was once a school, the State Gallery of Fine Arts has a comprehensive collection of 19th- and

The State Gallery of Fine Arts, in an imposing Neo-Classical building

20th-century Bulgarian paintings. Solemn 19th-century portraits hang alongside idyllic scenes such as Ivan Angelov's *Women Gathering Hay* (1903), and some typically vibrant works by Vladimir Dimitrov-Maistora. Large, bold canvases on the second floor represent more recent Bulgarian painting. Among the works here is *The Fire* (1977) by Svetlin Rusev, a monumental canvas in which a figure walks away from a furnace carrying a glowing ember into the darkness.

🏛 Hipokrat Pharmacy

ul. Saborna 16.
Open 10am–5pm Mon–Fri.

The fascinating Hipokrat Pharmacy (Apteka Hipokrat) has been preserved virtually as it was when it was a working pharmacy. It is lined with wooden drawers, and contains bottles labelled in Latin.

🏛 Georgi Bozhilov-Slona Gallery

Knyaz Tseretelev 1. **Open** 10am–6pm daily. 🌐

This attractive blue and white house contains a collection of paintings by Georgi Bozhilov-Slona (1935–2001). The artist, a key member of the Bulgarian Modernist movement, often painted abstract pictures of familiar objects, such as a still life with a chair, a stove and a cup. By using thick layers of oil paint and by blending textures and media he created striking images charged with emotion. Few of the paintings exhibited here are named or dated.

🏛 Icon Museum

ul. Saborna, 22. **Open** 9:30am–12:30pm, 1–5:30pm Mon–Fri, 10am–12:30pm, 1–5:30pm Sat & Sun. 🌐 (free on Thu).

This interesting museum is home to a valuable array of icons from the Plovdiv eparchy collection that was collected from churches under threat during the Communist years.

Icon of St Cyril and St Methodius in the Icon Museum

🏛 Nedkovich House

ul. Tsanko Lavrenov, 3. **Open** 9am–noon, 1–5pm Mon–Fri. 🌐

This grand house is a fine example of the symmetrical architecture so loved during the National Revival. An interesting feature is the courtyard structure with a window to the street known as the *clukarnik* (literally "gossip room") where the inhabitants could drink tea and chat to passersby. The first floor salon boasts a raised stage where musicians would entertain guests.

Room in Nedkovich House, built for a textile trader in 1863

Detail of one of the murals of European cities at Hindliyan House

Hindliyan House

ul. Artin Gidikov 4. **Open** 9am–5pm
Mon–Fri.

This elegant house, its pale blue
outer walls decorated with floral
motifs, looks onto a peaceful
courtyard garden. It was built in
1835–40, for Stepan Hindliyan, a
wealthy Armenian merchant. The
interior features murals depicting
the European cities that he
visited. The house also has a
hammam with a marble floor,
hot and cold water, and a domed
ceiling with tiny windows. The
spacious first-floor salon has
a stunning panelled ceiling and
a marble fountain.

Nebet Tepe

Dilapidated houses line ulitsa
Dr Chomakov, the street that leads
up to the equally ramshackle
Nebet Tepe (Prayer Hill). As the
city's highest point, the summit
was the site of a citadel. Today it
is an overgrown wasteland
strewn with boulders and the
barely visible foundations of the
ancient fortress. Even so, it is easy
to understand why the hill was
so prized by successive invaders.
Situated close to the Maritsa
River, it stands prominently in
the centre of the plain between
the Rhodope and Stara Planina
mountains. It is a good vantage
point from which to view most
of the city, spread out below.

Lamartine House

ul. Knyaz Tseretelev. **Closed** to
the public.

This attractive house is named
after the French poet Alphonse
de Lamartine, who stayed here
briefly in 1833, in the course of
travels that he described in
Voyage en l'Orient.

The house, now owned by the
Union of Bulgarian Writers, is
not open to the public, but from
the outside visitors can admire
its projecting floors supported
by wooden ribs.

Lamartine House, named after the French
poet who stayed here

Roman Theatre

ul. Hemus **Open** 9am–5:30pm
daily.

This impressive marble amphitheatre, set in the hillside
overlooking the city and the
Rhodope Mountains beyond,
was discovered during
construction work in 1972.
It was built in the 2nd century
AD, when Trimontium (Roman
Plovdiv) was at its height, and
formed part of the acropolis.
Today the theatre is used for
concerts and plays.

Trakart Cultural Centre

Podlez Arheologicheski. **Tel** (032) 631
303. **Open** 9am–7pm daily.
W trakart.org

Most pedestrians using the
Archaeological Underpass
(Podlez Arheologicheski) to
cross bul. Tsar Boris Osvoboditel
will not know that it is a Roman
street, paved with huge stone
slabs, dating back to the 3rd–
4th centuries AD. Alongside the
underpass is the Trakart Cultural
Centre, which exhibits the
foundations and mosaic floors
of a 4th-century Roman house
uncovered in the mid-1980s.
Supporting columns carved
with crosses date the building
to the late 4th century, when
Emperor Theodosius I made
Christianity the official religion.

The mosaics, preserved in situ,
are in remarkably good condition.
They include a portrait of
a woman thought to be
Penelope, the pagan goddess
of peace, who was adopted by
Christians as St Irene. The lead
pipe that supplied water to the
fountain in the house's main
reception room also survives.
Beside the fountain is a mosaic
with the words "happiness"
and "welcome" and geometric
designs bordered by bands of
swastikas and other motifs.
The remains of a corridor with
underfloor sewage channels
lead from the main entrance to
a room with a patterned mosaic
floor. An east-facing apse was
added later, as a meeting room
or chapel.

The centre, which is funded
by the US Embassy, also hosts
art exhibitions, and sells replicas
of ancient ceramics.

The well-preserved Roman Theatre, with seating for 6,000 spectators

⑳ Bachkovo Monastery

Бачковски манастир

See pp146–7.

㉛ Haskovo

Хасково

75 km (47 miles) E of Plovdiv. **Map** D5.
🏔 75,600. 🛈 bul. Rakovski 1a (038
666 444). 🚗 🚌 🚊 daily.
🌐 haskovo.bg

With pedestrianized streets,
neat flowerbeds and splashing
fountains, Haskovo has an
appealing town centre. It was
established in the 14th century,
and was predominantly Muslim
until the overthrow of Ottoman
rule in 1912 led to an influx of
ethnic Bulgarians.

Of the town's original seven
mosques only two remain. One
of them, the Eski Mosque, is the
oldest in the Balkans, although
its plastered façade and wood-
panelled interior largely conceal
the building's original features.

Haskovo was a centre of
southern Bulgaria's once-
thriving tobacco industry. This
period of the town's history is
documented at the History
Museum, which has a display
of machinery used to process
tobacco. Other rooms contain
collections of antique cigarette
boxes and photographs.

On the other side of the town,
on bulevard Bulgariya, is the
19th-century Church of Sveta
Bogoroditsa, a simple stone
building with an intricately
carved iconostasis and
bishop's throne. Nearby is
the Paskalevata Kûshta, a

Street in Haskovo, with the minaret of Eski
Mosque in the background

National Revival house with
a small art gallery. It is the birthplace of Aleksandûr Paskalev,
who laid the foundations of
publishing in Bulgaria.

🅲 Eski Mosque
ul. San Stefano 12.

🏛 History Museum
pl. Svoboda 19. **Tel** (038) 624 237.
Open 9am–noon, 1–4pm Tue–Fri. 🗺

⛪ Church of Sveta Bogoroditsa
Corner of bul. Bulgariya and ul.
Berkovski. **Tel** (038) 624 835. **Open**
8am–5pm daily. 🕐 8am Fri, Sun.

🏠 Paskalevata Kûshta
ul. Bratya Minchevi. **Tel** (038) 624 237.
Open by request, call ahead. 🗺

Islamic-style building in Kûrdzhali, now the
town's History Museum

㉜ Kûrdzhali

Кърджали

53 km (33 miles) south of Haskovo.
Map D5. 🏔 43,800. 🚗 🚌 🚊
🌐 kardjali.bg

Named after the legendary
Turkish commander Kûrdzha Ali,
who died during an attack on
the eastern Rhodopes in the
14th century, Kûrdzhali has
always been a mainly Muslim
town. Today, ethnic Turks make
up 62 per cent of its population.
Many have migrated to Turkey,
as reduced demand for the
region's tobacco in recent years
has lead to economic decline.
The main attraction for visitors
to Kûrdzhali is the History
Museum, in a splendid Islamic-
style building. Originally a
Muslim college, it has rows
of arched windows flanking
a grand central balcony topped
with a lead dome. The

museum's excellent
archaeological, natural history,
and ethnographic collections
are laid out on three floors.
Highlights include a nephrite
swastika pendant of the
6th millennium BC, and an
impressive bronze statue of
Apollo of the 3rd century BC.
Others include a replica of
a hefty metal-plated battle
catapult, and a collection of
medieval iron and bronze
crosses found at Perperikon.

🏛 History Museum
ul. Republikanska 4. **Tel** (0361) 63587.
Open 9am–noon, 1–5pm Tue–Sun.
🗺 🏛

㉝ Madzharovo Nature Reserve

Защитена местност около
Маджарово

35 km (22 miles) SE of Haskovo.
Map D5. 🚌 🛈 **Open** 9am–5pm
daily. 🌊 🚲 🏠 🗺 Accommodation
and guided tours should be booked in
advance, (0888) 420 159.

One of the few European
breeding grounds for black,
Egyptian and griffon vultures,
this reserve is of great interest
to birdwatchers. The vultures
nest on steep crags beside the
meandering Arda River, and
so as to maintain, or even
increase, their numbers, a diet
of carrion is provided by the
reserve warden.

Eight species of falcon and
nine of woodpecker, as well as
many other birds, also inhabit
the reserve.

Rocky cliffs in Madzharovo Nature Reserve,
habitat of vultures

❸ Eastern Rhodopes Tour

As they descend eastwards towards Kûrdzhali, the Rhodope Mountains become less dramatic. This dry, hilly landscape is dotted with extraordinary rock formations, most of which were formed by volcanic activity some 40 million years ago and slowly shaped by the erosive action of wind, sand and rain. This region, with small villages among tobacco fields and flocks of sheep and goats, was the first part of Bulgaria to be conquered by the Ottomans, and it still has a large population of ethnic Turks.

Tips for Walkers

Road Map D5.
Starting point: Stone Mushrooms, near Beli Plast, 20 km (12 miles) north of Kûrdzhali.
Length: 140 km (87 miles).
Getting there: Perperikon (from which the Stone Mushrooms are one hour's walk away) and Tatul (where the ruins are just outside the village) are accessible by bus. The other rock formations are best reached by car.

① Stone Mushrooms
The puffy pink Stone Mushrooms (Kamennite gûbi) are up to 2.5 m (8 ft) high. The green hue of their caps and their brown flecks are produced by traces of iron, manganese and other oxides.

③ Stone Wedding
Gently moulded columns of pink tufa make up the Stone Wedding (Vkamenenata svatba). The "bride" and "groom" are surrounded by other formations, their "guests".

Haskovo

Chernoochene
Yavorovo
Varbentsi
Stremtsi
Zayhar 507m
Most
Dazhdovnitsa
Chiflik
Perperek
Padartsi
Enchets
Kûrdzhali
Kurdzhali Lake
Shiroko Pole
Studen Kladenets Lake
Volovartsi
Gruevo
Raven
Nanovitsa
Mishevsko
Momchilgrad
Lale
Dzhebel
Komotini
Pripek
Mrezhichko
General Geshevo

② Perperikon and Ahridos
Cut deep into a rocky hilltop, Perperikon was a settlement founded in 6000 to 5000 BC. The spectacular ruins include a fortified acropolis. At the foot of the hill are the remains of Ahridos, thought to have been the capital of the eastern Rhodopes c.AD 1000.

④ Rock Window
The massive Rock Window (Skalen Prozorets) is 10 m (33 ft) high and 7 m (23 ft) wide. More of a table than a window, it consists of a limestone slab on two fat columns.

⑦ Stone Forest
This collection of rock stumps, up to 4 m (13 ft) wide and 1.5 m (5 ft) high, is known as the Stone Forest (Vkamenenata gora). The stones may be fossilized tree trunks or, more likely, the result of intense underwater volcanic activity during the early Eocene period.

⑤ Rocks at Ustra
Perhaps the most impressive of the eastern Rhodopes' rock formations, the Rocks at Ustra (Skalite na Ustra) have been sculpted by the elements into huge pillars and cones.

⑥ Tatul
A pair of tombs carved into the rock crown this site, once a Thracian hilltop temple. Other remains include a circular altar, a Roman wall, and a deep grain store.

0 kilometres 10
0 miles 10

Key
▬ Tour route
═ Main road
═ Other road
▬ Railway
△ Peak

⊕ Bachkovo Monastery

Бачковски манастир

At the foot of the forested slopes of the Rhodope Mountains lies Bachkovo Monastery, its serene courtyards filled with flowerbeds, exotic trees and drinking fountains. The monastery was founded in 1083 by Grigori and Abbasi Bakouriani, Georgian brothers who were commanders in the Byzantine army. In the 13th century, the monastery was sponsored by Tsar Ivan Assen II and his successor Ivan Aleksandŭr. Destroyed by the Ottomans in the 16th century, it was restored by the 17th century. Because of its fine architecture and frescoes, this great monastery, the second-largest in Bulgaria after Rila Monastery, is a UNESCO World Heritage Site.

The Ossuary
This is the only surviving part of the 11th-century monastery. The frescoes inside are so delicate that it is not open to visitors.

★ Last Judgment
In the porch of the Church of Sveti Nikola is a dramatic fresco of the Last Judgment by Zahari Zograf, with sinners falling into the fires of Hell.

Church of Sveti Nikola
A door to the left of the main courtyard leads to the Church of Sveti Nikola, which was built in 1834. It contains frescoes by Zahari Zograf and other renowned painters.

Fresco in the Dome
The dome of the Church of Sveti Nikola is decorated with a fresco of Christ Pantocrator, encircled by exquisitely painted portraits of saints.

Church of Sveta Bogoroditsa
This 17th-century church is richly decorated with frescoes. Themes include the Devil addressing Christ from the mouth of a monster, and Death shadowing an angel.

VISITORS' CHECKLIST

Practical Information
Bachkovo, 30 km (19 miles) S of Plovdiv. **Map** C4. **Tel** (03327) 277. **Open** 8am–5pm daily. 🎫 📷 🎫 🎫 🎫 for the Refectory.

Transport
🚌 from Plovdiv or Asenovgrad. Ⓜ

★ Iconostasis
The Church of Sveta Bogoroditsa also contains a highly ornate 17th-century gilt iconostasis, which gleams in the soft light of hundreds of flickering candles.

At the Miracle Icon of the Virgin, worshippers gather to kiss the silver-plated Icon of the Virgin, painted in 1310.

Main entrance

Ayazmoto

Procession of the Miraculous Icon

The refectory wall on the left of the courtyard bears the largest panoramic wall painting in Bulgaria. Painted by Alexi Atanasov in 1846, it depicts the procession with the Icon of the Virgin on 15 August, the day of the Assumption of the Virgin. After Orthodox Easter, the icon is carried to Ayazmoto.

Ayazmoto
On a nearby hill is a chapel known as Ayazmoto. The Icon of the Virgin was once hidden from the Ottomans here.

★ Refectory
A solid stone table and wooden benches stretch the length of the 17th-century refectory. The vaulted ceiling is covered with frescoes by pupils of Zahari Zograf.

Procession of the Miraculous Icon of the Virgin Mary

CENTRAL BULGARIA

The Stara Planina Mountains form a mighty wall across the heart of Bulgaria. To north and south lie wooded hills, fertile plains and the vast rose fields of the Sredna Gora valley. The region is renowned both for its natural beauty and its ancient remains, which include Neolithic settlements, Thracian tombs, the Roman towns of Nikopolis ad Istrum and Hisarya, and the majestic citadel of Tsarevets.

The Ottoman policy of granting regional towns local autonomy and tax privileges in return for guarding mountain passes allowed places such as Koprivshtitsa, Tryavna, Troyan and Kotel to prosper both financially and culturally. Merchants grew rich from sheep and cattle farming, and from the export of such goods as leather items, woollen cloth, pottery, rose oil and silk.

In the early 19th century, turning the weakened state of the Ottoman Empire to their advantage, these merchants used their wealth to establish and fund Bulgarian language schools and to restore long-neglected churches and monasteries. This fostered the sense of national identity that was to become the keystone of the National Liberation movement.

From the 1860s, central Bulgaria was a hotbed of revolutionary activity. The rebel leader Vasil Levski established secret revolutionary committees throughout the region, and it was from Koprivshtitsa that the April Rising of 1876 began. In 1877, the region witnessed the bloodiest battle of the War of Liberation when a Russian army, supported by Bulgarian militias, dug in at the Shipka Pass, from where they eventually defeated the Ottomans.

Though the *kurdzhali* raids of the early 19th century destroyed much of the area's architectural heritage, restored buildings in several picturesque museum towns and villages give an insight into 18th- and 19th- century rural life. The region's natural beauty has also been safeguarded by the creation of the reserves that form the Central Balkan National Park.

Traditional shuttered windows of a National Revival-style house in Koprivshtitsa

◀ Dazzling gold domes of the Shipka Memorial Church

Exploring Central Bulgaria

The Central Balkan National Park, a paradise for
wildlife as well as for hikers, dominates the western
part of the region. Central Bulgaria is also rich
in archaeological sites, including the Valley of
the Thracian Kings, near Kazanlŭk, and the Roman
town of Nikopolis ad Istrum and fortress of Hisarya.
The region has many historic towns such as Bozhentsi,
Tryavna and Koprivshtitsa, each with outstanding
architecture not to mention four famous monasteries.
Bulgaria's famous rose fields, at their best in May
and June, line the valley between Kazanlŭk
and Karlovo, below the towering Stara
Planina mountains.

RItual drinking vessel from the Valley
of the Thracian Kings

0 kilometres   25

0 miles   25

Sights at a Glance

1. Glozhene Monastery
2. Ribaritsa
3. Teteven
4. Troyan
5. Troyan Monastery
6. Central Balkan National Park *pp154–5*
7. Lovech
8. Emen Gorge
9. Gabrovo
10. Etura Complex
11. Bozhentsi
12. *Tryavna pp158–9*
13. *Veliko Tŭrnovo pp160–64*
14. Dryanovo
15. Kilifarevo Monastery
16. Preobrazhenski Monastery
17. Nikopolis ad Istrum

18. Sveta Troitsa Convent
19. Arbanasi
20. Kŭpinovo Monastery
21. Elena
22. Kotel
23. Zheravna
24. Sliven
25. Yambol
26. Stara Zagora
27. Kazanlŭk
28. Shipka
29. Karlovo
30. Hisarya
31. Starosel Tombs
32. *Koprivshtitsa pp176–9*

Tours

28. Valley of the Thracian Kings

Sveta Troitsa Convent, on the Yantra River,
north of Arbanasi

Getting Around

The main Sofia–Burgas road runs west to east, via Karlovo, Kazanluk and Sliven, along the southern slopes of the Stara Planina Mountains. The Sofia–Veliko Tûrnovo road runs north of the mountains. These two routes are connected by the Zlatishki, Troyan and Shipka passes. A railway runs parallel to the Sofia–Burgas road, with a branch veering north beyond Kazanlûk to Veliko Tûrnovo. Troyan and Lovech have rail connections, but most of the northern half of the region can only be reached by bus.

Fresco in the Church of Sveti Nikola, Elena

Ruse

Polski Trambesh

NIKOPOLIS AD ISTRUM ❶❼

SVETA TROISTA CONVENT ❶❽

Strazhitsa

vlikeni

Rositsa

Varna

REOBRAZHENSKI MONASTERY ❶❻

Gorna Oryahovitsa

❽

ARBANASI ❶❾

MEN VELIKO ❶❸
RGE TURNOVO 🏛🏠🏛 53 Zlataritsa

YANOVO 🏛🏠❶❹

❶❺ KUPINOVO MONASTERY ❷⓿

46

BOZHENTSI MONASTERY 🏛🏠

KILIFAREVO MONASTERY

ELENA ❷❶

❶❶

❶❷ TRYAVNA

BROVO 🏛🏠

KOTEL 🏛 ❷❷

ZHERAVNA ❷❸
53 🏛🏠

❶⓿ ETURA COMPLEX

Chumerna
1536 m

B a l k a n s

55

❷❾ SHIPKA 🏠🏛

Tvarditsa Shivachevo

❷❽ VALLEY OF THE THRACIAN KINGS Gurkovo

🏛 ❷❹ SLIVEN

7 Burgas

❷❼

Zhrebchevo Lake

6

AZANLUK 🏛🏠 Maglizh
Tundzha

Straldzha

5

n e n a G o r a

66

Kermen

❷❺ YAMBOL ⓒ

Nova Zagora

A1

❷❻ STARA ZAGORA 🏛🏠

55

53

A1

57

Sazliyka

7

5 Radnevo

Ovcharitsa Lake

Tundzha

Chirpan

Merichleri

Galabovo

Elhovo

79

Bolyarovo

Marica

Haskovo

Malko Sabrkovo Lake

Key

▬▬ Motorway

= = Motorway under construction

▬▬ Expressway

▬▬ Main road

▬▬ Other road

— Railway

▬▬ International border

△ Peak

Part of Veliko Tûrnovo, once the historic capital of Bulgaria

For additional map symbols see back flap

❶ Glozhene Monastery

Гложенски манастир

11 km (7 miles) NW of Teteven.
Map C3. **Tel** (01960) 388. **Open**
8am–9pm daily. 🕕 6pm daily. 🖥

Of all Bulgaria's many monasteries, this one probably has the most impressive setting. It perches on sheer cliffs that tower high above the Vit River valley. The monastery's fortress-like stone lower walls support rickety wooden upper storeys roofed with the roughly cut stone slabs characteristic of the region.

Founded in 1224, the monastery was dedicated to St George the Victorious by Prince Glozh, a Ukrainian who brought with him a miracle-working icon of St George from Kiev Monastery. The icon now in the monastery church is a copy; the original is in Lovech bishopric.

In the 13th and 14th centuries Glozhene Monastery was a thriving centre of learning, with schools for the study of literature and religion. The residential buildings around the central courtyard were built in 1858. It was where, in a secret underground chamber, that Vasil Levski hid from the Ottoman authorities

(see p173). The trapdoor to this hideout is now part of the **History Museum**, which also contains the room in which Bishop Kliment was imprisoned in 1893 after falling out with the Stambolov government. His meagre diet of salt fish and water was secretly supplemented by monks, who passed him a supply of food through a hole in the ceiling.

The earthquake of 1913 destroyed the old monastery church, although its 16th-century gilt iconostasis survives. The present church dates from 1931.

🏛 History Museum

Open 9am–6pm daily. 🐾

❷ Ribaritsa

Рибарица

12 km (7 miles) SE of Teteven.
Map C3. ℹ (06902-472).

The village of Ribaritsa lies on the picturesque Vit River. It is popular as a weekend retreat for Bulgarians, who stay in the village's many hotels or their villas on the wooded slopes of

Tour sign, Tsarichina Reserve, near Ribaritsa

the Stara Planina Mountains. Although Ribaritsa's main industry is tourism, it also benefits from cultivating raspberries and cattle farming. Fishing is a popular pastime here, as are pony trekking, hunting and walking in the neighbouring Tsarichina Reserve, part of the Central Balkan National Park (see pp154–5). The beech, fir and spruce forests in the reserve are the habitat of Bulgaria's seven species of owl as well as wolves, brown bears, red deer and otters (see pp30–31). South of the village is the Benkovski Monu-ment, which marks the spot where Georgi Benkovski was killed by the Ottomans after his participation in the fateful April Rising of 1876 (see p178). The event is re-enacted each year on 25 May.

❸ Teteven

Тетевен

72 km (45 miles) SW of Lovech.
Map C3. 🚉 11,500. 🚌 ℹ pl. Sava
Mladenov (0678-4217). 🛒 Sat.
🔗 teteven.bg

The forested peaks and rocky cliffs of the Stara Planina Mountains loom over Teteven, a quiet town that straddles the Vit River. Under Ottoman rule, Teteven, like several other settlements in the region, was granted self-government in return for providing troops to guard the mountain passes.

This relative autonomy boosted the town's craft-based economy, and its merchants profited from the export of locally made goods to Western Europe and Asia. In recognition of its skilled goldsmiths, the town became known as Golden Teteven, but this attracted the unwelcome attention of marauding *kurdzhali* bandits, who pillaged the town in 1801, supposedly killing over 5,000 and leaving only three houses standing.

Apart from its picturesque setting, the town's main attraction for visitors is its

Interior of Glozhene Monastery church, with a 16th-century iconostasis

Teteven, set in a valley amid the peaks of the Stara Planina Mountains

History Museum. The large collection begins with an array of Neolithic stone tools and clay figurines, Roman silverware, bronze coins and medieval swords, spears and axes, and flintlock rifles and pistols used by 19th-century revolutionaries. Teteven rugs, with typical diamond patterns in red, yellow and green, and 19th-century Bulgarian costumes make up much of the ethnographic display upstairs.

▥ History Museum
pl. Sava Mladenov 3. **Tel** (0678) 52005.
Open summer: 9am–noon, 2–5pm daily; winter: 9am–noon, 2–5pm Mon–Fri.

❹ Troyan
Троян

36 km (22 miles) S of Lovech. **Map** C3.
▨ 22,000. ▨ ▨ **ℹ** ul. Vasil Levski 133 (0670-60964). ▨ Rakiya Festival (last Sat in Sep). **ⓦ** troyan-bg.com

Thracians founded a settlement at this spot on the slopes of the Stara Planina Mountains about 3,000 years ago. In the 14th century Troyan grew into a centre of craftsmanship, exporting goods to Serbia, Romania and Constantinople. Today it is known for *Troyanska rakiya* (fruit brandy), which is celebrated at an annual festival.

It was the clay from the banks of the Ossum River that enabled potters to create Troyan's famed ceramics. They developed skilled techniques, including mixing metal oxides with the clay to produce a wider range of

colours. *Angoba*, the resulting brown ceramics with horizontal bands of colour and ripple effects have long been seen as a very traditional type of Bulgarian pottery.

The **Museum of Traditional Crafts** provides an excellent overview of the town's great potting industry. Other displays are devoted to woodcarving, and to Troyan's production of *kalpakchiite*, the bullet-shaped fur hats worn by men in the 18th and 19th centuries. The

Glazed jug at Troyan's History Museum

History Museum, next door, documents the exploits of local citizens during the April Rising (*see p178*).

▥ Museum of Traditional Crafts
pl. Vazrazhdenie. **Tel** (0670) 62063.
Open 9am–5pm daily.

▥ History Museum
pl. Vazrazhdenie. **Tel** (0670) 62062.
Open 9am–5pm daily.
Admittance by request at Museum of Traditional Crafts.

❺ Troyan Monastery
Троянския манастир

10 km (6 miles) SE of Troyan.
Map C3. **Tel** (06952) 2480. ▨
Open 8am–6pm daily. **✝** 5pm daily.
▨ ▨ ▨

Its central cobbled courtyard lined by wooden balconies be-decked with flowers, Troyan Monastery has an atmosphere of peaceful intimacy. One of Bulgaria's largest monastic establishments, it was founded in 1600 but most of its existing buildings date from the mid-19th century.

The main Church of Sveta Bogoroditsa was completed in 1835. Zahari Zograf (*see p110*) painted many of the church's superb exterior and interior murals and his brother Dimitŭr was responsible for the realistic portraits that adorn its elaborate Tryavna iconostasis. The façade features Zahari's signature scenes of Hell: devils torture sinners before rivers of fire sweep them into the jaws of monsters, while saints and Christ look down from Heaven.

In the outer courtyard is the **Hiding-Place Museum**, where visitors can see the room and secret cupboard where Vasil Levski (*see p173*) hid from the Ottomans while attempting to set up a revolutionary committee in the monastery. In an adjoining room is a display of assorted ecclesiastical objects.

▥ Hiding-Place Museum
Open 9am–5pm daily.

Detail of a fresco by Zahari Zograf at Troyan Monastery

❻ Central Balkan National Park

Национален парк "Централен Балкан"

Established in 1991, the Central Balkan National Park was created to preserve specific wildlife habitats. Covering a narrow strip stretching 85 km (53 miles) from east to west along the central Stara Planina, it includes nine reserves with magnificent granite and limestone peaks, as well as deep gorges, sheer cliffs, cave systems and sub-alpine meadows. Ancient forests of beech and fir constitute over half the park's extent. Bears, wolves, wild cats, otters, martens and 224 species of birds make up the animal population, and rare plants include nine locally endemic species and 67 endemic to the eastern Balkans. A network of paths and mountain huts allow hikers to enjoy this rugged and pristine wilderness.

Balkan chamois on the steep slopes of the Kaloferska Planina

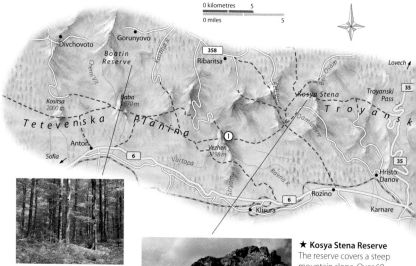

Boatin Reserve
With trees over 250 years old, the reserve has one of the largest protected beech forests in Europe. It is home to brown bears, wolves and wild boar.

★ Kosya Stena Reserve
The reserve covers a steep mountain slope. Over 60 species of birds, including the black woodpecker and Ural owl, nest here. There are also more than 40 species of rare plants, such as moonwort, edelweiss, and mountain avens.

Sub-alpine ecosystems
At lower altitudes, a gentler climate allows grassy vegetation to grow and provide a superb habitat for wildlife. In spring and early summer, the meadows are carpeted with wildflowers.

Key

⎓ Major road

⎓ Other road

- - Trail

▬ Railway

△ Peak

⌣ Pass

Steneto Reserve

Established to protect the Steneto Gorge, this reserve consists largely of lush beech forest. It is home to the greatest diversity of bird species in the Balkans. These include golden and booted eagles, eagle owls, and woodpeckers.

★ Raiskoto Praskalo

Bulgaria's highest waterfall, Raiskoto Praskalo (Paradise Gusher) cascades 124 m (407 ft) over sheer cliffs below Mount Botev. The park's other great waterfalls are Vidimskoto Praskalo (80 m/263 ft) and Kademliskoto Praskalo (72 m/236 ft).

Exploring the Park

The park and the reserves within it have a network of marked footpaths and a small number of mountain-biking trails, and chalets and lodges that offer basic to comfortable accommodation. As this is wild, harsh terrain, with an unpredictable climate, walkers should be suitably equipped before setting off on hikes.

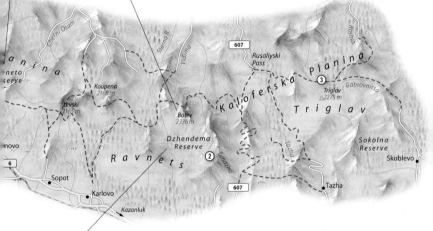

★ Dzhendema Reserve

Stark granite and limestone cliffs, dramatic gorges, and thundering waterfalls make up Dzhendema Reserve, the largest in the park. At lower altitudes there are ancient beech and fir forests as well as sub-alpine meadows.

KEY

① **Mount Vezhen**, at 2,198 m (7,214 ft), is one of the highest peaks in the park. Its challenging ascent attracts experienced mountaineers.

② **Spectacular cliffs** and dramatically eroded rock formations, which are frequently shrouded in swirling mist, gave Dzhendema its name, Hell Reserve.

③ **The Singing Rocks**, in Peeshti Skali Reserve, on the easternmost side of the park, are a cluster of rock formations that emit a melodious sound when the wind blows.

Pokritya most, or Covered Bridge, across the Osûm River at Lovech

❼ Lovech
Ловеч

35 km (22 miles) S of Pleven. **Map** C2. ⓘ 36,600. 🚌 🚏 🏛
🌐 lovech.bg

Because its position gave it control of the Troyan Pass, to the south, the site that Lovech occupies has been inhabited since Thracian times. In the 16th century the town's population was swelled by the arrival of thousands of Ottoman Turks, who stamped their mark on Lovech's cultural life by building mosques and Muslim schools here. Lovech's Bulgarian minority remained in the Varosha quarter, the old town on the slopes of Hisarya hill. Pokritya most ("Covered Bridge"), across the Osûm River, links Lovech's old and new quarters. It was built in 1874 by National Revival architect Kolyo Ficheto and is now filled with souvenir shops.

Many of the National Revival houses in the Varosha quarter form part of an architectural preservation area. The town's **Ethnographic Museum** occupies two of them, one filled with 19th-century European furniture and Ottoman floor cushions and low tables, the other furnished in early 20th-century style. The cellars contain wooden wine barrels, a wine press and a still for making *rakiya*, a potent spirit.

Further along the street is the **Vasil Levski Museum**. In 1870 Levski *(see p173)* made Lovech the headquarters of Bulgaria's Central Revolutionary Committee and the town contributed significantly to the Liberation movement. The museum contains a huge mural of the legendary rebel leader, as well as his dagger, sword and pistol, and other items relating to his life. The **Church of the Assumption** (1834) overlooks the museum. The murals in its simple interior are undergoing restoration.

A huge statue of Levski stands on Hisarya hill next to Hisar fortress. Originating in the 9th century, the fortress was prominent during the Second Bulgarian Kingdom (1185–1393) but fell into disrepair after the Ottoman invasion and is now in ruins.

🏛 **Ethnographic Complex**
ul. Hristo. **Tel** (068) 601 399.
Open 8am–noon, 1–5pm daily. 🖼

🏛 **Vasil Levski Museum**
ul. Marin Poplukanov 14. **Tel** (068) 601 407. **Open** 8am–noon, 1–5pm daily. 🖼

⛪ **Church of the Assumption**
ul. Marin Poplukanov.
Open 8am–8pm daily.

❽ Emen Gorge
Еменски каньон

Emen village, 25 km (16 miles) W of Veliko Tûrnovo. **Map** D2. 🚌

The magnificent Emen Gorge was carved out by the action of water over thousands of years. From Emen village, visitors can follow a trail that leads deep into the gorge via rocky paths and wooden walkways. The trail, which takes two hours to walk, culminates at Momin skok waterfall. Here cascades spill over a 10-m (30-ft) drop into a small lake that is suitable for swimming. This pristine area was declared a nature reserve in 1980.

Dramatic cliffs of Emen Gorge, carved out by the Negovanka River

🮥 Gabrovo
Габрово

46 km (29 miles) SW of Veliko Tûrnovo.
Map D3. 🮮 58,950. 🮮 🮮 🮮
🛈 pl. Vazrazhdane 3, (066 818 406).
🮮 Festival of Humour and Satire
(May). 🆆 **gabrovo.bg**

Officially Bulgaria's longest
town, Gabrovo is strung out
along the Yantra River for over
10 km (6 miles). Thanks to its
textiles industry, which
flourished during the 19th
century, it became known as
the Manchester of Bulgaria.

Gabrovo has long been the
butt of jokes about its citizens'
thriftiness. According to one
anecdote, the townspeople
avoid paying for musicians by
dancing in soundless sheepskin
slippers to tunes being played in
neighbouring Sevlievo. Gabrovo
has shrewdly encouraged this
image. In 1972, it opened the
House of Humour and Satire.
The intriguing displays here
include humorous paintings,
cartoons, clownish costumes
and photographs from around
the world, and some comical
cost-saving devices.

A visit to the **Museum of
Education** is a more sobering
experience. It is in the Aprilov
School – Bulgaria's first secular
school, founded in 1835. Starting
with early monastic schools, the
museum charts the development
of Bulgaria's education systems.
Across the river is **Detchko
House**, the smartly restored
National Revival home of Hadzhi
Detchko, a local merchant.

The **History Museum** traces
the town's development from

Copperware and other traditional objects in the History Museum, Bozhentsi

its origins in the 13th century
to the 1940s. The museum also
has a gallery of paintings by
20th-century local artists.

🏛 **House of Humour & Satire**
ul. Bryanska 68. **Tel** (066) 807 229.
Open 9am–6pm daily. 🮮 🮮
🆆 **humorhouse.bg**

🏛 **Museum of Education**
ul. Aprilovska 15. **Tel** (066) 800 770.
Open 8:30am–5:30pm daily. 🮮 🮮

🏛 **Detchko House**
pl. 10 Yuli 2. **Tel** (066) 806 905.
Open 9am–5pm Tue–Sat. 🮮

🏛 **History Museum**
ul. Nikoloayevska 10.
Tel (066) 809 767. **Open** 9am–5pm
Mon–Fri, 11am–4pm Sat. 🮮

🮥 Etura Complex
Етъра

9 km (6 miles) S of Gabrovo. **Map** D3.
Tel (066) 801 830. 🮮 **Open** summer:
9am–6pm daily; winter: 9am–4:30pm
daily. 🮮 🮮 🮮 🮮 🮮 **etar.org**

This open-air museum was
created to preserve Gabrovo's
crafts heritage. It is laid out as a
village where visitors can see
craftsmen at work using the
water-powered machinery that
once drove Gabrovo's booming
economy. In open-fronted
workshops spread out along
the banks of the Sivek River,
they work with wood, metal,
clay, silver and cloth to produce the souvenirs that are
sold in the bazaar quarter.
Shops also line a cobbled street
of re-created National Revival
buildings. A church, a clock tower
and stone fountains add detail
to this fascinating reconstruction
of 19th-century town life.

🮥 Bozhentsi
Боженци

16 km (10 miles) E of Gabrovo.
Map D3. 🮮 500. 🮮 🛈 (066) 804 422.

This enchanting village of
cobbled streets and stone-
roofed houses nestles among
woods in the Stara Planina
Mountains. It was founded by
Bulgarians seeking a safe haven
after the fall of Veliko Tûrnovo
to the Ottomans in 1393. For
centuries the village prospered
from its weaving and potting
industries, but declined in the
early 1900s as its inhabitants
left in search of work.

In 1962 the village was
declared a listed site. Since then
over 100 houses have been
restored and are now museums,
guest houses, inns and shops.
The **Museum of History**
contains farming and domestic
implements that illustrate daily
life. A beautiful old house on
the other side of the village
contains the **Doncho Popa
Museum**. Constructed over
a cavernous barn, the first floor
has a cosy open hearth,
Ottoman-style wall benches
and a baby-sized hammock.
The flat sink stones in the
balcony allowed dirty water
to be disposed of. Marked
footpaths connect the village
with Gabrovo, Tryavna and
Dryanovo Monastery.

🏛 **Museum of History**
Open 9am–6pm daily. 🮮
🮮 Admittance by request at
tourist information office.

🏛 **Doncho Popa Museum**
Open 9am–6pm daily. 🮮
🮮 Admittance by request at
tourist information office.

An exhibit at the House of Humour
and Satire in Gabrovo

⑫ Tryavna
Трявна

Tryavna's eminence as a crafts town is evident both in the remarkable houses of its old quarter and in its traditional workshops, which now produce souvenirs. The town was founded in the 15th century and, because good arable land was scarce, its inhabitants turned to crafts. By the late 18th century silk, rugs, rose oil and gold jewellery underpinned the town's flourishing economy. Tryavna's builders and woodcarvers earned fame for the quality of their workman-ship, and its painters provided icons for many of the churches and monasteries that were built during the National Revival period.

🏛 Shkoloto
pl. Kapitan Dyado Nikola 7. **Tel** (0677) 2517. **Open** May–Sep: 9am–6pm daily; Oct–Apr: 9am–5pm daily.
🖼 🎟 📷

Entered through a low stone archway off the main square, Shkoloto is a beautiful old building that was originally a school. It opened in 1839, and has a galleried courtyard lined with rooms that once provided accommodation for teachers and pupils.

The school room now holds an exhibition of paintings by Dimitûr Kazakov (1933–92) and wooden sculptures by his brother Nikola (b. 1935). Dimitûr's moody works, which often feature strong lines and limited colours, depict simple figures in abstract landscapes. Nikola's sculpture include intriguing wooden figures with a naïve character.

An adjoining room contains a small collection of antique clocks. The oldest, made in 1700, has a mechanism that is weighted with stones.

🏠 Raikov House
ul. Profesor Raikov 1. **Open** summer: 9:30am–1:30pm, 2–5pm Wed–Sun; winter: 9:30am–1:30pm, 2–4:30pm Wed–Sun (entry via Shkoloto). 🖼 🎟

This imposing residence, roofed with rough stone slabs, was the home of Professor Pencho Raikov, who is considered to be the father of Bulgarian chemistry. The white-washed house was built in 1846, and has large windows and spacious rooms. The furnishings and paintings inside indicate a comfortable middle-class lifestyle.

⛪ Church of the Archangel Michael
pl. Kapitan Dyado Nikola. **Tel** (0677) 3442. **Open** 7am–noon, 3–5pm daily. ⛪ 8am Sun. 📷

Founded in the 12th century and rebuilt in 1821, this charming church is set below ground level, in accordance with Ottoman requirements. The projecting roof, of rough stone slabs, almost reaches to the ground. The interior has a curved balcony

for female worshippers. The iconostasis, by members of the Vitanov family of Tryavna, is superbly decorated with carvings of fruit and flowers. On the walls are frescoes by members of the Zahariev family.

Church of the Archangel Michael, with paintings and woodcarvings

🏠 Daskalov House
ul. Slaveykov 27a. **Tel** (0677) 2517. **Open** summer: 9am–7pm daily; winter: 9am–5pm daily. 🖼 🎟 📷

Walled gardens surround this beautiful house, built in 1804 for Hristo Daskalov, a wealthy rose oil and silk merchant. The symmetrical building consists of two separate dwellings connected by a veranda. The interiors feature a pair of panelled ceilings, each with a finely carved sun motif.

The ceilings are result of a competition held between a master woodcarver, Dimitûr Oshanetsa, and his apprentice, Ivan Bochukovetsa. While the latter's work is notable for its swirling central rays, the master framed his sun with floral motifs. Oshanetsa was declared the winner, but the woodcarvers' guild recognized Bochukovetsa as a master.

An adjacent building contains an absorbing exhibition of Tryavna woodcarving. Items include icon frames, walking sticks, portrait busts, and statues of knights and bishops.

🏠 Slaveykov House
ul. Slaveykov 50. **Tel** (0677) 2278. **Open** May–Sep: 9:30am–1:30pm, 2–6pm Wed–Sun; Oct–Jun: 9am–5pm Wed–Sun. 🖼 🎟 📷

Two literary giants lived in this cozy house. Petko Slaveykov (1827–95) was an important National Revival figure who published Bulgarian-language

Open cobbled courtyard at Shkoloto, once Tryavna's school house

For hotels and restaurants in this region see pp225–6 and pp236–8

newspapers and magazines. He made a significant contribution to the campaign for an autonomous Bulgarian church. Pencho (1866–1912), the youngest of his nine children, published a modernist literary magazine. He was the director of Sofia's national theatre and library, and was nominated for the Nobel Prize.

The house, which is simply furnished, contains family portraits and literary items.

🏛 Museum of Icon-Painting

ul. Breza 1. **Tel** (0896) 755 938. **Open** summer: 9am–6pm daily; winter: 9am–4:30pm daily. 🅿 📷 📱

This museum, in a churchlike building in a park above the town, contains a large and captivating collection of boldly coloured 19th-century icons.

The Tryavna School of icon-painting, Bulgaria's oldest, originated in the late 17th century. It continued the style of medieval Bulgarian art, with some elements of Renaissance realism. Over two centuries, more than 200 icon painters were trained at Tryavna, and many were from the Vitanov and Zahariev families. While

Portrait of the Madonna and Child at the Museum of Icon-Painting

the Vitanovs were painters and woodcarvers who worked in the classic Tryavna style, the Zaharievs had a tendency towards greater realism and innovation. Much of these artists' early work was lost during *kurdzhali* attacks on churches and monasteries in the 18th century.

🏛 Angel Kŭnchev House

ul. Angel Kŭnchev 39. **Tel** (0896) 755 935. **Open** summer: 9:30am–1:30pm, 2–6pm Wed–Sun; winter: entry via Shkoloto. 🅿 📷

Angel Kŭnchev (1850–72) was a leading rebel who, with Vasil Levski *(see 173)*, worked to set up revolutionary cells around the country. He shot himself

VISITORS' CHECKLIST

Practical Information
245 km (150 miles) E of Sofia.
Map D3. 🚹 9,800. 🛈 ul. Angel
Kŭnchev 33 (0677-2247).
🅆 tryavna.bg

Transport
🚆 🚌

after his arrest in 1872 to avoid divulging secrets.

The house where he was born was built in typical Tryavna style, with low door-ways and ceilings, and ample wood panelling. There is also a display of rifles and pistols, bullet belts and swords.

Room at Angel Kŭnchev House, with hearth and woven rug

Tryavna Town Centre

① Shkoloto
② Raikov House
③ Church of the Archangel Michael
④ Daskalov House
⑤ Slaveykov House
⑥ Museum of Icon-Painting
⑦ Angel Kŭnchev House

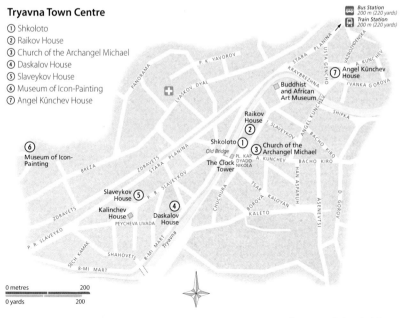

0 metres 200
0 yards 200

For map symbols *see back flap*

⑬ Veliko Tûrnovo
Велико Търново

With a picturesque hillside setting, fine architecture and a wealth of historic sights, Veliko Tûrnovo is one of Bulgaria's most beautiful cities. Tall, narrow houses teeter on sheer cliffs that rise high above the meandering Yantra River, and to the east are the ruins of the majestic fortress of Tsarevets. The city has a proud history as the mighty capital of the Second Kingdom (1185–1393), and later as the seat of liberated Bulgaria's first National Assembly. By day Veliko Tûrnovo bustles with local people, students and visitors. After dark, the focus switches to the city's lively bars and nightclubs.

Samovodska Charshiya, the bazaar in the Varusha quarter of the city

🏠 House of the Little Monkey
ul. Vustanicheska 14.
Closed to the public.

This house, one of many in Veliko Tûrnovo designed by the great local architect Kolyo Ficheto (1800–81), dates from 1849. It is set on a hillside, with the ground floor accessible at street level, and entrances to the two projecting upper floors at the rear. It features a pair of bay windows, attractive red and white brickwork, and a tiny statue of a monkey that gives the house its name.

🏛 Church of SS Kiril i Metodii
ul. SS Kiril i Metodii, Varusha quarter.
Open 8am–7pm daily. 🏛 8am Sun.

High up in the hills, in the city's old Varusha quarter, this small church was built by Kolyo Ficheto in 1860, but lost its dome and belfry during the earthquake of 1913. A curved wooden balcony at the back of the church was designed for the segregation of female worshippers.

🏛 Church of Sveti Nikolai
ul. Vustani Cheska 43, Varusha quarter.
Open 8am–7pm daily. 🏛 8am Sun.

This sturdy church, with a simple stone exterior and a red-tiled roof, was designed by Kolyo Ficheto. The iconostasis, with dragons, eagles and a central sun motif lighting the church's gloomy interior, is a stunning example of the work of the Tryavna School (see pp158–9). The bishop's throne features an allegorical carving of a dragon (Turkey) attacking a lion (Bulgaria) that is being suffocated by a snake (the Orthodox Church).

🏠 Samovodska Charshiya
Varusha quarter.

It was in the 19th century that Samovodska Charshiya developed into a thriving bazaar, with stalls, workshops and a caravanserai for visiting merchants. The bazaar is in the pleasant historic Varusha quarter of the city, which rises steeply above the old town. The attractive stone houses that line the bazaar's narrow cobbled streets are now occupied by souvenir shops selling local craft items.

🏛 Asenevtsi Monument
Asenevtsi Park.

Unveiled in 1985, to mark the 800th anniversary of the founding of the Second Bulgarian Kingdom, this monument features a mighty sword, with Asen, Petûr, Ivan Asen II and Kaloyan astride horses. The four tsars ruled the kingdom from 1185 to 1241. The monument is an excellent point from which to admire the city's old houses, precariously perched on the cliffs opposite.

🏛 Art Gallery
Asenovtsi Park. **Tel** (062) 638 941.
Open 10am–6pm Tue–Sun. 🅿 🔲

Bulgarian painting of the 19th and 20th centuries makes up this fine collection. Charcoal landscapes by Boris Denev (1883–1969) fill much of the ground floor. In the upper rooms are works by Dimitûr Kazakov (1933–92), with sharply outlined figures in abstract compositions. Among several monumental works are *Veliko Tûrnovo in the Past* by Naiden Petkov (1918–89) and *People Say Goodbye to Patriarch Evtimii* by Svetlin Rusev (b. 1933).

🏠 Sarafkina House
ul. Gûrko 88. **Open** Apr–Oct: 9am–noon, 1–6pm Tue–Sat; Nov–Mar: 9am–5:30pm Tue–Sat. 🅿

With stone walls below and whitewashed walls above, shuttered windows and a tiled roof, this house is typical of the

Church of Sveti Nikolai, built by the 19th-century architect Kolyo Ficheto

Luxurious interior of Sarafkina House

city's 19th-century domestic architecture. It was built in 1861 for Dimitûr Sarafkina, a wealthy banker, and is set on sheer cliffs above the river. The interior has Western-style furniture, and a display of photographs and period outfits.

🏛 Archaeological Museum

ul. Ivanka Boteva 2. **Tel** (062) 601 528. **Open** Apr–Oct: noon–6pm Mon, 9am–6pm Tue–Sun (Nov–Mar: to 5pm). 🎨

The courtyard of this grand old building is littered with Classical columns and busts. Although several precious artifacts were stolen in 2006, most of this absorbing collection remains in place.

The well-guarded centrepiece is a replica of a burial known as Kaloyan's Grave. It was

discovered in 1972, by the Church of the Forty Martyrs in the Asenova quarter *(see p164)*. On the skeleton was a gold ring and seal with the name Kaloyan, which suggested that these may be the remains of Tsar Kaloyan (1197–1207). In an adjoining room the gold seal of Tsar Ivan Asen II (1218–41) is displayed under a magnifying glass. Downstairs are finds from the Roman city of Nikopolis ad Istrum *(see p166)*.

🏛 Museum of the National Revival and Constituent Assembly

pl. Suedenenie 1. **Tel** (062) 629 821. **Open** Apr–Oct: noon–6pm Tue, 9am–6pm Wed–Mon (Nov–Mar: to 5:30pm). 🎨

Built by Kolyo Ficheto for the city's Ottoman governor in 1872, this vast edifice became Bulgaria's first parliament building after the Liberation. A copy of the new state's first constitution, signed in 1879, is on display. Material relating to the revolt against Ottoman rule fills the ground floor.

VISITORS' CHECKLIST

Practical Information
220 km (137 miles) NE of Sofia.
Map D3. 🚩 85,000. ℹ️ ul. Hristo Botev 5 (062 622 148).
🌐 velikoturnovo.info

Transport
🚋 🚌 🚇

🏛 Modern History Museum

pl. Suedenenie 1. **Open** 9am–5:30pm Mon–Sat. 🎨 🌐 **museumvt.com**

Housed in a former prison, the museum's exhibits cover the Balkan Wars and Bulgaria's role in the First World War. A small display recalls the life of the prime minister Stefan Stambolov, who was born in Veliko Tûrnovo.

Archaeological Museum, a fine arcaded building with a courtyard

---

Veliko Tûrnovo City Centre

1. House of the Little Monkey
2. Church of SS Kiril i Metodii
3. Church of Sveti Nikolai
4. Samovodska Charshiya
5. Asenevtsi Monument
6. Art Gallery
7. Sarafkina House
8. Archaeological Museum
9. Museum of the National Revival and Constituent Assembly
10. Modern History Museum

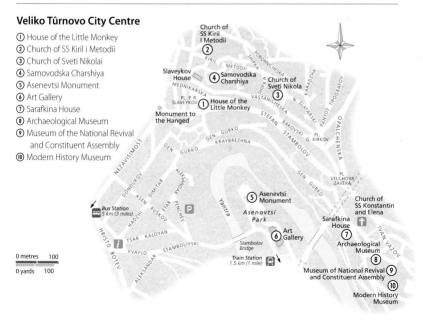

0 metres 100
0 yards 100

For map symbols see back flap

Tsarevets
Царевец

The impressive hilltop fortress of Tsarevets occupies a commanding position on a rocky hill that is nearly completely encircled by the Yantra River. This vantage point was occupied almost continuously from the 4th millennium BC, and in 1186, Tsar Petûr made it the capital of the Second Bulgarian Kingdom. From that time, the kings of Bulgaria inhabited the Royal Palace and many aristocrats and foreign diplomats set up residence in the citadel. When the Second Kingdom fell to the Ottomans in 1393, Tsarevets was reduced to rubble. Of the original 400 buildings and 22 churches only a small number have been fully restored.

★ Light Show
A fantastic light show, with a rousing sound track, takes place almost every night in summer. Waves of colour light up the fortress, and the spectacle culminates with bell ringing and fireworks.

Church of Sveti Georgi
This small church contains frescoes of Orthodox saints. The paintings, badly damaged and heavily restored, once covered almost the entire interior.

To Veliko Tûrnovo

Main Gate

Asenova Gate
Reconstructed in 1976, this three-storey gate tower was used by the artisans and clerics who lived in the Asenova Quarter below the fortress.

★ Baldwin's Tower
Named after Emperor Baldwin of Flanders, who was held here in the 13th century, this tower guarded the rock's southernmost point. Earlier, it was known as the Frenk Hisar Gate, and was used by foreign merchants living outside the complex.

KEY

① **Church of the Forty Martyrs**

② **Church of the Dormition**

③ **The Church of SS Petûr i Pavel** is a medieval church notable for its openwork capitals, frescoes of St Peter and St Paul, to whom it is dedicated, and depiction of the Pietà.

Church of Sveti Dimitŭr
The church is dedicated to St Demetrius, patron saint of the Second Bulgarian Kingdom. Medieval frescoes, repainted at a later date, decorate the interior.

VISITORS' CHECKLIST

Practical Information
Tsarevets.
Map D3.
Tel (062) 638 841.
Open Apr–Oct: 8am–7pm daily; Nov–Mar: 9am–5pm daily.
(free last Thu of month).
Light Show on all Bulgarian public holidays.

Rock of Execution
At the northernmost point of the fortress, the Rock of Execution juts out above sheer cliffs and the River Yantra far below. It was from here that traitors and criminals were pushed to their deaths.

★ Royal Palace
Built in the 12th century, the Royal Palace was an enclosed complex with a central courtyard. Now a partially reconstructed ruin, it has modern concrete staircases that visitors can climb for magnificent views of the surroundings.

Patriarchate
Perched at the rock's highest point is the 13th-century Church of the Patriarchate. Defended by thick walls, it was once part of the patriarch's residential complex. Startling modern murals adorn the interior.

| 0 metres | | 50 |
| 0 yards | | 50 |

Asenova Quarter

Асенова махала

This quiet district of Veliko Tûrnovo straddles the banks of the Yantra River, below the towering fortress walls of Tsarevets. For centuries, the quarter was inhabited by a thriving community of artisans and clerics, but they were forced to abandon it after an earthquake struck in 1913. This tremendous cataclysm flattened Asenova's old houses and seriously damaged its precious medieval churches.

Church of the Forty Martyrs, burial place of Bulgarian tsars

🏛 Church of the Forty Martyrs

ul. Sveti Kliment Ohridski 9. **Open** 9:30am–5:30pm daily.

Following a lengthy period of reconstruction, the church has a gleaming marble iconostasis and bright new icons. It was built in 1230 to commemorate Tsar Ivan Asen II's triumph over the Byzantines at Klokotnitsa, on the Feast of the Forty Martyrs. Of the six stone pillars that support the church's roof, three bear inscriptions by Bulgarian tsars.

The most famous, opposite the entrance, is by Khan Omurtag (ruled 816–31). It reads: "*A man, no matter how happy his life, eventually dies and another is born. May the man born later, while looking at this inscription, remember the man that made it.*" The pillar on the left opposite the entrance has an inscription by Khan Krum (ruled 803–14) and was brought from his frontier fortress of Rodesto. That to the right of the entrance was inscribed by Asen I with a list of his conquests.

🏛 Church of the Dormition

ul. Sveti Kliment Ohridski. **Open** 9am–6pm daily. 🕊 8am Sun.

This simple church, dedicated to the Dormition of the Virgin, was built in 1923 on the site of a

14th-century nunnery. Its plain interior walls are offset by a large wooden iconostasis with many portraits of saints.

🏛 Church of SS Petûr i Pavel

ul. Sveti Kliment Ohridski. **Open** 9am–6pm daily.

This small 13th-century church lost its roof in the terrible earthquake of 1913, but was later carefully restored. Two rows of stone columns flank the central aisle and fragments of original frescoes, depicting haloed saints, can be seen in an archway to the left of the entrance. The biblical scenes on the south wall were painted

Frescoes in a side chapel at the Church of SS Petûr i Pavel

in 1441, and the exterior wall, covered by a gallery, was painted with frescoes in the 17th century. It was at this church that the Ottomans slaughtered 110 Bulgarian nobles when they conquered Veliko Tûrnovo in 1393.

🏛 Church of Sveti Georgi

ul. Tsar Ivan Asen II. **Tel** (062) 636 954. **Open** Apr–Oct: 9am–6pm daily; Nov–Mar: by request.

According to an inscription in Greek at the entrance, this small church was built with funds provided by a local man and his wife, and it was constructed in no more than two months, in 1616. It stands on the foundations of a medieval church. The paintings inside include original frescoes depicting Orthodox saints.

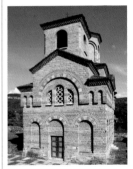

Church of Sveti Dimitûr, dedicated to the First Kingdom's patron saint

🏛 Church of Sveti Dimitûr

ul. Patriarh Evtimii. **Tel** (062) 636 954. **Open** Apr–Oct: 9am–6pm daily; Nov–Mar: by request.

From this church in 1185, the year of its consecration, two local noblemen, Petûr and Asen, launched a revolt against Byzantine rule. As a result, the Second Bulgarian Kingdom was established, with Petûr ruling as tsar, and Sveti Dimitûr became the new kingdom's patron saint.

Reduced to ruins by the earthquake of 1913, the church was painstakingly restored. Its walls consist of alternating layers of stone and brick, and the arches of its blind niches are ornamented with coloured ceramics.

Dryanovo Monastery, with craggy cliffs behind

⑭ Dryanovo

Дряново

25 km (16 miles) southwest of Veliko Tŭrnovo. **Map** D3. 🚂 8,000. 🚃 🚌
ℹ️ ul. Shipka 65 (0676-98097).
🌐 dryanovo.com

Named after the cornel tree
(dryan), Dryanovo was founded
in the 12th century. It was its
school of National Revival
woodcarvers and stone masons
that made the town famous in
the 19th century.

Today Dryanovo is known
chiefly as the birthplace of the
itinerant master builder Kolyo
Ficheto (1800–81), who constructed many houses, public
buildings, churches and bridges
in the region. He began an
apprenticeship in Teteven at the
age of 10, studied stonemasonry
in Albania in his teens, and
later learnt the art of building
churches, bell towers and
bridges. He achieved the status
of master builder at the age of 36.

Dryanovo's **History Museum**
is devoted to Ficheto's life
and work. The exhibits include
models of his most important
projects, which include the
covered bridge at Lovech
(see p156), the bridge at Byala,
and the Church of Sveti Nikola
in Dryanovo.

Environs

A little to the south of town
lies Dryanvo Monastery. After
a troubled history, its present
iteration consists of a cluster
of whitewashed buildings set
around pretty gardens and a
church. Founded in the 12th
century, the monastery became
a centre of Hesychasm *(see
p167)* in the 14th century.
Ottoman troops torched it

early in the 15th century and
again in the 17th century after it
had been restored. It was rebuilt
in the 1840s and later became a
secret meeting place for Veliko
Tŭrnovo's Central Revolutionary
Committee, headed by Vasil
Levski *(see p173)*. After the April
Rising of 1876, a group of 100
rebels led by Priest Hariton and
Bacho Kiro held out in the
monastery for nine days against
an overwhelming Ottoman
force. Most were killed and the
monastery burned once again.

A path beside the monastery
leads to Bacho Kiro Cave,
with a gallery some 1,200 m
(4,000 ft) long.

🏛️ History Museum
ul. Shipka 82. **Tel** (0676) 72097.
Open 8am–noon, 1–5pm daily. 📷

⛪ Dryanovo Monastery
4 km (3 miles) south of Dryanovo.
Open 7am–10pm daily. 🏨 6pm daily.
📷 📷

🕳️ Bacho Kiro Cave
500 m (550 yards) beyond Dryanovo
Monastery. **Tel** (0676) 72332.
Open Apr–Oct: 9am–6pm daily;
Nov–Mar: 10am–4pm daily. 📷 📷

⑮ Kilifarevo Monastery

Килифаревски манастир

14 km (9 miles) south of Veliko
Tŭrnovo. **Map** D3. **Open** 8am–7pm
daily. 🏨 7pm daily. 📷 📷

Now a nunnery, this attractive
riverside monastery was
founded in the 14th century
by Teodosi Tŭrnovski, with funds
from Tsar Ivan Asen II. In 1350
the Kilifarevo Literary School,
a leading promulgator of
Hesychasm *(see p167)*, was
established here. Medieval

literature was copied and
studied at the school, and it was
also where Evtimii, last patriarch
of the Second Kingdom,
received his education.
The monastery was several
times destroyed and rebuilt
during the Ottoman period.
Its principal church, dedicated
to St Demetrius of Salonika,
was built by Kolyo Ficheto in
1842. It incorporates two
16th-century chapels.

Fresco by Zahari Zograf inside
Preobrazhenski Monastery's church

⑯ Preobrazhenski Monastery

Преображенски манастир

7 km (4 miles) north of Veliko Tŭrnovo.
Map D2. **Open** 8:30am–8pm daily.

Set below rocky cliffs high in
the hills above the Yantra River,
the monastery was founded in
the 14th century. It was destroyed
during the Ottoman period, and
its reconstruction began in 1825.

The master builder Dimitŭr of
Sofia began work on the Church
of the Transfiguration in 1834
but, in 1835, his implication in
a plot to overthrow the Ottomans
led to his execution. Kolyo
Ficheto was commissioned to
complete the work. In 1863 he
added the tower, with a bell
donated by Alexander II of
Russia. Many of the icons and
murals were painted by Zahari
Zograf *(see p106)*. He also
painted the bold Wheel of Life,
turned by angels while devils
cast sinners into a monster's
mouth, on the façade.

The monastery's other
buildings have suffered
damage from rock falls and
are rather dilapidated.

Ruins of a building at the Roman town of Nikopolis ad Istrum

⓱ Nikopolis ad Istrum

Никополис ад Иструм

20 km (12 miles) N of Veliko Tûrnovo. **Map** D2. **Open** Apr–Oct: 9am–6pm daily; Nov–Mar: 10am–4pm daily.

This once magnificent Roman town was founded by the emperor Trajan in AD 102. It had temples, baths and theatres, and gladiatorial games were held here. By the 3rd century the town had developed into the most powerful settlement between the Danube to the north and the Stara Planina Mountains to the south. However, in the 6th century much of the town was destroyed by Goths and Slavs and many of its inhabitants resettled in present-day Veliko Tûrnovo (see pp160–61).

Nikopolis ad Istrum has been partially excavated but the site is overgrown. Even so, the ancient paved road that leads into it, and the surviving columns, walls and tombs give a good idea of its ancient glory. Artifacts from the site are on display in Veliko Tûrnovo's Archaeological Museum.

⓲ Sveta Troitsa Convent

Манастир "Света Троица"

4 km (3 miles) N of Veliko Tûrnovo. **Map** D2. **Open** 8am–6pm daily.

Sveta Troitsa Convent stands on the site of an 11th-century monastery that rose to prominence in the 14th century,

when pilgrims seeking spiritual guidance flocked to the nearby cave inhabited by the hermit Teodosi Tûrnovski. Patriarch Evtimii, a pupil of Tûrnovski, established the Tûrnovo School of Literature here, dedicated to the study of medieval Bulgarian, Greek and Russian texts. When the Second Bulgarian Kingdom fell in 1393, the monastery's 300 monks were put to death by the Ottomans for refusing to convert to Islam. According to legend, Evtimii himself was spared when the Ottomans seemingly received a divine warning, and decided to send him into exile instead.

In 1847 a new church was built on the site, but it was destroyed in the earthquake of 1913. The present convent buildings date from 1927.

⓳ Arbanasi

Арбанаси

4 km (3 miles) NE of Veliko Tûrnovo. **Map** D3. ⛰ 300. 🚌 ℹ (062-636 954). **W** arbanassi.org

The verdant pastures that surround Arbanasi were once densely populated by the cattle from which local merchants grew rich. Set on a limestone plateau overlooking Veliko Tûrnovo (see pp160–61), the picturesque town consists of an intriguing warren of dusty streets and massive fortress-like houses.

It is thought that Arbanasi was established either by Ottomans for the resettlement of Christian Albanian prisoners of war in the 15th century, or by ethnic Bulgarians who chose to speak Greek and take Greek names until the Liberation of 1878. In return for guarding the pass giving access to Veliko Tûrnovo, Arbanasi's inhabitants were granted autonomy and

Sveta Troitsa Convent, set against rocky cliffs in the Yantra River

The colourfully decorated interior of the Church of the Nativity, Arbanasi

fiscal privileges. This benefited its merchants, who prospered from exporting locally produced leather as far as India and Persia. The sturdy houses that they built to protect them in times of trouble failed to shield them from the brutal attacks of *kurdzhali* in 1798. Continuing insecurity in subsequent years led many of Arbanasi's residents to move to Veliko Tûrnovo. Today the town attracts large numbers of visitors and its restored houses have become retreats for wealthy Bulgarians.

One of the finest of Arbanasi's residential buildings is the 17th-century **Konstantsliev House**, west of the centre. Hefty stone foundations support a wooden upper floor, where various wood-panelled rooms are filled with period furniture. The upstairs toilet simply consisted of a hole in the floor through which human waste was delivered to hungry pigs below.

Southeast of the centre is the 17th-century **Church of the Archangels Michael and Gabriel**, which is decorated with 18th-century murals. But Arbanasi's greatest attraction is the **Church of the Nativity**, southwest of the centre. The simple exterior of this 17th-century church belies its fantastic interior. Strikingly colourful murals depicting saints and biblical scenes, interspersed with inscriptions in Greek, cover the walls and barrel-vaulted ceiling.

Further west is the **Monastery of Sveta Bogoroditsa**, which was founded as a convent in the 13th century. It was abandoned in 1393, after the end of the Second Kingdom, but was reopened in 1680 only to be destroyed by marauding *kurdzhali* bandits in 1798. The present cluster of simple stone buildings topped with red tiles dates from the mid-19th century, when the monk Daniel of Troyan launched the convent's restoration. The monastery church's miracle-working icon depicting a three-handed Madonna attracts a constant stream of pilgrims.

🏛 **Konstantsliev House**
Open 9am–6pm Tue–Sun.
📷 If closed, admission by request at Church of the Nativity.

⛪ **Church of the Archangels Michael and Gabriel**
Open 9am–noon daily. 📷 If closed, admission by request at Church of the Nativity.

⛪ **Church of the Nativity**
Open 9am–6pm daily. 📷 🎥 🏛

⛪ **Monastery of Sveta Bogoroditsa**
Open 8am–6pm daily.

㉒ Kapinovo Monastery
Капиновски манастир

18 km (11 miles) SE of Veliko Tûrnovo. **Map** D3. **Open** 8am–7pm daily.

This sturdy stone structure was rebuilt in 1825 with defence in mind, as the original 13th-century monastery was repeatedly destroyed under Ottoman rule. The church was built in 1835 and features icons by the Vitanov family of Tryavna. Above its entrance is a glowing Last Judgment mural (1845) by Yovan Popovich. It shows Christ flanked by legions of haloed saints watching devils poke sinners into a river of fire that sweeps them into hell. The monastery was a key educational and cultural centre during the National Revival movement of the 19th century.

Hesychasm

Developed by the monks of Mount Athos, in Greece, in the early 14th century, Hesychasm, a mystic Orthodox religion, was propagated from Kilifarevo Monastery by Sveti Teodosii Tûrnovski. Demanding the rejection of social activity, it was based on silent contemplation. Hesychasts constantly repeated prayers in the hope of reaching an ecstatic state in which they might experience God's divine light. Hesychasm's widespread popularity has sometimes been blamed for further weakening the declining Second Kingdom at a time when citizens were needed to defend the state rather than retreat into prayer.

Portal at Kilifarevo Monastery, once a centre of Hesychasm

㉑ Elena
Елена

40 km (25 miles) SE of Veliko Tŭrnovo.
Map D3. 🚆 6,500. 🚌 W elena.bg

Set amid forested hills, Elena was founded in the 15th century. Under Ottoman rule it was granted autonomy in exchange for guarding mountain passes in the vicinity, and this allowed it to prosper and develop as a centre of learning. It was here that Bulgaria's first teacher-training college was established, in 1843.

Much of Elena's quaint old town was consumed by fire during the War of Liberation (1877–8), but some fine houses and churches in the National Revival style survived. A notable example is **Ilarion Makariopolski House**, a handsome riverside mansion with dark wooden walls and a large veranda. Ilarion Makariopolski was born here in 1812. As Bishop of Constantinople, he played a key role in persuading the Ottoman authorities to establish an independent Bulgarian exarchate in 1870 (see pp26–7), a significant step towards liberation.

The National Revival Complex, a nucleus of fine 19th-century buildings above the town square, is centred on the large

Colourful carpets and weaving instruments at the Carpet Exhibition, Kotel

hilltop Church of the Assumption. Next to it is the smaller 16th-century **Church of Sveti Nikola**, whose barrel-vaulted interior glows with bright murals. In a former inn further down the hill is the **Ethnographic Museum**, with a display of Elena's colourful rugs, and garments made from *aba*, a locally produced woollen cloth.

🏛 **Ilarion Makariopolski House**
ul. Doino Gramatik 2. **Tel** (06151) 2214.
Open 9am–5pm daily. 📷

⛪ **Church of Sveti Nikola**
National Revival Complex, ul.
Tsarkovna 1. **Tel** (06151) 2129.
Open 9am–5pm daily. 📷

🏛 **Ethnographic Museum**
National Revival Complex, ul.
Tsarkovna 1. **Tel** (06151) 2129.
Open 9am–5pm daily. 📷

㉒ Kotel
Котел

54 km (34 miles) NW of Sliven.
Map E3. 🚆 6,200. 🚌

Founded in the 16th century as a sheep-farming centre, Kotel enjoyed relative autonomy under Ottoman rule in return for guarding a local mountain pass and providing the Ottoman authorities with sheep. While Kotel's shepherds tended their flocks, the womenfolk wove the carpets for which Kotel is renowned.

A variety of these beautiful examples of traditional handicraft is on display at the **Carpet Exhibition** in the old Galata quarter. The exhibition is housed in Kotel's former school house (1869), one of the few wooden buildings to have survived a fire that swept through the town in 1894. More of Kotel's carpets are displayed at the **Ethnographic Museum** nearby, in a house built in 1872. Its wood-panelled rooms are furnished in the comfortable domestic style of the late 19th century.

The large modernist stone building in the town centre is the **Pantheon**, dedicated to Kotel's most illustrious sons, Dr Petŭr Beron (1799–1871) and Georgi Rakovski (1821–67). Preserved here is the pickled heart of Dr Beron, who contributed greatly to the country's education system. Another room contains the bones of Georgi Rakovski, one of Bulgaria's first active revolutionaries.

A vivid scene of the Last Judgment at the Ethnographic Museum, Elena

For hotels and restaurants in this region see pp225–6 and pp236–8

West of the town is Izvorite Park, with bubbling springs and woodland, and the **Natural History Museum**, with an array of stuffed wildlife.

🏛 Carpet Exhibition
ul. Izvorska 17. **Tel** (0453) 42316.
Open 8am–noon, 1:30–5:30pm daily.

🏛 Ethnographic Museum
ul. Altunlu Stoyan 5. **Tel** (0453) 2315.
Open 8am–noon, 1:30–6pm daily.

🏛 Pantheon
pl. Vuzrazhdanie. **Tel** (0453) 42549.
Open 8am–noon, 1–5pm daily.

🏛 Natural History Museum
Izvorite Park. **Open** 9am–5pm daily.

㉓ Zheravna
Жеравна

14 km (9 miles) S of Kotel. **Map** E3.
525. **W** jeravna.com

With cockerels and goats wandering at liberty, and donkeys that pick their way along cobbled streets, this museum-village owes its charm to its authenticity. Like Kotel, Zheravna was granted autonomy by the Ottomans in return for guarding a local mountain pass. This helped to preserve the town's Bulgarian customs and culture.

Most of Zheravna's inhabitants were sheep or cattle farmers, and several museum-houses offer an insight into their lives. One is Sava Filaretov House, built in the early 19th century, with carved wood panelling in its rooms. Next to the hearth is a raised floor where the family slept during the winter. The early 18th-century Russi Chorbadzhi House is of a similar design, with arched doorways and intricately carved panelling. The cellar contains an ethnographic exhibition and a display of Zheravna carpets.

Another highlight is the small stone Church of Sveti Nikolai, with a beautiful gilt iconostasis topped with dragons and eagles. Yovkov House celebrates the life and work of Yordan Yovkov (1880–1937), author of *Legends of the Stara Planina Mountains*, in which he described Zheravna.

㉔ Sliven
Сливен

110 km (68 miles) W of Bourgas.
Map E3. 91,620.

Although undistinguished, this large town is pleasant enough. It is of interest chiefly through its association with *haidouki*, or Bulgarian rebels (mountain bandits who fought the Ottomans). The *haidouk* Hadzhi Dimitûr, who was born here in 1840, made frequent raids from Romania into Bulgaria before he was killed by Turkish soldiers in 1868. The **Hadzhi Dimitûr Museum**, in a 19th-century building that was the family house, is devoted to his life. The town also has an interesting **History Museum**, where exhibits include the skeleton of a horse from a Thracian tomb.

Sliven's other main attraction is its proximity to the Blue Rocks (*Sinite Kamûni*), in the Karandila area on the eastern side of the town. The rocks, once the hideout of *haidouki*, can be reached by means of a chair lift (12:30–6:30pm Mon, 8:30am–6:30pm Tue–Sun).

🏛 Hadzhi Dimitûr Museum
ul. Asenova 2 (off bul. Stefan Karadzha). **Tel** (044) 622 496.
Open 9am–noon, 2–5pm daily.
Closed Sun in winter.

🏛 History Museum
bul. Tsar Osvoboditel 18. **Tel** (044) 622 494. **Open** 9am–noon, 2–5pm daily.

㉕ Yambol
Ямбол

28 km (17 miles) SE of Sliven.
Map E3. 74,100.

Signs of ancient settlement discovered near Yambol show that the vicinity has been in-habited since Neolithic times. Yambol's immediate prede-cessor was the Thracian town of Kabile, located about 10 km (6 miles) to the northwest.

Under Roman rule, Yambol was enlarged, and in AD 293 it was renamed Diospolis by Emperor Diocletian. In the 4th century the town was destroyed by invading Goths, and through the Middle Ages its name changed several times as it came under the control of different peoples.

Window in Ebu Bekir Mosque, Yambol

Yambol still has a sizeable Turkish minority, whose presence here dates back to Ottoman times, and its oldest buildings are Islamic. The **Ebu Bekir Mosque**, off the town's central square, was built in 1413. Its massive stone walls support a single dome and minaret and, inside, a small section of the original murals has survived. Another notable Islamic building is the Bezisten Bazaar, opposite the mosque. Built in the 15th century, it is an elegant arched structure crowned with domes.

🟦 Ebu Bekir Mosque
pl. Osvobodzhenie. **Open** daily.

Hadzhi Dimitûr Museum, Sliven, with cobbled courtyard and open veranda

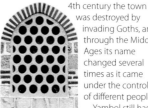

㉖ Stara Zagora
Стара Загора

90 km (56 miles) NE of Plovdiv. **Map** D3.
🚩 138,400. 🚌 🚐 🚊 *i* bul.
Ruski 27 (042 627 098). 🌐 **tour.
starazagora.bg**

Having been destroyed during
the War of Liberation, Stara
Zagora was rebuilt at the end of
the 19th century. Although it is
a rather undistinguished town,
it is of interest for its important
Neolithic site.

In the grounds of the hospital
west of the modern town,
this site consists of several
Neolithic Dwellings (*Neolitni
zhilishta*). Two have been
preserved, and such features
as hearths can be made out.
The dwellings were largely
destroyed by fire in about
5500 BC but enough remains
for visitors to gain an insight
into daily life 8,000 years ago.
There is also a museum, where
many of the objects unearthed
at the site are displayed.

Memorial to the defenders of Stara Zagora,
Russo-Turkish War 1877–8

A building that dates from a
much later phase in Stara
Zagora's history is the **Roman
Theatre**, near the town centre,
with partially restored marble
columns and tiered seating.
Nearby, modern buildings
surround the **Museum of 19th-
Century Town Life**. The period
furnishings and other objects
on display here illustrate middle-
class life during the National
Revival period. A few streets
south is the Eski Mosque, built
in 1409. It is currently closed.

🏛 **Neolithic Dwellings**
ul. Armeiska 20. **Tel** (042) 622 109.
Open 9:30am–noon,12:30–5pm
Tue–Sat. 🖼 🚫 📷

🎭 **Roman Theatre**
Bul. Mitropolit Metodii Kusev 33.

🏛 **Museum of 19th-Century
Town Life**
ul. Dimitŭr Naumov 68. **Tel** (042) 919
214. **Open** 9am–6pm Tue–Sun. 🖼

㉗ Kazanlŭk
Казанлък

36 km (22 miles) NW of Stara Zagora.
Map D3. 🚩 53,700. 🚌 🚐 🚊
i ul. Iskra 4, off ploshtad Sevtopolis,
(043 62817). 🌹 Rose Festival (1st
weekend in Jun). 🌐 **kazanlak.bg**

Though famed as the capital
of Bulgaria's rose-oil industry,
Kazanlŭk is also the centre of
an area of Thracian settlement
now known as the Valley of the
Thracian Kings. The valley is
dotted with Thracian tombs

Detail of the painting on the cupola of the
Kazanlŭk Tomb in Kazanlŭk

that date from the 5th to the
3rd centuries BC *(see opposite)*.
Many were found to contain
superb wall paintings and
exquisite gold and silver
objects. These are displayed
in the **Iskra Museum**.

In Tyulbe Park, in the
northeast of the town and
within walking distance of the
centre, is the **Kazanlŭk Tomb**.
The original tomb, with its
exceptionally fine frescoes is
closed to the public, but visitors
can see an exact replica nearby.

Aspects of life in Kazanlŭk's
much more recent history
are presented at the **Kulata
Ethnographic Complex**. The
restored 19th-century houses
here include the home of a
rose-farming family. Kazanlŭk's
rose-oil industry is documented at the small **Museum
of the Rose-Oil Industry** on
the outskirts of the town.

🏛 **Iskra Museum**
Corner of il. Kiril i Metodii and ul.
Slaveykov. **Tel** (0431) 63762.
Open 9am–5:30pm daily. 🖼 📷 🚫

🏛 **Kulata Ethnographic Complex**
ul. Nikola Petkov 18. **Tel** (0431) 21733
(summer), (0431) 63741 (winter).
Open 9am–5pm daily. 🖼

🎭 **Kazanlŭk Tomb**
Tyulbe Park. **Tel** (0431) 62817.
Open 9am–5pm daily; by request in
winter. 🖼 🚫 📷

🏛 **Museum of the
Rose-Oil Industry**
bul. Osvobozhdenie 49. **Tel** (0431)
63762. **Open** Apr–Oct: 9am–5:30pm
daily; Nov–Mar: by prior arrangement.
🖼 📷

Bulgaria's Rose-Oil Industry

Rosa damascena, the red rose from which attar of roses, or rose oil, is
made, was introduced to central Bulgaria by the Turks in the 19th
century. The region's soil and climate were perfect for its cultivation
and, by the 20th century, production of rose oil had developed into a
major industry. The roses, which are grown in plantations that stretch
for over 30 km (20 miles) along the valley between Karlovo and

Girl in traditional costume at the
Kazanlŭk Rose Festival

Kazanlŭk, bloom from late May
until mid-June, and the flowers
are harvested before dawn so
as to preserve their oil content.
About 3.5 tonnes of petals
produce 1 kilo (just over 2lb)
of rose oil, which is worth about
€6,000 (£4,200). The week-
long Kazanlŭk Rose Festival
culminates on the first weekend
of June, with music, dancing and
the election of a Rose Queen.

㉘ Valley of the Thracian Kings

The Tundzha Valley, northwest of Kazanlûk, was a holy place for the inhabitants of Seuthopolis, the capital of Seuthes III, who ruled the powerful Odrysae tribe in the 4th century BC. It was in this valley that many Thracian kings and nobles were buried, in elaborate stone tombs that were sealed and covered with earth. Excavation of these burial mounds (*mogili*), some of which seem to have been used as places of ritual and sacrifice, has shed light on Thracian rituals. About 15 of the tumuli have so far been excavated, but only a few are open to visitors.

VISITORS' CHECKLIST

Practical Information
About 20 km (12 miles) NW of Kazanlûk, on the road to the Shipka Pass. **Map** D3. **Open** Visits to the tombs can be arranged through the Iskra Museum in Kazanlûk; **Tel** (0431) 63762. 🅿 🅿 Ⓦ **kazanlak.bg**

Transport
For visitors without their own transport, the tombs are best reached by taxi from Kazanlûk.

★ **Mogila Shoushmanets**
A pair of stone doors with carvings of sun discs open into the burial chamber. A single column topped by a stone disc thought to symbolize the sun supports the domed ceiling.

Mogila Griffin
A corridor leads deep into the tumulus. The stone seats in its circular central chamber suggest that it was used as a temple. There are even iron hooks for the priests' robes.

★ **Mogila Helvetia**
Named after Switzerland, which provided the funds for its excavation, this tomb contains a temple and an antechamber where horses were regularly sacrificed and where priests made divinations from their blood.

Sarafova Tomb

Mogila Golyama Kosmatka
This tomb consists of three linked chambers, one of which contains the sarcophagus of Seuthes III and some remarkable gold and silver treasures.

Kazanlûk Tomb

Mogila Golyama Arsenalka
As it was found to be empty when it was excavated, this tomb is thought to have been plundered in ancient times. A corridor leads to a circular domed chamber with a concave central floor tile that represents the sun.

★ **Mogila Ostrousha**
Beneath a mound 20 m (65 ft) high, the Ostrousha Tomb contains six chambers. The northern room was carved from a single block of stone. The paintings on its walls include this tiny portrait of a red-haired girl.

Key

═══ Main road

─── Other road

- - - Trail

—•— Railway

Gabrovo
Schipchenska Planina
Shipka
56
5
Pavel Banya
Sheynovo
5601
Hadzhidimitrovo
Enina
Kran
Kazanluk
Sliven
608

0 kilometres   5
0 miles   5

For map symbols *see back flap*

Freedom Monument, Shipka Pass, a memorial to Russian and Bulgarian soldiers

❷❾ Shipka
Шипка

12 km (7 miles) north of Kazanlŭk.
Map D3. 🚠 2,500. 🚌

The gleaming golden domes of **Shipka Memorial Church** pinpoint the village of Shipka from afar. Sheltered by dense forest, this magnificent church was built in 1902 as a memorial to Russian and Bulgarian soldiers who died in the War of Liberation (see p51).

Environs
From Shipka village a winding mountain road leads up to Shipka Pass. It was here that General Gŭrko and his Russian army, supported by Bulgarian militia using cherry tree cannons and rocks for weapons, repulsed fierce Ottoman attacks in 1877. From the pass, several hundred steep steps lead up to the **Freedom Monument**, which crowns the summit of Mount Shipka, at an altitude of 1,326 m (4,352 ft). Standing 32 m (105 ft) high and built of roughly cut stone, the grand

memorial contains a small museum, with a collection of weapons and illustrations of the battle. A lofty observation platform offers stunning views of the memorial's mountainous surroundings.

🏛 **Shipka Memorial Church**
Open 8am–6pm daily. ✝ 8am Sun.
📷

🏛 **Freedom Monument**
Open 8:30am–5:30pm daily. 📷

❸❷ Karlovo
Карлово

35 km (22 miles) N of Plovdiv. **Map** C3.
🚠 25,500. 🚍 🚌 🚇 ℹ ul. Vodopad 35 (0335 953 373). 🌐 **karlovotur.com**

The highest mountains in the Central Balkans loom over Karlovo, birthplace of Vasil Levski, Bulgaria's most celebrated revolutionary. The town's 19th-century quarter is a jumble of National Revival buildings and cobbled streets centred on the rough stone **Church of Sveta Bogoroditsa** (1851). Its blue bell tower was

added in the late 19th century. The pink-walled **History Museum**, housed in a former boys' school, stands off ulitsa Vasil Levski, just south of the church. The museum's collections include various prehistoric artifacts, traditional costume, weaponry used by Bulgarian revolutionaries, and woollen socks made in Karlovo. Kurshum Mosque, at the top of ulitsa Vasil Levski, was built in 1485, with large blocks of stone framed by red bricks, but its large wood-panelled porch was added in the late 19th century. The mosque is disused and is not open to visitors.

A few streets to the west is the **Vasil Levski Museum**, in the house where Levski (see box) grew up. It features the dyeing room used by Levski's widowed mother, the family's winter quarters, with low tables and stools, and open first-floor summer rooms adorned with family photographs and portraits. A small chapel in the grounds contains a lock of Levski's hair sealed inside a glass case.

Environs
The small town of **Sopot** straddles the busy Sofia–Burgas road. Its main point of interest is the **Ivan Vazov Museum**, in the house where Bulgaria's literary hero was born. Ivan Vazov (1850–1922) is best known for his novel Under the Yoke, in which he described village life at the time of the April Rising. The building is a typical 19th-century house, and the exhibits include a

Fresco of Vasil Levski in the Church of Sveta Bogoroditsa, Karlovo quirky set of costumed manikins playing musical instruments while one of their number shaves himself in a barber's chair.

🏛 Church of Sveta Bogoroditsa
ul. Vasil Levski. **Open** 8am–7pm daily. 🕤 9am Sun.

🏛 History Museum
ul. Vazrozhdenska 4. **Tel** (0335) 94728. **Open** 8am–noon, 1–5pm daily. 🗎 📷

🏛 Vasil Levski Museum
ul. General Kartsov 57. **Tel** (0335) 93489. **Open** 8:30am–1pm, 2–5pm daily. 🗎

🏛 Ivan Vazov Museum
ul. Vasil Levski 1, Sopot. **Tel** (03134) 8650. **Open** 8:30am–5:30pm daily. 🗎

Kamilite Gate, one of four gates into the ancient town of Hisarya

❶ Hisarya
Хисаря

43 km (27 miles) N of Plovdiv. **Map** C3. 🏛 8,400. 🚍 🚌

Hisarya lies in a depression at the eastern end of the Sredna Gora Mountains. Springs drew Thracian settlers here in the 1st millennium BC, and later the Romans developed the settlement into a luxurious spa town. In AD 251 Hisarya was devastated by invading Goths, but it was rebuilt, with the addition of colossal walls, as much as 10 m (33 ft) high in places, and four gates. Of these, only one, the Kamilite Gate (named after the camel caravans that passed through it), remains.

In AD 293 the Romans renamed the town Diocletianopolis in honour of Emperor Diocletian, and prosperity returned until the collapse of the Byzantine Empire in the 6th century. One thousand years later, the town recovered its fortunes when the Ottomans rediscovered its healing mineral springs.

One of the temple-tombs near Starosel, burial place of Thracians

Today Hisarya's town walls enclose gardens, outdoor cafés and fountains. The small **Archaeology Museum** contains objects found during excavations of the town, including artifacts made by the Bessi, a Thracian tribe of the 1st millennium BC, votive tablets from the Roman period, and a marble bust of Diocletian.

🏛 Archaeology Museum
ul. Alexander Stamboliiski 8. **Tel** (0337) 62796. **Open** 8am–noon, 1–4:30pm daily. 🗎

❷ Starosel Tombs
Тракийска гробница – Старосел

N of Starosel village. **Map** D3. 🚍 **Open** 9am–5pm daily. 🗎 📷 📷

Of the 120 tumuli in the vicinity of Starosel, only a few have been fully excavated, but six of those were discovered to be Thracian temple-tombs. Their close proximity suggests that the area was particularly sacred to Thracians. Only two of the tombs are open to the public.

The Horizont tomb lies 3 km (2 miles) outside the village of Starosel. In 2002 archaeologists

uncovered a rectangular Thracian temple with steps leading to the entrance, and ten stone pillars that once supported the roof. The temple dates from the 5th century BC and was later used as the tomb of an unknown Thracian ruler, who was buried with a collection of arrowheads, silver beads and leather armour covered with plates of beaten gold.

The Chetinyova tomb, excavated in 2000, is 3 km (2 miles) further on. It dates from the 6th century BC and is thought to have been the burial place of the legendary Thracian ruler Sitalkes. The entire hilltop site is encircled by a wall of dressed granite. Granite steps lead up to the tomb's outer entrance, where a corridor opens onto a burial chamber 5.4 m (18 ft) in diameter, the largest so far discovered in Bulgaria.

The complex's early use as a temple is indicated by the wine trough for ritual libations behind the hill, the sacrificial pits dug near the entrance, and the fact that the site is aligned in such a way that, at the winter solstice, a shaft of sunlight beams into the central chamber.

Vasil Levski (1837–73)

One of Bulgaria's most active revolutionaries, Vasil Levski fervently believed that the only way for Bulgaria to win freedom was for its own people to rise up against Ottoman rule rather than await foreign intervention. Levski was a prominent member of the Central Revolutionary Committee and spent many years establishing secret revolutionary organizations in towns and villages throughout Bulgaria. His arrest and execution for treason in 1873 dealt a mighty blow to the liberation movement.

Monument to Vasil Levski in Karlovo

Ruins of the grand fortress of Tsarevets, Veliko Tŭrnovo ▶

㉝ Koprivshtitsa
Копривщица

Thanks to its many fine National Revival houses, Koprivshtitsa is one of Bulgaria's most attractive towns. It was founded in the 14th century, as a rich centre of cattle farming. Under Ottoman rule its citizens were granted autonomy in return for collecting taxes on behalf of the Ottoman Empire. In the early 19th century, Koprivshtitsa's prosperity attracted bandits (*kûrdzhalii*), who plundered and torched the town on several occasions. However, it quickly recovered, and it is during that period of reconstruction that its colourfully painted wood and stone houses were built. Koprivshtitsa was also the home of several of Bulgaria's leading revolutionaries, and it was here that the momentous April Rising of 1876 was declared.

🏛 Debelyanov House
ul. Dimcho Debelyanov. **Tel** (07184) 2077. **Open** May–Oct: 9:30am–5:30pm Tue–Sun; Nov–Apr: 9am–5pm Tue–Sun.

This delightful house has a picturesque setting above the town, against a backdrop of forested hills. Its projecting red-tiled roof contrasts with bright blue lower walls and the dark wood of the upper storey.

It is the birthplace of the Symbolist poet Dimcho Debelyanov (1887–1916), who was killed in action during World War I.

The house contains personal possessions, such as books, that Debelyanov took with him to war, photographs and paintings, including a portrait of him by Georgi Mashev. In the garden is a brooding statue of his mother, awaiting the son who was never to return.

Statue in the garden of Debelyanov House

↑ Church of Sveta Bogoroditsa
ul. Dimcho Debelyanov 26. **Open** irregular hours. 🕐 8am Sun.

The blue-walled Church of Sveta Bogoroditsa played a memorable role in Bulgarian history. On 20 April 1876, its bell rang out to announce the beginning of the April Rising.

The church was built in 1817, on the site of an earlier church that was destroyed by *kurdzhali* bandits. Surrounded by thick stone walls, it was built slightly sunken into the ground so as to comply with Ottoman regulations governing the height of Christian churches. The three-storey bell tower was added in 1896.

The church's interior is plain, but it has a superb iconostasis by woodcarvers of the Tryavna School, with biblical scenes interwoven with animals and flowers. Some of its icons were painted by Zahari Zograf (*see p110*). Tragically, the church's original murals were destroyed in the course of misguided renovation, and replaced with newly painted icons.

🏛 Kableshkov House
ul. Todor Kableskov 8. **Tel** (07184) 2054. **Open** May–Oct: 9:30am–5:30pm Tue–Sun; Nov–Apr: 9am–5pm Tue–Sun.

The upper floor of this imposing residence juts out over the stone wall round its cobbled courtyard. It was built in 1845, to a symmetrical design, the central salons on both floors flanked by identical rooms. The central bay on the upper floor makes a pleasant summer sitting area. This was the home of Todor Kableshkov

Train Station
12 km (7.5 miles)

Debelyanov House ①

Oslekov House ⑥ ℹ

DEBELYANOV

GARANILO

Aprilts Mausoleum

Cemetery

Church of Sveta Bogoroditsa ②

Kableshkov House ③

PÛRVA PUSHKA

Lyutov House ⑤

Bridge of the First Shot ④

NIKOLAI BELODEZHDOV

0 metres   100
0 yards   100

The Church of Sveta Bogoroditsa, whose bell proclaimed the April Rising

Kableshkov House, elegant home of the leader of the April Rising

VISITORS' CHECKLIST

Practical Information
110 km (68 miles) E of Sofia.
Road Map C3. 🚂 3,000.
🛈 pl. 20 April (07184 2191).
📅 Fri. 🎭 Re-enactment of
the April Rising (1–2 May),
International Folk Festival (every
five years, next in summer 2015).
🌐 **koprivshtitza.com**

Transport
🚌

(1851–76), leader of the April Rising *(see p178)*. After studying in Plovdiv and Istanbul, where he became fluent in French, Greek and Turkish, he returned to Koprivshtitsa to chair the town's secret revolutionary committee. On 20 April 1876 he declared the start of the uprising with his infamous Bloody Letter, written in the blood of the revolutionaries' first Turkish victim. In the aftermath of the uprising's failure, Kableshkov was captured and imprisoned in Gabrovo, where he shot himself. He was buried at the Church of the Assumption in Koprivshtitsa.

🌉 Bridge of the First Shot
ul. Pŭrva Pushka.

Over a small stream in a quiet location southwest of the town centre is the Bridge of the First Shot. As the spot where the first Turk was killed during the April Rising, the humpbacked bridge is a hallowed site in Bulgarian history. A statue of Todor Kableshov, leader of the April Rising *(see above),* stands nearby.

Detail of a room at Lyutov House, with elaborate painted decoration

🏛 Lyutov House
ul. Nikola Belovezhdov 2. **Tel** (07184) 2138. **Open** May–Oct: 9:30am–5:30pm Wed–Mon; Nov–Apr: 9am–5pm Wed–Mon. 🎟

With a huge curved gable, symmetrical layout and decorative features, Lyutov House typifies Plovdiv architecture. It was designed and built in 1854 by master-craftsmen from Plovdiv, and in 1906 it was acquired by Petko Lyutov, a Koprivshtitsa milk merchant, who decorated the building with the Viennese furniture on display here today.

A double staircase leads up to the central salon. The room has an impressive elliptical vaulted ceiling edged with murals of the cities that Lyutov visited. The rooms on either side of the salon are furnished with Ottoman-style benches and European furniture. The walls feature niches and coving painted with elaborate floral motifs and further cityscapes. An exhibition of 18th- and 19th-century grey felt rugs made in Koprivshtitsa is on the ground floor.

Sights at a Glance

[map with labels: olnitsa, PETAR ZHIKOV, ⑦ avelov ouse, BULEVARD HADZHI NENCHO PALAVEEV, GEORGI BENKOVSKI, Bus station, age ool, odno-talishte, Market, Topolnitsa, Benkovski Monument, Benkovski House ⑧]

Bridge of the First Shot, an historic spot

🏛 **Karavelov House**

ul. Hadzhi Nencho Palaveev 39. **Tel** (07184) 2176. **Open** May–Oct: 9:30am–5:30pm Tue–Sun; Nov–Apr: 9am–5pm Tue–Sun.

Home to one of the National Liberation Movement's key ideologists, Karavelov House consists, in fact, of two separate buildings. The winter quarters were constructed in 1810, while the summer house, built over the main entrance, was added in 1835.

Lyuben Karavelov, born here in 1834, was a prolific writer, publisher and fervent revolutionary. He spent time among Bulgarian émigrés in Bucharest, where he published the influential *Liberty* and *Independence* newspapers and chaired the Bulgarian Revolutionary Central Committee. The printing press

Panorama of Koprivshtitsa as seen from the Benkovski monument

Pretty exterior and courtyard of Karavelov House, Koprivshtitsa

that he bought in Serbia in 1871 is on display in the winter quarters along with some of the publications he put together with Vasil Levski and Hristo Botev. During the Russo-Turkish War of 1877–8, he returned to Bulgaria before succumbing to tuberculosis. Petko, his younger brother, was three times prime minister of the new Bulgarian state.

🏛 **Benkovski House**

ul. Georgi Benkovski 5. **Tel** (07184) 2030. **Open** May–Oct: 9:30–5:30pm Tue–Sun; Nov–Apr: 9am–5pm Tue–Sun.

Its rickety wooden façade and pretty garden give Benkovski House the appearance of a fairytale cottage and the

Benkovski monument, unveiled in 1908

homely interior suggests that the Hlutev family led a modest and cozy existence. The asymmetrical design consists of low winter quarters topped by summer rooms grouped around a veranda that displays a replica of one of the cherry-tree cannons used in the April Rising. Adjoining rooms contain Benkovski's revolutionary district flag, uniforms, his Winchester rifle and faded family photographs.

He was born Gavril Hlutev and grew up here, studying to become a tailor before moving abroad at the age of 22. In Romania he was revolutionized by a group of Bulgarian émigrés and returned to Koprivshtitsa in 1875 under the assumed name of Georgi Benkovski. He formed what was to become the legendary "winged" cavalry detachment that rallied support from local villages during the April Uprising. The detachment managed to escape to the Balkan Mountains following the failure of the uprising, but Benkovski was betrayed and later killed on 25 May 1876.

The massive granite monument on the hillside above Benkovski House portrays a cloaked Benkovski astride a leaping horse looking over his shoulder to rouse his rebel army. The words *"Stavaite robove az neshta yarem"* (Rise up slaves, I don't want a yoke) are carved boldly across its base.

The April Rising, 1876

Initially planned for May, the April Uprising of 1876 relied upon the local populace to rise up against the Ottomans when called upon. Itinerant revolutionary agitators had spent several years priming and arming local groups in preparation for the revolt. Kableshkov, chairman of Koprivshtitsa's revolutionary committee, was forced to declare an early start on 20th April when Turkish officials tried to arrest him. The uprising disastrously failed to raise the support it needed from locals too fearful of Turkish retribution; villages that did participate were brutally punished – the most notorious case being at Batak *(see p130)*. Though many died in this apparently fruitless sacrifice, universal international outrage at the barbaric Ottoman reprisals lead to Russia's declaration of war on Turkey a year later and Bulgaria's liberation in 1878. The Apriltsi Mausoleum was built in 1928 in Koprivshtitsa's main square to honour those who died.

The Apriltsi Mausoleum

Oslekov House

Ослековата къща

Commissioned by the wealthy merchant and tax collector Nincho Oslekov, the house was built in 1856 by Samokov craftsmen. Because of space restrictions, it is asymmetrical, but is otherwise typical of National Revival buildings. The ground-floor winter quarters have low ceilings and small windows to conserve heat. The first floor, used in summer, has a spacious salon with large windows and adjoining rooms. Oslekov's support for the National Liberation movement brought him a death sentence after the April Uprising. He was hanged in Plovdiv in 1876.

★ Red Room
Like other rooms in the house, the Red Room has a fretted wooden ceiling. On the walls are paintings of mansions and the original symmetrical plan for Oskelov House.

Men's Room
This was where Oslekov would receive his guests and engage in business. The murals throughout the building reveal foreign places he visited while on business.

The women's room
displays a colourful collection of woollen socks along with a horizontal loom and a spinning wheel.

First floor

First-Floor Salon
Cloth-covered benches line the walls of this impressive room. This was a weaving workshop, but was also used for festivities and family events. It was here that rebel uniforms were clandestinely produced for the April Rising.

Ground floor

Main entrance

Ground floor salon

The ground-floor living room, decorated with murals of female musicians, was used in winter. The mix of eastern and western influences is typified by the European dining table with Turkish-style wall benches.

★ Main Façade
Views of Venice, Padua, Rome and other European cities, painted by Kosta Zograf of Samokov, decorate the façade. The columns are of cedarwood imported from Lebanon.

NORTHERN BULGARIA

With dramatic contrasts, northern Bulgaria encompasses jagged mountains and pine forests in the northwest and fertile sunflower-covered flatlands and low vine-covered hills near the banks of the Danube. The region also has a rich cultural heritage, with Stone Age cave paintings, medieval castles and Muslim holy sites that illuminate the complex fabric of Bulgarian history.

Much of the region is mountainous, with the eastern spurs of the Balkan range presenting a formidable obstacle to the main transport routes leading north from Sofia. The trip through Iskûr Gorge, just north of the capital, is one of Bulgaria's classic journeys, past a tortured sequence of rocky outcrops. The limestone cliffs of Vratsata Gorge are no less dramatic, although little beats the sandstone pillars of Belogradchik. Further north, the prehistoric paintings of Magura Cave are evidence of one of Europe's earliest cultures.

North and east of the mountains lie flatlands watered by the tributaries of the Danube, a river that has played a major role in Bulgarian history. The stately fortress of Baba Vida at Vidin defended the state from northern invaders, while the city of Ruse grew rich on the profits of river trade. Ruse is the gateway to the Rusenski Lom, a twisting canyon where medieval monks turned caves near Ivanovo into a unique community of rock-cut monasteries. Above the southern end of the Rusenski Lom hovers the cliff-top citadel of Cherven, one of Bulgaria's most atmospheric medieval sites.

Further east, Lake Sreburna is a famous feeding ground for migrating birds, including Dalmatian pelicans. Rolling hills of pasture and fruit trees provide an idyllic setting for Sveshtari, a site whose Thracian tombs and Muslim shrines still radiate a spiritual aura. The major urban centre of the northeast is Shumen, a former fortress town whose modern café-lined boulevards have a delightfully relaxing feel.

Belogradchik fortress, first built in Roman times using the natural terrain to maximum advantage

◀ Rock Monastery of Sv. Dimitûr Basarbovski, situated on the banks of the Rusenski Lom in northern Bulgaria

Exploring Northern Bulgaria

A region that embraces the eastern spur of the Balkan mountains, the Danubian Plain and the rolling hills of the northeast, northern Bulgaria has some of the country's most varied terrain. The mountains of the northwest offer plenty of opportunities for hiking, especially around the karst outcrops of the Vrachanski Balkan and the rock pillars of Belogradchik. Vidin and Pleven are historic towns, but it is the 19th-century port of Ruse that offers the best urban attractions. The cluster of tombs near Sveshtari are among the finest Thracian sites in the country, and the enigmatic Madara Horseman, near Shumen, is equally unmissable. Lake Sreburna, in the east, is one of the country's top birdwatching sites.

Kilims at Chiprovtsi, with typical geometric motifs woven in bright colours

Key

- ▬▬ Motorway
- ▬▬ Expressway
- ▬ Major road
- ▬ Other road
- ⁓ Railway
- ▬▬ International border
- △ Peak

Rock formations, once used as a stronghold, above Belogradchik

Sights at a Glance

1. Vidin
2. Magura Cave
3. Belogradchik
4. Montana
5. Berkovitsa
6. Chiprovtsi
7. Vratsa
10. Pleven
11. Nikopol
12. Svishtov
13. *Ruse pp190–91*
15. Sveshtari
16. Sreburna Nature Reserve
17. Silistra
18. Shumen
19. Madara
20. Veliki Preslav

Tours

8. Vrachanski Balkan Tour
9. Iskûr Gorge Tour
14. Rusenski Lom Tour

Iconostasis, with haloed figures, in the
Church of Sveti Nikola, Pleven

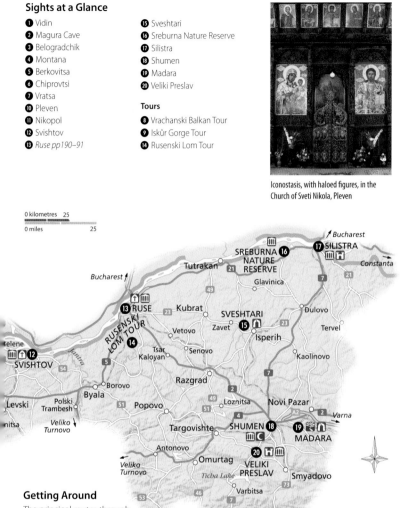

Getting Around

The principal routes through
the region are the main road and rail
lines running north from Sofia to Vratsa,
Montana and Vidin, and those running
northeast from Sofia to Pleven and
Ruse. From Ruse, onward travel to
either Silistra or Shumen is fairly easy.
Shumen itself is connected to the Black
Sea city of Varna by a fast stretch of
dual carriageway. Some of the most
scenic parts of northern Bulgaria, such
as Iskûr Gorge, the rock formations near
Belogradchik and the Rusenski Lom,
can only be reached on minor
roads, where progress may be slow.
Unfortunately, the river Danube has
little potential as a tourist itinerary:
there is no passenger transport on the
river itself, and the roads along its banks
are in poor condition.

Ornately decorated cupola of Tombul Mosque in Shumen

For additonal map symbols *see back flap*

❶ Vidin

Видин

200 km (125 miles) N of Sofia.
Map A1. 🏙 48,000. 🚆 from Sofia.
🚌 from Sofia.

Set on the Danube, Vidin is Bulgaria's westernmost port and of strategic importance to successive waves of settlers. First were the Celts, who arrived in the 3rd century BC, followed by Romans, Byzantines, Ottomans and Bulgarians. Today Vidin is an important river crossing, with ferries shuttling across the Danube to the Romanian port of Calafat.

Central Vidin centres around ploshtad Bdin, a broad square lined with modern buildings. A short walk northeastwards along ulitsa Tûrgovska is the **History Museum**, in the much-modernized residence of Vidin's governor in Ottoman times. The museum contains an absorbing collection of floor mosaics and marble sculpture from the 2nd-century Roman settlement of Ratiaria, a frontier fort 25 km (16 miles) southeast of Vidin, near the village of Archar.

Northeast of ploshtad Bdin, and parallel to the banks of the Danube, are the Riverside Gardens, with lawns and trees. On the western side of the gardens is Vidin's only surviving mosque, built by the soldier and governor Osman Pazvantoglu in the 1790s. The attractive domed building in the mosque's enclosed garden originally served as a *kitabhane*, or Koranic library.

Dominating the northern end of the park are the imposing towers and bastions of **Baba Vida**, the 13th-century fortress that once guarded the northwestern approaches to the medieval kingdom of Bulgaria. Baba Vida is one of the best-preserved castles in Bulgaria, largely because it was so valuable to successive Ottoman occupiers that it remained in constant use. The core of the castle, with towers and turrets, is still largely intact. From here visitors can enjoy sweeping views of the river.

Walking back towards central Vidin along ulitsa Knyaz Boris I, visitors will pass the Cross-shaped Barracks (Krustata kazarma) built during the reign of Osman Pazvantoglu. The barracks now contain the town's **Ethnographic Museum**. Its collection includes local costumes, textiles woven by the nomadic, sheep-rearing Vlachs, a local ethnic minority who speak a language similar to modern Romanian.

Behind the nearby Church of Sveti Nikolai is one of Vidin's oldest churches, Sveti Panteleimon, built by the 17th-century Despot of Wallachia, Ioan Matei Basarab, whose portrait graces the entrance.

🏛 **History Museum**
Tel (094) 601 710. **Open** 9am–5pm Mon–Fri, 10am–5pm Sat–Sun. 🖋

🏰 **Baba Vida**
Tel (094) 601 705. **Open** summer: 8:30am–5:30pm Mon–Fri, 9am–5:30pm Sat & Sun; winter: 9am–5pm Mon–Fri, 10am–5pm Sat & Sun. 🖋

🏛 **Ethnographic Museum**
Tel (094) 601 709. **Open** 9am–5pm Mon–Fri, 10am–5pm Sat–Sun. 🖋

Prehistoric rock paintings of men and animals at Magura Cave

❷ Magura Cave

пещерата "Магура"

Rabisha village, 35 km (22 miles) SW of Vidin. **Map** A2. **Tel** (0894) 481 964. **Open** summer: 10am–5pm daily; winter: 10am–4pm daily. 🖋 🖋 🖳

Both on account of its mineral formations and its prehistoric paintings, this is one of Bulgaria's most spectacular limestone caves. It is located just outside Rabisha, a village in the foothills of the Western Balkan range. The cave has unusually large galleries, some with ceilings 25 m (80 ft) high, and zestful rock paintings that date from the 2nd millennium BC.

The route descends 2 km (over 1 mile) down the cave, with some steep and slippery sections. The first two caverns, the Triumphal Hall and Gallery of the Stalactones, contain stunning stalactites and stalagmites. A tunnel-like side chamber off the main route leads to the Gallery of Drawings, where paintings executed in bat droppings show stylized sun and star shapes, hunters wielding bows and a variety of exotic beasts. Most striking are the scenes of ritual celebration, in which female figures dance with their arms above their heads, observed by sexually excited males.

Along the main route, visitors will come to the Chamber of the Fallen Pine. It is named after the tapering stalagmite, 11 m (36 ft) long and 6 m (20 ft) in diameter, which collapsed in the chamber.

The cave is also near Lake Rabisha, which is popular with local fishermen because of its rich stocks of catfish and carp.

The fortress of Baba Vida, built to defend the Danube crossing at Vidin

For hotels and restaurants in this region see pp226 and pp238–9

The natural fortress above Belogradchik, transformed into a citadel by Romans, Bulgarians and Ottomans

❸ Belogradchik
Белоградчик

50 km (31 miles) SW of Vidin. **Map** A2. 🚠 5,330. 🚌 from Vidin.

The small hillside town of Belogradchik is surrounded by some of the most dramatic rock formations in Bulgaria. The Belogradchik rocks (Belogradchiskite skali) were formed millennia ago, when thick deposits of sandstone were forced upwards by the movement of tectonic plates. Erosion by wind and rain then shaped them into an other-worldly assortment of pillars, cones and mushroom forms.

The hill above the town is crowned by a dramatic circle of rocky pinnacles. Forming a natural fortress, they were used as an almost impregnable citadel by Romans, Bulgarians and Ottomans. The inner stronghold commands stunning views of the surrounding landscape. Yet more spectacular rock formations, with names such as the Bear, the Horseman and the Monks, can be seen by following footpaths through a vale west of Belogradchik.

In a glade outside the town is a **Natural History Museum**, with stuffed examples of birds and forest-dwelling mammals of northwestern Bulgaria.

🏛 **Natural History Museum**
Tel (0936) 53231. **Open** 9am–noon, 2–5pm daily. 🖼

❹ Montana
Монтана

80 km (50 miles) SE of Vidin; 90 km (56 miles) N of Sofia. **Map** B2. 🚠 43,800. 🚆 from Sofia. 🚌 from Sofia.

Although it grew from the Roman fort of Castra ad Montanesium, modern Montana has the appearance of a 20th-century town. The spacious main square, with fountains and flowerbeds, is an example of Communist urban planning. Just off the square is a small **History Museum**, with traditional costumes of the Karakachani, nomadic shepherds of the western Balkans. Few genuine Karakachani now remain, as most have adopted settled lifestyles.

🏛 **History Museum**
Tel (0963) 305 489. **Open** 8am–noon, 1–5pm daily. 🖼

Fountains in Montana's large pedestrianized main square

❺ Berkovitsa
Берковица

24 km (15 miles) south of Montana. **Map** B2. 🚠 13,460. 🚆 from Montana. 🚌 from Sofia.

In the 19th century Berkovitsa was a prosperous centre of woodworking and pottery-making. It became a minor health resort in the early 20th century, when Sofians discovered its pure mountain air. The town is also the starting point of a hiking trail to Mount Kom, 12 km (7 miles) to the west.

Evidence of Berkovitsa's 19th-century heritage is displayed in the **Ivan Vazov Museum**, in the house where the novelist lived while serving as magistrate. Appointed in 1879, Vazov *(see p85)* soon left to pursue a writing career in Plovdiv. His former home features handsomely carved wooden ceilings, luxurious carpets and some copperware.

The **Ethnographic Museum** celebrates Berkovitsa's ceramics industry with a display of pots and jugs glazed in vivid yellow and green. Local craftsmanship can also be seen in the Church of the Birth of the Virgin.

🏛 **Ivan Vazov Museum**
ul. Poruchnik Grozdanov 11. **Tel** (0953) 88045. **Open** 8am–noon, 2–5pm Mon–Fri (from 9am Sat & Sun). 🖼

🏛 **Ethnographic Museum**
ul. Poruchnik Grozhdanov 7. **Open** 8am–noon, 2–5pm Mon–Fri (from 9am Sat & Sun). 🖼

Ruins of the Cathedral of Sveta Maria, Chiprovtsi

❻ Chiprovtsi
Чипровци

25 km (16 miles) W of Montana.
Map A2. 🚐 2,100. 🌐 chiprovtsi.bg

Wedged into an attractive mountain valley, Chiprovtsi is a small, unassuming town that betrays few signs of its former greatness. From the 13th century, when it was populated largely by Saxon immigrants of Catholic faith, Chiprovtsi was one of the most important centres of gold- and silver-mining in the Balkans. Its prosperity survived the Ottoman conquest, and the town became a great centre of Catholic learning. After an un-successful uprising against the Ottomans in 1688, the town was laid waste and its inhabitants banished. Chiprovtsi was not repopulated until 1737. It was then that carpet-weaving became the town's main industry, as it still is today.

The **Town Museum** illustrates aspects of Chiprovtsi's past. Exhibits include examples of the intricate jewellery that was made by the town's goldsmiths in the 17th century. There is also a display of colourful Chiprovtsi kilims, and an example of the vertical looms on which carpets are still woven in the town today.

Next door to the museum is the Church of the Ascension, which contains a fine 19th-century iconostasis. Nearby are the meagre ruins of the medieval Cathedral of Sveta Maria.

🏛 **Chiprovtsi Town Museum**
ul. Vitosha 2. **Tel** (09554) 2168.
Open 8am–noon, 1–5pm Mon–Fri, 9am–5pm Sat–Sun. 🎫 (free on Thu).

❼ Vratsa
Враца

110 km (68 miles) N of Sofia. **Map** B2.
🚐 61,000. 🚉 🚌

Vratsa is an ideal starting point for touring the Vrachanski Balkan (*see opposite*) whether by foot or car. However, it should not be overlooked as an attraction in its own right.

Vratsa's main square is dominated by a statue of the poet and revolutionary Hristo Botev (1848–76). In May 1876, Botev entered Ottoman-occupied Bulgaria at the head of a band of patriot exiles. He and all his followers perished, having made their last stand on Mount Okolchitsa, just outside Vratsa.

Botev is also remembered at Vratsa's **History Museum**.

However, the real attraction here is some of finest Thracian gold and silver yet discovered in northern Bulgaria. A room is devoted to the Rogozen Treasure (Rogozensko sukrovishte), a collection of more than 150 silver ewers and bowls discovered in 1983. Made for a Thracian noble family between the 5th and 4th centuries BC, the vessels are richly decorated, some with abstract swirls and stripes, others with mythological subjects and hunting scenes. A particularly impressive piece is a pitcher with a powerful portrait of the Thracian mother-goddess astride a lion.

Another room contains the Vratsa Treasure (Vrachanska sukrovishta), a collection of artifacts from the grave of a Thracian noblewoman. Notable pieces include an exquisite gold wreath and a bronze shin-guard bearing the tattooed face of a deity.

Vratsa's **Ethnographic Museum**, in a restored 19th-century schoolhouse, contains a collection of colourful Bulgarian costumes. There is also a display of musical instruments that illustrates the history of brass bands in northern Bulgaria.

🏛 **History Museum**
pl. Hristo Botev 2. **Tel** (092) 620 220.
Open 9am–5:30pm Mon–Fri, 9am–noon, 1pm–5:30pm Sat & Sun. 🎫 Joint ticket for History Museum and Ethnographic Museum (free on Mon).

🏛 **Ethnographic Museum**
ul. David Todorov 2. **Open** 🎫 See History Museum.

Chiprovtsi Carpets

Brightly coloured traditional Chiprovtsi carpets

Chiprovtsi is one of the few Bulgarian villages where carpet weaving is still widely practised, and where skills are passed down from mother to daughter. Woven on vertical looms, the carpets feature brightly coloured patterns that feature a centuries-old repertoire of stylized motifs. Many of these originated as fertility symbols. They include bird motifs known as *piletata* (chickens), abstract zig-zags known as *lozite* (vines), and the mysterious cluster of black triangles known as *karakachka* (black-eyed bride).

Traditional costumes at the Ethnographic Museum, Vratsa

❽ Vrachanski Balkan Tour

The highland region that stretches out to the west of Vratsa is known as the Vrachanski Balkan. Its landscape, most of which is protected as a nature park, consists of pasture-covered hills, forested valleys and jagged outcrops of limestone. The region's most dramatic feature is the deep Vratsata Gorge, which starts just west of Vratsa. The hills on either side of the gorge provide lush grazing for cows and sheep, and from their milk local dairies produce some of the best Bulgarian yoghurt.

Tips for Drivers

Map: B2. **Starting point**: Vratsa.
Length: 60 km (37 miles).
Stopping-off places: There are several hotels, restaurants and cafés in Vratsa, and you can get light refreshments at villages such as Pavloche and Chelopek. There is a hostel at Ledenika.
Ledenika Cave
Open summer: 9am–5pm daily; winter: 9am–4pm daily.

② Vratsata Gorge
Cutting a great swathe through the landscape, Vratsata Gorge is formed by sheer cliffs that rise almost vertically from the valley floor. The terrain above consists of pasture and majestic outcrops of rock.

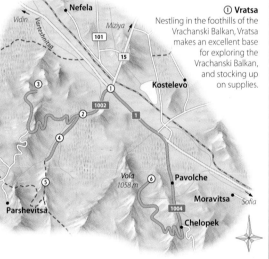

① Vratsa
Nestling in the foothills of the Vrachanski Balkan, Vratsa makes an excellent base for exploring the Vrachanski Balkan, and stocking up on supplies.

③ Ledenika Cave
Formed by seeping rainwater over a period of 2 million years, the cave contains a sequence of subterranean halls, with spectacular stalactites and stalagmites. The cave is also inhabited by a large colony of bats.

④ Zgorigrad
Largely agricultural and with horses and carts still serving as a popular mode of transport, Zgorigrad is a pleasant example of a northwest Bulgarian village.

⑤ Vrachanski eco-trail
Upstream from the village of Zgorigrad, this well-signed nature walk (Eko puteka) ascends a narrowing ravine, passing through forests of lime, beech and walnut.

⑥ Okolchitsa
This historic peak, where the poet and revolutionary Hristo Botev was killed, has a cross at the top and panoramic views overlooking the valley.

Map labels: Nefela, Vidin, Vratenitsa, Miziya, 101, 15, 3, 1, Kostelevo, 1002, 2, 1, 4, Vola 1058 m, 5, 6, Pavolche, Moravitsa, Sofia, 1004, Parshevitsa, Chelopek

Key
- ▬▬ Tour route
- ═══ Main road
- ═══ Other road
- – – Trail
- ⌁ Railway
- △ Peak

0 kilometres 5
0 miles 5

❾ Iskûr Gorge Tour

Rising on the slopes of Mount Vitosha, the Iskûr River flows north to join the Danube just west of Nikopol. Its course cuts through the limestone of the western Balkans to form the Iskûr Gorge, a defile that runs for 156 km (97 miles) between Sofia and Mezdra, where the river emerges onto the open plains. The gorge is famous for its dramatic rock formations, and the monasteries nearby are important places of pilgrimage.

Tips for Drivers

Map: B3. **Length of tour**: approximately 105 km (65 miles). **Getting there**: Road and rail routes follow the gorge, providing easy access to the scenic stretches. **Stopping-off places**: There are picnic spots and café-restaurants at Gara Lakatnik, right beneath the Lakatnik rocks.

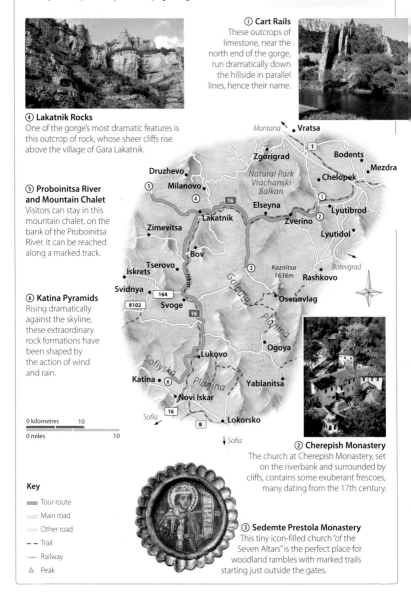

① Cart Rails
These outcrops of limestone, near the north end of the gorge, run dramatically down the hillside in parallel lines, hence their name.

④ Lakatnik Rocks
One of the gorge's most dramatic features is this outcrop of rock, whose sheer cliffs rise above the village of Gara Lakatnik.

⑤ Proboinitsa River and Mountain Chalet
Visitors can stay in this mountain chalet, on the bank of the Proboinitsa River. It can be reached along a marked track.

⑥ Katina Pyramids
Rising dramatically against the skyline, these extraordinary rock formations have been shaped by the action of wind and rain.

② Cherepish Monastery
The church at Cherepish Monastery, set on the riverbank and surrounded by cliffs, contains some exuberant frescoes, many dating from the 17th century.

③ Sedemte Prestola Monastery
This tiny icon-filled church "of the Seven Altars" is the perfect place for woodland rambles with marked trails starting just outside the gates.

Key

- ▬▬ Tour route
- ══ Main road
- ── Other road
- − − Trail
- ─── Railway
- △ Peak

0 kilometres 10
0 miles 10

The Panorama, one of several reminders of the Siege of Pleven

⑩ Pleven
Плевен

160 km (99 miles) NE of Sofia.
Map C2. 🚆 107,000. 🚌 🚐
ℹ️ pl. Vazrazhdane 1 (064 824 004).
🌐 tourinfo.pleven.bg

An important centre of trade in the 19th century, Pleven is remembered today primarily for the decisive role that it played in the Russo-Turkish War of 1877–8 *(see p51)*. In July 1877 the Russian army advanced on Pleven, but the Ottoman garrison, under the command of Osman Pasha, stood resolute. After a five-month siege, Pleven finally surrendered, and this was soon followed by the collapse of Ottoman resistance throughout Bulgaria.

Several public buildings in the town recall the event. A **Mausoleum** commemorating Russian casualties in the siege is the central feature of ploshtad Vazrazhdane, Pleven's main square. Inside are plaques engraved with the names of the fallen. Pleven's main shopping street, ulitsa Vasil Levski, leads northward to the **Museum of Liberation**, in which the Siege of Pleven is remembered.

Nearby is the 14th-century Church of Sveti Nikola. It was rebuilt in 1834 after being pillaged by *kŭrdzhalii* (roving bandits). Inside are a wooden iconostasis carved by Master Peter of Gabrovo, and icons by Dimitŭr Zograf *(see p110)*.

In a former barracks just south of the town centre, the **History Museum** displays more weaponry dating from the

siege, as well as an extensive archaeological collection that includes mosaics and sarcophagi from the Roman settlement of Oescus, 35 km (22 miles) north of Pleven.

On high ground west of the town centre, defensive earth-works dating from the Ottoman period underlie the lawns

Roman sculpture in the History Museum, Pleven

and trees of Skobelev Park. At its centre is the **Skobelev Museum**, which honours the Russian general who commanded Cossack detachments during the siege. At the northern end of the park is the **Panorama**, a cylindrical monument unveiled in 1977 to mark the centenary of the siege. Its interior is lined with a long panoramic painting that depicts the decisive moment when Osman Pasha tried to break the siege.

🏛 **Mausoleum**
pl. Vuzrazhdane. **Tel** (064) 830 033.
Open 9am–noon, 1–6pm Tue–Sat. 🖼

🏛 **Museum of Liberation**
ul. Vasil Levski 157. **Tel** (064) 843 558.
Open 9am–noon, 1–5pm Tue–Sat.

🏛 **History Museum**
ul. Stoyan Zaimov 3. **Tel** (064) 822 623.
Open 9am–noon, 1–5pm Tue–Sat.

🏛 **Skobelev Museum**
Park Skobelev. **Tel** (064) 830 251.
Open summer: 9:30am–noon, 12:30–6pm daily; winter: 9am–noon, 12:30pm–5:30 pm daily.

🏛 **Panorama**
Park Skobelev. **Tel** (064) 830 251.
Open summer: 9am–noon, 1–6pm daily (winter: to 5pm). 🖼 🖼

⑪ Nikopol
Никопол

55 km (34 miles) N of Pleven.
Map C2. 🚆 4,976. 🚌 🚐

Situated in a cleft in a chalky escarpment over the Danube, Nikopol is a sleepy rural settlement that betrays few signs of its historical importance. In Roman times, when it was known as Nikopolis, it was a garrison town. It was later developed by Byzantine and Bulgarian rulers,

and by the Middle Ages, it was the most important fortress on the lower Danube. In 1396, Nikopol was the site of a significant battle, when Crusaders led by King Louis of Hungary were crushed by Ottoman forces. Today there are only scant remains of the fortress on the bluff, east of the town.

⑫ Svishtov
Свищов

95 km (59 miles) NE of Pleven.
Map D2. 🚆 30,200. 🚌 🚐

Now a quiet provincial town, in the 19th century Svishtov was the busiest ferry-crossing point on the Bulgarian stretch of the Danube (Dunav).

The most prominent building that recalls this golden age is the Church of Sveta Troitsa, built in 1867 by Kolyo Ficheto *(see p165)*. Down the hill from the church is the **Aleko Konstantinov House**, where the furniture and personal effects of Aleko Konstantinov, Bulgaria's greatest 19th-century satirical writer, are displayed. In 1897 Konstantinov was assassinated, and the remains of his bullet-perforated heart are preserved in a glass jar in the house.

🏛 **Aleko Konstantinov House**
ul. Klokotuitsa 6. **Tel** (0631) 60467.
Open 8am–noon, 1–5pm Mon–Fri. 🖼

Church of Sveta Troitsa in Svishtov, built by Kolyo Ficheto

⑬ Ruse

Русе

With handsome 19th-century municipal buildings and Art Nouveau villas, the Danube port of Ruse has a strong Central European flavour. Ruse owes much to Midhat Pasha, its governor from 1864 to 1868. This enlightened Turkish administrator transformed the Ottoman garrison town into a modern European city. After the Liberation, Western investment increased, and Ruse became Bulgaria's wealthiest city. Many of its most atmospheric neighbour-hoods are in its northwesterly section, among the grid of streets between ulitsa Aleksandrovska and the Danube. Its focal point is ploshtad Svoboda, the central square traversed by the pedestrianized ulitsa Aleksandrovska, one of Bulgaria's most vibrant shopping streets.

🏛 Church of Sveta Troitsa

pl. Sveta Troitsa 9. **Tel** (082) 824 277.
Open 7:30am–7pm daily.

Built in 1632, this church is an eyecatching blend of Baroque and Muscovite styles. Steps lead down to a nave that lies 4 m (13 ft) below street level, a reminder that, during the Ottoman period, churches could not rival mosques in height or magnificence. The main iconostasis bears splendid Russian icons from the Sergiev Monastery in Moscow.

🏛 Ploshtad Svoboda

Central Ruse revolves around ploshtad Svoboda (Liberation Square), a broad pedestrianized area with well-kept lawns and shrubs. At its centre stands the Liberation Monument (1909), in the form of a soaring pillar topped by a figure symbolizing liberty.

On the southwestern side of the square is the Drama Theatre, built in 1900 as an entertainment and shopping centre. The ground floor was leased to shopkeepers, and it

Palace of Aleksandûr Batenberg, now the Regional History Museum

became known as Dohodnoto Zdanie (Revenue Building). The figure of Mercury on the roof is a city landmark.

🏛 Regional History Museum

pl. Aleksandûr Batenberg 3.
Open 9am–6pm daily. **Tel** (082) 825 002. 📷 🌐 **museumruse.com**

From Ploshtad Svoboda, a short walk southwest along ulitsa Aleksandrovska leads to ploshtad Aleksandûr Batenberg, one of Ruse's most elegant squares. At its western end is the former palace of Prince Aleksandûr Batenberg, now the Regional History Museum.

The first floor is devoted to Bulgaria's prehistoric, Roman and medieval periods. The centrepiece is the Borovo Treasure, a ceremonial bowl and drinking horns made for Thracian rulers in the 4th century BC. Other rooms recall Ruse's belle époque, with re-creations of pre-World War I high-street shops. There is also an ethnographic section, with traditional wedding costumes.

🏛 Sexaginta Prista

ul. Tsar Kaloyan 2. **Tel** (082) 825 002.
Open 9am–noon, 1–5:30pm Tue–Sat. 📷

Just north of pl. Aleksandûr Batenberg, along ul. Tsar Kaloyan, a path leads to the site of Sexaginta Prista (Port of Sixty Ships). This Roman naval base was built in the 1st century, during the reign of the emperor Vespasian. Traces of its fortifications are visible, and there is a fascinating collection of Roman tombstones and inscriptions.

To the north lies Ruse's 19th-century port area, where luxury goods from western Europe arrived by barge, to be stored in the fine red-brick warehouses that still stand.

🏛 Zahari Stoyanov Museum

bul. Pridunavski 12. **Tel** (082) 825 002.
Open 9am–noon, 1–5pm Mon–Fri. 📷

From the port area, bulevard Pridunavski rises to a bluff above the Danube. Among the handsome villas on the landward side is the Zahari Stoyanov Museum, devoted to the revolutionary who took part in the April Rising and who wrote a stirring firsthand account of the event. With photographs, muskets, revolutionary banners and some of Stoyanov's personal belongings, the museum documents Bulgaria's struggle for liberation.

🏛 Kaliopa House

ul. Tsar Ferdinand 36. **Tel** (082) 825 002. **Open** 9am–noon, 1–5:30pm Tue–Sat. 📷

A little way northeast of the Zahari Stoyanov Museum is the 19th-century villa once

Iconostasis with Muscovite icons, in the Church of Sveta Troitsa

An opulently furnished room at Kaliopa House

inhabited by Maria "Kaliopa" Kalitsch, wife of the Prussian consul. It is now home to the Museum of Urban Lifestyles.

Lavishly decorated by Kalitsch and a succession of subsequent owners, the house is a perfect example of how Ruse's upper classes lived prior to World War I. A fresco depicting Cupid and Psyche dominates the stairwell, while the upstairs rooms have stuccoed ceilings, hand-painted wall decorations and opulent furnishings.

Transport Museum

ul. Bratya Obretenovi 13. **Tel** (082) 222 012. **Open** 9am–noon, 1–5pm Mon–Fri.

Bulevard Pridunavski continues northeast along the riverfront towards the Ruse Transport Museum. Here Ruse's railway heritage is celebrated with a display of historic locomotives. One of Midhat Pasha's most important initiatives was the construction of a railway line from Ruse to Varna (from where steamships sailed to Istanbul), thus opening up Ruse to international investment. Among the museum's exhibits is an opulent carriage built for Empress Eugenie of France, who travelled through Ruse on her way to the opening of the Suez Canal in 1869.

Pantheon of National Revival Heroes

Park na Vûzrozhdentsite. **Open** 9am–noon, 1–5:30pm Sun–Thu.

South of the Transport Museum lie two large parks. Park na Vûzrozhdentsite (Park of the Men of the Revival) is dotted with small mausolea commemorating those who fought for independence in the 19th century. Its main feature is the Pantheon of National Revival Heroes, a concrete ziggurat with a gilt dome. Inside, an eternal flame burns in memory of those who fell in the struggle for freedom. There are also symbolic statues

VISITORS' CHECKLIST

Practical Information
330 km (200 miles) NE from Sofia.
Map D2. 149,700. ul. Aleksandrovska 61 (082 824 704).
March Music (classical).
tic.rousse.bg

Transport
from Sofia, Pleven, Varna.
from Sofia.

and tombs of guerrilla leaders and of Bulgarian volunteers who fought in the Russo-Turkish War. Because it was built over one of the city's oldest cemeteries, the Pantheon has aroused controversy. In 2001 the site was symbolically re-Christianized, when a cross was added to the Pantheon's dome.

Pantheon of National Revival Heroes, in Park na Vûzrozhdentsite

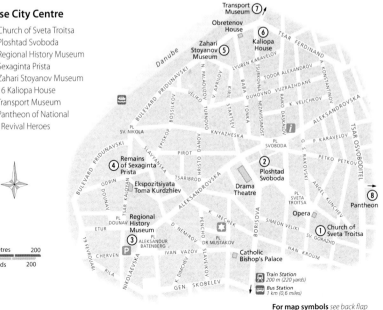

Ruse City Centre

1 Church of Sveta Troitsa
2 Ploshtad Svoboda
3 Regional History Museum
4 Sexaginta Prista
5 Zahari Stoyanov Museum
6 Kaliopa House
7 Transport Museum
8 Pantheon of National Revival Heroes

0 metres   200
0 yards   200

Train Station
200 m (220 yards)

Bus Station
1 km (0,6 miles)

For map symbols see back flap

⑭ Rusenski Lom Tour

South of Ruse, the Rusenski Lom river winds its way through a dramatic series of canyons. This unique and unspoiled natural environment is home to tortoises, lizards and snakes, eagles, buzzards and a few Egyptian vultures. The inaccessible nature of the valley made it popular with medieval hermits, who established monasteries in the caves, decorating them with sumptuous frescoes. Further up the valley at Cherven, medieval Bulgarian rulers built a magnificent cliff-top city, whose crumbling ruins are as dramatic as any in the country.

Tips for Drivers

Map: D2–E2.
Length: 40 km (25 miles).
Starting point: Ruse. Follow the main highway to Sofia as far as the city outskirts then take the turn-off to Basarbovo.
Stopping-off places: There is a restaurant and a couple of simple cafés in the village of Ivanovo. The parking lot at the entrance to the Ivanovo Rock Monasteries is the starting point for some relaxing riverside walks.

① Rock Monastery of Sv. Dimitûr Basarbovski

Built into a sheer cliff east of Basarbovo, this is the only still-functioning rock monastery in Bulgaria. The icon-filled church founded in the 15th century and named after the holy man and healer Dimitûr of Basarbovo, is reached by a zig-zagging stone staircase.

② Ivanovo Rock Monasteries

In the 14th century a large community of monks lived here. Only the Tsurkvata cave has been kept as a museum and is filled with vivid New Testament frescoes.

③ Ivanovo

Up on a plateau, the village of Ivanovo preserves an agricultural way of life. A handful of B&Bs and family hotels cater for tourists drawn by the beauty of the valley below.

④ Cherven Fortress

Originally fortified by the Byzantines in the 6th century, Cherven and its fortress became a key strategic point for Bulgaria's 13th-century tsars. A flourishing city full of churches and civic buildings, it was sacked by the Ottomans in 1388 and never recovered, leaving an evocative collection of hilltop ruins for today's visitors to explore.

⑤ Cherven

With its red-tiled houses perched on hilltops above the river, rustic Cherven is one of the most picturesque settlements in northern Bulgaria.

0 kilometres 5
0 miles 5

Key

▬ Tour route
═ Main road
═ Other road
⊸ Railway

Map labels: Bucharest, Ruse, 5, 501, 2, Danube (Donau), Rusenski Lom, Varna, 52, Krasen, 202, 501, Bozhochen, Shtraklevo, 5, Natural Park, Beli Lom, Pleven, Rusenski Lom, Koshov, Nisovo, Cherni Lom, Malki Lom, 501, Tabachka, Popovo

Mound of Ginina Mogila, most important of the Thracian tombs outside the village of Sveshtari

⓰ Sveshtari

Свещари

95 km (59 miles) SE of Ruse. Map E2.
🚌 from Isperih.

The large number of Thracian burial mounds around the village of Sveshtari suggests that the area was a major civic and religious centre before the Roman conquest. The largest cluster of burial mounds (mogili) are located just west of the village, in an area that is now the Sboryanovo History and Archaeology Reserve. Visits to the mounds are arranged through the **Sveshtari Mogili Information Centre** at the entrance to the reserve.

There are 26 burial mounds in all. Ginina Mogila, a tomb of the 3rd-century BC excavated in 1982 and now a UNESCO World Heritage Site is the most famous, and most important in archaeological terms. Beyond the ornately carved portal at its entrance, a tunnel-like passageway leads to the burial chamber of a Thracian noble and his wife. Ten caryatid-like female figures, which may represent an archetypal mother goddess, line the walls. A mural just below the barrel-vaulted ceiling depicts the deceased on horseback, being presented with a wreath and other gifts by a goddess and her servants. On either side of this main chamber are two smaller chambers in which the skeletons of ritually slaughtered horses were found. Two of the other tombs nearby are as impressive in their construction, but not as richly decorated.

Just beyond the tombs, a path descends for 2 km (1¼ miles) towards Pette Pûrsta, a natural spring at the bottom of a cliff. The spring seems to have been sacred to local people since Neolithic times.

Beside the spring is Demir Baba Tekke, the shrine of a 16th-century Muslim holy man. Set beneath cliffs, it consists of a domed chamber containing a stone sarcophagus about 4 m (13 ft) long.

Demir Baba, a semi-legendary figure, is still highly revered by the mixed Muslim-Christian community around Sveshtari. As a place of pilgrimage, the tekke is particularly popular among the Aliani, a local community of Muslims whose forebears came from Iran and Azerbaijan. Aliani regularly come to pray at Demir Baba's shrine or to tie coloured cloths to its window-frames to bring them good luck.

A short distance beyond the Pette Pûrsta locality are the remains of a fortified city dating

Entrance to Ginina Mogila, in the side of the mound

from the 3rd century BC. It is thought to be the capital of the Getae, who were a strong Thracian tribe c. 5th century BC. The Greek historian Thucydides mentions the Getae in connection with their prowess in horsemanship. This provides an interesting link with the horses in Ginina Mogila, which were almost certainly slaughtered to provide the dead with mounts in the afterlife. Both the accounts of Greek historians and the artifacts discovered in the tombs around Sveshtari have thrown light on the Getae's religious beliefs and rituals.

▥ Sveshtari Mogili Information Centre
1 km (¾ mile) W of Sveshtari.
Open Mar–Nov: 9am–noon, 1–5pm Wed–Sun. 🐾 📷

▥ Demir Baba Tekke
3 km (2 miles) W of Sveshtari.

Burial chamber inside Ginina Mogila, with stone couch and female figures

Rock Monastery of Sv. Dimitûr of Basarbovo, Rusenki Lom ▶

Lakeland and reed beds at Sreburna Nature Reserve

⑯ Sreburna Nature Reserve

резерват "Сребърна"

17 km (11 miles) W of Silistra.
Map F1. 🚌 from Silistra.

One of Bulgaria's richest wildfowl habitats, this expanse of pristine wetland is a UNESCO Biosphere Reserve. At its centre is Lake Sreburna, a shallow stretch of fresh water cut off from the Danube by a narrow spit of sand and marshland.

Surrounded by reeds and rushes, and filled with frogs and insects, the lake makes an ideal feeding ground for a multitude of birds, many species of which are rarely seen elsewhere in Bulgaria. While it has a permanent population of several species of ducks and herons, Sreburna also attracts large numbers of cormorants, spoonbills and Dalmatian pelicans during the spring nesting season. So as not to disturb the birds, access to the lakeshore is restricted, but the **Natural History Museum** on the western side of the lake has a viewing terrace.

🏛 Natural History Museum
Tel (08677) 2469. **Open** 9am–noon, 2–6pm Mon–Fri. 📷

⑰ Silistra

Силистра

122 km (76 miles) NE of Ruse. **Map** F1.
🚆 35,230. 🚌 from Sofia & Ruse.

The easternmost of Bulgaria's ports on the Danube, Silistra has been important since the mid-1st century AD, when Emperor

Claudius made it the base of the 11th Legion. Under Byzantine rule, Silistra became an episcopal see and in the Middle Ages it served as the Bulgarian kings' foremost military base on the lower Danube.

While a scattering of Byzantine and medieval ruins can be seen in Silistra's riverside park, an overview of the city's past is provided by the **History Museum**, whose collection includes some fine Roman tombstones and a 1st-century stone sundial with a depiction of Orpheus.

Medzhiditabiya Fortress, on a ridge 3 km (2 miles) west of the town centre, was built by the Ottomans in the 18th century. It has huge stone walls and angular bastions giving sweeping views of the river below.

Statue of Pegasus in Silistra

🏛 History Museum
ul. Simeon Veliki 72. **Tel** (086) 822 075.
Open 9:30am–5pm Mon–Fri. 📷
(free on Mon).

⑱ Shumen

Шумен

90 km (56 miles) SW of Dobrich; 106 km (66 miles) SE of Ruse. **Map** E2.
🚆 80,500. 🚏 from Sofia & Varna.
🚌 from Ruse, Varna & Sofia. 🛈 bul. Slavyanski 17 (054-857 773).

One of northeastern Bulgaria's major urban centres, Shumen is rich in monuments associated with the medieval Bulgarian state and later Ottoman rule. Bulevard Slavyanski, a café-lined, tree-

shaded strip, runs through the town centre. In a park nearby is the **History Museum**, where finds from the medieval cities of Veliki Preslav and Pliska, and a replica of a Thracian war chariot, are displayed.

Several attractive 19th-century buildings, which are open to the public 9am–5pm weekdays, line ulitsa Tsar Osvoboditel, which lies parallel to bulevard Slavyanski. Among the scattering of interesting small museums in this part of town is the House of Pancho Vladigerov (1899–1978), devoted to the life of Bulgaria's leading symphonic composer. Nearby, the Lajos Kossuth House-Museum honours the famous Hungarian nationalist leader who briefly made his home in Shumen in 1849. Also nearby is the Panaiot Volov Memorial House, family home of one of the leaders of the ill-fated April Rising of 1876.

To the west of the town centre are two reminders of the Ottoman era. One is the Bezisten, an oblong, stone-built market hall where traders from Dubrovnik set out their stalls. The other is the huge **Tombul Mosque**. This masterpiece of Ottoman architecture is the largest functioning mosque in the country. It was built in 1744, and the interior is decorated with wall paintings in which plant motifs are entwined with lines from the Koran written in elegant Kufic script. In the west wing of the mosque is a Koranic school, with a beautiful arcaded courtyard in the centre of which is a canopied fountain for ritual washing.

Dominating the Ilchov bair ridge immediately south of the town centre (accessible via a steep flight of steps) is the **Monument to the Creators of the Bulgarian State**. This was erected in 1981 to mark the 1,300th anniversary of Bulgar Khan Asparuh's arrival in the Balkans (see p46). Its central tower is adorned with reliefs of Asparuh and his successors. An audiovisual display describes the glories of the medieval kingdom of Bulgaria.

Crowning a hill about 3 km (2 miles) west of the town centre is **Shumen Fortress** (Shumenska krepost). This defensive construction was a major component of the ring of castles built to defend Pliska and Preslav, capitals of the First Bulgarian Kingdom. The outer walls have been partially rebuilt, and give an idea of what the fortress looked like in the 14th century.

History Museum
bul. Slavyanski 17. **Tel** (054) 063 429. **Open** summer: 9am–6pm daily; winter: 9am–5pm Mon–Fri, by prior arrangement on Sat & Sun.

Tombul Mosque
ul. G.S. Rakovski 21. **Tel** (054) 802 875. **Open** 9am–6pm daily.

Monument to the Creators of the Bulgarian State
Ilchov bair. **Tel** (054) 872 107. **Open** May–Sep: 8am–8pm daily; Oct–Nov: 8:30am–5pm daily.

Shumen Fortress
Tel (054) 875 487. **Open** 9am–5pm daily.

⑲ Madara
Мадара

12 km (7 miles) E of Shumen. **Map** F2. 1,300. from Shumen & Varna.

With sheer cliffs towering above it, the village of Madara is one of the most compelling historical locations in Bulgaria. Central to the site's mystique is the Madara Horseman, an 8th- or 9th-century relief carved into the rockface above the village. It depicts a king on horseback,

The courtyard, with central fountain, at Tombul Mosque, in Shumen

accompanied by a hunting dog, striking a lion with his spear. Inscriptions in Greek beside and below the relief refer to the military campaigns of three Bulgar *Khans* – Tervel, Krumesis and Omurtag. Both a statement of dynastic power and a tribute to the gods of hunting and horsemanship, it is a powerful and charismatic piece of sculpture.

To its right, a path leads to the Cave of the Nymphs, an atmospheric limestone cavern with moss and trickling water, used as a shrine by Thracians in the 4th century BC. To the left of the horseman, a steep rock-cut stairway leads to the top of the cliff and out onto a plateau, where the scant ruins of an 8th-century Bulgar fortress can be explored.

⑳ Veliki Preslav
Велики Преслав

20 km (12 miles) SW of Shumen. **Map** E2. 8,950. from Shumen.

Lying immediately south of the modern town of Preslav, the old city of Veliki Preslav (Great Preslav) was the capital of Bulgaria from 893 to 969. It emerged as Bulgaria's spiritual centre soon after the country's conversion to Christianity in 865. Tsar Boris I retired to a monastery here in 889, and his son Simeon probably trained as a monk here. Veliki Preslav's days as state capital ended when Prince Svyatoslav of Kiev sacked it in 969.

The ruins of Veliki Preslav include two rings of fortifications built with huge blocks of stone. Inside are traces of civic buildings, a palace complex and a rotunda known as the Golden Church because of the gold-plated dome that once crowned it. An **Archaeological Museum** at the northern end of the site has a rich collection of medieval pottery and coins, and some delicate gold jewellery from the grave of a medieval noblewoman.

Archaeological Museum
Veliki Preslav. **Tel** (0538) 42630. **Open** 9am–5pm daily.

The Madara Horseman, an ancient relief carved in rock above Madara

BLACK SEA COAST

Golden sandy beaches with clear blue sea and hot summers with cloudless skies are the Black Sea coast's greatest attractions. Away from its resorts, which are crowded with visitors at the height of the season, lie stretches of wild coastline, small fishing villages and nature reserves that attract many migratory birds.

Sunny Beach, Golden Sands and Albena are the Black Sea coast's three major resorts. It is to these that the vast majority of summer visitors come. The coast's smaller resorts, such as Sveti Sveti Konstantin and Elena, and Rusalka, cater for those in search of quieter, smaller-scale, family-oriented facilities.

Traditional fishing and farming towns along the coast have begun to exploit the possibilities offered by their own glorious stretches of sand. Here, hotels and apartment blocks have sprung up with startling alacrity, and tourism now accounts for much of the region's revenue. Although many of these hotels are brash, large-scale commercial concerns, there are also smaller, family-run establishments. These usually offer a friendlier alternative to the large resorts. In ancient times, the Black Sea coast was a thriving hub of trade. Originally populated by sophisticated Thracians, it was later colonized by Greek traders until the Romans took control of much of the coast in the 1st century BC. The coast was conquered by both the First and Second Bulgarian Kingdoms, and it is to the latter period that Nesebûr's small 13th- to 14th-century churches belong. After the cultural stagnation of centuries of Ottoman rule, the National Revival of the mid-19th century inspired the construction of the picturesque half-timbered houses in Sozopol and Nesebûr.

Today, the region is still in a period of transition. Construction continues apace and, with massive investment in tourist facilities and infrastructure, the Black Sea coast seems set to maintain its popularity in the future.

The beach at Golden Sands, one of the largest and most popular resorts on the Black Sea coast

◀ Picturesque rocky headlands found in parts of the northern Black Sea coast

Exploring the Black Sea Coast

With long sandy beaches and a pleasant climate, Bulgaria's Black Sea coast is the country's main holiday region. Major resorts include Albena, Golden Sands, Varna and Sunny Beach. Away from these centres, the coastline is much less developed. To the north, it is wild and rocky, while to the south lies the wilderness of Strandzha Nature Park. The coast is also a stopping place for migrating birds, thousands of which rest or overwinter in the wetlands around Durankulak, Pomorie and Burgas. Settled by Greek traders in the 6th century BC, the coast has a rich history. A glimpse of its fascinating past is revealed at the Archaeological Museum in Varna, and in the ancient towns of Kaliakra, Nesebûr and Sozopol, now popular holiday resorts.

Ceiling painting at the Church of Sveti Atanas in Varna

Steep cliffs on the headland at Cape Emona, between Obzor and Sunny Beach

Sights at a Glance

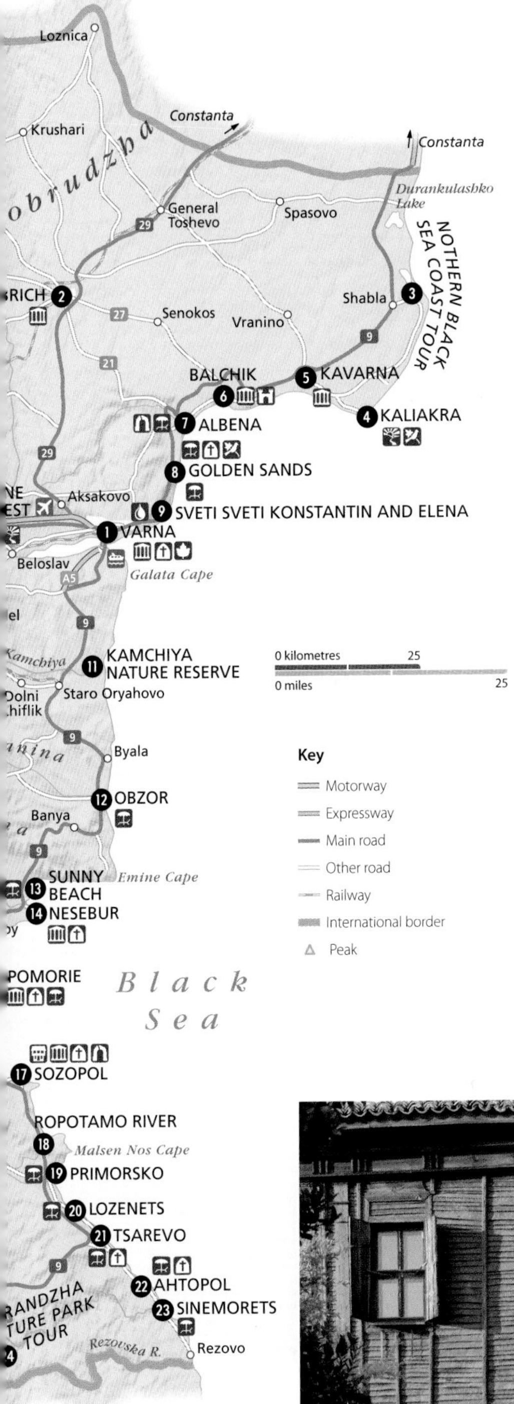

Loznica

Krushari

Constanta

Constanta

o b r u d z h a

General Toshevo

Spasovo

Durankulashko Lake

NOTHERN BLACK SEA COAST TOUR

RICH **2**

Senokos

Vranino

Shabla **3**

BALCHIK 5 KAVARNA

6

7 ALBENA

4 KALIAKRA

8 GOLDEN SANDS

Aksakovo

9 SVETI SVETI KONSTANTIN AND ELENA

NE EST

Beloslav

1 VARNA

Galata Cape

el

Kamchiya

11 KAMCHIYA NATURE RESERVE

Dolni hiflik

Staro Oryahovo

nina

Byala

12 OBZOR

Banya

a

13 SUNNY BEACH

Emine Cape

14 NESEBUR

oy

POMORIE

B l a c k S e a

17 SOZOPOL

ROPOTAMO RIVER

18

Malsen Nos Cape

19 PRIMORSKO

20 LOZENETS

21 TSAREVO

22 AHTOPOL

23 SINEMORETS

RANDZHA TURE PARK TOUR

Rezovska R.

Rezovo

| 0 kilometres | 25 |
| 0 miles | 25 |

Key

═══ Motorway

═══ Expressway

─── Main road

─── Other road

┄┄ Railway

▓▓▓ International border

△ Peak

Beach at Golden Sands, one of Bulgaria's most popular resorts

Getting Around

Whether you reach the Black Sea coast by plane, train, bus or car, your starting point will be Burgas or Varna. Burgas is the gateway to Sunny Beach, Nesebûr, Sozopol and the Strandzha region, while from Varna a road leads north to Golden Sands, Albena, Balchik and beyond. The region has an extensive bus network, with frequent services between and around Burgas and Varna. Further north and south, however, bus services are progressively sparser and less frequent. In summer, these outlying regions are served by minibuses, although they run according to demand rather than to a set timetable. Taxis are ubiquitous, and all large towns and resorts have car hire agencies.

Wooden house in Sozopol's historic district, on the peninsula

For additional map symbols *see back flap*

❶ Varna
Варна

With wide pedestrianized boulevards, shady Sea Gardens, and a sandy beach, Varna has the tranquil air of a coastal resort, despite its being a centre of commerce and Bulgaria's third-largest city. As Varna's remarkable ancient necropolis shows, the city's history goes back to the 5th millennium BC. In the 6th century BC, it was settled by Greeks. The thriving colony fell to the Romans in the 1st century BC, but retained its role as one of the Black Sea's key ports. Varna became part of Bulgaria in the 8th century. It was taken by the Ottomans in 1393, but after the Liberation of 1878 it rapidly grew to become the bustling modern city, port and resort that it is today.

🏛 Archaeological Museum

bul. Maria Luisa 41. **Tel** (052) 681 011.
Open summer: 10am–5pm Tue–Sun; winter: 10am–5pm Tue–Sat. 🅿 📷 📱 📷 **W** amvarna.com

Over 100,000 ancient artifacts discovered in and around Varna fill this fascinating museum. It was founded in 1888 by the Czech archaeologist Karel Skorpil, who settled in Varna after the Liberation and pioneered the exploration of Bulgaria's ancient past.

The collection fills 40 rooms on two floors. The most intriguing section is that devoted to Varna's necropolis, west of the modern city. It was in use from 4400 to 4200 BC, and was discovered in 1972. Many of the 294 graves that were excavated contained some stunning gold objects, among which were some of the earliest examples of gold jewellery ever found. No fewer than 850 pieces, including gold animal figures, were found in a single grave. Visitors can also see the replica of a grave in which the body of a powerful leader or a priest was covered with gold items such as a penis sheath, and surrounded with copper and flint tools.

Another important exhibit is the gold jewellery of a Thracian noblewoman. Dating from the Hellenistic period (4th–1st century BC), it consists of a bull's-head pendant and two beautifully detailed earrings that are miniature statuettes of Nike, goddess of victory. Among the many Roman artifacts in the

Archaeological Museum exhibit

collection is a large array of marble tombstones carved with scenes of funeral banquets.

The museum's upper floor is devoted to the medieval period. Here visitors can see a fine display of pottery, weaponry, jewellery and religious art, including some superb altarpieces with silver motifs, and a collection of radiant icons of the 16th to the 19th centuries.

⛪ Cathedral of the Assumption

pl. SS Kiril i Metodii. **Tel** (052) 613 005. **Open** 8am–6pm daily. 🕐 8:30am daily, also 6pm Sat. 📷

The second-largest place of Christian worship in Bulgaria after the Alexander Nevski Memorial Church in Sofia (see pp76–7), the cathedral was built to commemorate the Russian soldiers who died in the fight for liberation from Ottoman rule. Its construction was funded by Varna's citizens, and it was

completed in 1886. Designed by the Russian architect Maas, with golden onion domes, the cathedral is similar to St Petersburg's cathedral. Its surprisingly compact interior is covered with over-life-size murals painted under the supervision of another Russian, Professor Rostovtsev, in 1949. Master craftsmen from Debur, in Macedonia, carved the splendid bishop's throne, which features a pair of winged panthers, and created the vast iconostasis in 1912. Hearing the cathedral's male-voice choir, which

[Map of Varna showing Varna Airport, SOFIA, Cathedral of the Assumption, Clock Tower, Market, Stoyan Bachvarov Drama Theatre & Varna Opera-House, Ethnographic Museum, Train Station, and streets including BUL VARNENCHIK, BULEVARD MARIA LO, PRESLAV, DRAGOMAN, etc.]

```
Varna Airport
8 km (5 miles)
✈ SOFIA                    GENERAL KOLEV
                                          Archaeol
                                          Mu
        BUL VARNENCHIK    BULEVARD    DRAGOMAN
                                        BULEVARD MARIA LO
        ✚
              ② Cathedral of
                 the Assumption      BDIN
        ℹ                                        PETAR PARC
              PL                    DRAGOMAN
              MITROPOLIT                          SHIKAR
              SIMEON      PL          SHUMEN
                          NEZAVI-
              Clock        SIMOST
              Tower    ROUSSE
Market                              PL
                                    NEZAVI-
                  Stoyan Bachvarov  SIMOST
        PRAGA     Drama Theatre &              KNYAZ BO
                  Varna Opera-House    PRESLAV
        KAP PETKO VOIVODA
                          DEBAR
        KRALI MARKO    DR ZAMENHOF
                                    S VRACHANSKI
              DEBAR    TSAR SIMEON
                                    Ethnographic  P
                                    Museum ③  TSARIBROD
                                              DRUZ

0 metres          400
0 yards           400
                          Train Station
                          200 m (220 yards)
                          ← BUL
```

Iconostasis, made by Macedonian craftsmen, Cathedral of the Assumption

sings at weekend services, is a memorable experience.

🏛 Ethnographic Museum

ul. Panagyurishte 22. **Tel** (052) 630 588.
Open May–Oct: 10am–5pm daily;
Nov–Apr: 10am–5pm Tue–Sat. 🅿 📷

In an imposing 19th-century National Revival-style house surrounded by high stone walls, this is one of Bulgaria's largest ethnographic museums. The ground floor is dedicated to farming, with displays of tools used for sowing, harvesting and threshing, and beekeeping and viniculture.

In the rooms upstairs, traditional costumes are on display. Among them are the single-colour costumes that were predominant in the Varna region until settlers introduced multicoloured outfits. This section includes a wedding scene of costumed dummies, with the bride in a wooden wedding sled, men in black hats, and the village matchmaker, who holds a black cockerel.

VISITORS' CHECKLIST

Practical Information
380 km (235 miles) E of Sofia.
Map G2. 🚉 343,500. 🛈 sv. Kiril i
Metodiy (052 820 690). 🛒 daily.
🎭 Varnensko Lyato (Varna
Summer; Jul–Sep).

Transport
✈ 🚆 🚋 🚌 Ⓜ

The church contains Varna's oldest icon, a 13th-century depiction of the Virgin, whose silver plating has been worn smooth by the lips of believers who venerated and prayed to her. The elaborate iconostasis was carved by craftsmen from Debur in Macedonia, who provided the wood-work for the Cathedral of the Assumption.

Part of the Roman Thermae, a baths complex of the 2nd–4th centuries AD

🏛 Roman Thermae

ul. Han Krum. **Open** summer:
10am–5pm Tue–Sun; winter:
10am–5pm Tue–Sat. 🅿

A monument to the ingenuity of Roman architects, this huge public baths complex covers over 7,000 sq m (75,000 sq ft). It was built in the 2nd century AD for what was then the Roman city of Odessos.

Although in ruins, enough of the complex survives to give an idea of Roman bathing habits. Having disrobed in the *apodyteria* (dressing rooms), visitors would pass through to the *frigidarium* (cold pool), *tepidarium* (warm pool), and *caldarium* (hot pool), then repeat the process. Warm air circulated in cavities between the walls and under the floors, and doorways were staggered so as to prevent cold draughts. The cost of the baths' upkeep is thought to have caused their decline in the 3rd–4th centuries.

On the top floor of the museum is the re-creation of a Gagauz farmer's house. The Gagauz are a Turkish-speaking Christian people who settled on the Black Sea coast in the 12th century. There are still Gagauz villages around Varna today, but few Gagauz still speak their original language. Also on this floor is a re-created interior of the house of a wealthy early 20th-century family, furnished in a combination of Oriental and European styles.

🏛 Church of the Assumption

ul. Han Krum 19. **Tel** (052) 633 925.
Open 7:30am–6pm daily.
🏛 10am Sun.

This tiny church is known to local people as the Little Virgin (*Malka Bogoroditsa*). It was built in 1602, and is set below ground level, in accordance with the requirement that churches should be no higher than a man on horseback, lest they outshine mosques. The church's attractive wooden bell tower was added after the Liberation.

Sights at a Glance

1. Archaeological Museum
2. Cathedral of the Assumption
3. Ethnographic Museum
4. Church of the Assumption
5. Roman Thermae
6. Church of Sveti Atanas
7. City History Museum
8. Museum of Medical History
9. Navy Museum
10. Armenian Church
11. City Art Gallery
12. Sea Gardens
13. Evksinograd Palace

⛪ Church of Sveti Atanasii

ul. Graf Ignatiev 19. **Tel** (052) 639 716.
Open summer: 7:30am–6pm daily;
winter 8am–5pm daily. ✝ 9am Sun.

Peaceful gardens next to the
Roman Thermae *(see p203)*
are the setting of this National
Revival church. The focal point
of the interior is a dramatic
iconostasis that is completely
covered with intricately carved
figures and motifs. It was made
in the 19th century by master
woodcarvers from Tryavna, who
also made the richly decorated
bishop's throne and pulpit.
Originally built in the late
17th century, the church was
destroyed by fire in 1836 and
was rebuilt in 1838.

🏛 City History Museum

ul. 8 Noemvri 3. **Tel** (052) 632 677.
Open Nov–Apr: 10am–5pm
Tue–Sat.

This building, constructed in
1851 as the Belgian Consulate, is
one of Varna's oldest surviving
houses. The museum that it now
accommodates traces the history
of Varna from the late 18th
century, when it was a
neglected coastal town,
to the mid-20th, when
it had become a
major port
and popular
seaside resort.
    Some of the most
interesting exhibits
here are the tools
and implements
used by Varna's
craftsmen and
tradesmen of the
past. Photographs provide other
historical documentation.
Upstairs are the uniforms and
military paraphernalia of Varna's
citizens who fought in the
Serbo-Bulgarian War, Balkan
Wars, and both world wars.

Printing press at the City
History Museum, Varna

🏛 Museum of Medical History

ul. Paraskeva Nikolau 7. **Tel** (052) 639
729. **Open** 10am–4pm Mon–Fri.

The somewhat gruesome
collection of the Museum of
Medical History occupies a
building that was once Varna's
first hospital, opened in 1869.
An array of 10th-century skulls
and skeletons demonstrate
mysterious practices such as
deliberate deformation of the
skull by binding it, and
trepanation (the practice
of drilling holes in the skull).
    Upstairs is an exhibition of folk
medicine, the only kind of
medical treatment that was
available under Ottoman rule.
Surgical instruments are displayed
alongside antique examination
chairs and the re-creation of a
19th-century pharmacy.

🏛 Navy Museum

bul. Primorski 20. **Tel** (052) 632 018.
Open summer: 10am–6pm Wed–Sun;
winter: 9am–5:30pm Tue–Sat.

The prize exhibit here is the
Druzhki (Intrepid), a torpedo boat
displayed outside the museum.
In 1912, during the First Balkan
War, the *Druzhki* secured the
Bulgarian navy's
only victory in
the conflict
when it sank
a large Turkish
cruise ship,
the *Hamidie*.
Inside the
museum are
exhibits
relating to
navigation on
the Black Sea in ancient times,
starting in the 6th century BC.
There are also models of mines
and battleships, and photographs of great naval figures.
    The yard behind the museum
is filled with an assortment of

helicopters, artillery cannon and
boats, and a working submarine
periscope, through which visitors
can admire views of Varna Bay.

Nave and main altar at the Armenian
Church, Varna

⛪ Armenian Church

ul. Han Asparuh 15. **Tel** (052) 619 382.
Open 8am–6pm daily. ✝ 10:30am Sun.

Built in 1842, this light, airy
church was renovated in 2003.
Like most Armenian churches,
the interior is quite plain, with
no iconostasis, murals or icons.
However, the walls are hung with
naïve paintings of St Sargis, to
whom the church is dedicated,
and scenes from the life of Christ.
Recordings of Armenian chanting,
which play throughout the day,
create a magical atmosphere.
    A monument commemorates
Ottoman atrocities against the
Armenians in 1894 when an
estimated 300,000 were killed.
Known as the "Great Massacres",
they were overshadowed by the
1915 genocide which claimed
over 1.5 million lives.

🏛 City Art Gallery

ul. Lyuben Karavelov 1. **Tel** (052) 612
363. **Open** 10am–5pm Tue–Sun.

This collection concentrates on
the development of Bulgarian
painting since the early 20th
century. Several works by
Vladimir Dimitrov (1882–1960)
are on display, and there are also
portraits by the 17th-century
Flemish painter Anselmus von
Hulme. The gallery also hosts
temporary exhibitions of Bulgarian
and international art. The main
hall is often used as a venue for
concerts and poetry readings.

The torpedo boat *Druzhki* at the entrance of the Navy Museum in Varna

For hotels and restaurants in this region see pp227 and pp240–41

Varna's popular Sea Gardens, above the town's long sandy beach

Sea Gardens

Aquarium Tel (052) 632 064.
Open May–Sep: 9am–8pm daily;
Oct–Apr: 9am–5pm daily.
Planetarium Tel (052) 684 441.
Call ahead to book group shows.
Zoo Open May–Sep: 8am–8pm daily;
Oct–Apr: 8:30am–4:30pm daily.
Dolphinarium Tel (052) 302 199.
Open shows at 10:30am, noon, 3:30pm,
5pm in summer, at noon in winter.
dolphinarium.festa.bg
Terrarium Tel (052) 302 571.
Open 9am–9pm daily.

The Sea Gardens' (Morskata
Gradina) first trees were planted
in 1862. The Czech landscape
architect Anton Novak spent
much of his life laying out this
urban park, with trees and
plants from Bulgaria and from
around the Mediterranean. With
neat flowerbeds and shaded
paths, the gardens provide
welcome respite from the
sweltering summer heat.

Closest to the centre of the
gardens is the ivy-covered
Aquarium, whose graceful pair
of stingrays are the stars of a
somewhat neglected collection.
Further along, the **Planetarium**
offers daily shows in various
languages. To reach the **Zoo** it is
best to take the road train that
winds its way through the park
on a 2-km (1-mile) circuit. The
zoo's inhabitants range from
camels and deer to emus and
pelicans. Although they seem
content enough, they are
housed in fairly cramped
concrete quarters. Nearby is the
Dolphinarium, where dolphins
entertain audiences with games
of basketball and a variety of

tricks. A little way beyond is the
Terrarium, with a spine-tingling
collection of black widow spiders
and venomous snakes, and a
crocodile, among other reptiles.

Varna's long sandy beach
stretches out below the Sea
Gardens. As it is lined with
outdoor restaurants, cafés and
bars, it is not particularly
peaceful but it is ideal for
sybaritic days of swimming,
sunbathing, eating and
drinking. After dark, the beach is
one of the Black Sea's liveliest
spots, with clubs pumping out
loud music until the small hours.

Evksinograd Palace

8 km (5 miles) north of central Varna.
Tel (052) 393 140. **Open** 10am–3pm
Mon–Fri, 9am–2pm Sat & Sun, only for
pre-booked groups of at least 5.

The spectacular Evksinograd
Palace and its beautiful gardens
are located in Varna's northern
suburbs, on the main road out of
the city. The palace grounds also
incorporate the Evksinograd
winery, which produces some of
Bulgaria's finest wines and *rakiyas*.

This chateau-like palace was
built for Prince Aleksandûr
Batenberg I *(see p51)* and was
completed in 1886. It was
designed by the Viennese
architect Rumpelmeyer and its
gardens were laid out by French
landscape designers in the late
19th century.

The palace was the summer
residence of Bulgarian royalty
until the Communists came to
power in 1944. It then became
the holiday home of the party
élite. It is still state property.

❷ Dobrich
Добрич

93 km (60 miles) SE of Silistra, 55 km (34
miles) NW of Varna. Map F2. 90,375.
from Varna or Sofia. dobrich.bg

Dobrich lies at the centre of a rich
agricultural region that is known
as Bulgaria's breadbasket.
The largely modern town
centre encloses an open-air
ethnographic complex, Stariya
Dobrich (Old Dobrich). It contains
about 30 workshops, where
artisans practise traditional crafts,
and a café that serves Turkish
coffee accompanied by a
spoonful of *sladko* (cherry jam).

The small **Archaeological
Museum** in the complex
contains gold jewellery from a
necropolis of the 5th millennium
BC. The **Ethnographic Museum**
has displays of folk costumes and
traditional embroidery, and a
traditional cottage garden.

Dobrich's **Art Gallery** contains
paintings by many major
Bulgarian painters, including
Vladimir Dimitrov-Maistora
and Zlatyu Boyadzhiev.

Archaeological Museum
ul. Konstantin Stoilov 18. **Tel** (058) 603
256. **Open** summer: 9am–6pm Mon–
Fri; winter: 8am–5pm Mon–Fri; by
request on Sat & Sun.

Ethnographic Museum
ul. Alen Mak 5. **Tel** (058) 602 642.
Open See Archaeological
Museum.

Art Gallery
ul. Bulgaria 14. **Tel** (058) 604 602.
Open See Archaeological Museum.

Fertility, a painting by Keazim Issinov at the
Art Gallery in Dobrich

❸ Northern Black Sea Coast Tour

Thanks to its rocky shore and short summer, the northern Black Sea coast has escaped intensive development. In this flat landscape, fields of sunflowers and wheat stretch for miles in every direction. The coast is punctuated with sleepy villages, whose inhabitants still subsist from small-scale fishing and farming. Dramatic cliffs line the wide sandy beaches of Krapets. This part of the Black Sea coast is also rich in bird and plant life, and is littered with archaeological remains.

Tips for Drivers

Map G2. **Length of route**: approximately 40 km (25 miles). **Stopping-off points**: There are hotels, guesthouses, campsites, restaurants and cafés along the route, but most especially in Kavarna, Shabla and Krapets. **Place of further interest**: The Archaeological Park on an island in Durankulak Lake has remains of prehistoric habitation.

① Durankulak

Located on the Via Pontica, the nature reserve at Durankulak Lake attracts thousands of migratory birds. Species include the white pelican, bittern and pygmy cormorant, and most of the world's red-breasted geese.

② Cape Shabla Lighthouse

This red and white lighthouse marks the headland, where there is a small settlement, east of the village of Shabla some 5 km (3 miles) inland.

③ Tyulenovo

The village's tiny harbour shelters clusters of colourful fishing boats. Rusting oil tanks dotted all over the surrounding grassy clifftops pump out hot sulphuric mineral water.

④ Kamen Briag

The village of Kamen Briag is set on limestone cliffs riddled with caves. An Eternal Flame, fed by natural gas rising from deep below, burns near memorials to people who have fallen from the cliffs.

⑤ Yailata

Cave dwellings, a cliffside necropolis and a ruined medieval fortress are preserved in the archaeological park here. The park is also home to many plants, birds and snakes.

⑥ Rusalka

The Holiday Village here is a tranquil and isolated resort. It's much quieter than those further south and caters for all ages.

Key

▬▬ Tour route
═══ Main road
─── Other road
– – Trail

Map labels: Constanta, 9, 2904, Staevtsi, Durankulak Lake, Vaklino, Krapets, Bozhanovo, Ezerets, Ezeretzko Lake, Shablensko Lake, Shabla, 9, Gorun, Poruchik Chunchevo, Kavarna, Sveti Nikola, 901, Kavarna

0 kilometres 5
0 miles 5

❹ Kaliakra
Калиакра

56 km (35 miles) from Dobrich.
Map G2. 🚌 **Open** 10am–7pm daily.
🖼️ 🚻 💻 🏪

Meaning "fine nose" in Greek, Kaliakra is a rocky promontory that extends 2 km (over 1 mile) into the sea. Locals attribute the reddish colour of its limestone cliffs to the blood of the many people who died in battles for control of this strategic point. The ruins of a grand fortress of the 4th century BC remain; it was successively held by Greeks, Romans, Bulgarians and Ottomans. According to legend, 40 maidens tied their hair together and jumped into the sea to escape a worse fate at the hands of invading Ottoman soldiers.

Ruins of the fortress at Kaliakra, subject of many legends

❺ Kavarna
Каварна

61 km (38 miles) north of Varna.
Map G2. 🚍 11,600. 🚌 🚏 🏖️ daily.
ℹ️ ul. Dobrotitsa 27 (0570-81818).
🌐 **kavarna.bg**

Although its main street is dominated by dour Socialist-era architecture, Kavarna is a pleasant town, with lively cafés and bars. Its origins go back to the 6th century BC, when a settlement known as Bizone was founded by Greek colonists. Bizone thrived until it was flattened by an earthquake in the 1st century BC. Later rebuilt, it was ruled successively by Romans, Slavs and Ottomans.

Since the Middle Ages the town has been known as Kavarna. Liberated from Ottoman rule in 1878, the town became part of Romania in 1913. It was returned to Bulgaria in 1940.

Kavarna's **Ethnographic Museum**, in a National Revival house, features displays on the daily life of its 19th-century inhabitants. The **Art Gallery** has a collection of local seascapes and organizes exhibitions of the work of Bulgarian and international artists.

Artifacts related to sea trade in ancient times fill the **Marine Museum**, in a 15th-century *hammam* off the road to the seafront. Exhibits here include stone anchors, amphorae, coins and bronze figures. Immediately behind is the **History Museum**, which documents Kavarna's more recent past.

Just outside the town is the seafront district of Chirakman, a resort zone with restaurants, hotels and a small beach.

🏛️ **Ethnographic Museum**
ul. Sava Ganchev 16. **Tel** (0570) 85017.
Open 8am–noon, 1–5pm Mon–Fri.
🖼️ 🚻

🏛️ **Art Gallery**
ul. Aheloi 1. **Tel** (0570) 84236.
Open See Ethnographic Museum. 🖼️

🏛️ **History Museum**
ul. Chernomorska 1b. **Tel** (0570) 82150. **Open** See Ethnographic Museum. 🖼️

🏛️ **Marine Museum**
ul. Chernomorska 1. **Tel** (0570) 84288.
Open See Ethnographic Museum. 🖼️

❻ Balchik
Балчик

43 km (27 miles) north of Varna.
Map G2. 🚍 12,500. ℹ️ ul. Primorska 25a (0579-76951). 🚌 🚏

Because it has only a small beach, Balchik does not attract crowds of visitors, so it remains pleasantly quiet throughout the summer. In Greek times, when it was a busy port and wine producer, Balchik

was known as Dionisopolis, in honour of the god of wine. Like Kavarna, it was part of Romania between 1913 and 1940.

Balchik's small **National Revival Complex** is set in pretty gardens next to the Church of Sveti Nikolai (1866). Its centrepiece is a re-creation of the town's first Bulgarian school, established in 1848. The small collection at the **History Museum** documents Balchik's past. Just opposite is a large half-timbered old house. This is the **Ethnographic Museum**, with costumes and exhibits relating to local trades. The **Art Gallery** has a collection of 20th-century paintings and sculptures related to Balchik. They include vivid modernist depictions of the town by Svetlin Rusev (b. 1933).

Statuette, Marine Museum, Kavarna

Environs
About 2 km (over 1 mile) outside Balchik is the delightful seafront **Palace of Queen Marie**. It was built in 1924 by King Ferdinand of Romania as a retreat for his British-born wife Marie, one of Queen Victoria's grand-daughters. The palace gardens contain Europe's second-largest collection of cacti.

🏛️ **National Revival Complex**
ul. Hristo Botev 4. **Tel** (0579) 72177.
Open summer: 9am–5pm Mon–Sat, by request on Sun; winter: 7:30am–4pm Mon–Fri. 🖼️

🏛️ **Ethnographic Museum**
ul. Dimitûr Zhelev 3. **Tel** (0579) 72177. **Open** See National Revival Complex. 🖼️

🏛️ **History Museum**
ul. Dimitûr Zhelev 2. **Tel** (0579) 72177. **Open** See National Revival Complex. 🖼️

🏛️ **Art Gallery**
ul. Otets Paisii 4. **Tel** (0879) 998 916.
Open 9am–noon, 1–5pm Mon–Fri. 🖼️

🏰 **Palace of Queen Marie**
2 km (over 1 mile) west of Balchik.
Tel (0579) 74552. **Open** summer: 8am–8pm daily; winter: 8:30am–5pm daily. 🖼️ 💻 🏪 🌐 **dvoreca.com**

Sun and relaxation on Albena's long sandy beach

Environs

About 7 km (4 miles) inland from Golden Sands is **Aladzha Monastery**. The hermits who settled here in the 6th century cut dozens of cells and chambers into the limestone cliff, and evidence of Stone Age dwellers has also been discovered here. The caves are now linked by sturdy metal steps, but the monks reached them by scrambling up and down perilous ledges using the footholds that are still visible in the cliff face.

❼ Albena

Албена

34 km (21 miles) N of Varna. **Map** G2.
🚌 🏨 🌐 albena.bg

Like Golden Sands and Sunny Beach, Albena's superb beach has received the Blue Flag award for its cleanliness. It is 5 km (3 miles) long and up to 500 m (550 yds) wide, and with shallow water for some distance offshore, it is perfect for water sports *(see p249)*.

Although Albena is a major resort, its hotels are spread over extensive parkland, giving it a spacious feel. It was built in the 1970s, with a tasteful planning ethic that resulted in buildings melding with the natural environment. Largely because of this (and its cleanliness) Albena has a calmer atmosphere than its neighbour Golden Sands. Besides water sports, Albena has a horse-riding centre, and offers driving safaris to Cape Emona, 150 km (90 miles) to the south.

Environs

Just outside the dusty village of Obrochishte, about 15 km (8 miles) inland from Albena, is the 16th-century **Ak Yazula Baba Tekke**. This pentagonal monastery contains the grave of Ak Yazula Baba, a 14th-century holy man who followed the dervish path of poverty and austerity and who was venerated by local Muslims. As it is also the alleged burial place of St Athanius and Knyaz Boris I, Bulgaria's first Christian ruler, the site is popular with Christians too.

❽ Golden Sands

Златни пясъци

18 km (11 miles) N of Varna. **Map** G2.
🚌 🏨 🌐 goldensands.bg

Bulgaria's second-largest coastal resort after Sunny Beach, Golden Sands (Zlatni Pyasåtsi) amply lives up to its name. Wooded hills, part of the Golden Sands Nature Park, slope down towards the sea and an almost continuous line of newly built hotels. In season, parasols in uniform grid patterns dominate the crowded beach and a full range of water sports is on offer.

Golden Sands' downside is that, as at Sunny Beach, rampant development has continued unchecked for years and the infrastructure has failed to keep pace. With few noise restrictions, loud music emanates from many nightclubs in the heart of the hotel zone, making this a paradise for some and a hell for others.

❾ SS Konstantin and Elena

Свети Константин и Елена

9 km (5 miles) N of Varna. **Map** G2.
🚌 🏨 🌐 stconstantine.bg

A far smaller coastal resort than its northern neighbours, Sveti Sveti Konstantin and Elena appeals to families in search of easily accessible facilities. The seafront has short beaches and rocky coves backed by a woodland. This gives the resort a tranquil atmosphere. Several of the hotel complexes along the seafront have hot mineral baths and saunas, and offer therapeutic massages.

In the heart of the resort is the tiny **Monastery of SS Konstantin and Elena**. It was founded in the 17th century but was destroyed during the Russo-Turkish War of 1828–9. Two brothers from Veliko Tŭrnovo *(see pp160–61)* rebuilt the monastery and, after the Liberation of 1878, it became

Visitors on the beach at the popular Golden Sands resort

For hotels and restaurants in this region see pp227 and pp240–41

Luxury health resort pool at Sveti Sveti Konstantin and Elena

a fashionable spot for weekend breaks. From 1946 its popularity led to the location being developed as Bulgaria's first beach resort.

🏠 Monastery of SS Konstantin and Elena

Tel (052) 362 076. **Open** 8am–6pm daily. 🆆 **varnamonastery.bg**

Massive tree-like pillars of the 50-million-year-old Stone Forest

❿ Stone Forest
Побитите камъни

18 km (11 miles) W of Varna, on the road to Devnya.

As its name suggests, the Stone Forest *(pobiti kamûni)* is a cluster of weirdly tree-like stone columns. Spread over a barren landscape, they stand in seven groups of more than 300 each. Some are as much as 6 m (20 ft) high and up to 9 m (30 ft) in circumference.

The stones are believed to be 50 million years old, and their origins have long been the subject of scientific speculation. From the numerous theories advanced by experts, it is generally agreed that they

formed when separate layers of chalk merged through a layer of sand. Some scientists, however, still support the theory that they are the fossilized trees of an ancient forest.

⓫ Kamchiya Nature Reserve
резерват "Камчия"

25 km (16 miles) S of Varna. **Map** F3.

Just before it reaches the sea, the Kamchiya, eastern Bulgaria's longest river, flows through the nature reserve that takes its name. Established in 1951, the reserve is internationally recognized as a site of ornithological importance. Its densely forested marshland, known as the Longoza, is home to an abundance of rare species, including pelicans and kingfishers. Regular boat trips take tourists up and down the river.

Just outside the reserve is a long sandy beach that has so far escaped development into a resort. It is therefore almost deserted, even at the height of summer, and this may explain its popularity with nudists.

⓬ Obzor
Обзор

62 km (39 miles) S of Varna.
Map F3. 🅰 1,970. 🚍 🏠
🆆 **grad-obzor.com**

Named Heliopolis (City of the Sun) by the Greeks and later occupied by the Romans, the small town of Obzor is now a thriving, if somewhat brash, coastal resort. Broken columns from the Roman Temple of Jupiter are scattered throughout the town's leafy park, which is surrounded by open-air restaurants and cafés.

Obzor's main attraction is its great beach, in the outskirts to the north. However, as developers are rapidly expanding it, this part of Obzor currently resembles a huge building site.

⓭ Sunny Beach
Слънчев бряг

35 km (22 miles) N of Burgas.
Map F3. 🚍 🚆 🚲
🆆 **sunnybeach-bg.com**

Established in the 1960s, Sunny Beach (Slûnchev bryag) was one of Bulgaria's first coastal resorts. It is now the country's largest, and it continues to expand in all directions. Palatial hotels, apartment blocks and Socialist-era leisure complexes stretch out behind a beautiful beach 8 km (5 miles) long.

Sunny Beach, which has Blue Flag status, is particularly popular with families and with visitors on package holidays. Besides a wide range of water sports, the resort also has a multitude of shops, bars, restaurants and nightclubs.

The Kamchiya River estuary, part of the pristine Kamchiya Nature Reserve

Statue of St Nicholas in the Nesebûr harbour, Black Sea coast ▶

⑭ Nesebûr
Несебър

Set on a rocky peninsula, Nesebûr's beautiful old town is densely packed with historic houses and churches. The site was first settled by Thracians, who founded a town known as Mesembria. It was later taken by Greeks and then by Romans, to whom it capitulated rather than suffer destruction. In the 9th century, when Mesembria was renamed Nesebûr, the town became part of the First Bulgarian Kingdom, but it was in the 13th to 14th centuries, as a powerful city-state, that it reached its commercial and cultural zenith. Today, as a well publicized World Heritage Site, Nesebûr is popular with visitors. Because of this it tends to become very crowded in the summer season.

Aerial view of Nesebûr, a town whose origins go back to Thracian times

🏛 Archaeological Museum
ul. Mesembriya 2a. **Tel** (0554) 46019. **Open** summer: 9am–8pm Mon–Fri, 9:30am–1:30pm, 2–7pm Sat & Sun; winter: 9am–5pm Mon–Fri, by request on Sat & Sun. 🅿 🚻 ⌂ 🔲 **ancient-nessebar.com**

The collections laid out here provide a fascinating insight into Nesebûr's long history. The displays begin with stone anchors and decorated pottery from the Thracian period (2nd–1st millennium BC), and coins minted in Mesembria in the 5th century BC, which indicate its independence and importance after it became a Greek colony in the 6th century BC. Other exhibits from this period include delicate gold jewellery from Mesembria's necropolis and architectural elements carved with swastikas symbolizing the sun. Red glazed pottery, marble grave-stones and reliefs of Hercules and Thracian horsemen are among exhibits representing the town's Roman period.

Nesebûr's prosperity during the Middle Ages is illustrated by a display of gold coins and gold jewellery, and some fine decorative architectural elements. The collections end with an outstanding array of icons from Nesebûr's churches, some from the 13th century.

⛪ Church of Christ Pantokrator
pl. Mesembriya. **Open** 9am–11pm daily. ⌂

This attractive church near the centre of the old town is typical of the churches built during Nesebûr's resurgence in the 13th and 14th centuries. The building's façade features a row of blind arches built with alternating courses of stone and brick, and with decorative motifs in the form of turquoise inlay and red brick swastika motifs. Inside is an art gallery selling works by local artists.

⛪ New Metropolitan Church Sveti Stefan
ul. Ribarska. **Open** summer: 9am–8pm Mon–Fri, 9:30am–1:30pm, 2–7pm Sat & Sun; by request in winter. 🅿 🚻 ⌂

Popularly known as the Church of Sveti Stefan, the New Metropolitan Church Sveti Stefan was founded in the 11th century. It supplanted the Old Metropolitan Church in the 15th century and was enlarged in the 16th.

The interior is breathtaking with its 16th- to 18th-century frescoes depicting scenes from the life of the Virgin. Other notable features of the interior are the 16th-century painted iconostasis, the ornate bishop's throne, and an elaborately carved 18th-century wooden pulpit.

⛪ Church of St John Aliturgitos
ul. Ribarska 12. ♿

This ruined church is set in an isolated spot overlooking the Black Sea, its east window framing stunning sea views. It was built in the 14th century and was reduced to ruins by an earthquake in 1913. Concrete pillars now support what remains of the roof. Built in stone and brick, the church has blind arches decorated with motifs, such as stars, squares and swastikas, which symbolize the sun and the continuity of life.

Façade of the Church of Christ Pantokrator, with Byzantine-style arches

Ruins of the Old Metropolitan Church, still the centrepiece of old Nesebûr

🏛 Ethnographic Museum
ul. Mesembriya 2. **Tel** (0554) 46019.
Open 10am–1pm, 2–6pm Mon–Sat.

Occupying Muskoyanin House, the Ethnographic Museum re-creates domestic life as it was lived in this fine 18th-century residence. There is also a display of traditional local costumes worn for various seasonal rituals. They include a selection of *lazarki* outfits worn by young girls to celebrate the arrival of spring.

🏠 Old Metropolitan Church
ul. Mitropolska.

Although it is in ruins, the Old Metropolitan Church (Starata Mitropoliya) is still the focal point of Nesebûr's old town. The church, the oldest and largest in Nesebûr, was founded in the 5th century. It originally formed part of the bishop's palace, but was destroyed by Venetians in the 13th century. Only part of its walls survive. A two-tiered brick and stone arcade culminates in a large central apse that is now a popular meeting point and the venue for plays and concerts.

🏠 Church of Sveta Paraskeva
ul. Venera 9. **Open** 8am–10pm daily.

The Byzantine style of this 13th-century church is very similar to that of the Church of Christ Pantokrator. Green ceramics set between layers of red brick and stone decorate the façade's blind arches. The church now houses a private art gallery that sells seascapes painted by local artists.

🏠 Church of Sveti Spas
ul. Briz 6. **Open** summer: 10am–5pm Mon–Fri, 10am–3pm Sat & Sun; by request in winter.

Like many others built during the Ottoman period, the 17th-century Church of Sveti Spas (Church of the Saviour) is set below street level. The exterior is plain, but within are colourful frescoes, most of which show scenes from the lives of Christ and the Virgin. A curiosity of the frescoes is that some have been marked with graffiti of sailing boats. They were created by sailors praying for safety at sea. The floor also houses a Byzantine princess's gravestone.

VISITORS' CHECKLIST

Practical Information
Map F3. 🚗 8,700.
ℹ ul. Mesembriya 10 (0554 42611). 🏠 daily.

Transport
🚌 from Sunny Beach, Burgas, and Varna (in summer).
⛴ Sunny Beach.

Early 17th-century frescoes in the Church of Sveti Spas

Nesebûr Old Town
① Archaeological Museum
② Church of Christ Pantokrator
③ New Metropolitan Church
④ Church of St John Aliturgetos
⑤ Ethnographic Museum
⑥ Old Metropolitan Church
⑦ Church of Sveta Paraskeva
⑧ Church of Sveti Spas

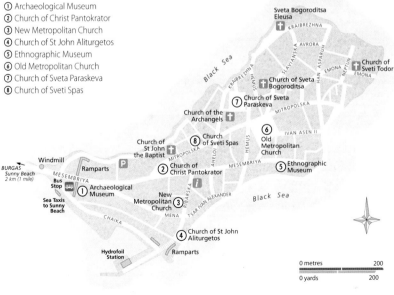

0 metres 200
0 yards 200

For map symbols see back flap

⓯ Pomorie
Поморие

20 km (12 miles) N of Burgas. **Map** F3.
🏘 13,650. 🚌 🚍 🛥 daily.

Today, as in ancient times, Pomorie is known for its salt pans and its dry white wine, *Pomoriiski dimyat*. Largely destroyed by fire in 1906, this coastal town was rebuilt in the 1950s, which explains the rather unsightly concrete buildings that line its streets. One survivor of the fire is the Church of the Transfiguration (1763), with 17th-century icons.

Next to Lake Pomorie, just outside the town, a working salt pan at the **Salt Museum** accompanies an exhibition about the trade in "white gold" that brought the town prosperity. The lake itself is a magnet for birdwatchers, who come to spot storks and pelicans resting here on their migration route across the Black Sea.

🏛 Salt Museum
Tel (0596) 25344. **Open** summer: 8am–6pm Mon–Fri, 10am–6pm Sat & Sun; winter: 8am–4pm Mon–Fri. ♿ ♿

Salt pans at the Salt Museum on the outskirts of Pomorie

⓰ Burgas
Бургас

160 km (100 miles) S of Varna. **Map** F3.
🏘 200,300. ✈ ⛴ 🚉 🚌 🚍 🛥 daily. 🌐 bourgas.net

Although it tends to be overlooked as Varna's *(see pp202–3)* ugly sister, Burgas is in fact a pleasant city, whose pedestrianized centre has benefited from recent refurbishment. In the early 1800s, Burgas

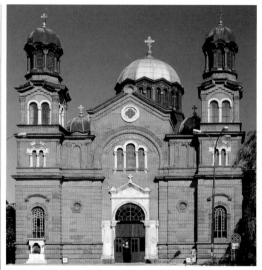
The Church of SS Kiril i Metodii in Burgas, completed in 1905

was depopulated after attacks by *kŭrzdhalii* bandits, but by the mid-19th century it had recovered to enjoy an economic boom based on craftsmanship and the export of grain.

Burgas has several fine churches and interesting museums. The **Ethnographic Museum**, in a 19th-century house, contains a collection of local traditional costume, including women's aprons whose distinctive and colourful designs were unique to their villages. Also on display are some intimidating *kukeri* costumes *(see p106)*, complete with bells and wooden swords. Nearby is the bulky **Church of SS Kiril i Metodii**, designed by Ricardo Toskanini, the Italian architect who strongly influenced Burgas's architecture in the early 20th century. At the **Natural History Museum** visitors can see a glittering array of Bulgarian minerals and giant Brazilian crystals, as well as butterflies, insects, crustaceans and stuffed mammals.

On the corner of ulitsa Mitropolit and ulitsa Lermontov, the little Armenian Church (variable opening hours) is a striking sight. Its attractive exterior belies its dour interior. Built in 1853, it serves Burgas's small Armenian community.

Close by is the **Archaeological Museum**. Its small but captivating display begins with axe heads, stone anchors and knives dating back ten thousand years. Bronze Age pottery is followed by various items from the period of Greek colonization. The most striking exhibits are a gold necklace and earrings found at the cremation site of a Thracian priestess. Burgas's **Art Gallery**, in a former synagogue, offers the opportunity to see some fine 18th- and 19th-century icons, as well as works by modern Bulgarian painters and local artists.

Just outside the town centre, at the far end of bulevard Bogoridi, are the attractive Sea Gardens. They were laid out in 1910, with open-air cafés and restaurants that command sea views. Some intriguing Eastern-bloc sculptures of the 1970s are dotted about between flowerbeds.

Environs
Just outside Burgas, on the road to Sozopol, is **Lake Poda**, a haven for rare birds and plants. Managed by the Bulgarian Society for the Preservation of Birds, the lake and its environs are of international importance as a habitat for breeding colonies of spoonbills, ibises and herons.

iii Ethnographic Museum
ul. Slavianska 69. **Tel** (056) 842 587.
Open summer: 10am–5:30pm Mon–
Fri, 10am–6pm Sat; winter: 9am–5pm
Mon–Fri.

⬆ Church of SS Kiril i Metodii
pl. Sveti Kiril i Metodii. **Open** variable.
8am, 9am Sun.

iii Natural History Museum
ul. Fotinov 30. **Tel** (056) 843 239.
Open 10am–5:45pm Mon–Sat.
burgasmuseums.bg

iii Archaeological Museum
ul. Bogoridi 21. **Tel** (056) 843 541.
Open 10am–5:45pm Mon–Sat.
burgasmuseums.bg

iii Art Gallery
ul. Mitropolit Simeon 24. **Open** 9am–
noon, 2–6pm Mon–Fri.

⓱ Sozopol
Созопол

32 km (20 miles) S of Burgas. **Map** F3.
5,750. Apollonia Arts Festival (first 10
days in Sep). sozopol.com

With sandy bays to the north
and south, Sozopol's historic old
town stands on a peninsula
jutting out into the Black Sea.
The cobbled streets of this
picturesque fishing port are
densely lined with attractive
old houses.

Ancient artifacts discovered
in the harbour area suggest
that the site has been inhabited
since the 5th millennium BC.
Thracians settled on the
peninsula in the 2nd millennium
BC, but it was from the early 7th
century BC, when it became the
Greek colony of Apollonia Pontica,
that this fishing port rose to
power and prosperity. Romans
conquered and destroyed the
town in 72 BC, and in AD 330
Apollonia was absorbed into
the Byzantine Empire. It was
then renamed Sozopolis
("Saved Town"), in reference
to its adoption of Christianity.

During the Middle Ages,
Sozopol was one of the First
Bulgarian Kingdom's major
ports, and, despite coming
under Ottoman rule in 1453, it
remained an important centre
of shipbuilding, commerce and
fishing until it was overtaken by
Burgas in the mid-19th century.

Wooden houses along a street in
Sozopol's old town

The collections in the
Archaeological Museum
document Sozopol's long history.
Amphorae of various shapes predominate, but there are also some
superb Greek pottery vessels
decorated with scenes that
celebrate Dionysus, god of wine
and pleasure. Upstairs there is a
fascinating display of figurines
from Apollonia's necropolis,
which was in use from the 4th
to the 3rd centuries BC. Simple
stone anchors of the 2nd–1st
millennium BC attest to early
trading relations between
the Thracians of Sozopol and
the eastern Mediterranean.

Remains of Sozopol's
fortifications, built from the 4th
to 14th centuries AD, form part
of the **South Fortress Wall and
Tower Museum**. Most of the
town's medieval churches were
destroyed in the Ottoman period,
but later examples remain.
Among them are the 15th-
century Church of Sveta
Bogoroditsa, with elaborate
wooden iconostases, and the

Church of Sveti Georgi (1836),
which has colourful icons. The
Church of Sveti Zosim, dedicated
to the Orthodox patron saint of
seafarers, has icons by Dimitar of
Sozopol, an artist of the National
Revival period. At the end of
the peninsula is Sozopol's **Art
Gallery**, with seascapes by
local artists. Sozopol hosts the
Apollonia Arts Festival
(see p40).

iii Archaeological Museum
pl. Han Krum 2. **Tel** (0550) 22226.
Open May–Oct: 8:30am–6pm daily;
Nov–Apr: 8:30am–12:30pm, 1:30–5pm
Mon–Fri.

**⬆ South Fortress Wall and
Tower Museum**
ul. Milet. **Tel** (0550) 220267.
Open 9:30am–9:30pm daily.

iii Art Gallery
ul. Kiril i Metodii 78. **Tel** (0550) 22202.
Open 10am–6pm Mon–Fri.

⓲ Ropotamo
Nature Reserve
резерват "Ропотамо"

18 km (11 miles) S of Sozopol. **Map** F4.
Open 9am–9pm daily.

The wide estuary of the
Ropotamo River forms part of
the Ropotamo Nature Reserve,
set up in 1940 to protect
extensive marshland and the
largest expanse of sand dunes
in Bulgaria. Covering 1,000 ha
(2,470 acres), the reserve is home
to over 200 species of birds and a
variety of rare plants and flowers,
including the endemic sand lily.
Regular boat trips carry tourists
along the river, where its famous
water lilies flower spectacularly
from June to October.

The estuary of the Ropotamo River, part of Ropotamo Nature Reserve

⓳ Primorsko
Приморско

55 km (34 miles) S of Burgas. **Map** F4. 3,700. daily.

This bustling town is set on a peninsula between two estuaries. With 10 km (6 miles) of sandy beaches to the north and south, it has long been a popular spot for holidaymakers. In high season the streets in the town centre are uncomfortably cluttered with souvenir stalls and the beaches are densely covered with parasols. But those who venture slightly further will find quiet creeks, pristine dunes and rocky pools, with the forested Strandzha Mountains in the background.

⓴ Lozenets
Лозенец

60 km (37 miles) S of Burgas. **Map** E4. 470.

Lozenets was once a quiet coastal backwater, but it has now become one of the Black Sea's most fashionable resorts. While wealthier visitors frequent the resort's small number of smart bars, restaurants and clubs on the main street, elsewhere simple garden restaurants cater to humbler holidaymakers.

The extensive beaches just north of Lozenets attract windsurfers and kitesurfers. Several watersports schools also operate here during the summer season.

Windsurfing in warm summer waters at the resort of Lozenets

㉑ Tsarevo
Царево

70 km (43 miles) S of Burgas. **Map** F4. 5,900. *i* in the bus station. daily.

Founded in the 7th century BC as a Greek colony, Tsarevo is now a well established beach resort, with a small harbour that bustles with fishing boats. On the promontory south of Tsarevo, well away from the noise and bustle of the town in high season, is the **Church of Uspenie Bogorodichno** (1810). It contains an impressive collection of 19th-century icons and from its pretty garden there are beautiful views of Tsarevo and its coastline. A long beach stretches away north of the town, but unfortunately much of it is being developed.

🏛 Church of Uspenie Bogorodichno
Vasiliko quarter. **Open** 8am–8pm daily. 8am, 9am Sun.

㉒ Ahtopol
Ахтопол

85 km (53 miles) S of Burgas. **Map** G4. 1,200. daily.

Set on a rocky peninsula at the foot of the Strandzha Mountains, Ahtopol is another popular coastal resort, with a large sandy beach on its northern side. In summer, the town centre becomes very crowded with Bulgarian holiday-makers as well as foreign visitors.

However, Ahtopol's old town offers greater tranquillity. The streets of this picturesque district are lined with wooden houses shaded by fig trees. The **Chapel of the Ascension**, built in 1796, contains brightly painted antique icons.

🏛 Chapel of the Ascension
ul. Briz. **Open** 8am–noon, 3:30–8:30pm daily.

Beach at Sinemorets, at the southern end of Bulgaria's Black Sea coastline

㉓ Sinemorets
Синеморец

90 km (56 miles) S of Burgas. **Map** G4. 260.

As it fell within Bulgaria's post-war border zone, Sinemorets was inaccessible during the Communist period. After 1989, the first visitors to come here found just a tiny village with pristine beaches. For a time, Sinemorets was the haven of young Bulgarians, who camped along the coast. But the village has now been discovered by the tourism industry and is suffering the same fate as coastal towns further north. Hotels and apartment blocks are springing up along the coast-line, but there are still unspoiled beaches south of the village.

Church of Uspenie Bogorodichno, on a promontory south of Tsarevo

㉔ Strandzha Nature Park Tour

Locked into Bulgaria's border zone until 1989, Strandzha's vast oak and beech forests escaped the ravages of logging. The park was created in 1995 and covers 1,160 sq km (450 sq miles) between the central Strandzha Mountains and the Black Sea. The five reserves within the park provide a secure habitat for endangered animals such as golden eagles, grey-headed woodpeckers, wolves, pine martens and otters. Rare plants include the Strandzha whortleberry, Caucasus primrose and cherry laurel.

Tips for Drivers

Road map F4.
Length of tour: approximately 55 km (34 miles).
Stopping-off places: There are guesthouses, restaurants, bars and cafés in Brushlyan. Also if there's time it's worth considering a detour to Gramatikovo.

① Bûlgari
This tiny hilltop village is renowned for its annual fire-dancing ceremony, which takes place on 3 and 4 June, the feast day of St Konstantin and St Elena.

② Silkossia Reserve
Bulgaria's oldest reserve, this is one of the few places in the country where the delightful Strandzha rhododendron flourishes. Its pinkish-mauve violet flowers blossom in May.

Tsarevo

907

Zabernovo

Kondolovo ①

②

9

Burgas

Veleka

Petrova Niva

H a s e k i y a t a

Gramatikovo

Kosti

⑤

98

Stoilovo

9

Avdere

Veleka

9

n Bratanova Cave

Kîrklareli

④

③

△ Gradishte 710m

Dense beech and oak forests
dominate the park. Strandzha's border zone location has protected its nature from destructive human activity.

③ Malko Tûrnovo
Interesting archaeological finds from the region, as well as items from the more recent past, fill the village's History Museum, in a National Revival building.

0 kilometres 5

0 miles 5

⑤ Brûshlyan
With attractive 18th-century wooden houses and a 17th-century walled and sunken church, the small village of Brûshlyan is an architectural reserve. Its church school and picturesque peasant dwellings are of particular interest.

④ Mishkova Niva
A Thracian burial ground and a Roman necropolis were discovered here. Of the park's many archaeological sites, this is one of the easiest to reach. Visits can be arranged through the History Museum in Malko Tûrnovo.

Key
▬▬ Tour route
══ Main road
⋯⋯ Other road
− − Trail
▬▬ International border
△ Peak

For additional map symbols *see back flap*

TRAVELLERS' NEEDS

WHERE TO STAY

From luxurious hotels in the major towns and cities to family-run B&Bs in rural areas, Bulgaria offers an ever-increasing choice of accommodation. In recent years there has been a boom in the construction of new hotels, especially in the four-star category and above. Sofia, Plovdiv, seaside towns and skiing resorts now offer accommodation ranging from convenient self-catering apartments to luxurious spa hotels. In rural areas, basic but comfortable accommodation, with traditional hospitality, is offered in private homes, and by the country's growing number of bed-and-breakfast establishments, very often situated in historic houses.

Hotels

There is a profusion of hotels in Sofia, on the Black Sea coast and in mountain skiing areas. In contrast, in parts of northern and central Bulgaria, where the tourist industry is not as well developed, the choice of accommodation is much more limited.

Bulgarian hotels are graded according to the international five-star system. Even so, the number of stars allocated to particular a establishment can sometimes seem a little too generous. As a general rule, a four-star hotel in Bulgaria is roughly equal to a three-star hotel elsewhere.

Rooms in most recently built hotels with a three-star rating or above have bathrooms with baths or shower cubicles. In some slightly older hotels, however, rooms still have old-style Bulgarian bathrooms with an open, un-curtained shower and a drain in the middle of the floor.

Room in the five-star Grand Hotel, in central Sofia *(see p222)*

In Sofia, in ski resorts and in coastal towns and cities, most hotels in the four-star category and above have a gym and a sauna and in many cases a swimming pool as well. Chic design hotels and boutique hotels are increasingly becoming evident in Bulgaria's main cities.

Nearly all Bulgarian hotels have satellite or cable television broadcasting programmes in the major European languages, although they may put an extra charge for access to premium film channels.

Spa Resorts

Many areas of Bulgaria are renowned for their natural mineral springs. Health tourism has long been popular here, and the growing popularity of spa and wellness travel has led to increasing provision of well-equipped four- and five-star spa hotels.

Bulgaria's main spa centres are Sandanski and Kyustendil, south of Sofia, Velingrad and Devin, in the Rhodope Mountains, and Albena and Sveti Sveti Konstantin and Elena, on the Black Sea coast. All have hotels with swimming pools filled either with warm water from mineral springs or with sea water, depending on their location. The hotels also have wellness centres with saunas and steam baths, and offer many beauty treatments.

Apartments

Self-catering apartments are an increasingly common feature on the Black Sea coast and in inland skiing resorts. Many form part of apartment hotels. These generally offer two-bedroom, family-size apartments or studios, but also provide the usual hotel facilities, such as a reception desk, chambermaids and, in many cases, a breakfast room. Many apartment owners advertise their accommodation on internet booking sites such as booking.com and hostelworld.com. Booking is relatively problem-free provided you read descriptions and user-reviews carefully before committing yourself.

Private Accommodation

In mountain and seaside areas, many Bulgarian families rent

Aquapark as seen from a hotel balcony at Sunny Beach, on the Black Sea

private rooms (*chastni kvartiri*) to visitors during the summer season. Compared to those of hotels, prices for rooms in private houses are very low and the hosts are usually extremely hospitable. However, bear in mind that you will be sharing your hosts' bathroom and that in most cases breakfast is not included in the price. Accommodation in private houses is organized by the tourist offices and travel agencies in each area. It can be booked on arrival at the location.

Bed and Breakfast

Family-run bed-and-breakfast establishments (B&Bs) are an increasingly common feature of rural or mountain regions. Although most B&Bs are in modern family homes, some, such as those in historic mountain villages like Koprivshtitsa, Kovachevitsa and Zheravna, are in beautiful restored 19th-century houses, and frequently have rooms furnished with sheepskin rugs and hand-woven textiles. Details of many Bulgarian B&Bs can be found on popular websites such as booking.com and hostelworld.com.

Hostels, Campsites and Monasteries

Sofia, Plovdiv, Veliko Tŭrnovo and several coastal towns are well supplied with informal, backpacker-friendly hostels. These commonly have one or more dormitory rooms with bunk beds, as well as a small communal area, and approachable English-speaking

Campsite at Oazis Beach, on the Black Sea coast

staff. Many Bulgarian hostels also offer self-contained double rooms, and breakfast is often included in the room rent.

Spending a few nights at a campsite (kŭmping) is another inexpensive, albeit increasingly elusive, option. There were once many campsites outside Bulgaria's most scenic towns and along the Black Sea coast. However, since many of them have now been sold off to property developers, their number has fallen dramatically in recent years. The continued existence of those that remain is far from certain. Camping anywhere but in a designated campsite is illegal in Bulgaria.

Basic accommodation is also available in the simply-decorated cells of some of Bulgaria's larger monasteries, such as Rila and Troyan. To book a room, it's best to contact the monasteries directly.

Reservations

Bulgaria can be very busy in season, with Black Sea hotels filling up in summer and ski resorts proving similarly popular in winter. It is, therefore,

always advisable to reserve in advance. All establishments can be booked directly via email or telephone, although staff in rural hotels or B&Bs might not speak English.Luckily, most Bulgarian accommodation options are bookable via popular Internet sites such as eurobookings, booking.com, hostelworld and expedia.

Recommended Hotels

The hotels listed in this guidebook have been chosen for a wide range of reasons and criteria. They are all representative of their context, be that bustling Sofia, the Black Sea coast, the rustic villages of northern Bulgaria or the country's many spa resorts. Each stands out and has earned a good reputation for hospitality and charm. Listings cover a vast variety of accommodation, from rural guesthouses, hostels and self-catering apartments, to full-service hotels with modern amenities. There is also a good choice of luxury hotels and intimate boutique establishments. A warm welcome earns plenty of points, as do those little extras like coffee-and tea-making facilities and allowing guests use of the kitchen.

The DK Choice label means the hotel is particularly outstanding. It may stand in beautiful surrounds, have a spectacular outlook, be a historically important landmark building, offer outstanding service, a romantic atmosphere, be particularly charming, have a great spa, or a noteworthy sustainable outlook. Whatever the reason, it is a guarantee of an especially memorable stay.

DIRECTORY

Hotel Booking Websites

Booking
w booking.com

Eurobookings
w eurobookings.com

Expedia
w expedia.com

Hostelworld
w hostelworld.com

Modern hotel in a traditional-style house, with a large swimming pool

Where to Stay

Sofia

Art Hostel €
Hostel **City Map** 3 B3
ul. Angel Kanchev 21a
Tel (02) 987 0545
W art-hostel.com
Full of art with a charming garden
and communal kitchen. There's
even a bar-gallery for exhibitions.

Canape Connection Hostel €
Hostel
ul. William Gladstone 12a
Tel (02) 441 6373
W canapeconnection.com
With a touch of quirky design, this
comfortable hostel offers a choice
of dorms and private doubles.

Apartment House Dunav €€
Modern **City Map** 2 E2
ul. Dunav 38
Tel (02) 983 3002
W dunavaparthouse.com
Smartly done, studio to family-
unit apartments, with wood
floors and modern bathrooms.

Bulgari €€
Modern
ul. Pirotska 50
Tel (02) 831 0060
Located in one of Sofia's oldest
shopping areas. Rooms are neatly
done and have TV and desk space.

Diter €€
Modern **City Map** 3 C3
ul. Han Asparuh 65
Tel (02) 989 8998
W diterhotel.com
Charming 19th-century mansion
in a cobbled street, with elegant
rooms done up in warm colours.

Favorit €€
Modern
ul. Knyaz Boris I 193
Tel (02) 931 9391
W hotelfavorit.bg
Friendly hotel located midway
between the train station and
city centre. Well-equipped rooms.

Kolikovski €€
Modern
ul. Hristo Belchev 46
Tel (02) 933 3000
W kolikovski.com
Centrally located smart hotel
offers well-equipped rooms
and suites.

Niky €€
Modern
ul. Neofit Rilski 16
Tel (02) 951 6091
W hotel-niky.com

Close to major attractions. Offers
choice of double rooms and self-
catering apartments.

Ogosta House €€
Boutique
ul. Ogosta 5
Tel (02) 946 1042
W ogostahouse.com
Three cosy apartments with
stylish interiors, amid a host of
shops and cafés.

Red Bed and Breakfast €€
Guesthouse **City Map** 4 E4
ul. Lyuben Karavelov 15
Tel (02) 988 8188
W redbandb.com
Well-located B&B with richly
furnished rooms. Erstwhile home
of sculptor Andrey Nikolov.

Scotty's Boutique Hotel €€
Boutique **City Map** 1 B3
ul. Ekzarh Yosif 11
Tel (02) 983 6777
W scottyshotel.biz
Elegantly transformed block has
themed rooms decorated in
bright colours and kitschy fabrics.

Apartment House Sofia €€€
Luxury
ul. Golo Burdo 2-4
Tel (02) 960 2888
W aphouse-sofia.com
Centrally-located stylish building.
Upscale studios to 2-bedroom
family apartments, all with
excellent kitchen facilities.

Art 'Otel €€€
Luxury
ul. William Gladstone 44
Tel (02) 980 6000
W artotel.biz

Quirky decor at the Canape Connection
Hostel, Sofia

Price Guide

Prices are based on a one night's stay in
high season for a standard double room,
including tax, service charges and
breakfast unless otherwise stated.

€	up to €35
€€	€35 to 70
€€€	over €70

Four-star hotel, a short walk from
Sofia's main shopping boulevard.

Central Park Hotel €€€
Luxury
bul. Vitosha 106
Tel (02) 805 8181
W centralparkhotel.bg
Upscale hotel with well-equip-
ped and spacious rooms, most
with excellent views of the park.

Festa €€€
Luxury
bul. Bulgariya 83
Tel (02) 818 9628
W festahotels.com
Classy establishment on Sofia's
southern fringes. Contemporary
rooms with great views.

Grand Hotel Sofia €€€
Luxury
ul. Gûrko 1
Tel (02) 811 0801
W grandhotelsofia.bg
Leading full-service hotel with
majestic rooms and efficient
service. Prime central location.

Hilton €€€
Luxury
bul. Bulgariya 1
Tel (02) 933 5000
W sofia.hilton.com
Modern hotel set before Mount
Vitosha, offers excellent comforts
and award-winning cuisines.

Kempinski Zografski €€€
Luxury
bul. James Bouchier 100
Tel (02) 969 2222
W kempinski.com
Stunning hotel with exquisite
restaurants, bars, shopping, spa
and a Japanese garden.

Les Fleurs €€€
Boutique
bul. Vitosha 21
Tel (02) 810 0800
W lesfleurshotel.com
Luxury, convenience and style
with a floral theme.

Radisson Blu Grand Hotel €€€
Luxury
pl. Narodno sûbranie 4
Tel (02) 933 4334
W radissonblu.com/hotel-sofia

Modern hotel with excellent rooms and suites, phenomenal city views and great service.

Sheraton Sofia Hotel Balkan €€€
Luxury
pl. Sveta Nedelya 5
Tel *(02) 981 6541*
w sheratonsofia.com
Sheer opulence, complete with chandeliers, grand rooms with plush furnishings and more.

Sofia Plaza €€€
Luxury
bul. Hristo Botev 154
Tel *(02) 813 7912*
w hotelsofiaplaza.com
Conveniently located for the city's historic and cultural spots. Chic rooms and apartment suites.

DK Choice

Sofia Residence Boutique Hotel €€€
Boutique
ul. Oborishte 63
Tel *(02) 814 4888*
w residence-oborishte.com
A cosy hotel in a leafy residential area with stylish two-room apartments that feature wood floors, bold colours and modern design.

Southern Bulgaria

BACHKOVO: Djamoura €
Guesthouse Map C4
ul. Osvobozhdenya 74
Tel *(03327) 2320*
w djamura.com
Cosy rooms and suites in a restored house, next to Bulgaria's second-largest monastery.

BANSKO: Alpin €
Guesthouse Map B4
ul. Neofit Rilski 6
Tel *(0749) 84343*
w alpin.bansko.bg
Rooms with pine furniture and wooden floors in the historic Old Town area. Organizes hiking trips.

BANSKO: Dedo Pene €€
Guesthouse Map B4
ul. Aleksandar Buynov 1
Tel *(0749) 85073*
w dedopene.bg
Atmospheric inn with traditional furnishings, blends old-time romance and modern-day comfort.

BANSKO: Kempinski Grand Hotel Arena €€€
Luxury Map B4
ul. Pirin 96
Tel *(0749) 88888*
w kempinski-bansko.com

The Kempinski Grand Hotel Arena in Bansko

Plush five-star hotel with service matching its fantastic mountain views. Perfect for ski-lovers.

BLAGOEVGRAD: Kristo €
Modern Map B4
Varosha Quarter, 2700 Blagoevgrad
Tel *(073) 880 444*
w hotelkristo.com
Beautiful resort set amid the greenery of the historic quarter. Majestic rooms with lovely views.

BOROVETS: Rila €€€
Luxury Map B4
Tel *(07503) 2295*
w rilaborovets.com
Bulgaria's largest ski hotel right next to the slopes, offers elegant rooms and superb facilities.

DEVIN: Ismena €€
Spa Map C4
ul. Osvobozhdenie
Tel *(03041) 4872*
w ismena.bg
This complex of traditional buildings offers modern facilities including a mineral water pool, Jacuzzi, sauna and spa.

DEVIN: Persenk €€
Spa Map C4
ul. Druzhba 10
Tel *(03041) 3877*
w persenk.eu
Elegantly furnished rooms with five-star comfort amidst lush pine forests and fresh mountain air.

HASKOVO: Hotel Central €
Modern Map D4
ul. Vasil Drumev 20
Tel *(038) 660 333*
w hotel-central-haskovo.com
Centrally located hotel offers excellent value. Comfortable rooms with good views.

KOVACHEVITSA: Lavanda €€
Guesthouse Map B4
Tel 0898 680 468
w lavanda.bg

Modern rooms combine folksy furnishings at this B&B set in an enchanting stone house.

KYUSTENDIL: Strimon Spa Club €€€
Spa Map A4
ul. Tsar Simeon I 24
Tel *(078) 559 000*
w strimon-spaclub.com
Aristocratic five-star hotel with plush rooms and a range of beauty and medicinal treatments.

MELNIK: Despot Slav €
Guesthouse Map B5
Tel *(07437) 2248*
w melnik.bg
Charming hotel built in traditional Melnik style with wrought-iron furniture, wood doors and exposed stone walls.

MELNIK: Litova Kûshta €€
Guesthouse Map B5
Tel *(07437) 2313*
w litovakushta.com
Hotel built upon an ancient wine cellar; rooms with hand-painted borders and wood ceilings.

MELNIK: Lumparova Kûshta €€
Guesthouse Map B5
Tel *(07437) 2218*
w lumparovamelnik.com
Imposing old mansion with cosy rooms, great views and wine and food tastings. Traditional decor.

PAMPOROVO: Malina Villas €€
Modern Map C5
Tel *(03095) 8388*
w malina-pamporovo.com
Wooden chalets amid lush pine forest: each a fully-equipped, chic living unit with modern amenities.

PAMPOROVO: Orlovets €€€
Luxury Map C5
Tel *(03095) 9000*
w hotelorlovetz.com
Family-friendly five-star on a forested hillside. Winter skiing and summer biking facilities.

For more information on types of hotels *see p221*

Entrance to the Renaissance guesthouse in Plovdiv Old Town

PLOVDIV: Hikers Hostel €
Hostel Map C4
ul. Suborna 53
Tel *0885 194 553*
w hikers-hostel.org
Tastefully decorated, old house
offers rooms as well as dorms.
Close to the city's art and culture.

PLOVDIV: Star Hotel €
Modern Map C4
ul. Patriarh Eftimii 13
Tel *(032) 633 599*
w starhotel.bg
Rooms at this no-frills hotel have
vending machines instead of
breakfast. Excellent location.

PLOVDIV: Dafi €€
Modern Map C4
ul. Georgi Benkovski 23
Tel *(032) 620 041*
w hoteldafi.com
Intimate hotel in the maze-like
Kapana district: Plovdiv's prime
nightlife area.

PLOVDIV: Novotel €€€
Luxury Map C4
ul. Zlatyu Boyadzhiev 2
Tel *(032) 934 444*
w icep.bg
Overlooking the river, this high-
rise with modern decor offers a
wealth of on-site facilities.

**PLOVDIV OLD TOWN: Old
Plovdiv Guest House** €
Hostel Map C4
ul. Chetvurti Yanuar 3
Tel *(032) 260 925*
Friendly hostel-cum-guesthouse
with a choice of doubles, triples
and quad rooms.

**PLOVDIV OLD TOWN: Art
House Boris** €€
Luxury Map C4
ul. Suborna 49
Tel *(032) 266 379*
w borispalace.com
Lavishly restored 19th-century
mansion, offers opulent but
affordable rooms. Great service.

DK Choice

**PLOVDIV OLD TOWN:
Renaissance** €€
Guesthouse Map C4
pl. Vuzrazhdane 1
Tel *(032) 266 966*
w renaissance-bg.com
Done up in traditional 19th-
century style, this hotel on
the fringes of the Old Town,
offers rooms with period
furniture and hand-painted
walls, and a restaurant with
a walled courtyard.

**PLOVDIV OLD TOWN:
Residence** €€
Luxury Map C4
ul. Knyaz Tseretelev 11
Tel *(032) 632 389*
Stylish hotel with plush
furnishings, soft drapes, antique
beds and marble staircase.

**PLOVDIV OLD TOWN:
Hebros** €€€
Luxury Map C4
ul. Konstantin Stoilov 51a
Tel *(032) 260 180*
w hebros-hotel.com
Lavishly done with antique
furniture, these two 19th-century
houses combine romance,
comfort and classy service.

RILA MONASTERY: Gorski Kut €
Modern Map B4
Tel *(07054) 2170*
w gorski-kut.eu
Situated just a few miles from Rila
Monastery, this hotel has bright,
simple rooms and a restaurant
that overlooks the Rila River.

**RILA MONASTERY:
Tzarev Vrah** €€
Modern Map B4
Tel *(07054) 2280*
w tzarevvrah.com
Most rooms at this hotel offer
good views of the valley. Located
just outside Rila Monastery.

SAMOKOV: Sonata €€
Guesthouse Map B4
ul. Petŭr Beron 4
Tel *(0722) 60334*
w hotelsonata-samokov.com
Well-equipped hotel at the foot
of Rila Mountain. Great base for
the ski pistes at Borovets.

SANDANSKI: Sandanski €€€
Spa Map B5
ul. Makedoniya
Tel *(0746) 31271*
w interhotelsandanski.bg
Upscale hotel with a comprehensive range of medical and beauty
treatments. Tennis courts too.

SHIROKA LŬKA: Kalina €
Guesthouse Map C4
ul. Kapita Petko Voyvoda 63
Tel *(0888) 784 897*
w shirokaluka-kalina.com
Clean rooms with good
mountain views, furnished in
traditional Rhodope style: wood
panelling and thick woollen rugs.

SMOLYAN: Luxor €€
Modern Map C5
bul. Bulgariya 51
Tel *(0301) 63317*
w luxor-bg.com
Three-star hotel with spacious
rooms, contemporary furnishings, gym, sauna and casino.

SMOLYAN: Petko Takovata €€
Guesthouse Map C5
ul. Momchil Yunak 10
Tel *(0301) 80240*
w petko-takova.com
Cosy B&B in a traditional, old stone
house at the centre of town.

VELINGRAD: Olymp €€
Spa Map B4
ul. Tsar Samuil 1a
Tel *(0359) 56100*
w olymp-bg.com
Spa hotel with great views, high
standards of service and over 50
types of therapy.

VELINGRAD: Dvoretsa €€€
Spa Map B4
ul. Tosho Staykov 8
Tel *(0359) 56200*
w dvoretsa.com
Five-star hotel in a wooded park,
with luxurious rooms and broad
range of spa treatments.

**ZLATOGRAD: Pachilovska
Kŭshta** €
Guesthouse Map D5
ul. Evgenia Pachilova 4
Tel *(03071) 4166*
w eac-zlatograd.com
In the heart of the Ethnographic
Area Complex, this 19th-century
house has rooms that feature
antique wooden furniture.

Central Bulgaria

GABROVO: Gabrovo €
Modern Map D3
bul. Hemus 4
Tel *(066) 801 705*
W hotel-gabrovobg.eu
Contemporary establishment
south of the town centre, has
clean and spacious rooms.

DK Choice

**HISARYA: Hissar Spa
Complex** €€
Spa Map C3
ul. Gûrko 1
Tel *(0337) 62781*
W hotelhissar.com
Large hotel complex with a
host of health and beauty
facilities. Studios to suites
and apartments in both
'standard' and 'delux'
categories. Offers tennis,
bowling, billiards and more.

KARLOVO: Almond €€
Luxury Map C3
Bademika Quarter
Tel *(0335) 91555*
W almondbg.com
Splendid hotel, set amidst the
almond orchards in the hills
above Karlovo. Elegant rooms.

KAZANLÛK: Teres €
Modern Map D3
ul. Lyubomir Kabakchiev 16
Tel *(0431) 64272*
W hotelteres.com
Comfortatable rooms near the
Ethnographic Complex. Tour the
owner's rose oil workshop.

**KOPRIVSHTITSA: Bashtina
Kûshta** €
Guesthouse Map C3
bul. Hadzhi Nencho Palaveev 32
Tel *(07184) 3033*
W fhhotel.info
Blending traditional architecture
with modern interiors, this hotel
has smart, comfortable rooms.

KOPRIVSHTITSA: Kalina €
Guesthouse Map C3
bul. Hadzhi Nencho Palaveev 35
Tel *(0888) 224 788*
Attractive house with a pleasant
garden and cosy rooms that have
pine furniture and period fittings.

**KOPRIVSHTITSA:
Tryanova Kûshta** €
Guesthouse Map C3
ul. Gereniloto
Tel *(07184) 3057*
All-wooden house with comfort-
able rooms that feature tradi-
tional fabrics and pine furniture.

LOVECH: Hotel Varosha €
Modern Map C2
pl. Todor Kirkov 36
Tel *(068) 603 377*
W hotelvarosha.com
Well-equipped hotel with a
range of smartly furnished
rooms: studios to apartments.

LOVECH: Presidium Palace €€€
Luxury Map C2
ul. Tûrgovska 51
Tel *(068) 600 170*
W presidivm.com
Premier hotel with modern
design, stylish rooms and a wide
range of on-site facilities.

**RIBARITSA: Evergreen
Palace** €€€
Luxury Map C3
Tel *(06902) 2070*
W evergreen-palace.net
Picturesque hotel in dense
riverside forest, with a range of
chic rooms and villas.

SLIVEN: Imperia €€
Modern Map E3
Tel *(044) 667 599*
W hotelimperia.net
Well-equipped resort hotel near
the Sliven-Karandila chairlift.

**STARA ZAGORA: Hotel
La Roka** €€
Boutique Map D3
ul. Tsar Ivan Shishman 38
Tel *(042) 919 427*
W hotel-laroka.com
Stylish hotel in warm chocolate
and cinnamon colours. Family
rooms available.

STARA ZAGORA: Forum €€€
Luxury Map D3
ul. Hadzhi Dimitûr Asenov 94
Tel *(042) 631 616*
W hotelforum.bg
Classy establishment in a
restored 1890s building features
bright, elegantly furnished
rooms and suites.

TETEVEN: Villa Cherven €€
Modern Map C3
Konski Dol
Tel *(0888) 340 172*
W villacherven.com
Chalet-like hotel in the moun-
tains with smart, modern rooms.

TROYAN: Troyan Plaza €€
Modern Map C3
ul. Slaveikov 1
Tel *(0670) 64399*
W troyanplaza.com
Plush hotel on the banks of Belli
Ossum River. Organizes visits to
natural and cultural spots.

TRYAVNA: Ralitsa €
Modern Map D3
ul. Kaleto 16a
Tel *(0677) 62262*
W ralitsa.tryavna.biz
Large hotel on a wooded hill,
with comfortable rooms and
superb views. Great for walks.

TRYAVNA: Zograf €
Guesthouse Map D3
ul. Slaveykov 1
Tel *(0677) 64970*
W zograf.tryavna.biz
Set in a building with Revival
period architecture, this hotel has
comfortable, modern rooms.

VELIKO TÛRNOVO: Comfort €
Guesthouse Map D3
ul. Panayot Tipografov 5
Tel *(062) 628 728*
W hotelcomfortbg.com
Intimate hotel in the
Ethnographic and Architectural
complex. Rooms with great views.

**VELIKO TÛRNOVO:
Hikers Hostel** €
Hostel Map D3
ul. Rezervoarska 91
Tel *(0889) 691 661*
W hikers-hostel.org
Quirky wooden furniture.
Summer terrace has great views
of Tsarevets fortress.

Elegantly-appointed room at Hotel Forum, Stara Zagora

For more information on types of hotels *see p221*

Pelican Lake Guesthouse, Sreburna, located in beautiful environs

VELIKO TŬRNOVO: Studio €€
Boutique   Map D3
ul. Teodor Lefterov 4
Tel (062) 604 010
W studiohotel-vt.com
Stylish hotel with warm and chic interiors, located near the entrance to Tsarevets fortress.

VELIKO TŬRNOVO: Yantra Grand Hotel €€€
Luxury   Map D3
ul. Opalchenska 2
Tel (062) 600 607
W yantrabg.com
Upscale hotel with richly furnished rooms and stunning views of Tsarevets.

YAMBOL: Tundzha €
Modern   Map E3
ul. Buzludzha 13
Tel (046) 662 771
W hotel-tundzha.domino.bg
An old-style Socialist-era building at a pleasant riverside location. Simple rooms.

ZHERAVNA: Eko €
Guesthouse   Map E3
Tel (04585) 389
W ekohotel.jeravna.com
Modern amenities blend with history in this 18th-century Revival house with wood-panelled rooms.

Northern Bulgaria

BELOGRADCHIK: Madona €
Guesthouse   Map A2
ul. Hristo Botev 26
Tel (0936) 5546
W hanmadona.com
Friendly B&B on a quiet residential street, with small, comfortable rooms and superb home-cooked breakfast pastries.

CHIPROVTSI: Torlacite €
Guesthouse   Map A2
ul. Pavleto 31
Tel (0887) 892 790
W torlacite.com
Owned by a family of kilm weavers, this centrally-located B&B has rooms with folksy furnishings. Carpet weaving courses too.

DOBRICH: Villa di Poletta €
Modern   Map F2
ul. Hristo Botev 1
Tel (058) 849 000
W villadipoletta.com
Convenient, downtown family hotel has spacious, stylish rooms.

RUSE: Luliaka €
Modern   Map D2
Zapaden Park
Tel (082) 821 161
W luliaka.com
Mix of rooms and apartments at this tastefully restored villa. River-facing balconies.

RUSE: Bistra & Galina €€
Modern   Map D2
ul. Han Asparuh 8
Tel (082) 823 344
W bghotel.bg
This fully-equipped hotel has spacious rooms, a fitness centre, indoor pool, Jacuzzi and more.

RUSE: City Art Hotel €€
Boutique   Map D2
ul. Veliko Tŭrnovo 5
Tel (082) 519 848
W cityarthotel.com
Restored 1890s building, once a hat maker's home and workshop, now a grand hotel with uniquely done rooms and apartments.

RUSE: Danube Plaza €€
Modern   Map D2
pl. Svoboda 5
Tel (082) 822 929
W danubeplaza.com
Main-square hotel with a mix of simple and more plush rooms, the latter with deep-pile carpets.

RUSE: Vega Boutique Hotel €€
Boutique   Map D2
ul. Aleksandrovska 48
Tel (082) 525 555
W hotelvegaruse.com
A 19th-century town house, with a retro, belle-époque theme and a relaxing ground-floor café.

RUSE: Anna Palace €€€
Luxury   Map D2
ul. Knyazheska 4
Tel (082) 825 005
W annapalace.com
Historical city-centre mansion with majestic rooms that have great views of the Danube River.

SHUMEN: Kyoshkove €
Modern   Map E2
Park Kyoshkove
Tel (0899) 989 621
W kyoshkove.eu
Simply-furnished rooms in a leafy park. The restaurant has terrace with views of the pines.

SHUMEN: Shumen €€
Modern   Map E2
pl. Oborishte
Tel (054) 800 003
W hotel-shumen.com
Huge four-star hotel with a range of standard to luxury rooms, choice of excellent restaurants, indoor pool and more.

SILISTRA: Drustar €€
Luxury   Map F1
ul. Kapitan Mamarchev 10
Tel (086) 812 200
W hoteldrustar.com
Smart five-storey hotel with deep-pile carpets, designer furniture, kids' play area and tennis courts.

DK Choice

SREBURNA: Pelican Lake Guesthouse €
Guesthouse   Map F1
ul. Petko Simov 16
Tel (085) 15322
W srebarnabirding.com
Mere steps from Sreburna Nature Reserve, this friendly B&B, set in a beautifully renovated house, offers meals with a vegetarian slant and even lets guests use the kitchen. Its very knowledgeable owners organise nature tours.

VIDIN: Anna Kristina €€
Modern   Map A1
ul. Baba Vida 2
Tel (094) 606 037
W annakristinahotel.com
Elegant hotel in a 19th-century mansion, with well-equipped rooms and an outdoor pool.

VIDIN: Neptun €€
Modern   Map A1
ul. Dunavska 8
Tel (094) 680 039
W hotelneptunvidin.com
Full-service hotel with rooms that have bright, sensuous colours and great views of the Danube.

VRATSA: Chaika €
Modern   Map B2
Vratsata Gorge
Tel (092) 621 369
W chaika.net
With a great lake for boating, this chalet-style building, offers dramatic views of the cliffs. An ideal base for hiking.

Black Sea

AHTOPOL: Hotel Agata Beach €€
Boutique   Map G4
ul. Cherno More 37
Tel (0590) 62288
W hotelagatabeach.com
Modern hotel, near the sea cliffs at
the eastern tip of this peninsular
town. Sea-facing terrace bar.

ALBENA: Laguna Beach €€
Spa   Map G2
Tel (0579) 62959
W albena.bg
Pyramid-shaped structure right
on the beach. Excellent facilities,
including a huge pool, a cinema
and childcare facilities.

BALCHIK: Bisser €
Modern   Map G2
ul. Zalez 43
Tel (05797) 2717
W bisserhotel.com
Simple hotel near Queen Marie's
palace. Some rooms offer great sea
views and there's an outdoor pool.

BALCHIK: White House €€
Modern   Map G2
ul. Geo Milev 18
Tel (05797) 3822
W whitehousebg.com
Efficiently run hotel next to
Balchik's marina. Most rooms
have stripped pine floors and
balconies with sea views.

BALCHIK: BlackSeaRama €€€
Luxury   Map G2
5 km north of Balchik on the E87 road
Tel (05797) 960 11 00
W blacksearama.com
Opulent villas in varying sizes,
walking distance from the beach
and Bulgaria's finest golf course.

BURGAS: Bulgaria €€
Modern   Map F3
ul. Aleksandrovska 21
Tel (056) 841 291
W bulgaria-hotel.com
Sophisticated 17-storey building
with fantastic views of Burgas.

BURGAS: Primoretz Grand
Hotel & Spa €€€
Luxury   Map F3
bul. Knyaz Aleksandŭr Batenberg 2
Tel (056) 812 345
W hotelprimoretz.bg
Known for high standards of
comfort, this grand hotel and spa
offers a vast range of wellness,
fine dining and leisure options.

GOLDEN SANDS:
Kamchia Park €€
Modern   Map G2
Tel (052) 355 511
W hotelkamchia.com

Comfortable resort hotel, just 150
metres from the beach. Room
balconies have excellent views.

KAVARNA: Hotel Karina €
Guesthouse   Map G2
ul. Hristo Botev 20
Tel (0570) 83520
W hotel-karina.info
Family-run hotel with well-kept
garden. Common kitchen where
guests can prepare breakfast.

KRAPETS: Kibela Destinations €€
Guesthouse   Map G2
Tel (0888) 880 281
W villakibela.com
Beautiful single-storey house
with walled garden and pool,
in a sleepy fishing village.
Lets out rooms, a suite or the
entire villa.

LOZENETS: Friends €€
Guesthouse   Map F4
ul. Ribarska 43
Tel (0888) 606 575
W friendshotel.org/lozenec
Comfortable rooms and an
excellent sushi restaurant at this
hotel situated in a garden near
the beach.

NESEBŬR: Trinity €€
Guesthouse   Map F3
ul. Venera 8
Tel (0887) 422 466
W trinity-nessebar.com
Old fishing hut in the archaeological
reserve, has rooms done up in
traditional decor. Good sea views.

SINEMORETS: Casa Domingo €€
Luxury   Map G4
ul. Ribarska
Tel (0550) 66093
W casadomingo.info
Tranquil establishment with
rooms around a central
courtyard and pool. Boat trips
and canoeing are also organized.

Spa centre at the Graffit Gallery Hotel
in Varna

SOZOPOL: Fotini-Sozopol €
Guesthouse   Map F3
ul. Dimitŭr Tashev 2
Tel (0550) 22800
W fotini-sozopol.com
Modern rooms and apartments
at two locations: one in the Old
Town, the other near the beach.

SOZOPOL: Orion €€
Guesthouse   Map F3
ul. Vihren 28
Tel (0550) 23193
W hotel-orion.net
A modest establishment with ten
rooms and six apartments that
offer good views of the bay.

SVETI KONSTANTIN: Piero €€
Guesthouse   Map G2
Tel (052) 362 424
W hotelpiero.com
Charming house near the beach
with spacious, smartly done rooms.

VARNA: Hi Boutique €€
Boutique   Map F2
ul. Han Asparuh 11
Tel (052) 657 777
W hotel-hi.com
Plush hotel, in a leafy and historic
area, with chandeliers, gilded
mirrors and retro furnishings.

VARNA: Panorama €€
Modern   Map F2
bul. Primorski 31
Tel (052) 687 300
W panoramabg.com
Rooms at this hotel in the city's
centre have designer furnishings.

VARNA: Boutique Splendid €€
Modern   Map F2
ul. Bratya Shkorpil 30
Tel (052) 681 414
W boutiquesplendid.net
Comfortable rooms and suites in
a restored 19th-century building,
with fine views of the cathedral.

DK Choice

VARNA: Graffit Gallery €€€
Boutique   Map F2
bul. Knyaz Boris I 65
Tel (052) 989 900
W graffithotel.com
This stylish building holds
four floors of chic rooms, each
floor done in a different colour.
Luxurious rooms and bath-
rooms, spa centre and gym.

VARNA: Grand Hotel London €€€
Boutique   Map F2
ul. Musala 3
Tel (052) 664 100
W londonhotel.bg
Elegantly-restored 19th-century
building with Art Nouveau
touches and top-notch comfort.

For more information on types of hotels see p221

WHERE TO EAT AND DRINK

As new restaurants continue to open almost everywhere in Bulgaria, the range of eating options throughout the country is also increasing. Styles of the restaurants vary from folksy eateries offering the best of traditional Bulgarian cooking, to elegant establishments specializing in modern European cuisine. In the middle range are restaurants serving national and international food. The most

common types of restaurant, and the most authentically Bulgarian, are *mehani* (taverns) and *kruchmi* (inns), which serve traditional Bulgarian dishes, often accompanied by local wines. Bulgaria also has good gourmet restaurants, notably in Sofia and on the Black Sea coast. Italian-style pizza and pasta restaurants can be found everywhere, and inexpensive Chinese restaurants are common in large cities.

Beachside tables outside a restaurant in Sozopol, on the Black Sea

Choosing a Restaurant

The most widespread type of restaurant in Bulgaria is the *mehana,* or tavern, an informal establishment serving a range of Bulgarian dishes and regional specialities. Most *mehani* also have a long list of Bulgarian wines *(see pp32–3)* and a full range of other alcoholic drinks. *Mehani* are usually homely places, often with brightly coloured tablecloths and a decor of folkloric objects, such as traditional pottery laid out on shelves and old agricultural implements as decorations on the walls. In popular tourist areas, *mehani* often have live musical entertainment in the form of regional folk-singing evenings.

A *kruchma* (inn) is similar to a *mehana* in its informal, folksy style. Traditionally the *kruchma* was where the men of the village gathered to drink and play cards. Today, however, the word *kruchma* is often appropriated by smart regional restaurants so as to convey a

sense of welcoming rustic authenticity. At a *mehana* or *kruchma* you can spend a whole evening lingering over a full meal, but it is also perfectly acceptable simply to sit at the bar and enjoy a drink while nibbling at a snack or salad.

Any establishment calling itself a restaurant *(restorant)* is likely to offer a mixture of Bulgarian and international food. Service in a restaurant is usually slightly more formal

Salads form an important part of Bulgarian cuisine

than in a *mehana* or *kruchma,* and the decor often follows international rather than local styles. In Sofia and the major Black Sea resorts, an increasing number of restaurants specialize in French, Italian or Japanese cuisine. While they are inexpensive, many of these restaurants have high culinary standards.

As almost everywhere else in the world, every Bulgarian city has at least one Chinese restaurant *(Kitaiski restorant).* Most offer a familiar range of Chinese food, frequently served in large portions and at very reasonable prices.

Pizzerias are springing up almost everywhere in Bulgaria. However, the pizzas they serve are usually made with locally produced ingredients, and are rarely the equal of the authentic Italian- or American-style pizzas that are available in other countries.

When to Eat

Mehani and restaurants are usually open from 11am until 11pm or midnight. Little distinction is made between lunch *(obyad)* and dinner *(vecherya),* and the same menu of dishes is usually offered all through the day.

Reservations

Bulgaria's best restaurants generally attract a large clientele, so it is a good idea to reserve a table, especially at weekends. As restaurant staff may not always have a good command of English, or any other European language, it is

One of the pleasant dining areas at Evergreen Palace, in Ribaritsa *(see p237)*

often best to make your reservation by calling at the restaurant in person rather than booking by phone.

Reading the Menu

Both in *mehani* and restaurants, menus are written in Cyrillic script *(see pp282–4)*. In Sofia and in tourist resorts, menus in English are often available. However, as translations are rarely perfect, some thought and imagination may be required to make out precisely what is on offer. Most menus are divided into sections, typically covering snacks, salads, hors d'oeuvres, main dishes and desserts. Vegetarian dishes are listed as *yastiya bez meso* ("meatless dishes") or as *postno yadene* ("fasting food").

Vegetarians

There are only a handful of dedicated vegetarian restaurants in Bulgaria, and most of these are in Sofia. Mainstream *mehani* and restaurants rarely include meat-free options in their list of main courses, but there are always plenty of salads and hors d'oeuvres that are suitable for vegetarians. Combining two or three of these makes a healthy and filling meal.

Bulgarian salads are particularly noted for the fresh vegetables that make up most of their ingredients. Among traditional hors d'oeuvres are various combinations of cheese, eggs and vegetables baked in earthenware pots, a wide range of vegetables fried in breadcrumbs, and cubed vegetables grilled on a kebab skewer. Common Bulgarian hors d'oeuvres include *chushka byurek* (a large pepper stuffed with cheese and fried in batter or breadcrumbs) and aubergine *(patladzhan)* fried and served with yoghurt.

Vegetarians should be wary of vegetable soups and stews. Many of these apparently meat-free dishes are made with meat stock.

The Bill and Tipping

Like the menu, the bill *(smetkata)* is usually written in Cyrillic. If you are confused about the names of dishes you ordered or about the amount you have been charged, refer back to the original menu.

Credit cards are only accepted in smarter restaurants in Sofia and other major towns and cities. Restaurant bills rarely include service, and it is customary to leave a tip of about 10 per cent.

Smoking

Smoking is still a widespread habit in Bulgaria. Smoking is banned from the interiors of restaurants and bars, but is permitted on the outdoor terraces that spring up in spring and summer, ensuring that cigarette smoke can be difficult to avoid.

Recommended Restaurants

The restaurants listed in this guidebook have been chosen for a wide range of reasons and criteria. They are all representative of their setting, be that Sofia, the Black Sea coast, the traditional small towns of Central Bulgaria or the Rila Mountains. Each stands out and has earned a noteworthy reputation.

Listings cover a variety of eateries, from the traditional Bulgarian taverns and inns that specialize in regional dishes to simple pizzerias, restaurants serving fish and seafood, chic bistros, vegetarian cafés and fine dining in smart restaurants.

The DK Choice label means the restaurant is outstanding and warmly recommended. It may serve especially memorable meals with local specialities, offer excellent value for money, be located in beautiful surrounds, be a historically important landmark building, have a romantic atmosphere or be particularly charming. Whatever the reason, it is a guarantee of an especially memorable meal.

Live music at the Hadzhidraganovite Kûshti restaurant in Sofia *(see p232)*

The Flavours of Bulgaria

Bulgarian food is similar in many ways to that of the Greece and Turkey: filo pastries *(byurek)*; tomato, cucumber and white cheese salad *(shopska salata)*; moussaka *(musaka)* and stuffed vine leaves *(sarmi)* are among the shared dishes. But there are important differences too, not least the use of sunflower instead of olive oil for cooking and flavouring. Away from the Black Sea, there is less emphasis on fish dishes and a stronger reliance on vegetables and fruit. A salad or a selection of *meze* often begin a meal, both traditionally accompanied by a glass of *rakiya*, the local brandy.

Bunch of fresh dill

Farmer from Dobarsko, showing off the tomato crop

The Mountains

Geography plays the biggest role in regional variations of Bulgarian cuisine. Livestock farming in the lower mountain ranges – most notably in the Rhodopes, Stara Planina, Rila, Strandzha and Pirin – is a tradition that goes back thousands of years. The omnipresent *kiselo mlyako* (sour yoghurt made with ewes', cows' or buffalo milk) is usually eaten plain, but it also forms the base for *tarator* soup and the drink *ayryan*. Bulgarian *sirene* cheese will be a familiar sight and taste for most visitors, since it is very similar to Greek *feta*. However, it is inadvisable to compare them in front of a Bulgarian – unless it's to say that the Bulgarian version is better. *Sirene* turns up in a huge number of dishes, from filo pastry *banitsa* to *shopska salata*. The hard, yellow cheese *kashkaval* is not as widely used, but it is an essential part of any *meze*. Also key to any group of *meze* dishes are examples of Bulgaria's huge range of sausages and cured meats. Spicy sausages such as *sudzhuk*, *banski staretz* and *strandzhanski dyado*, and the air-cured ham

Tarama Kyopolou Cured ham Sarmi Country bread
Sudzhuk salami Sirene cheese Kashkaval cheese

Selection of the many dishes that make up a Bulgarian *meze*

Bulgarian Dishes and Specialities

Many of the traditional dishes of Bulgaria feature yoghurt, cheese, spices and herbs. *Chubritsa* is a herb similar to oregano and appears dried and crumbled onto soups, stews and even bread. Dill-scented *tarator* soup is wonderfully cooling on a hot summer day. Many dishes are meatless, such as the "monastery-style" bean soup of white kidney beans and vegetables, believed to have originated with one of the country's many religious orders. Bulgarians love stuffed vegetable dishes, peppers being a favourite. Usually baked, in summer peppers are filled with *sirene* cheese and egg and deep-fried. Carp, from the rivers such as the Danube, is the traditional dish for the important feast day of St Nicholas and, at Christmas and New Year, *banitsa* will have lucky charms hidden among its filo leaves.

Kidney beans

Tarator, the national dish, is a creamy, chilled soup made with yoghurt, dill, walnuts and sunflower oil.

Bulgarian fruit and vegetables, piled high on a Sofia market stall

The Coast

The dwindling fish stocks of the Black Sea are slowly on the mend and it is possible once more to enjoy excellent grilled bonito and stewed or fried scad when they arrive at the end of summer. Sprats, served fried or marinated, are available throughout the year. Mussels are plentiful and good, but must come from pollution-free sources. Bulgarian fish soup, *ribena chorba*, is seasoned with thyme, and may be made with fresh or saltwater fish.

ON THE MENU

Banitsa Savoury filo pastry pie filled with *sirene* and egg, vegetables or minced meat.

Kavarma Veal pork, chicken or lamb, stewed with onions and good local red wine.

Kyopolou Aubergine, pepper and tomato dip with garlic, parsley and red wine vinegar.

Kyufteta Spiced roasted, fried or grilled meatballs.

Shkembe chorba Soup made of veal tripe flavoured with garlic, said to be an infallible cure for a hangover.

Sirene po shopski Layers of cheese, peppers and tomato topped with an egg and baked in a small pot.

Tarama Creamy dip made from salted fish roe blended with chopped onion, soaked bread and sunflower oil.

elenski but, seasoned with herbs, all stem from the need to preserve meat to last through the long and bitter mountain winters. Hearty stews are a mountain tradition too, with *kavarma* and pork ribs with kidney beans among the tastiest and most popular.

The Plains

The best of Bulgaria's fruit and vegetables are grown on the plains to the south and north of the Stara Planina range, usually without fertilizers. Berries, orchard fruits, melons and grapes (for the table as well as for wine) are among the many superb fruits. The peppers, tomatoes, cucumbers, onions, aubergines (eggplant), potatoes and courgettes (zucchini) are arguably the best in Europe and certainly among the cheapest. They feature prominently in a wide range of stews that go by the generic name of *gyuvetch*. Many salad dishes, such as *shopska* and *ovcharska* (shepherd's salad), originated on the plains and are at their very best here because of the freshness of the produce.

Fields of sunflowers in the countryside around Bozhentsi

Shopska salad is a delicious mix of chopped tomatoes, cucumbers, peppers, onions and grated white cheese.

Sweet peppers are filled with a variety of stuffings, from rice or cheese and egg to meat, and baked or fried.

Baklava, filo pastry layered with walnuts and cinnamon and doused in syrup, is also eaten in Greece and Turkey.

Where to Eat and Drink

Sofia

100 Grama Sladki €
Café **City Map** 3 B2
ul. Angel Kanchev 18
Tel *(02) 846 7212*
Small café with plenty of cakes and
tarts to go along with coffee, tea
and hot chocolate. Has excellent
chocolates and biscuits as well.

Boom! €
Bistro **City Map** 3 A1
ul. Kurnigradska 15
Tel *(0894) 420 440*
Stylish restaurant with minimalist
furnishings, serves gourmet
burgers and grilled steaks made
with fresh ingredients.

Boyansko Hanche €
Bulgarian
pl. Sborishte 1
Tel *(02) 856 3016*
A folk-style restaurant offering
the full range of Bulgarian cuisine
and a sprinkling of international
steak and chicken dishes. Live
performances of traditional song
and dance every evening.

Ciccione Panini Bar €
Café **City Map** 3 B1
ul. Hristo Belchev 6
Tel *(0882) 503 040*
This Italian café and delicatessen
is great for a quick espresso
and pastry. Also serves fresh
sandwiches with Italian ham,
salami and other fillings.

Halbite €
Bulgarian **City Map** 4 C3
ul. Neofit Rilski 72
Tel *(02) 980 4147*
Pub-restaurant with wooden
tables, popular for its traditional
grilled meats, vegetarian dishes
and wide range of beers.

SkaraBar €
Bulgarian
Zaimov Park
Tel *(02) 483 0696*
Chic bar-restaurant under the
Sfumato Theatre, offers a modern
menu with great Bulgarian grilled
meat staples. Side orders include
salads, peppers and beans.

Supa Star €
Bistro **City Map** 4 E2
ul. Tsar Ivan Shishman 8
Counted amongst the first and
the best of the little cafés that
have sprung up in Sofia. Menu
changes daily, and comprises
excellent and well-priced soups.

Barbarossa €€
Italian **City Map** 3 B3
ul. Hristo Belchev 32
Tel *(02) 590 7954*
Set in a 19th-century house with
a pleasant courtyard, this homely
restaurant serves fresh pasta,
authentic pizzas and freshly
baked breads. Often used as
a venue for tango evenings.

Before & After €€
International **City Map** 3 B2
ul. Hristo Belchev 12
Tel *(02) 981 6088*
Enjoy a full meal, like pan-fried
fish, or savour a cake and coffee
at this delightful café, with an Art
Nouveau theme, located in the
centre of the city.

Bulgari €€
Bulgarian **City Map** 2 F3
bul. Knyaz Dondukov 71
Tel *(02) 843 5419*
This 19th-century house,
artfully done with old and
new photographs of Sofia,
offers a menu with the national
favourites: roast lamb, barbecued
meats and oven-baked stews.

Chevermeto €€
Bulgarian
pl. Bulgariya 1
Tel *(0885) 630 308*
Traditional Bulgarian stews and
grills are served at this large
restaurant that has a folklore
theme, complete with traditional
carpets and sheepskin rugs. Try
the signature spit roast lamb.

Egur Egur €€
Armenian **City Map** 4 E2
ul. Sheinovo 18
Tel *(02) 946 1765*
This classy restaurant serves
delicious skewer-grilled meats,
exotic sweet-and-sour stews and
intriguing vegetarian dishes
featuring aubergines, courgettes,
mushrooms and peppers. There
is a second Egur Egur at ul.
Dobrudzha 10.

Hadzhidraganovite Kûshti €€
Bulgarian
ul. Kozlodui 75
Tel *(02) 931 3148*
An elegant restaurant, with dining
rooms done in traditional folk
style, offering an extensive menu
of authentic national dishes.

Olive's €€
International **City Map** 3 B2
ul. Graf Ignatiev 12
Tel *(0894) 654 837*
Centrally located café-restaurant
with a bit of everything: burgers,
pizzas, pastas and salads for a
quick bite; and steak and seafood
as a fuller meal.

One More Bar €€
International **City Map** 4 E2
ul. Tsar Ivan Shishman 12
Tel *(0877) 693 735*
Roomy spot in an elegant villa at
the centre of the city, with an
enticing menu of international
salads, quality sandwiches and
hard-to-resist desserts.

Pastorant €€
Italian **City Map** 3 A2
ul. Tsar Asen 16
Tel *(02) 981 4482*
Friendly restaurant offering
freshly made pasta served with
authentic Italian sauces. The
cakes and puddings make for
some excellent desserts.

Authentic Bulgarian food at the Hadzhidraganovite Kûshti in Sofia

Checkpoint Charly, named after the best-known crossing point on the Berlin Wall

DK Choice

Pod Lipite €€
Bulgarian
ul. Elin Pelin 1
Tel *(02) 866 5053*
Just over the road from the Borisova Gradina Park, "Under the Limes" perfectly re-creates the atmosphere of a 19th-century country tavern with its wood-beamed interior and delicious home cooking. The emphasis is on grilled and oven-baked meats, although there is a healthy choice of vegetarian dishes on the starter menu.

Pri Yafata €€
Bulgarian **City Map** 3 A2
ul. Solunska 28
Tel *(02) 980 1727*
Enjoyable folk-themed restaurant, with a vast range of Bulgarian specialities and quality wines from every region of the country.

Sluntse Luna €€
Vegetarian **City Map** 3 C3
ul. 6 Septemvri 39
Tel *(0899) 138 411*
With a relaxed air and a rustic theme, this eatery offers an imaginative range of Bulgarian

and global recipes. The on-site bakery has a menu of fresh cake and bread takeaways.

Sushi Bar €€
Japanese **City Map** 3 A1
ul. Ivan Denkoglu 18
Tel *(02) 981 8442*
Chic but by no means too formal, Sushi Bar offers a huge choice of expertly prepared sushi in small helpings or set menus.

Tavite €€
Bulgarian **City Map** 3 B2
ul. William Gladstone 58
Tel *(0882) 880 901* **Closed** *Sun*
Charcoal-grilled Bulgarian food served in a bright, arty interior, with fine cuts of meat and Black Sea fish.

Brasserie €€€
International **City Map** 3 B2
pl. Raiko Daskalov 3
Tel *(02) 980 0398*
A fashionable place specializing in European-Asian fusion dishes and tapas-style snacks. Live music on Thursdays.

Checkpoint Charly €€€
International **City Map** 4 D2
ul. Ivan Vazov 12
Tel *(02) 988 0370*
Minimalist decor blends with iconic Communist era details at this stylish restaurant, known for its excellent selection of wines and food ranging from pasta to steak and duck.

Ego €€€
International **City Map** 4 D1
bul. Tsar Osvoboditel 12
Tel *(02) 980 8989*
Upscale bar-nightclub, also serves a well-executed list of pastas and seafood with an Italian influence.

Enoteca Uno €€€
International **City Map** 4 D4
bul. Vasil Levski 45
Tel *(02) 981 4372*

Sophisticated restaurant offering modern European cuisine with a strong Mediterranean flavour, backed up by a wide range of international wines.

Gioia €€€
Italian **City Map** 1 A1
ul. Tsar Samuil 60
Tel *(02) 986 0854*
Exquisite Italian fare in an intimate setting. Excellent fresh pasta, veal cutlets and a long list of fine fish dishes.

La Capannina €€€
Italian **City Map** 4 E1
pl. Narodno sŭbranie 1
Tel *(020) 980 4438*
Situated right across the Bulgarian parliament, this fine dining restaurant is renowned for its delectable Mediterranean and Italian fare and delicacies such as asparagus and truffles.

Lebed €€€
Seafood
Samokovsko shose 83
Tel *(02) 992 1111*
"Swan", a beautiful restaurant on the shores of Lake Pancharevo, is famous for its fish specialities, refined service and a list of well-chosen international wines.

L'Etranger €€€
French **City Map** 1 C2
ul. Tsar Simeon 78
Tel *(02) 983 1417*
Upscale family-run bistro serving well-made dishes, from simple quiches to full meals. French wines add to the experience.

Manastirska Magernitsa €€€
Bulgarian **City Map** 3 C3
ul. Han Asparuh 67
Tel *(02) 980 3883*
This plush villa with antique furnishings has an amazing menu of traditional Bulgarian dishes, with plenty of choices for vegetarians too.

The stylish and trendy dining room of Ego in Sofia

For more information on types of restaurants *see p229*

Maraia Fusion €€€
International **City Map** 4 D1
ul. G.S. Rakovski 123
Tel (02) 980 6260
Mixing the informality of a diner with haute cuisine standards, this upscale option serves an imaginative range of European-Asian dishes alongside excellent sushi. Full menu of cocktails.

Shades of Red €€€
International **City Map** 3 C1
ul. Gûrko 1
Tel (02) 811 0811
Classy restaurant attached to the Grand Hotel Sofia, offers a wide variety of Mediterranean and French dishes, augmented by Argentinian steaks.

Sidoniya €€€
International
ul. Slavovitsa 51a
Tel (0893) 688 884
Imaginative fusion of modern European and Bulgarian cuisine, with the menu changing regularly.

The Chefs €€€
International
Lake Pasarel
Tel (0896) 723 222 **Closed** Mon, Tue, Wed, Thu
Award-winning, weekend-only restaurant, 17km southeast of town. Offers contemporary European cuisine combining inventiveness and flair. Menu changes daily.

Southern Bulgaria

BACHKOVO: Djamoura €
Bulgarian **Map** C4
ul. Osvobozhdenie 74
Tel (03327) 2320
Great place for grilled meats, excellently done local trout and vegetarian dishes. Dine in the warmth of an open fire, or on the open terrace.

BACHKOVO: Vodopada €
Bulgarian **Map** C4
Tel (03327) 2389
Enjoy large portions of well-cooked lamb and local fish on outdoor tables next to the gushing waterfall near the Bachkovo Monastery entrance.

**BANSKO:
Makedonska Kruchma** €€
Bulgarian **Map** B4
ul. Tûrgovska 1
Tel (0888) 792 299
In the little village of Dobrinishte, near Bansko ski resort, the "Macedonian Inn" serves traditional Bulgarian food in a dining room artfully done with timber furniture.

BANSKO: Molerite €€
Bulgarian **Map** B4
ul. Glazne 41
Tel (0886) 559 595
Spread over two floors, this restaurant, with wooden beams and traditional decor, serves lavish portions of grilled and roast meats.

**BANSKO:
Obetsanova Mehana** €€
Bulgarian **Map** B4
pl. Vazrazhdane 1
Tel (0878) 555 611
Converted from an old National Revival-style house into a tavern with a large garden. Serves well-prepared Bansko specialities such as kapama (pork or chicken with vegetables) and chumlek (slow-cooked shin of beef).

BANSKO: Come Prima €€€
Mediterranean **Map** B4
ul. Pirin 96
Tel (0749) 88888
A sophisticated affair in the Kempinski Hotel, with an open kitchen and a menu that runs from home-made pasta to seafood.

**BLAGOEVGRAD:
Mehana Vodenitsata** €€
Bulgarian **Map** B4
Bachinovo Park
Tel (0898) 625 959
This folk-style restaurant, 2km south of central Blagoevgrad, has a park-like setting, complete with a kids' playground and mini zoo.

DEVIN: Elit €€
Bulgarian **Map** C4
ul. Yundola 2
Tel (03041) 2240
Elegant restaurant with a summer garden, serves traditional dishes as well as mussels, squid and freshwater and Black Sea fish.

DEVIN: Ismena €€
Bulgarian **Map** C4
ul. Guritsa 4
Tel (0884) 707 970
A good place to try traditional Rhodope dishes, with a smart interior and an outdoor terrace that has lovely mountain views.

HASKOVO: Uno Piu €
Pizzeria **Map** D4
bul. Dobrudzha 10
Tel (0886) 361 111
A classy family-friendly pizzeria with a summer garden and play area for kids.

HASKOVO: Alafrangite €€
Bulgarian **Map** D4
ul. Milin Kamûk 7
Tel (038) 664 400

The elegantly decorated Come Prima in Kempinski Hotel, Bansko

Delectable Bulgarian cuisine is served at this elegant, 1815 house. Choose between dining in its traditionally furnished rooms or in the lovely garden outside.

KOVACHEVITSA:
Kruchma Bratyata €
Bulgarian Map B4
Tel *(0888) 347 478*
Serves traditional local dishes featuring home-grown vegetables. Local wines and brandies, too.

KÛRDZHALI:
Mehana Rodopchani €€
Bulgarian Map D5
Road to Ardino
Tel *(0898) 690 057*
Bulgarian fare served with flair in a traditional setting. Located 3 km west of the centre.

KYUSTENDIL: Strimon €€€
International Map A4
ul. Tsar Simeon I, 24
Tel *(078) 559 000*
Sophisticated restaurant serving high-class cuisine with French and Mediterranean influences.

LESHTEN: Leshten Mehana €€
Bulgarian Map B4
Tel *(0888) 544 651*
This charming stone house at the centre of the village serves Bulgarian dishes prepared from fresh local produce. Great home-made wines too.

MELNIK: Despot Slav €
Bulgarian Map B5
Tel *(07437) 248*
A good balance between vegetarian and meat dishes, with excellent rabbit, duck and pork among the options.

MELNIK: Mencheva Kûshta €
Bulgarian Map B5
Tel *(07437) 339*
An old house with a distinct character; the perfect place to sample traditional dishes and fiery fruit brandies.

PAMPOROVO: Chanove €€
Bulgarian Map C5
Tel *(03095) 8212*
With hunting trophies and a roaring fireplace, Chanove serves old-style Bulgarian dishes, including goose lungs, chicken hearts and delicious bean soup.

PAMPOROVO: White House €€
Bulgarian Map C5
Tel *(03095) 8550*
This elegant eatery, done with a rustic theme complete with exposed wooden beams and cow bells, has a menu of traditional Rhodope dishes, pasta and pizza.

Grilled and stewed squid cooked in Greek tomato sauce, served at Hemingway in Plovdiv

PLOVDIV: Erevan €
Armenian Map C4
ul. Otets Paisii 15
Tel *(0894) 762 779*
Stylish restaurant serving traditional grills and Anatolian wines.

PLOVDIV: Veda House €
Vegetarian Map C4
ul. Georgi Benkovski 50
Tel *(032) 622 760*
Two-storey café-restaurant known for tasty vegetarian dishes, leaf teas, home-made biscuits and desserts. Daily menu is good value.

PLOVDIV: XIX Vek €€
Bulgarian Map C4
ul. Tsar Kaloyan 1a
Tel *(032) 886 856*
A local favourite that has walls decorated with traditional implements reminiscent of a 19th-century village, offers a wide choice of local dishes.

PLOVDIV: Gusto €€
Italian Map C4
ul. Otets Paisii 26
Tel *(032) 653 882*
This city-centre restaurant is well-known for its good-value fare, with authentic pizzas, pasta and salads.

DK Choice

PLOVDIV: Art Café
Filipopolis €€€
International Map C4
ul. Suborna 29
Tel *(032) 624 851*
More of a restaurant, this café has an elegant interior and an oudoor terrace with sweeping views of modern Plovdiv. The mains menu has competently handled steaks, duck and freshwater fish, while the tempting desserts include apple strudel and walnut pie.

PLOVDIV: Hemingway €€€
International Map C4
ul. Gûrko 10
Tel *(032) 267 350*

Bohemian decor combines with comfort at this upscale BBQ & Grill that has a well-stocked bar.

PLOVDIV: Salt & Pepper €€€
Seafood Map C4
ul. Han Kubrat 1
Tel *(032) 275 671* **Closed** *Sun*
Located in a modern building with a small terrace, this first-floor restaurant specializes in Mediterranean seafood, a wide range of fish dishes, excellent pastas and risottos.

PLOVDIV OLD TOWN:
Alafrangite €€
Bulgarian Map C4
ul. Kiril Nektariev 13
Tel *(0888) 312 433*
Bulgarian classics are served in the rooms of this beautifully preserved 19th-century, Revival-style house.

PLOVDIV OLD TOWN:
Konyushite na Tsarya €€
Bulgarian Map C4
ul. Saborna
Tel *(0898) 542 787*
A summer-only establishment, this restaurant and bar is also popular for Bulgarian grills. Gets crowded on weekends.

PLOVDIV OLD TOWN:
Hebros €€€
International Map C4
ul. Konstantin Stoilov 51
Tel *(032) 260 180*
The seasonally-changing menu at this award-winning high-class restaurant focuses on French-Modern European cuisine, made with fresh ingredients.

PLOVDIV OLD TOWN:
Petr I €€€
Russian Map C4
ul. Knyaz Tseretelev 11
Tel *(032) 620 789*
Though its decor tends to border on kitsch, this expensive Russian restaurant offers a splendid dining experience. The terrace has delightful views of the city.

For more information on types of restaurants *see p229*

Freshly-tossed salad, a popular side dish with many Bulgarian meats

This elegant restaurant has a Mediterranean theme complete with faux Greco-Roman pillars. The menu comprises well-made pasta, seafood and salads.

SHIROKA LŮKA:
Mehana pri Slavchev €
Bulgarian **Map** C4
Tel (0888) 784 897
Sample Rhodope specialities such as patatnik (savoury potato bake), while being serenaded by bagpipers, at this restaurant located in the heart of an idyllic village.

SMOLYAN: Riben Dar €€
Seafood **Map** C5
ul. Snezhanka 16
Tel (0301) 63220
Tucked away in a hillside residential area, Riben Dar offers a wide-ranging menu of freshwater fish and Aegean seafood.

VELINGRAD: Aquatonik €€
International **Map** B4
ul. Nikola Vaptsarov 122
Tel (0359) 51010
Modern restaurant in the Aquatonik spa centre, serves a range of well-prepared European and Mediterranean dishes.

VELINGRAD:
Rodopsko Selo €€
Bulgarian **Map** B4
bul. Suedinenie 149
Tel (0887) 509 020
A folk restaurant with outdoor tables in a walled courtyard, the "Rhodope Village" has national dishes, wines and fermented fruit rakiyas (brandies).

Central Bulgaria

ARBANASI: Izvora €€
Bulgarian **Map** D3
ul. Opŭlchenska 2
Tel (062) 627 917

Attractive garden restaurant with an open grill and a good selection of oven-baked dishes.

ARBANASI: Payak Mehana €€
Bulgarian **Map** D3
Tel (062) 606 810
Traditional mehana, in an old stone house done up with typical Bulgarian decor, serves hearty grilled meats and shashlik kebabs.

GABROVO: Pizza Tempo €
Pizzeria **Map** C3
ul. Pencho Slaveykov 1
Tel (066) 806 920
Stylish Italian restaurant with an open kitchen, offers tasty thin-crust pizzas and a wide selection of pasta dishes.

GABROVO:
Strannopriemnitsa €
Bulgarian **Map** C3
ul. Opŭlchenska 15
Tel (066) 807 121
Folk-style restaurant with a balcony and courtyard, serves delightful local grilled meat dishes.

GABROVO: Rest €€
International **Map** C3
ul. Stara Planina 4
Tel (066) 876 543
This charming old house, with a gated garden, aims to please diners with European and Bulgarian meat and poultry dishes.

HISARYA: Panorama €€
International **Map** C3
ul. Gŭrko 1
Tel (0337) 62781
With great views from the fifth-floor terrace, this quality restaurant offers Rhodope specialities alongside Arabic and European fare.

KARLOVO: Vodopad €
Bulgarian **Map** C3
ul. Vodopad 41
Tel (0335) 93127

PLOVDIV OLD TOWN:
Puldin €€€
Bulgarian **Map** C4
ul. Knyaz Tseretelev 3
Tel (032) 631 720
Feast here on the superbly prepared and presented traditional cuisine, including fish and vegetarian dishes. Choose between the ambience of a modern restaurant upstairs or the more traditional tavern below.

RILA MONASTERY:
Drushliavitsa €€
Bulgarian **Map** B4
Tel (0888) 278 756
With hearty Bulgarian dishes and freshly-caught trout dominating its menu, and a gurgling stream running under its overhanging terrace, this restaurant adjoining the monastery walls offers a fine dining experience.

RILA MONASTERY:
Tzarev Vrah €€
Bulgarian **Map** B4
Tel (0898) 705 399
The rustic ambience at this eatery above the Rila River provides a nice setting for traditional regional cuisine, with grilled meats and local trout.

SAMOKOV: Starata Kŭshta €
Bulgarian **Map** B4
ul. Zahari Zograf 13
Tel (0888) 723 118
Set in a charming 19th-century house, this traditional restaurant has a relaxed air, with plenty of salads and grilled meat on the menu.

SANDANSKI: Plomari €€
International **Map** B5
ul. Makedoniya 1
Tel (0746) 33035

The homely and welcoming dining area of Rest in Gabrovo

The contemporary-style garden of Forum, Stara Zagora

Uncomplicated grilled food is served at this traditional *mehana* with plenty of outdoor tables, located next to the Suchurum waterfall *(vodopad)* on the outskirts of Karlovo.

KARLOVO: Edno Vreme　€€
Bulgarian　**Map** C3
ul. Rakovska 9
Tel *(0879) 201 105*
"Once Upon a Time" excels with a traditional menu of grilled meats, freshwater fish and healthy salads. Set, of course, in an endearing house with a lovely walled garden.

KAZANLŭK: Teres　€
Bulgarian　**Map** D3
ul. Lyubomir Kabakchiev 16
Tel *(0431) 64272*
Part of the Teres hotel, serves well-prepared Bulgarian cuisine, freshwater fish and pizza. Outdoor seating in a relaxing and well-kept garden.

**KOPRIVSHTITSA:
20 April Tavern**　€
Bulgarian　**Map** C3
pl. 20 April
Tel *(0889) 368 220*
Mehana on the town's main square, named after the date of the April Rising of 1876. Serves good Bulgarian food on the outdoor terrace in summers and in the warmth of its fireplace during winters.

**KOPRIVSHTITSA:
Chuchura**　€
Bulgarian　**Map** C3
ul. Hadzhi Nencho Paleveev 66
Tel *(0888) 347 770*
Historic house with walled courtyard, serves great central Bulgarian fare. *Tutmanik* (cheese bread) and *patatnik* (potato bake) are the house specialities.

DK Choice

**KOPRIVSHTITSA:
Dyado Liben**　€€
Bulgarian　**Map** C3
ul. Hadzhi Nencho Palaveev 47
Tel *(07184) 2109*
This romantic restaurant in a beautifully restored mansion offers a short but excellent menu of grilled meats and oriental sweets typical of the Balkan peninsula.

LOVECH: Pri Voivodite　€
Bulgarian　**Map** C2
ul. Marin Pop Lukanov
Tel *(0888) 837 513*
Hidden behind stone walls in the Varosha quarter, this local favourite serves excellently prepared regional fare.

LOVECH: Apollo　€€
International　**Map** C2
ul. Tŭrgovska 51
Tel *(068) 600 170*
An upmarket restaurant with an inventive menu featuring steaks, seafood and Mediterranean dishes. Good list of international wines.

**RIBARITSA:
Evergreen Palace**　€€
International　**Map** C3
Tel *(06902) 2066*
Plush restaurant with fantastic mountain views, serving well-prepared fresh trout, goose and duck. Also has a good selection of Bulgarian wines.

STARA ZAGORA: Forum　€€
International　**Map** D3
ul. Hadzhi Dimitŭr Asenov 94
Tel *(042) 631 616*
This upscale restaurant is known for its meticulously prepared Bulgarian and international fare, backed by excellent wines.

TETEVEN: Maksim　€
Bulgarian　**Map** C3
ul. Emil Markov 27
Tel *0885 671 367*
Regional cuisine in a medieval-period ambience, complete with suits of armour, shields and stained-glass windows.

TETEVEN: Teteven Mehana　€
Bulgarian　**Map** C3
ul. Simeon Kumanov 46
Tel *0899 955 314*
Traditional stone house tavern, with local and national dishes.

TROYAN: Mehana Troyan　€
Bulgarian　**Map** C3
ul. Slaveykov 54
Tel *(0670) 64399*
With a full-size wagon as part of its decor, this fun interpretation of a traditional tavern in the Troyan Plaza hotel offers local dishes.

TRYAVNA: Pizza Domino　€
Pizzeria　**Map** D3
ul. Angel Kanchev 36
Tel *(0677) 2322*
Modern restaurant with delicious, inexpensive thin-crust pizzas, pastas and a choice of salads.

Evergreen Palace in Ribaritsa, nestled between the Stara Planina Mountains

For more information on types of restaurants *see p229*

The historic Hadzhi Nikoli in Veliko Tûrnovo, offering Bulgarian and international cuisine

TRYAVNA: Starata Loza €
Bulgarian   Map D3
ul. Slaveykov 44
Tel *(0677) 4501*
Whether dining on the vine-shaded terrace or in the traditionally-styled room, feast on local specialities such as stewed calf's tongue and fried brains.

TRYAVNA: Zograf Mehana €
Bulgarian   Map D3
ul. Slaveykov 1
Tel *(0677) 4970*
An old-style tavern with an open fire and wooden furniture, offering a good range of local food including trout and rabbit.

VELIKO TÛRNOVO:
Mehana Gurko €
ul. Gûrko 33
Tel *(062) 627 838*
Traditional *mehana* serving local specialities together with a long list of wines and *rakiyas* (brandies), in folksy surroundings.

VELIKO TÛRNOVO:
Pizza Tempo €
Pizzeria   Map D3
ul. Ivailo 4
Tel *(062) 606 920*
Popular restaurant serving a good range of pizzas, pastas and Bulgarian staples. Rustic environment with exposed-brick walls and overhead wood beams.

VELIKO TÛRNOVO: Ego €€
International
ul. Nezavisimost 17
Tel *(062) 601 804*
Main street pizzeria and grill, with pasta, steaks and other international dishes filling out an extensive menu.

VELIKO TÛRNOVO:
Shtastlivetsa €€
Bulgarian   Map D3
ul. Stefan Stambolov 79
Tel *(062) 600 656*

Lively restaurant with a huge menu covering almost everything in Bulgarian cuisine, plus pizzas and pastas.

VELIKO TÛRNOVO:
Hadzhi Nikoli €€€
International   Map D3
ul. Rakovska 39
Tel *(062) 651 291*
This well-appointed restaurant in an old *caravanserai* offers an inventive range of modern European and Bulgarian dishes. Has a list of excellent wines.

VELIKO TÛRNOVO:
Klub na Arhitekta €€€
International   Map D3
ul. Velcho Dzhamdzhiyata 14
Tel *(062) 621 451*
Built into a steep hillside above Yantra River, the "Architect's Club" serves European classics in a candlelit, cave-like interior.

VELIKO TÛRNOVO: Yantra €€€
International   Map D3
ul. Opalchenska 2
Tel *(062) 600 607*

An appetizing 'Cherga' salad, made with a variety of fresh vegetables

One of the town's best, this capacious restaurant offers an excellent choice of Bulgarian and international cuisine, along with great views of the Tsarevets citadel.

YAMBOL: Pizza Nostos €
Pizzeria   Map E3
ul. Tsar Samuil 1
Tel *(046) 664 099*
One of the better pizzerias in town, with a good choice of thin-crust pizzas and a special menu for vegetarians.

ZHERAVNA: Starcha €
Bulgarian   Map E3
Tel *(0887) 495 555*
Newly-built, traditional-style restaurant, with succulent barbecued meats and salads made from fresh local produce.

Northern Bulgaria

BELOGRADCHIK: Madona €
Bulgarian   Map A2
ul. Hristo Botev 26
Tel *(0936) 5546*
Family-run *mehana* with views of Belogradchik's famous rocks. Specialities include *chorba od kopriva* (nettle soup) and *grohchano* (diced pork with onions and garlic).

BERKOVITSA:
Krusteva Kûshta €
Bulgarian   Map B2
ul. Sheinovo 5
Tel *(0953) 88099*
Regional fare, comprising salads and meat dishes, served in a charming 19th-century house that has a walled garden.

CHIPROVTSI:
Gostopriemnitsa Kipro €
Bulgarian   Map A2
ul. Balkanska 46
Tel *(09554) 2947*
Homely restaurant with wooden bench-and-table seating. Serves Bulgarian grilled meat dishes and local specialities such as *kachamak* (polenta with white cheese).

DOBRICH: Residence €€
International   Map F2
ul. Batovska 20
Tel *(058) 602 300*
Smart and elegant eatery with a good mixture of mainstream Bulgarian and Central European dishes.

PLEVEN: Bulgarski koren €
Bulgarian   Map C2
ul. Naicho Tsanov 4
Tel *(064) 829 090*

Traditional food in a National Revival-style house with a shaded garden and a pretty stream. The *gyuveche* dishes (meat and vegetables baked in a clay pot) are excellent.

PLEVEN: Paraklisa Klub €
International   Map C2
ul. Knyaz Boris III 1
Tel *(064) 820 020*
City-centre restaurant that gets rather packed with young drinkers in the evenings, especially over weekends. Serves pretty much everything, from steaks to pizza.

RUSE: Pizza Roma €
Pizzeria   Map D2
ul. Tsurkovna nezavisimost 16
Tel *(082) 879 999*
Intimate cellar-bound restaurant serving well-made thin-crust pizzas, pasta dishes and salads. Leave room for the tiramisu.

RUSE: La Strada €€
International   Map D2
ul. Aleksandrovska 77
Tel *(0882) 557 799*
European restaurant serving an eclectic range of meat, fish and fowl dishes, prepared in a variety of classic styles.

RUSE: Mehana Chiflika €€
Bulgarian   Map D2
ul. Otets Paisii 2
Tel *(082) 828 222*
This fine restaurant, with agricultural implements as part of its decor, is a great place to try traditional Bulgarian cuisine.

RUSE: Leventa €€€
Bulgarian   Map D2
Leventa Complex
Tel *(082) 862 880*
Bulgarian classics are given lavish haute-cuisine treatment at this restored 19th-century fortress, which has seven dining halls richly decorated with hand-painted frescoes. The wine house, amid grand vaults of wine barrels, serves excellent red and white wines.

RUSE: Panorama €€€
International   Map D2
bul. Pridunavska 22
Tel *(0899) 955 095*
From its top floor perch, this classy restaurant offers command-ing views of the Danube, and serves classic European fare with old-school standards of presentation and service.

SHUMEN: Panorama €€
International   Map E2
Tel *(0882) 990 499*
Pan-European fare including steaks, pasta and fish, served with style at this top-floor hotel-restaurant with grand views of the city.

SHUMEN: Popsheytanova Kŭshta €€
Bulgarian   Map E2
ul. Tsar Osvoboditel 158
Tel *(054) 802 222*
Traditional restaurant famous for its charcoal-grilled meats and wide range of cuts, including rabbit and lamb.

DK Choice

SILISTRA: Nikulden €
Seafood   Map F1
ul. Pristanishtna 2
Tel *(086) 822 214*
This riverside eatery, with wood-panelled walls and plants, is renowned for its selection of fish from the Danube. Succulent fillets of *som* (catfish), *sharan* (carp) and other catch-of-the-day are served grilled or pan-fried, according to choice. A glass of the local *kaisieva rakiya* (apricot brandy) makes for a perfect aperitif.

SVISHTOV: Bai Ganyu €
Bulgarian   Map D2
ul. Dragan Tsankov 12
Tel *(0631) 23403*
Inexpensive Bulgarian fare (including Danube fish) and a wide variety of salads and vegetable-based starters are served at this homely eatery hidden away in a residential street a few steps away from Svishtov's main square.

SVISHTOV: Svishtov €
Bulgarian   Map D2
ul. Dimitûr Shishmanov 10
Tel *(0899) 877 887*
Friendly place to sample roast-meat dishes such as *dzholan* (pork calves) and Danube fish. Has domestic bric-à-brac aesthetically hung on its stone walls.

VIDIN: Anna Kristina €
Bulgarian   Map A1
ul. Baba Vida 2
Tel *(094) 606 038*
Charcoal-grilled cuts of pork and beef dominate the menu of this pleasant restaurant. Its speciality is the shashlik-style skewered kebabs. Try the red Gumza wine.

VIDIN: Zodiac €€
International   Map A1
ul. Pazarska 2
Tel *(094) 606 184*
Smart fine-dining restaurant with a menu offering expertly-handled steaks, pizzas, freshwater fish and good local wines.

VRATSA: Chaika €
Bulgarian   Map B2
Vratsata Gorge
Tel *(092) 622 367*
Garden restaurant at the foot of the cliffs of Vratsata Gorge, where traditional Bulgarian grilled dishes and fried freshwater fish are prepared to high standards. Try the home-baked bread buns.

A live performance at the luxurious and elegant La Strada in Ruse, Northern Bulgaria

For more information on types of restaurants *see p229*

Black Sea Coast

BALCHIK: Korona €€
International   **Map** G2
Dvoretsa
Tel *(0579) 76847*
Barbequed meats and a wide
choice of fish and seafood dishes,
served in a stone building near
the Botanical Gardens. Outdoor
seating beneath a pergola.

BALCHIK: Veroni €€
Bulgarian   **Map** G2
ul. Dunav 3
Tel *(0579) 76868*
Popular for its Bulgarian and
Italian options. Lovely garden.

BALCHIK: White House €€
International   **Map** G2
ul. Geo Milev 18
Tel *(0579) 73951*
With its shaded terrace overlooking the marina, this place
offers high-quality food at reasonable prices. Impeccable service.

BURGAS: Grolsch €€
Bulgarian   **Map** F3
Primorski Park
Tel *(056) 813 426*
Barbecue restaurant in the Sea
Garden, serves generous portions
of meat and fish. Has a nice list of
local beers and wines.

BURGAS: Rose €€
International   **Map** F3
ul. Bogoridi 19
Tel *(0897) 200 000*
A 19th-century building with
quirky decor and a menu that
covers seafood and Mediterranean
dishes, including good risottos
and excellent desserts.

BURGAS: Salini €€€
International   **Map** F3
ul. Aleksandûr Batenberg 2
Tel *(0897) 096 398*

Attached to Primoretz hotel,
this elegant restaurant offers
an amazing variety of beautifully-
presented Mediterranean, seafood
and local Bulgarian cuisines.

DURANKULAK: Zlatna Ribka €
Seafood   **Map** G2
Durankulak Lake
Closed *Mon*
The "Golden Fish" is hugely
popular on account of the freshly-
caught fish served and its garden
seating on the lake's edge.

GOLDEN SANDS: Parmy €€€
International   **Map** G2
Kraybrezhna aleya
Tel *(0888) 205 023*
This friendly restaurant in a
mega-resort has a satisfying
menu of grilled meats, seafood,
fish and pizzas.

KAMEN BRIAG:
Trite Kestena €
Seafood   **Map** G2
Village Centre
Tel *(05704) 2759*
One of the oldest restaurants in
the area, with a large courtyard
shaded by vines and plum trees.
Its menu comprises of fresh fish
and home-grown vegetables.

KAVARNA:
Midena Ferma Dulboka €€
Seafood   **Map** G2
*Midway between Kavarna and
Bulgarevo*
Tel *(0899) 911 377*
Occupying a spectacular spot
on the water's edge at the foot
of the cliffs, this legendary
seafood restaurant serves
mussels from its own farm,
cooked in many different ways.

LOZENETS: Starata Kûshta €
Bulgarian   **Map** F4
ul. Georgi Kondolov 2
Tel *(0550) 57257*

"Old House" follows the
traditional Bulgarian theme of
red-and-white tablecloths and
rustic wooden tables to serve
the vast range of grilled meats
it is widely popular for.

LOZENETS: Friends €€
International   **Map** F4
ul. Ribarska 45
Tel *(0888) 606 575*
Well-prepared sushi, local
seafood dishes and meaty grills
are the trademarks of this cool
and stylish restaurant.

NESEBÛR: Plakamoto €
Seafood   **Map** F3
ul. Ivan Aleksandûr 8
Tel *(0554) 45544*
In a restored 19th-century
building with a terrace shaded
by fig trees, this idyllic restaurant
offers a variety of Black Sea fare.
Try the mussels and conger eel.

NESEBÛR:
Kapitanska Sreshta €€
Seafood   **Map** F3
ul. Mena 22
Tel *(0554) 42124*
Occupying a lovely old house with
a shaded terrace overlooking the
harbour, the "Captains' Meet" has
a long, impressive menu of fish
dishes, covering conger eel, shark
and swordfish.

NESEBÛR: Neptun €€
Seafood   **Map** F3
ul. Neptun 1
Tel *(0554) 44133*
Charming restaurant that has
a menu of Black Sea and Aegean
fish, shellfish, calamari and
prawns. Great sea views.

POMORIE: Kotvata €
Seafood   **Map** F3
bul. Yavorov 2
Tel *(0554) 22422*
A pleasant outdoor restaurant
with superb sea views, "The
Anchor" offers a good choice of
fish and delectable desserts.

SHABLA: Bai Pesho €
Seafood   **Map** G2
Tel *(0888) 221 771*
Atmospheric eatery right on
the shore, famous for its no-frills
menu of grilled fresh fish. Its fish
soup is legendary.

SINEMORETS:
Sinyata Akula €€
Seafood   **Map** G4
ul. Butamya 11
The "Blue Shark" offers Black Sea
fish and Mediterranean food,
with excellent risotto and pasta
dishes served alongside healthy
salads and great desserts.

The unconventional interior of Rose, Burgas

Wine bottles lining the walls of Di Wine in Varna

SINEMORETS:
Casa Domingo €€€
International Map G4
ul. Ribarska
Tel *(0590) 66093*
Sit under refreshing vines around the central pool of this upscale restaurant, and choose from a wide variety of meticulously prepared Mediterranean dishes and local seafood.

SOZOPOL: Rusalka €€
Seafood Map F3
ul. Milet 36
Tel *(0550) 23047*
Waves crash against rocks directly below Rusalka, which offers great views and an equally amazing variety of seafood, pasta and pizza.

SOZOPOL: Urania €€
International Map F3
ul. Milet 34
Tel *(0550) 22717*
Refined dining with carefully prepared Black Sea fish, steaks and a few inventive dishes that feature rabbit and duck.

SUNNY BEACH:
Hanska Shatra €€€
Bulgarian Map F3
Tel *(0554) 22811*
This restaurant, a massive concrete replica of a Bulgarian Khan's tent, offers a vast range of national and international cuisine, accompanied by endless floorshows.

TYULENOVO: Delfina €
Seafood Map G2
Next to Tyulenovo Harbour
Tel *(05743) 42221*
Meat dishes and locally caught fish crowd the menu of this small hotel-restaurant. The terrace overlooks a tiny harbour full of fishing boats.

VARNA: My Café €
Café Map F2
bul. Slivnitsa 16
Tel *(0878) 193589*
Main-street patisserie with a French theme that is probably the best place in Varna to enjoy coffee and croissant. Also has a delicious selection of eat-in or take-out cakes and sandwiches.

VARNA: Bodega €€
Spanish Map F2
bul. Slivnitsa 9
Tel *(0899) 115055*
Centrally located wine and tapas bar with a wide choice of seafood dishes, succulent Spanish hams and *montaditos* (small sandwiches) to nibble on.

VARNA: Garibaldi €€
Italian Map F2
ul. Tsar Osvoboditel 9
Tel *(052) 604 080*
This majestic restaurant is just the place for great Italian cuisine: *prosciutto* (cured ham) starters, fresh-made pasta, veal cutlets and an excellent tiramisu.

VARNA: Pri Monahinite €€
Bulgarian Map F2
ul. Primorski 47
Tel *(052) 611 830*
One of Varna's most charming and imaginative restaurants, "At the Nun's" has a vast menu filled with dishes from almost every region of the country. Extensive wine list, too.

VARNA: Acant Rouge €€€
International Map F2
ul. Knyaz Aleksandûr Batenberg 41
Tel *(052) 696 336*
An upscale and intimate restaurant with a French theme, offers exquisite preparations of fish, lamb and rabbit dishes. Excellent home-made ice cream.

VARNA: Di Wine €€€
International Map F2
Bratya Shkorpil 2
Tel *(052) 606 050*
Elegant city-centre wine bar, as well-suited for a quick snack as it is for a full meal. Menu extends from tapas-style nibbles to excellent steaks, lamb chops and superb desserts.

VARNA: Modus Bistro €€€
International Map F2
ul. Stefan Stambolov 46
Tel *(052) 660 910*
Smart and sleek restaurant with a mainstream European menu that strikes a good balance between meat, fish and vegetarian options. Classic desserts as well.

VARNA: Musala €€€
International Map F2
ul. Musala 3
Tel *(052) 664 175*
Located in Grand Hotel London, this sophisticated restaurant, with velvet upholstery and silver cutlery, serves a European menu with élan. Try the duck, venison or Black Sea fish.

DK Choice

VARNA: Red Canape €€€
International Map F2
bul. Knyaz Boris I 65
Tel *(0882) 005 005*
With a splash of sensuous reds and cool greys, this elegant restaurant in Graffit Gallery Hotel scores perfectly on being both a haute-cuisine restaurant and a design-conscious bistro. Its menu covers cuisine with a distinct French- and Mediterranean-influence, along with Black Sea fish, with everything prepared and served with attention to detail.

For more information on types of restaurants *see p229*

SHOPPING IN BULGARIA

Bright modern malls and shops selling clothes by major international labels are an increasingly common feature of Bulgaria's town and city centres. By contrast, and quite untouched by international retail culture, Bulgaria also has a wealth of shops, open-air markets and stalls selling everything from Bulgarian-made soaps to *rakiya*, Bulgarian brandy. In every town centre there is a market, with stalls stacked with fruit, vegetables and flowers, and street kiosks with meticulously arranged trays of dried fruit, nuts and sweets. Bulgaria's rich handicrafts tradition includes the distinctive pottery from Troyan, weaving and embroidery, woodcarving and metalwork. In coastal resorts and other areas frequented by visitors, streets and promenades are lined with souvenir stalls offering dolls in traditional costume, replicas of antique icons and local craft items.

Opening Hours

In major towns and cities and in holiday resorts, shops are open from 10am to 8pm Monday to Saturday, and often stay open later during the summer season. In Sofia and in towns along the Black Sea coast, shops also open on Sundays, closing at various times between 2pm and 6pm.

Food shops and super-markets in major towns and cities are open from 7am to 10pm Monday to Saturday, and from 7am to 6pm on Sunday. In smaller towns, shops may close much earlier, and may also close at lunchtime.

Markets

Every town in the country has an open-air market, where fresh fruit and vegetables, all sorts of Bulgarian cheeses and sausages are sold. While markets in cities follow regular shop hours, those in smaller towns may be open only in the morning, or on certain days of the week.

Several of Bulgaria's most picturesque outdoor markets sell not only fresh produce, clothing and household goods but also handicrafts. The liveliest of these markets are the daily **Zhenski pazar** in Sofia, the daily market in Varna, and the Sunday morning market in Bansko.

The daily **Bric-à-Brac market** in front of the Aleksandŭr Nevski Memorial Church in Sofia is the best place to go for antiques, old postcards, and Communist-era medals and militaria.

Payment Methods

Cash is still the most common means of paying for goods in Bulgaria. Cheques are rarely accepted, and credit cards can only be used in the more prestigious shops in Sofia and other major cities.

It is not customary to haggle, except when you are shopping for bric-à-brac or craft items in the more informal markets, where prices are not marked.

Window of a clothes shop on bulevard Vitosha in Sofia

Crafts and Souvenirs

High-quality craft items predominate on Bulgaria's souvenir stalls, with ceramics, embroidery and traditional textiles among the most popular items. Pottery from the central Bulgarian town of Troyan, decorated with flowing patterns in bright colours, is one of the most typically Bulgarian souvenirs. While Troyan plates and jugs are available throughout the country, the widest choice of the finest-quality pieces can be found at the **Arts and Crafts Exhibition** in Oreshak, near Troyan Monastery.

Traditional Bulgarian textiles include vividly patterned kilims hand-woven on vertical looms by the womenfolk of highland villages such as Kotel and

Stall with fresh fruit and vegetables at Rimska Stena market, Sofia

Chiprovtsi. Other hand-woven items include fleecy rugs (*guberi*) from villages in the Rhodope Mountains, and tufted goat-hair rugs (*kozyatsi*) from highland villages all over Bulgaria. Brightly coloured blouses, delicately embroidered with folk motifs, are usually also of a high quality.

Bulgaria is a major producer of attar of roses, an essential oil extracted from the damask rose, which is used all over the world as an ingredient of perfumes and beauty products. Locally made soaps, skin creams and eau de cologne made from Bulgarian attar of roses are available in high-street pharmacies and supermarkets throughout the country. Other craft items that the visitor might consider buying include traditional copper pots and coffee sets, and hand-painted copies of Orthodox icons.

Souvenirs are sold on market stalls and in small shops in tourist resorts throughout the country. Specialist outlets selling the best-quality handicrafts include **Bŭlgarski Dyukyan** and the **Ethnographic Museum Shop** in Sofia. Shops in the Stariya Dobrich quarter in Dobrich, and the Samovodska charshiya in Veliko Tûrnovo, are good places to pick up good-quality items made by local craft workshops.

Embroidered blouses and other traditional clothes for sale in Bansko

Books and CDs

Bulgarian bookshops offer a wide range of books on the subject of Bulgaria's scenic beauty, historic sights and cultural heritage. Many are lavishly illustrated and have text in English. Bookshops are also good places to go to buy road maps and town plans.

The liveliest place to browse for books is the open-air book market on ploshtad Slaveykov in Sofia (*see p86*). Here, a multitude of stalls are loaded with books old and new. Books, as well as stationery, CDs and DVDs, can also be found in multimedia stores, which are increasingly common in larger towns and cities.

As might be expected in a country with such rich musical traditions, CDs of Bulgarian folk music are widely available on souvenir stalls, at museum shops and in music stores. However, as there are many low-quality recordings on the market, it is advisable to choose albums released by reputable labels such as Kuker and Gega, which specialize in traditional Bulgarian music. Although high-street multimedia stores carry a wide selection of traditional folk music recordings, the best places to go for advice on what to buy are specialist shops like **Dyukyan Meloman** in Sofia.

Wine and Rakiya

Most food shops and supermarkets carry a wide selection of Bulgarian wines. While Bulgarian Merlots and Cabernet Sauvignons are on a par with red wines from elsewhere in Europe, domestic varieties, such as Melnik from the southwest (*see pp120–21*) and Mavrud from the Asenovgrad region, have a much more distinctive character. Bulgarian wines of the highest quality are those produced by leading wineries such as Todoroff and

Bottle of Bulgarian *rakiya*

Damyanitza. These excellent wines are available in stores throughout the country.

Bottles of *rakiya* (grape or plum brandy) also make very good gifts. Look for bottles marked *otlezhala* (meaning "matured"), as these are likely to be of superior quality.

DIRECTORY

Markets

Zhenski pazar
ul. Stefan Stambolov, Sofia.
Map 1 A2. **Open** 8am–7pm daily.

Bric-à-Brac
pl. Aleksandŭr Nevski, Sofia.
Map 2 E4. **Open** 8am–dusk daily.

Clothes and Handicrafts
ul. Tsar Simeon, Bansko.
Open 8am–2pm Sun.

Clothes and Handicrafts
pl. Mitropolit Simeon, Varna.
Open 8am–3pm daily.

Crafts Shops

Bŭlgarski Dyukyan
ul. Pirotska 11a, Sofia.
Map 1 A3. **Tel** (02) 988 4139.

Ethnographic Museum Shop
pl. Aleksandŭr Batenberg 1, Sofia.
Map 1 C4.

Arts and Crafts Exhibition
Oreshak, near Troyan Monastery.

CD Shops

Dyukyan Meloman
ul. 6 Septemvri 7a, Sofia.
Map 4 D1.
Tel (02) 988 5862.

ENTERTAINMENT IN BULGARIA

Bulgaria's classical music, ballet and theatre season runs from the beginning of October to the end of June. During this time, the country's fine orchestras, opera and ballet companies perform at venues in Sofia and other major towns, and theatre companies stage productions of classic and contemporary plays.

Through the summer months, a succession of arts festivals take place in the towns of the Black Sea coast, with stimulating programmes of music, drama and dance. Bulgaria's vigorous folk culture also offers the opportunity to see and hear traditional Bulgarian dancing and music at one of several major summer folk festivals.

Classical Music, Opera and Dance

Bulgaria has a fine tradition of classical music. The quality is high, and tickets for concerts are very reasonably priced. The Bulgarian Philharmonic Orchestra, which performs weekly at the Bulgarian Hall (Zala Bulgariya) in Sofia, is the country's most prestigious orchestra. However, the provinces aren't forgotten and Plovdiv, Varna and Burgas also maintain good symphony orchestras. Many of Bulgaria's best orchestras and soloists perform at Varna Summer International Festival in July, a month-long orchestral, choral and chamber music event.

The leading opera and ballet companies in the country operate under the aegis of the **Bulgarian National Opera and Ballet** in Sofia. Close ties with Russian ballet schools have produced some excellent dancers and international companies often visit Sofia on tour. However, several regional cities do maintain pretty good opera companies. The **Plovdiv Operatic and Philharmonic Society, Stara Zagora Opera** and **Varna Opera and Philharmonic Society** are among the best. Plovdiv is definitely the best place to go for open-air opera. In summer, the town's Roman theatre is the venue for performances of Verdi's *Aïda* and other classics.

Poster at the National Theatre in Sofia

Theatre

Every sizeable town and city in Bulgaria has at least one theatre, where a varied programme of classic and modern drama is staged. Sofia, where there are between about 10 and 12 different plays to choose from on any evening during the season, offers the widest choice of productions.

For visitors from other countries, the main disadvantage is that almost all performances are in Bulgarian, with simultaneous translations very rarely provided. However, leading theatres, such as the **Ivan Vazov National Theatre** in Sofia, perform many classic plays (such as the works of Shakespeare), which English-speaking visitors may know well enough to allow them to follow the plot and enjoy the performance.

Bulgaria also has several imaginative and daring theatre directors, whose work is visually stunning, even if you cannot follow the dialogue. The **Sfumato Theatre Workshop** in Sofia has an international reputation for putting on contemporary and avant-garde plays. The main festival for challenging modern drama is Scene at the Crossroads (Stsena na krŭstopŭt), which takes place in Plovdiv in mid-September and in which international and Bulgarian actors take part. Excellent modern drama also forms part of Sozopol's Arts Festival, in early September.

Performance by members of the Bulgarian National Opera and Ballet, Sofia

Cinema

New Hollywood blockbusters and other international films reach Bulgaria a month or two after being premièred elsewhere. They are screened in their original language, with subtitles in Bulgarian.

Modern multiplexes with comfortable seats and high-quality sound are common in Sofia. Outside the capital, cinemas tend to be old-fashioned and badly ventilated. Both in Sofia and elsewhere, cinema tickets are inexpensive.

Folk Music and Dance

Performances of traditional folk music and dancing are a regular feature of folk-style restaurants in Sofia and in holiday resorts.

Authentic folk festivals are an important feature of the Bulgarian calendar. The leading folk festival is that held in Koprivshtitsa. The main event is the International Folk Festival, at which folk dancers and musicians from all over Bulgaria perform. This takes place every five years (the next in summer 2015) on a meadow outside the village. The Folklore Days festival, a smaller gathering featuring local folk singers and dancers, is held in central Koprivshtitsa in mid-August each year.

Other major events include Pirin pee ("Pirin Sings"), a celebration of Bulgarian-Macedonian music held at Predel, west of Bansko; and Rozhenskia Sûbor ("Rozhen Gathering"), a festival of Rhodopean music held on a mountainside near Smolyan.

The Arena Multiplex in Sofia

Pre-Christian rites are other occasions when traditional music is played. The *kukeri* rites *(see p106)* involve masked mummers dancing wildly to strident musical accompaniment.

Chervilo Club-Bar in Sofia, one of many nightclubs in the capital

Rock, Jazz and Nightclubs

Local bands playing popular rock and jazz standards are a frequent feature of bars and clubs in cities and holiday resorts. Big names in rock and pop perform at the National Palace of Culture in Sofia. Club culture is highly developed in Bulgaria, with local and international house and techno DJs spinning discs to large and appreciative audiences in Sofia and in coastal resorts during the season.

International jazz musicians gather for two important annual events: the Varna International Jazz Festival in early August, and the Bansko Jazz Festival in mid-August.

DIRECTORY

Classical Music, Opera and Ballet

Bulgarian National Opera and Ballet, Sofia
Tel (02) 987 7011.
w operasofia.bg

Plovdiv Opera and Philharmonic Society
Tel (032) 625 553.
w ofd-plovdiv.org

Stara Zagora Opera
Tel (042) 622 431.
w opera-starazagora.bg

Varna Opera and Philharmonic Society
Tel (052) 665 022.
w operavarna.bg

Theatres

Ivan Vazov National Theatre, Sofia
Tel (02) 811 9227.
w nationaltheatre.bg

Sfumato Theatre Workshop, Sofia
Tel (02) 944 0127.
w sfumato.info

Arts Festivals

Apollonia, Sozopol
w apollonia.bg

Folk dancers at the Apollonia Arts Festival, Sozopol

OUTDOOR ACTIVITIES

With the beaches of the Black Sea coast, which stretches for 354 km (220 miles) along the country's eastern border, and spectacular mountains in the interior, Bulgaria offers almost endless possibilities for active holidays. On the coast, well-organized beach resorts offer a great range of water sports, from windsurfing to kiteboarding, while the waters of nearby bays and rocky coves are perfect for learning scuba diving. The mountain resorts offer excellent skiing and snowboarding in winter, and in summer they become bases for hiking and mountain-biking. Other sports include rafting and kayaking on fast-flowing rivers, rock climbing and caving, and horse-riding. Bulgaria also has wide tracts of unspoilt countryside that is rich in flora and fauna. With wetlands and other pristine habitats attracting native as well as migratory birds, Bulgaria also offers unrivalled birdwatching.

Hiking

With four major mountain chains and several smaller ranges, Bulgaria offers a great variety of hiking trails that traverse stunningly beautiful scenery. It is easy to get away from it all as the country is roughly the size of England but the population is only around the 8 million mark.

The Rila and Pirin ranges south of Sofia are the easiest to explore, with winter-sports resorts such as Borovets and Bansko becoming convenient hiking bases in spring and summer. The pine-cloaked Rila massif culminates in Mount Musala, which at 2,925m (9,600 ft) is the highest peak in the Balkans. However, it is the breathtakingly beautiful Seven Lakes locality, in the western part of the range, that attracts most day-trip hikers.

The neighbouring Pirin range has a spectacular array of jagged limestone peaks, with 45 summits over 2,590m (8,500ft) high. The cable car from Bansko and chairlift from Dobrinishte

Chapel in the rock, Rusenski Lom National Park

make the Pirin one of the most accessible areas of mountain wilderness in Bulgaria, with gushing streams, mountain lakes and panoramic views awaiting those who make the trip. In both the Rila and Pirin ranges, paths are well marked and a network of mountain huts provides stopping places for walkers. The Rhodope Mountains, which dominate southern Bulgaria, feature coniferous forests and fragrant meadows, and are dotted with rustic villages and areas of karst landscape with such spectacular features as Trigrad Gorge and the Yagodina Cave.

The Balkan range runs the length of northern Bulgaria from east to west: along its main ridge runs the longest marked hiking route in Bulgaria. Walking the entire trail, which forms part of the trans-European E3 hiking route, will take about 20 days. Those who only have enough time to walk a short stretch of the Balkan Range should aim for the prettiest area, the Central Balkan National Park, south of the town of Troyan. Limestone cliffs, highland meadows and beech forests characterize the Iskûr Gorge, north of Sofia, and the nearby Vrachanski National Park.

Near the Danube port of Ruse, the canyons of the Rusenski Lom National Park are famous for their medieval rock-hewn monasteries and pretty wild flowers.

Reliable, up-to-date hiking maps are available for all the most popular hiking areas in Bulgaria. Although they are sporadically available from newspaper kiosks and tourist agencies in mountain resorts, it is best to buy them before you head for the mountains, from specialist shops in Sofia such as

Hikers at a pass high in the Pirin Mountains, in southwestern Bulgaria

the **Stenata** sports shop or at the office of **Zig Zag Holidays**. Zig Zag and **walkingbulgaria.com** can organise guided or self-guided holidays.

Mountain Biking

The vast network of gravel tracks and forestry roads that threads through Bulgaria's wooded mountains provides great potential for mountain biking. The sport is relatively undeveloped here, and few mountain biking routes are marked. So you're likely to have the mountain to yourselves. However, there are several signed trails around Velingrad and Momchilovtsi, in the Rhodope Mountains, and around Teteven and Troyan, in the Central Balkan range. Bansko in summer is also a good area for mountain biking; try **Mountain Tracks** in town or just rent a bike from a hotel (do check it out first though). The Velingrad-based agency **BikeArea** publishes mountain-biking maps of the vicinity and also organizes guided mountain-biking tours. Many places offer bikes for rent at reasonable prices.

Horse Riding

A wide variety of horse riding holidays is available in Bulgaria, ranging from invigorating gallops along Black Sea beaches to one-day or one-week treks through some stunning inland mountain scenery. Travelling on horse enables the visitor to

The ski resort of Borovets, in the northern Rila Mountains

cover a lot of ground and yet see the countryside close-up and at a comfortable pace. Stables offering excursions for all abilities are based at Albena, on the northern Black Sea coast, Ribaritsa and Uzana in the central Balkans, Trigrad in the Rhodopes and Beli Iskŭr in the Rila Mountains. Equine holiday specialists such as **Arkantours** and **Horseriding Bulgaria** can provide more details and arrange bookings.

Winter Sports

Skiing is a major aspect of Bulgaria's leisure industry but to date the country has really struggled to dispel its image as solely a budget or even downmarket option. This was brought on by a combination of poor ski facilities and bad food and accommodation. However, this is all changing and after substantial investment the resort

of Bansko now has a very modern ski-lift system, snowmaking facilities, good food and and lively après ski. With good pistes for skiers of all abilities, Bansko even has some exhilarating descents for advanced skiers. In addition, you can even go heli-skiing here for a fraction of the price you would pay elsewhere in Europe or North America. For novices or inexperienced skiers, the resorts of Borovets and Pamporovo, with their excellent ski schools and nursery slopes in or near the centre of the resort, are also recommended. For those staying in Sofia, Mt Vitosha, just outside the capital, makes an ideal destination for a weekend excursion.

All of these resorts have ski schools with instructors who speak good English. Most UK ski operators, such as **Inghams Travel**, offer ski holidays in Bulgaria but there are also plenty of Bulgarian companies such as **Bulgariaski** offering the same type of holidays, often at better prices.

Snowshoeing, which requires no previous experience, is an increasingly popular winter sport in Bulgaria thanks largely to the many mountain ranges available. It involves hiking across high-altitude snowfields in specially designed footwear, and provides memorable winter-landscape views. General outdoor trekking and adventure companies such as **Zig Zag Holidays** and walkingbulgaria.com will be able to arrange trips.

Group of mountain bikers on a country road in the Rila Mountains

Kayaker on Lake Pancharevo

Rafting and Kayaking

Wild rivers such as the Struma, in southwestern Bulgaria, the Iskŭr in the northwest, and the Rusenski Lom in the northeast, provide excellent opportunities for rafting. The sport is usually practicable only in the spring and early summer, when the rivers are at their fullest and fastest, thanks to meltwaters from the mountains above. This is when you will find the best whitewater action.

Those who would rather enjoy more gentle touring can try Lake Batak, in the western Rhodopes, the Kŭrdzhali reservoir in the eastern Rhodopes, or consider a leisurely kayak tour down the Danube. Specialist Bulgarian tour operators **Zig Zag Holidays** can also organize short kayaking tours like these.

Birdwatching

Bulgaria is home to an amazing variety of wild birds, with over 400 species that are either indigenous or passing through on seasonal migrations.

The best places for birdwatching are the Rhodope Mountains, the shores of the Black Sea and the coastal wetlands around Durankulak, Shabla and Burgas. The latter are important stopping places on the Via Pontica, the north–south migration route that thousands of birds take each autumn and spring on their flights to and from Asia.

Slightly inland, the reedy edges of Lake Sreburna, beside the Danube, is the nesting ground or overwintering place for over 180 species of birds. In the eastern Rhodope Mountains, the rocky, arid landscape of the Arda Gorge, near Madzharovo, provides the perfect habitat for three different species of vulture and numerous birds of prey. In the western Rhodope Mountains, the Trigrad Gorge is inhabited by several rare species of bird, including the wallcreeper.

Cormorant, one of Bulgaria's sea birds

Information on birdwatching in Bulgaria is available from the **Bulgarian Society for the Protection of Birds**.

Rock Cimbing

With a significant proportion of the countryside classified as mountain, Bulgaria has many opportunities for mountain climbers of all levels.

Bulgaria's prime rock climbing site is the Vratsata Gorge just outside Vratsa, where sheer limestone cliffs provide some challenging ascents. There's excellent free climbing opportunities of varying lengths. Gara Lakatnik on the Iskŭr Gorge is a popular extreme sport destination.

Other destinations such as the Rila and Pirin Mountains offer varied walking and climbing opportunities with peaks up to 2,900 m (9,500 ft).

Cavern inside the spectacular Magura Cave, near Belogradchik

Caving

Bulgaria also offers plenty of opportunities for cavers. Caves that are open to visitors include Ledenika Cave, near Vratsa; Magura Cave, near Belogradchik; and the Trigrad and Yagodina caves in the western Rhodope Mountains. Many tour operators offer short "caving trips" accompanied by trained speleologists, but most of the above caves are lit and can be explored without special equipment. Agencies that specialize in adventure holidays – such as **Odysseia-In**, among others – can arrange caving trips to other caves, notably Temnata Dupka, in the Iskŭr Gorge, Duhlata Cave on Mount Vitosha, and Orlova Chuka in the Rusenski Lom.

Colony of water birds at Lake Pomorie, near Varna

Windsurfers off a beach at Lozenets, on the southern part of the Black Sea coast

Windsurfing and Kiteboarding

Bulgaria is a good place for beginners to learn how to windsurf, although the gentle afternoon breezes may not meet the expectations of more experienced windsurfers. All the main resorts such as Sunny Beach, Golden Sands, Albena, Lozenets and Sozopol have windsurfing schools.

Kiteboarding, which involves being towed at high speeds by a giant parachute-like kite, can be enjoyed at Lozenets, Sunny Beach and Golden Sands.

Diving

Diving is increasingly popular in Bulgaria, and there are diving schools and centres in nearly all of the Black Sea resorts. **Deep Blue** has diving centres in Sofia, Golden Sands and Sunny Beach. The best areas for underwater exploration are the northern Black Sea coast around Kamen Briag and Tyulenovo, where divers can explore varied rock formations, submerged caves, colourful shoals of fish and exotic sea anemones. There are also several WWII shipwrecks north of Varna at Cape Shabla. However, the visibility is not especially good in the Black Sea and divers used to the rich underwater life of coral reefs may be slightly disappointed.

Paragliding

Bulgaria is an excellent place to learn how to paraglide as the cost is lower than in other European destinations. There's also plenty of hilly terrain to launch from and rocks and plateaux to create thermals. The best time of the year to try this sport is from March to October. **Super Sky Paragliding** is a Sofia-based outfit that can organize lessons and tours in any of the main venues such as Sopot in the central Balkan range, and the southeastern shoulder of Mount Vitosha, near Bistritsa.

Paragliding behind a speedboat, a popular sport on the Black Sea coast

SURVIVAL
GUIDE

PRACTICAL INFORMATION

With fine cities, a beautiful coastline and stunning mountain scenery, Bulgaria is an attractive destination all year round. On the Black Sea coast, the main holiday season runs from May to September, peaking in July and August, when temperatures are at their highest and the beaches fill with holidaymakers. The skiing season runs from late December to mid-March. Hiking in the country's spectacular mountains can be enjoyed from April through to October, while Bulgaria's historic cities, with their great churches, cathedrals, museums and art galleries, are rewarding places to visit at any time of year. Although travelling in Bulgaria may not be as quick and easy as in other European countries, there are no serious obstacles, and Bulgarians are helpful and courteous towards foreign visitors.

Passports and Visas

To enter Bulgaria, citizens of European Union countries do not need a visa but must have a full (not a visitor's) passport. Citizens of Australia, Canada, New Zealand and the USA do not need a visa for a stay of up to 90 days. Nationals of other countries should check current regulations with the Bulgarian Embassy or Consulate in their home country.

Sofia Airport, Bulgaria's main domestic and international air transport hub

Customs

Visitors entering Bulgaria from elsewhere in the European Union may bring with them a quantity of goods appropriate to the length of their stay. Visitors entering Bulgaria from a non-EU country can bring in, duty free, 200 cigarettes, 1 litre of spirits, 2 litres of wine and 60 ml. of perfume.

Works of art, antiques and rare coins cannot be taken out of the country without a permit from the Ministry of Culture.

Tourist Information

The availability of tourist information in Bulgaria differs greatly from one region to the next. A useful source is the National Information and Publicity Centre in Sofia, which is run by the Bulgarian Tourism Authority *(see p255)* and provides information on the whole country.

There is also a scattering of privately run regional information centres, mostly in areas of the country that are popular with hikers and skiers, and in towns, such as Bansko and Koprivshtitsa, that attract visitors on account of their historic and cultural interest. Tourist information centres in such places sell maps of their area and give advice on accommodation in the locality. Surprisingly, on account of its popularity as a holiday destination, there are very few tourist information centres on the Black Sea coast.

For details of local attractions and tourist excursions, and advice on local restaurants, ask at the reception desk of your hotel, or go to a privately run travel agency in the nearest town or city.

Opening Hours

Museum opening times are far from uniform. In popular tourist spots, museums are generally open from 9am to 5pm Tuesday to Sunday, but sometimes close at lunchtime. Many museums in these tourist areas frequently stay open longer in the evening during the summer season.

Tourist information center, with leaflets and postcards, in Koprivshtitsa

◄ Yellow taxi cabs gathered in front of the Parliament during a rally in Sofia

A beachside bar in one of Bulgaria's popular Black Sea resorts

Museums in smaller provincial towns are more likely to be open from 9am to 5pm Monday to Friday, with no weekend opening.

Churches and monasteries are open every day, and do not close for lunch. In small or remote villages, however, churches tend only to be open for religious services. A good time to visit is around 5pm, when evening services are commonly held, although visitors should, of course, be considerate and take care not to disturb worshippers.

Payphone for the use of wheelchair-users

Disabled Travellers

Bulgaria unfortunately lags behind most other European countries in terms of access to public buildings and facilities for disabled people. Pavements everywhere are uneven and unramped, and few public buildings, shops and visitor attractions are adapted for wheelchair users.

Many museums are in older buildings without lifts, and access to archaeological sites is also very difficult.

By contrast, hotels in well-established spa resorts such as Velingrad, Hisarya, Sandanski and Pomorie are likely to have facilities for wheelchair-users. In other parts of Bulgaria, only the newer and more upmarket

hotels have facilities for disabled people. Although most of Sofia's five-star hotels are easily wheelchair-accessible, there is no guarantee that the hotel rooms themselves have been adapted for disabled guests. It is therefore advisable to phone ahead, to check on accessibility and inform the establishment of your particular needs.

Gay & Lesbian Visitors

Although Bulgarian society is traditionally patriarchal and conservative, attitudes to gays and lesbians are slowly becoming more relaxed. Today, several openly gay men are prominent in the entertainment and media industries. Sofia has a handful of dedicated gay and lesbian bars and clubs, and a large number of mixed clubs where people of any sexual orientation are welcome.

Electrical Equipment

The main electricity supply in Bulgaria is 220/240V, and standard European two-pin plugs are used. To use their own electrical devices in Bulgaria, visitors from the UK will need to buy an adaptor before they travel. However, most rooms in hotels with a four-star rating or above are equipped with hair dryers.

Time

Bulgaria is in the Eastern European time zone, so that it is two hours ahead of the UK and seven hours ahead of east-coast USA.

In Bulgaria, as in most other European countries, clocks go back one hour in October and forward one hour at the beginning of April.

Body Language

Confusingly, Bulgarians shake their heads when they mean "yes" and nod when they mean "no". Younger Bulgarians, especially those who work in the tourist industry, may reverse these gestures in order to ease understanding. The best way for visitors to ensure that they are not misunderstood is to pronounce a clear yes (da) or no (ne) and not to rely on gestures.

Visitors at a wine-tasting in one of Bulgaria's wine-producing regions

Richly decorated interior of the Church of the Archangels at Arbanasi

Religion

Bulgaria is a religiously active country, with most of its population adhering to one of two faiths. While just over 82 per cent of Bulgarians are Christians of the Bulgarian Orthodox denomination, about 12 per cent are Muslims. There is also a small number of Jews.

Most Bulgarian Orthodox churches are beautifully decorated, with icons, frescoes and carved wooden furnishings. In city-centre churches, religious services are held daily, with the Sunday morning service the most important of the week. A timetable giving times of services is usually posted near the entrance of each church. In larger towns and cities, churches

Orthodox monks at one of Bulgaria's monasteries

are busy throughout the day, with local people coming in to light candles beside the altar or pray to a particular saint.

Bulgaria also has several important Orthodox monasteries. Many are set in beautiful highland areas that offer the perfect conditions for peace and contemplation. Monasteries are also important places of pilgrimage for Bulgarians, and most are open every day throughout the year, welcoming both sightseers and worshippers.

In the calendar of the Orthodox Church, Easter usually falls a week or two later than in the Catholic and Protestant calendars. It is the most important religious holiday of the year, and at midnight on Easter Saturday churches are filled with worshippers.

Although Muslim communities are distributed throughout Bulgaria, they are particularly concentrated in the Rhodope Mountains, around Kurdzhali and Haskovo in the southeastern part of the country, and around Shumen and Razgrad in the northeast. Each of the towns in these regions has at least one mosque, and from the top of the minaret the muezzin calls the faithful to prayer five times a day. Friday prayers, for which Muslims assemble on Friday afternoons, is the most important service of the week.

When visiting a church or mosque, visitors should show

respect and consideration, and observe certain customs. To avoid the risk of causing offence, visitors should be appropriately dressed. Women with bare arms and low-cut tops, and men with bare legs are likely to be frowned upon. When visiting a mosque, visitors are asked to remove their shoes and women should cover their head, arms and legs. As you walk around a mosque, take care not to pass in front of anyone kneeling in prayer: this is considered to be an act of basic courtesy.

Photography

Photography is not allowed in churches unless special permission has been given by the priest. Elsewhere, attitudes to photography are generally quite relaxed. At museums and archaeological sites, the use of cameras is allowed on payment of an extra fee. When photographing people, however, always ask their permission first.

Public transport tickets for sale at a street stall in Sofia

Admission Charges

All museums and archaeological and historic sites make a charge for admission, as do those churches and mosques that have the status of tourist attractions as well as places of prayer. Most museums offer a guided tour (beseda) for an extra charge. These tours are usually in Bulgarian only, but it is sometimes possible to arrange a tour in other languages by contacting the museum in advance.

Public Toilets

There are public toilets at main bus and train stations and privately run toilets in central Sofia and in resorts along the Black Sea coast. All museums and restaurants have toilets, as do most cafés, but if you want to use a café toilet you will be expected to stay for at least a cup of coffee.

There is a small charge for using public and private toilets, with an extra fee for toilet paper. While state-run public toilets are generally badly maintained, those that are privately run are considerably cleaner.

Addresses and Street Names

The most common terms used in Bulgarian addresses are ulitsa (street; abbreviated to ul.); ploshtad (square; abbreviated to pl.); and bulevard (boulevard; abbreviated to bul.). In addresses a building's street number always comes after the street name, so that "5 Freedom Square", for example, is written as "pl. Svoboda 5".

Women Travellers

Women travelling alone or together should exercise normal caution. Bulgaria is a relatively safe country, with no particular areas that should be considered dangerous to visit. However, as

Sign for a public toilet

in most other countries, all towns and cities in Bulgaria have insalubrious, badly-lit areas, especially in districts outside the centre. Women should avoid walking alone in these areas after dark.

In remote rural areas, where foreign visitors are still a novelty, lone women are likely to become the object of unwanted attention. Hitch-hiking, and travelling on overnight trains in a couchette compartment rather than a sleeper car, are inadvisable.

Fresh-fish stall with signage in Cyrillic script

Language

Bulgarian is a Slavonic language related to Russian, Serbian and Croatian, and more distantly to Czech and Polish. Most young Bulgarians speak a few words of English and certain other European languages. Bulgarians of the older generation are more likely to have Russian, which they studied at school, as their second language.

Many museums and art galleries have labels and information panels in Bulgarian only. But most restaurants, especially in holiday resorts, provide menus in English.

Bulgaria was the first country to adopt the Cyrillic alphabet, which was developed in the 9th century by the disciples of St Cyril and St Methodius. Cyrillic, rather than Roman, is still the dominant script in Bulgaria, and names of restaurants, cafés, museums and galleries are generally written in this script. Signs on main roads are usually in both Cyrillic and Roman script. In rural areas, road signs are usually in Cyrillic.

DIRECTORY

Embassies and Consulates

Ireland
ul. Bacho Kiro 26–28, Sofia.
Map 1 C3.
Tel (02) 985 3425.
info@embassyofireland.bg

South Africa
ul. Bacho Kiro 26, Sofia.
Map 1 C3.
Tel (02) 939 5015.
sofia.consular@dirco.gov.za

United Kingdom
ul. Moskovska 9, Sofia.
Map 2 D4.
Tel (02) 933 9222.
W ukinbulgaria.fco.gov.uk

United States
ul. Kozyak 16, Sofia.
Tel (02) 937 5100.
sofia@usembassy.bg

Tourism Organizations

Bulgarian Tourism Authority
pl. Sveta Nedelya 1, Sofia.
Map 1 B4.
Tel (02) 933 5845.
W bulgariatravel.org

Useful Websites

W bulgariainside.eu
W inyourpocket.com
W visitsofia.bg

Foreign visitors at a stall in a flea market in Sofia

Personal Security and Health

Although Bulgaria has a low crime rate, petty theft can be a problem in major towns and cities and in tourist spots. The best way to avoid becoming a victim of petty crime is to take basic precautions. In crowded areas such as shopping malls, markets and train or bus stations, take extra care of your bags and beware of pickpockets. At all times, keep documents, money and credit cards hidden from view, and keep valuables in the safe of your hotel room. When you park your car, never leave anything in view. Basic medical advice is available at pharmacies but, as hospitals are underfunded, make sure you have adequate medical insurance for private care.

Motorcycle traffic policeman on duty in a city centre

Beach at a popular resort on the Black Sea, with sun loungers and parasols

Drivers of vehicles with non-Bulgarian number plates receive a disproportionate amount of attention from traffic police. Foreign drivers are quite often flagged down at checkpoints on main highways, and subjected to spot fines for minor infringements that Bulgarian drivers routinely get away with. However, unless you are offered an official receipt, you are not legally obliged to pay these fines.

Beaches

During the holiday season, life-guards are employed on the beaches of major resorts. These beaches are regularly swept for litter and on almost all of them visitors can expect facilities such as showers. Sun loungers and parasols can be rented for a fee.

Outside the main resorts, many town beaches on the Black Sea charge a small access fee. The funds are supposed to finance the employment of lifeguards and litter collectors, but this is not always put into practice.

Some of Bulgaria's most beautiful beaches, particularly along the southern part of the Black Sea coast, are wonderfully wild and uncommercialized, but are without any facilities.

Personal Belongings

Before you leave home, it is wise to check that you are adequately insured against the loss or theft of luggage and valuable possessions.

Take photocopies of your passport and other important documents. If your passport is lost or stolen, photocopies will help your embassy or consulate to issue a new one. Also make a note of your credit card numbers and the emergency telephone number of the issuing bank, so that you can cancel them immediately if they are lost or stolen. Keep this information secure.

When you park your car, always lock it and make sure any items of value are out of sight. Cameras or camcorders should be carried on a strap or inside a case. Never leave your clothes and other belongings unattended on a beach, even if you are swimming just a few metres away.

Any incidence of theft should be reported immediately to the police. The loss or theft of a passport should be reported without delay to your country's embassy or consulate in Sofia (see p255).

Police

Bulgarian police are usually courteous in their dealings with visitors from other countries, but they may not have a good command of English or any other foreign language. If you have to report the loss or theft of property, bear in mind that Bulgarian police are slow in filling out reports, so be prepared to be patient.

A typical high-speed chase car used by the Bulgarian police

On beaches, exposure to strong sun can be a hazard from May to early October. Young children are especially vulnerable to sunburn. Sunhats, sunglasses, and a high protection factor suncream are essential. Also remember to carry bottled water with you to prevent dehydration, which can lead to heat exhaustion. During the middle of the day, it is best to stay under a parasol or go indoors, so as avoid exposure to the sun when its rays are at their strongest.

Pharmacy shop with distinctive blue and white signage and snake motif

Medical Care

Bulgaria is free from most dangerous contagious diseases, so that visitors need no immunizations. The tap water is also safe to drink.

Citizens of countries of the European Union are entitled to use the Bulgarian national health service free of charge. Citizens of other countries must pay for treatment. All foreign visitors, whether or not they are from another EU country, must pay for any but the most basic medicines. You should be able to claim some reimbursement from your insurance company if you keep the receipts.

Bulgarian state-run hospitals often lack the most effective medicines and the most up-to-date facilities. Because of this, it is probably best to seek treatment in a private clinic if you fall ill. Again, you will be able to claim reimbursement if your insurance policy covers this eventuality. Your hotel is likely to be able to recommend a reliable private doctor or a reputable private clinic.

Visitors to Bulgaria who are on package holidays should seek the advice of their local tour company representative.

Pharmacies

Bulgarian pharmacies are easily recognized by the word *apteka*, usually in white against a blue background, and the sign of the coiled Aesculapian snake. Most pharmacies keep normal shop hours (*see p242*). Every major town and city has a duty pharmacy, with an emergency counter that is open 24 hours a day. All pharmacies post details of the nearest duty pharmacy in their window.

Pharmacies are a good source of advice for minor medical problems, although it may be difficult to find one with English-speaking staff.

Although most Bulgarian pharmacies carry a selection of international-brand drugs, they may not stock the particular drug or remedy drugs that you are accustomed to using. If you need special prescription drugs, it is best to bring an adequate supply with you.

Every Bulgarian town and city has at least one herbal pharmacy (*Bilkova apteka*) offering natural remedies, very often made from locally sourced herbs and plants. The staff in such pharmacies have a good knowledge of herbal medicine and can offer advice on remedies, but are unlikely to speak English. However, you should be able to communicate adequately using a smile, a phrasebook and basic sign language.

Fire

Bulgaria's hot, dry summers create prime conditions for forest fires, which can spread with alarming speed. During excursions to forests, visitors should take extreme care to extinguish camp fires, and to dispose of cigarette butts and used matches carefully.

DIRECTORY

Emergency Services

Emergency
Tel 112

Police
Tel 166

Ambulance
Tel 150

Fire
Tel 160

Fire crew and fire engines at the ready at a station in Sofia

Banking and Local Currency

Bulgarian towns and cities are well provided with banks, and automatic cash machines can be found outside most major high-street branches. Credit cards are increasingly commonly accepted in larger hotels, the smarter restaurants and luxury shops, but they are not widely used elsewhere. Almost all other transactions, from paying for a stay in a hostel to buying souvenirs, are customarily made in cash.

Banks, Exchange and Cash Dispensers

Bank opening hours are 9am to 4pm Monday to Friday. A bank (banka) will change all major foreign currencies, basing its rate on the official exchange rates released by the Bulgarian National Bank each morning. Transactions in banks are slow and require a lot of form filling.

If you are changing cash, it can be quicker to go to an exchange bureau (obmenno byuro). Exchange bureaux usually have longer opening hours than banks and can be found on high streets in most towns, cities and resorts.

When using an exchange bureau, always check rates carefully: most bureaux offer

Postbank logo

the same exchange rates as the major banks, but some of those in busy tourist resorts offer disadvantageous deals. Many hotel reception desks also change money, but they rarely offer competitive rates. The easiest way to obtain Bulgarian currency is to use an automatic cash machine. These machines are now ubiquitous in Bulgaria's town centres, and they have instructions in English. Most ATMs accept Visa, MasterCard, Maestro and American Express. However, bear in mind that most banks and credit card companies in your home country make a small charge for each withdrawal you make abroad.

Exchange bureau in a tourist location, with signage in English

Traveller's Cheques and Credit Cards

Banks in Sofia and large resorts cash traveller's cheques by issuers such as American Express, Thomas Cook and major banks. Cashing traveller's cheques can be a lengthy process as it tends to involve a good deal of bureaucracy. Outside tourist areas, traveller's cheques are not widely accepted.

Credit cards can be used at the more upmarket hotels (with a three-star rating or above), in smart restaurants, and for car hire.

Currency

The currency of Bulgaria is the lev (plural: leva), which is divided into 100 stotinki. As Bulgaria is now a member of the European Union, it is planning to adopt the euro as soon as possible.

As leva are not widely available outside Bulgaria, you will need to change or withdraw currency when you arrive in the country. In 1999, after extraordinary inflation, the value of the lev was adjusted. Thus 1,000 leva became 1 lev. Banknotes issued before 1999 are now worthless.

DIRECTORY

Bulgarian Banks

ING Bank
bul. Bulgaria 49b
Sofia 1404.
Tel (02) 917 64 00.

Postbank
bul. Okolovrasten pat 260
Sofia 1766.
Tel 0700 18 555.

Lost Cards and Traveller's Cheques

American Express
Tel (44) 1273 696933
(Lost cards UK & US).

MasterCard
Tel 1 636 722 7111
(Lost cards UK & US).

Visa
Tel 00 800 0010 888 557 4446
(Cards UK & US).
Tel 1 303 967 1052
(Traveller's Cheques UK & US).

Banknotes

Banknotes are issued in denominations of 2, 5, 10, 20, 50 and 100 leva. The text on the notes is in Cyrillic, but their value is clearly displayed. Each is illustrated with the portrait of a historical figure who played an important role in the history or culture of the nation.

2 leva banknote

5 leva banknote

10 leva banknote

20 leva banknote

50 leva banknote

100 leva banknote

1 lev coin

50 stotinki coin

20 stotinki coin

10 stotinki coin

5 stotinki coin

Coins

Coins are issued in denominations of 1, 2, 5, 10, 20 and 50 stotinki, and 1 lev. Coins of 1 to 5 stotinki are copper-coloured, and those of 10 to 50 stotinki are silver-coloured. The 1 lev coin has a portrait of St John of Rila, patron saint of Bulgaria, on its reverse.

2 stotinki coin

1 stotinka coin

Communications

Bulgaria has national telephone and postal systems, both of which are reasonably efficient, although the postal service is a little slower than in some Western European countries. Bulgarians have enthusiastically embraced the internet, so that even in smaller towns visitors will have no trouble finding an Internet café. Foreign newspapers, by contrast, are more difficult to find. Even so, magazines and guides, aimed specifically at visitors, are available in a number of cities. Cable and satellite channels dominate Bulgarian television.

Mobile phone user in a city centre in Sofia

Sign for Vivacom, Bulgaria's telephone company

Using the Telephone

The main telephone network in Bulgaria is operated by Vivacom (Bulgarian Telecommunications Company). There are Vivacom centres in most large towns and cities. They are usually open from 8am to 6pm daily, but those in large towns and cities may be open 24 hours. To make a call from a Vivacom centre, obtain a token from the counter and use one of the booths.

Vivacom also runs the few public telephones that you will find on street corners, in hotel lobbies, and other public areas. These telephones are card-operated, with phonecards, or with credit cards for long-distance calls. Phonecards (fonokarti) can be bought in post offices and at newspaper kiosks. Buy a couple of different cards to widen the choice of phones available.

Most hotel rooms are equipped with telephones. But calls made from them are much more expensive than from a public telephone.

International calls can be made from all public telephones. To make an international call, dial 00, followed by the country code, the area code (omitting the initial zero), then the number. Useful country codes are: 44 for the UK, 1 for the USA and Canada, 353 for Ireland, 61 for Australia, 64 for New Zealand, and 27 for South Africa. The country code for Bulgaria is 359. Area codes in Bulgaria include 02 for Sofia, 056 for Burgas, 032 for Plovdiv, and 052 for Varna.

Bulgaria's mobile telephone network covers the whole country, although reception may be patchy in sparsely populated mountain valleys. Mobile phone usage is widespread in Bulgaria, and visitors who bring their own phone are unlikely to experience any problems.

Bear in mind that, in order to make and receive calls on your mobile phone while abroad, your roaming facility will have to be activated before you leave home. While abroad you will then be charged for both incoming and outgoing calls and text messages. For full details of call charges, contact your mobile phone operator before leaving home.

One way of avoiding high call charges is to buy a pre-paid SIM card from a Bulgarian mobile phone operator such as Mtel, Globul or Vivacom, and insert it into your phone so that you can make calls to Bulgarian numbers, at Bulgarian prices, during your stay. However, some mobile phones will automatically lock if you insert another network's SIM card into them, so check with your original operator before attempting this.

Using a card-operated telephone

1 Lift the receiver.

2 Insert the phonecard and wait for the dialling tone.

3 Dial the number and wait to be connected. The display panel tells you how much time you have left.

4 Replace the receiver at the end of your conversation and remove your card.

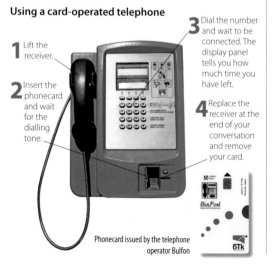

Phonecard issued by the telephone operator Bulfon

Postal Services

Post offices (*poshta*) are open 8am to 5pm Monday to Friday, and 8am to 1pm on Saturday. Post offices in large towns and cities may stay open until 7pm or 8pm Monday to Friday. Post offices have separate counters for buying stamps (*marki*), sending letters (*pisma*) and despatching parcels (*koleti*), so check that you are in the right queue. Postage stamps can also be bought at most shops that sell postcards.

By standard post, letters and postcards sent to destinations in Europe take about seven days to arrive. Post to North America takes about two weeks. For quicker delivery use the express service (*bûrza*) or airmail (*vûzdushna*).

Yellow postbox with horn logo and "poshta" in Cyrillic and Roman script

Post office in Smolyan, with post boxes outside

Television and Radio

Bulgaria's principal television channels are BNT 1, which is state-run, and BTV and Nova TV, which are both independently run. All three channels broadcast a mixture of domestically made programmes, imported dramas and live sport. Most bars, restaurants and hotels have televisions tuned to international cable channels. Larger hotels offer foreign-language channels, including CNN and BBC World.

The BBC World Service and Radio France Internationale are available on VHF in Sofia. Outside Sofia, however, it is difficult to tune in to foreign-language transmissions.

Press

Apart from tabloids, sold mostly in coastal resorts, and the *Financial Times* and *Herald Tribune*, sold in cities, few English-language newspapers are available in Bulgaria. The principal source of news about Bulgaria in English is the local news and information website **Novinite** (The News). It is updated several times a day and offers a wide range of stories on all subjects, from general news to business and sports. There is also an app available for smartphones.

Sofia In Your Pocket is a local edition of the excellent city guide series published around Europe. It is updated quarterly. There are also *In Your Pocket* guides for Veliko Turnovo and Plovdiv, although they are updated less frequently. Another useful tool is the **Sofia - The Insider's Guide**. This book is updated each year and is packed with information primarily aimed at expats. Available free of charge in hotels, restaurants and business centres, as well as places of culture and entertainment, the guide is a valued source of information for foreigners visiting or coming to live in Bulgaria's capital.

Internet

There are Internet cafés in all major holiday resorts, and in most towns and cities. They are usually open from 10am to 9pm, but hours are flexible and some remain open around the clock. Vivacom centres also offer Internet access.

Many hotels provide free Internet access to guests, in the form of one or two computer terminals in the lobby. For those who travel with their laptops or smartphones, an increasing number of hotels offer either wireless Internet (not always free) or plug-in Internet connections in their rooms. Most bars, cafés and restaurants in major towns and resorts also offer free Wi-Fi; just ask the staff for the password.

Newspaper kiosk, with a wide selection of papers and magazines

DIRECTORY

English-Language Media

Novinite
W novinite.com

Sofia – The Insider's Guide
W insidesofia.com

Sofia In Your Pocket
W inyourpocket.com

TRAVEL INFORMATION

Bulgaria is well connected with the rest of Europe by air, and this is the quickest and most economical way of reaching the country. Because of a lack of fast, modern roads and railways in southeastern Europe, travelling to Bulgaria by car, bus or train is somewhat arduous, and impractical for visitors with limited time. Bulgaria itself is served by a network of train and bus routes, to major towns and cities and most rural areas too. For complete independence, however, hiring a car may be the most attractive option.

Arriving by Air

Sofia, the capital of Bulgaria, is well served by direct flights from most European countries. **Bulgaria Air**, the national carrier, has daily scheduled flights to Sofia from London Gatwick, Amsterdam, Paris and other European capitals. Flight times from the UK are about three hours.

British Airways provides scheduled flights to Sofia from London Heathrow. The low-cost airlines **easyJet, Wizzair** and **NIKI** offer flights to Sofia, Burgas and Varna from the UK and from central Europe, while **Ryanair** flies from London to Plovdiv. Other low-cost carriers may start to provide services between the UK and Bulgaria at some time in the future; see www.skyscanner.net for the latest airlines and routes.

Direct flights to Bulgaria from North America and other non-European countries are rare. Most intercontinental routes involve a direct flight to a European hub such as London, Amsterdam or Frankfurt, and a connecting flight to Bulgaria.

Plane of the Bulgaria Air fleet at Sofia Airport

International Airports

Bulgaria's largest airport serves the capital, Sofia. The airport has convenient transport connections with the city centre, which is about 10 km (6 miles) to the west. Bus no. 84, from Terminal 1, and bus no. 284 from Terminal 2, depart for the city centre every 10–20 minutes. Taxis are also easy to find, and the fare inexpensive. Much of western and central Bulgaria is easily accessible from Sofia. Although it is not such a convenient entry point if you are heading for the Black Sea coast, there are connecting domestic flights to Varna, on the Black Sea. Alternatively, you can make the connection by car, bus or train, a journey time of 6–7 hours.

Other airports used by international traffic include Plovdiv, Burgas and Varna. These airports were originally built to handle package-holiday flights and are consequently less well provided with duty-free shops and cafés than Sofia Airport.

Air Fares

As with most destinations, air fares for flights to Bulgaria vary according to the time of year. They are generally highest during the summer months, although prices also rise significantly during the skiing season, which runs from mid-December to mid-March. Flights

The main entrance to Sofia Airport

A hall at Sofia Airport, Bulgaria's main air transport hub

during the Christmas and Easter periods are often fully booked well in advance.

Tickets for flights on low-cost airlines obviously offer excellent value, but to make the most of the lowest fares available travellers should book well in advance, preferably over the Internet. However, travellers should bear in mind that additional costs, such as taxes and buying food and drinks, can whittle down the initial difference in price between tickets offered by regular carriers and low-cost airlines.

In summer, charter flights from the UK serve airports such as Varna and Burgas. Seats on these flights are often only available as part of a package deal. See your travel agent for advice.

Domestic Flights

The only domestic flights in Bulgaria are the daily flights provided by **Bulgaria Air** between Sofia and Varna, on the Black Sea. Tickets are inexpensive and the flight time is less than one hour.

Trains

Travelling to Bulgaria by train is most suitable for those who enjoy rail travel and who are willing to spend at least two days reaching their destination. There are various routes, all of them offering rewarding journeys with much fine scenery and the chance to stop off in some interesting cities. However, the total cost of travelling to Bulgaria by train is

Electric train on a local route

likely to be higher than by air. It may also be difficult to buy a through ticket from western Europe to Bulgaria. Travellers may find is easier to buy one ticket to Budapest, for example, and another for onward travel from there. From continental Europe, the principal routes to Bulgaria are Salzburg to Sofia via Zagreb and Belgrade, and Budapest to Sofia via Belgrade or Bucharest. Sleeping cars are available on certain stretches.

Approaching Bulgaria from the south, there are direct trains to Sofia from Istanbul, in Turkey, with a journey time of 12–13 hours, and from Thessaloniki, Greece (7 hours). The best source of information in English on train travel to Bulgaria is **The Man in Seat 61**, a website run by rail travel enthusiasts.

DIRECTORY

Airlines

British Airways
Tel (02) 954 7000 in Bulgaria, 0844 493 0787 in the UK. w ba.com

Bulgaria Air
Tel (02) 402 0400 in Bulgaria, 020 8745 9833 in the UK.
w air.bg

easyJet
w easyJet.com

NIKI
Tel (02) 491 7506 in Bulgaria, 0871 5000 737 in the UK.
w flyniki.com

Wizzair
Tel 0900 63022 in Bulgaria, 0906 959 0002 in the UK.
w wizzair.com

Ryanair
Tel 0871 246 0002 in the UK.
w ryanair.com

Airports

Sofia
Tel (02) 937 2211.
w sofia-airport.bg

Varna
Tel (052) 573 323.
w varna-airport.bg

International Rail Travel

The Man in Seat 61
w seat61.com

Rail Europe
Tel 08448 484 064 in the UK, 1–800 622 8600 in the US.
w raileurope.com

Trainseurope
Tel 0871 700 7722.
w trainseurope.co.uk

КАТ.	НОМЕР	НАПРАВЛЕНИЕ	ПРЕЗ	ЧАС	КОЛ.	ЗАК.
Б	8615	БУРГАС - Bursas	Пловдив	13:40	4и	
Б	6691	КЮСТЕНДИЛ		14:00	1	
П	20111	Г. ОРЯХОВИЦА		14:15	10	
П	10113	ПЛОВДИВ - Plovdiv		14:15	1г	
П	50223	ДУПНИЦА - Dupnica		14:27	2г	
П	10210	ДРАГОМАН		14:35	8г	
П	50205	ПЕРНИК - Pernik		15:10		
Б	4613	РУСЕ - Ruse	Г. Оряховица	15:20		

ЗАМИНАВАЩИ DEPARTURE

Electronic departure board at Sofia's main railway station

Travelling by Train, Bus and Taxi

Bulgaria's rail network links all major towns and main cities, and a few smaller destinations as well. On some routes, particularly through the mountains, train travel offers the opportunity to enjoy some spectacular scenery. However, the country's railway system is in need of modernization and journey times are slow. An alternative option for travel on inter-city routes is to take one of Bulgaria's fast, clean, modern buses. Much of rural Bulgaria is reached by older, local buses, although more remote villages may only be served by one or two a day. For a tailor-made journey, another option is to negotiate a long-distance trip with a taxi driver.

Signs on a platform at Sofia's Central Train Station

Travelling by Train

The country's rail network is operated by **Bulgarian State Railways** (Bulgarska durzhavna zheleznitsa, or BDZh). There are three categories of train: the Accelerated Fast Train (Uskoren burz vlak, or UBV), which stops only at principal towns along a route, is the fastest. UBVs run between Sofia and major provincial towns such as Plovdiv, Varna and Burgas. Most UBVs have modern, comfortable carriages and a buffet car.

Inter-city routes are also served by Fast Trains (Burz vlak, or BV), which make more stops than UBVs. They have slightly older carriages, and do not always have a buffet car.

Slowest are the Passenger Trains (Putnicheski vlak, or PV), which stop at every station. Although some of these trains are modern, many are old and uncomfortable. On all classes of train, the toilets are often abominably badly maintained. Train tickets can be purchased

Main entrance to Sofia's Central Train Station

at station ticket offices. Both first-class (purva klasa) and second-class (vtora klasa) tickets are available for journeys on UBV and BV trains. On PV trains only second-class seating is available. If you are travelling long distances, first-class tickets are a good buy: by Western European standards they are not expensive, and will give you slightly more comfortable seats and more legroom. Reservations (zapazeni mesta) are advisable if you are travelling between Sofia and the Black Sea coast in summer, particularly at weekends. If you are travelling by overnight train between Sofia

and the Black Sea, it is advisable to book a place in a sleeping car (spalen vagon), as the regular carriages are uncomfortable and you may be at risk from petty thieves.

In Sofia, advance tickets of all kinds can be purchased from two city-centre bureaux; **Rila Agency**, for international tickets, and the **Transport Service Centre**, for domestic services. BDZh does not offer any kind of rail pass. However, EuroDomino, InterRail and City Star passes are valid for travel on Bulgarian railways. The complete Bulgarian train timetable is available online in English at www.bdz.bg.

Travelling by Bus

Bus services in Bulgaria are operated by several national and regional bus companies. Virtually every town and village in the country is accessible by bus, although the smaller, more remote villages may be served by only one or two buses a day.

Inter-city bus routes linking Sofia with the country's largest towns and cities (notably Plovdiv, Varna, Burgas, Pleven and Ruse) depart several times a day. Buses on these routes are usually modern, with comfortable

Train on one of Bulgaria's scenic mountain routes

seats and air conditioning, and there are regular stops for refreshments and the use of toilets. By contrast, buses on provincial routes are likely to be old, with uncomfortable seats.

Some provincial routes are served by minibuses rather than full-size buses. Minibuses are generally faster than buses, but cramped seating makes them uncomfortable.

Bus tickets can be bought from ticket counters at bus stations, but not on the buses themselves. On inter-city routes, advance reservations are advisable if you are travelling on a Friday or Sunday evening, or at any time during major public holiday periods such as Christmas or Easter. Advance reservations are also recommended if you are travelling between Sofia and the Black Sea coast in July and August. Tickets and information on bus travel throughout Bulgaria is available from **Sofia Central Bus Station**.

Private agent selling tickets for journeys on inter-city buses

Timetables and Information

Thanks to the Internet, planning your trip around Bulgaria is vastly simpler than it used to be. Sofia's Central Bus Station has clear arrival and departure times as well as prices, all in English.

Modern inter-city bus at Sofia's Central Bus Station

The privately run **Etap Bus Company** also has clear timetables in English on its web-site. However, while bus and train stations in large towns and cities often have information counters (marked "*informatsiya*"), the staff here seldom speak any other language than Bulgarian.

Bus and train stations usually also have a timetable (*razpisanie*) prominently displayed in the ticket hall, but this will invariably be in Cyrillic. Departures (*zaminavane*) and arrivals (*pristigane*) are listed in two different sections of the timetable. At smaller bus stations, timetables may be incomplete and ticket windows closed without explanation. In such cases your best option is to ask local people whether a particular service is running.

Private bus operator's inter-city timetable

Taxis

Taxi drivers in Bulgaria most usually take passengers on short journeys within towns and cities, or to and from airports. However, taxi drivers will often agree to undertake longer trips

if these are arranged in advance. Metered fares are relatively low, generally ranging from 0.70 to 2 Lv per km (roughly 1.20 to 4 Lv per mile). For a long journey, you may prefer to agree on a set fare with the driver in advance. This can be roughly calculated by multiplying the rate per kilometre (displayed on the vehicle's window) by the distance to be travelled.

For more information on travel by taxi, *see p269*. As always don't be tempted to get into a taxi that isn't yellow, even if the driver insists he is an official taxi.

DIRECTORY

Bus Information

Etap Bus Company
W etapgroup.com

Sofia Central Bus Station
bul. Knyaginya Mariya Luiza 100.
Tel 0900 21000.
W centralnaavtogara.bg

Train Information

Bulgarian State Railways
W bdz.bg

International Rail Tickets

Rila Agency
ul. Gurko 5, Sofia.
Tel (02) 987 0777.

Domestic Rail Tickets

Transport Service Centre
National Palace of Culture (NDK), Sofia. **Tel** (02) 865 8402.

Licensed taxis in Sofia

Travelling by Car

Exploring Bulgaria by car is an attractive option, as it gives greater freedom and allows you to explore remoter areas of the country that may not be well served by public transport. However, visitors should bear in mind that fast highways are relatively few, and that the condition of other roads often leaves much to be desired. It is best to avoid driving in major cities such as Sofia and Varna, as traffic flow is badly organized and time-consuming jams all too frequent. Road signs on main inter-city trunk roads are usually shown in both Cyrillic and Roman script. On minor roads and in rural areas, however, they may be in Cyrillic only.

Sign for an international car- and van-hire agency

Desk of a car rental company at one of Bulgaria's airports

Car Hire

By Western European standards, hiring a car in Bulgaria is inexpensive. Many international car-hire companies have offices at airports and in stations, and in central Sofia and other major towns and cities. Most Bulgarian travel agents can arrange car hire through one of the well-known international companies. Car hire desks can also be found in the lobbies of some of the larger resort hotels. Some of the small local car-hire companies offer extremely cheap deals on hatchbacks and other small cars, although the vehicles themselves may not be in the best condition.

To hire a car in Bulgaria you must be over 21 and must show a valid passport and valid driving licence (which you must have held for a minimum of two years). You will also be asked to show your credit card or to pay a cash deposit, and you may require a valid international insurance policy. If you know you will need to hire a car during your stay in Bulgaria, it may be easier, but not necessarily cheaper, to arrange this with one of the

Stack of road signs in a town

main international car hire companies before you leave home. Another option, if you want to reach a remote spot not well served by public transport, for example, is to hire a car with driver. You can do this through a car hire company, or by asking a taxi driver for a day rate *(see p265)*.

Roads

Although some of Bulgaria's highways are well maintained, most of the country's roads are in bad condition, so that travel by road tends to be slow. Many roads have uneven surfaces, ruts and potholes. In mountain areas road surfaces may also be degraded by rock falls and extreme weather conditions, such as heavy rain and ice. Added to this, and alarmingly for oncoming traffic, drivers often suddenly veer from one side of the road to the other so as to avoid these hazards. In rural areas, motorists should also be prepared to encounter slow-moving horse- or donkey-carts.

In winter, especially after heavy rainfall, or when there is snow and ice, rural roads can be slippery and dangerous, and along remote stretches help will not be readily to hand should you find yourself in difficulties. If you are thinking of venturing into the mountains in winter, it is advisable to carry snow chains.

Road signs on major routes are often in both Cyrillic and Roman script but on minor roads they may be in Cyrillic only. Navigation will be much easier with the aid of a reliable map *(see opposite)*.

Petrol station on a road in the outskirts of a town

The road to Rila Monastery, one of the better maintained stretches in Bulgaria

Fuel

Petrol (benzin) is cheaper in Bulgaria than in Western Europe. The most likely places to find filling stations (benzinostantsiya) are on the outskirts of towns and along main highways. In rural areas they can be hard to find, so fill up if you are about to venture off the beaten track. Another hazard, particularly at stations in out-of-the-way places, is dirty or adulterated petrol. To be safe, stick to stations run by Shell, BP or OMV.

Vignettes

To drive on public highways, but not on other roads, in Bulgaria drivers must display a windscreen sticker, or vignette (vinetka). Vignettes can be purchased at border checkpoints or at most petrol stations. They cost 10 Leva (€5) for one week, 25 Leva (€12) for one month, or 67 Leva (€34) for one year. Highways for which drivers need a vignette are clearly signed.

Sign for a tolled highway

Prices for vignettes at a petrol station

Rules of the Road

Speed limits on Bulgarian roads are 120 km/hr (75 mph) on main highways, 90 km/hr (56 mph) on minor roads, and 50 km/hr (31 mph) in urban areas. Seat belts are compulsory for front-seat passengers. Driving with more than 0.5 mg of alcohol in the bloodstream is strictly forbidden, and punishable by a heavy fine. Using a mobile phone while driving is only permissible with a hands-free set.

You may often notice local drivers flaunting these rules. However, foreign drivers should not emulate them, as the Bulgarian police rarely show lenience towards non-Bulgarians.

Highway police are authorized to levy on-the-spot fines for speeding and other traffic offences. If you are stopped and fined, be sure to see an official receipt before paying.

Maps

Up-to-date road maps of Bulgaria are widely available from petrol stations and bookstores throughout the country. They are usually available in Cyrillic and in Roman-script versions. Detailed area maps are much harder to find. However, in popular mountain areas, you will find local hiking maps on which minor roads are marked.

Maps of Sofia, Plovdiv and Varna, which are updated annually, can be purchased from local newspaper kiosks and bookstores, but maps of other urban areas appear more sporadically and sell out fast.

Assistance

For information on all aspects of driving in Bulgaria and assistance in case of breakdown, contact the **Union of Bulgarian Motorists**. The organization has 55 regional centres, and its website, in English and Bulgarian, offers information on everything from caravanning to traffic regulations. Through the union you can also arrange any extra insurance that you may need once in Bulgaria.

DIRECTORY

Car Hire

Avis
Tel (02) 826 1100. W **avis.bg**

Budget
Tel (02) 870 0001. W **budget.bg**

Europcar
Tel (02) 981 4626.
W **europcar.bg**

Holiday Autos
W **holidayautos.co.uk**

Driving Information

Union of Bulgarian Motorists
pl. Positano 3, Sofia.
Tel (02) 935 7935; for 24-hour emergency (02) 911 46 or 146 (mobile).
W **uab.org**

Getting around Sofia

Public transport in Sofia consists of an extensive network of trams, buses and trolleybuses, with a unified ticketing system, and a fleet of privately run minibuses. The city also has two modern metro lines. Another convenient way of getting around Sofia is to hail one of the capital's inexpensive yellow taxis. As in many other capital cities, however, public transport in Sofia is hampered by traffic congestion, particularly during the morning and early evening rush hours, when trams and buses are reduced to a crawl. Lengthy cross-town journeys may also involve changing from one form of public transport to another. Sightseeing trips around the city, as well as day excursions to places further afield, are provided by private tour operators.

Escalator at a station on one of Sofia's two metro lines

Train at one of the stations on Sofia's modern metro line

Metro

Sofia's clean, modern metro (*metropoliten*) consists of two underground lines. Line 1 (red line) starts from Tsarigradsko shose in the east of the city, runs beneath the city centre, and terminates in Obelya in the northwestern suburbs. Line 2 (blue line) starts at Obelya and runs from north to south to James Bourchier station. This line has an interchange with Line 1 at Serdika. There are also plans for a third line, to run from west to east, but as yet no firm date for the line's completion has been set.

Metro services generally run from 5am to 11:30pm daily. Tickets (*bileti*) for a single journey of any length cost 1 Lv and can be bought from the ticket counter in each station. A card valid for ten single trips costs 8 Lv.

Tram, Bus and Trolleybus

Trams (*tramvai*), buses (*avtobusi*) and trolleybuses (*troleybusi*) provide adequate if at times slow transport all over central Sofia and out to the suburbs. Like the metro, services run from 5am to 11:30pm daily. Information on routes is not always easy to find. Service numbers and route diagrams are displayed at some tram and bus stops, although details of destinations are invariably written in Cyrillic. The best option is to buy an up-to-date map of the city, which will have public transport routes marked on it.

A unified ticketing system applies to travel on trams, buses and trolleybuses (but not for the metro, for which a separate ticket must be bought, nor for minibuses, where you pay the driver). Tickets (*bileti*) can be purchased from kiosks near major bus and tram stops. They are also available at most newspaper kiosks throughout the city. Single tickets cost 1 Lv. A strip (*talon*) of 10 tickets costs 8 Lv. Note that the tickets in a strip are numbered 1 to 10 and should be used in sequence: for

Tram on one of the routes in Sofia's extensive public transport network

example, tickets 1 to 9 will not be considered valid unless you have ticket number 10 in your possession. When you board a tram, bus or trolleybus, remember to punch your ticket by inserting it in the small machine near the vehicle's door. Ticket inspectors are a regular presence on public transport, and failure to punch a ticket is likely to result in an on-the-spot fine. Travellers on buses, trams and trolleybuses are also officially required to buy an extra ticket for any large piece of luggage. This rule is, however, only really enforced on routes to and from the airport. Within the city it is widely ignored.

If you intend to make extensive use of public transport in Sofia, a pass can be a convenient option. A one-day pass which includes travel on the metro *(karta za edin den)* costs 4 Lv and a five-day pass *(karta za pet dena)* 15 Lv. Both are readily available at kiosks.

Orange "bendy" bus, with separate entry and exit doors, in Sofia

Trolleybus at a stop in Sofia

Tour Buses

Private tour companies have buses with routes taking in the city's major sights and attractions. Companies like **Traventuria** offer full-day and half-day excursions around the city, and arrange trips to other interesting locations within easy reach of the

capital, as well as other sights around Bulgaria.

Minibuses

Sofia's trams, buses and trolleybuses are augmented by a fleet of privately owned minibuses *(marshrutki)*. These operate specific express routes through the city, from 5am to 11:30pm daily. Although minibuses halt at many of the stops used by buses and trolleybuses, they can also be hailed along their routes and will stop en route to allow passengers to alight if asked.

Minibuses are often faster than trams and buses, but can frequently feel crowded and stuffy. The fare (1.50 Lv) is paid directly to the driver, and passengers must tender the exact coins.

Sign for taxi rank in central Sofia

Taxis

Several private companies run fleets of taxis in Sofia. All licensed taxis are yellow, and have a sticker displayed in the windscreen or side window indicating their rates in Bulgarian *leva* (Lv).

Taxi fares are quite low by Western European standards.

They range from 0.70 Lv per kilometre (about 1 Lv per mile) during the day and rise by about 30 per cent at night. It is customary to tip the driver 10 per cent of the fare.

There are taxi ranks at most major intersections in Sofia. Taxis can also be hailed as they cruise the streets of the city centre. A small green light inside the windscreen indicates that the taxi is available, and small red light indicates that it is taken.

Taxis can also be ordered by telephone but it is usually easier to ask the reception staff at your hotel to make the call.

Unlicensed taxis tend to congregate at locations such as airports and main railway stations, where disoriented foreign travellers may be easy to swindle. Never be tempted to get into a "taxi" that isn't yellow, no matter what the driver says. This advice should be followed throughout Bulgaria.

DIRECTORY

Tour Buses

Traventuria
ul. Veslets 45, Sofia.
Tel (02) 489 0885.

Taxis

OK Supertrans
Tel (02) 973 2121.

Radio CB Taxi
Tel (02) 91263.

Yellow Taxi 91119
Tel (02) 91119.

Yellow licensed taxi from one of Sofia's privately run fleets

General Index

Acknowledgments

Hachette Livre Polska would like to thank the following staff at Dorling Kindersley:

Publisher
Douglas Amrine

List Managers
Vivien Antwi, Christine Stroyan,

Managing Art Editor
Jane Ewart

Senior Editor
Hugh Thompson

Designers
Kate Leonard, Karen Constanti

Map Co-ordinator
Casper Morris

DTP Manager
Natasha Lu, Jamie McNeill

Additional Picture Research
Rachel Barber, Marta Bescos Sanchez, Ellen Root

Production Controller
Linda Dare

DORLING KINDERSLEY would like to thank all those whose contributions and assistance have made the preparation of this book possible:

Main Contributors
Jonathan Bousfield, Matt Willis

Factchecker
Petya Milkova, Matei Balazs

Proofreader
Stewart J Wild

Indexer
Hilary Bird

Additional Photography
Ian O'Leary, Frank Greenaway, Victor Milkov, Kim Taylor, Jerry Young

Additional Illustrations
Gary Cross, Chapel Design and Marketing Ltd.,

Cartography
Base mapping supplied by Cartographia Ltd., Budapest 2006.

Revisions and Relaunch Team
Jonathan Bousfield, Neha Dhingra, Vidushi Duggal, Amy Harrison, Mohammad Hassan, Priyanka Kumar, Jude Ledger, Catherine Palmi, Azeem Siddiqui, Julie Thompson, Nikhil Verma

Special Assistance
The Publishers would like to thank the staff at shops, museums, hotels, restaurants and other organizations in Bulgaria for their invaluable help. Particular thanks go to: Jolanta Antczak at BE&W; Ilian Dimitrov at PhotoTresor (AZ Press OOD); Desislava Haytova at Bulgaria Photos Net; Beata Ibrahim at Corbis; Carlo Irek at 4Corners Images, Tim Kantoch at Photolibrary Group; Nevena Nikolova at Unofficial Info site of the Museum Town Koprivshtitza; Csilla Pataky at Cartographia Ltd., Budapest; Boryana Punchewa, Director of the Bulgarian Institute of Culture in Warsaw; Milena Trapcheva at Sofia Photo Agency (Novinite Ltd).

Photography Permissions
The Publishers would like to thank all those who gave permission to photograph at musuems, palaces, churches, restaurants, hotels, shops and other sights too numerous to list individually. Particular thanks go to: Iliya Chernev, Executive Secretary of the International Bagpipe Festival in Shiroka Laka; Grazyna Chroszcz at Fotodesigner; Emil Iliev, General Manager of the International Jazz Festival in Bansko; ImagesFromBulgaria. com; Katya Ivanova at Strandja Nature Park Directorate; Yassen Jekoff, photographer; Bisjera Josifova at National Art Gallery in Sofia; Martin Mitov, photographer; Ivan Pajkinski, Director of the Museum of History, Vratza; Rumiana Pashaliyska Director of the National Museum of Literature in Sofia; Peter Petrov, photographer; Ana Rousseva, International Relations Officer at Apollonia Art Foundation; Diana Terzieva at Central Balkan National Park Directorate; Maria Vassileva, Chief Curator at Sofia Art Gallery; Kosu Zareb, Director of the Historical Museum in Kazanlak.

Picture Credits
t=top; tc=top centre; tr=top right; tl=top left; cla=centre left above; ca=centre above; cra=centre right above; cl=centre left; c=centre; cr=centre right; clb=centre left below; cb=centre below; crb=centre right below; bl=bottom left; bc=bottom centre; br=bottom right; b=bottom.

The Publishers are grateful to the following individuals, companies and picture libraries for permission to reproduce their photographs:

AKG Images: 26cla; Erich Lessing 88tr; Ullslein Bild – Archiv 26tr. **Alamy Images: A+P** 27tl; Vladimir Alexeev 30tr; Arco Images GmbH/P. Goll 228; David Ball 112cl; Rosen Dimitrov 58-9; Emil Enchev 31cra, 31bc; Bulgaria Alan King 26–7; Cephas/Mick Rock 22b; Craft Alan King 24bl; i creative 1c; Ilian Religion 52cl ilian studio 24clb; Image Register 044 28br; Isifa Image Service s.r.o/Kubes 114bl; johnrochaphoto 62-3; Moreleaze Travel London 230cla; Melvyn Longhurst 26clb, 52cr, 52br; Nikreates 29cr, 38cra, 53cra, 66bc, 123cr, 124tr, 125cra, 132cla, 132clb, 132br, 142bl, 143br, 146br, 149b, 252bl, 260tr, 260bl; Rolf Richardson 28bl; Robert Harding Picture Library 20t; /Peter Scholey 21tr; /Adam Woolfitt 25tl;

rochaphoto 112bc; Harry Studio 231tl; Travel Pictures 231cb; Gregory Wrona 23bc, 31tr. **Apollonia Arts Festival:** 40bl. **Ardea:** John Mason 30cb; Johan De Meester 31bl; Duncan Usher 30bl, 30cl; M. Watson 31crb; Wardene Weisser 31cb. **AZ Press OOD:** 34tr; 34cla; 34b; 35tl; 35c; 36bl; 38bl; 41bc; 46bc; 48br; 57tc; 65br; 78c; 78bl; 90tl; 91br; 103b; 106tr; 106bl; 108cla; 109tl; 109cra; 109br; 126cl; 127cr; 132tr; 133cra; 133crb; 134clb; 142cr; 147cra; 147bl; 170bl; 193br; 212cla; 244b; 247cr; 263c; Vladimir Alexeev 114tr; Jivko Aratov 24-5, 29bl; Rosen Dimitrov 24cb, 24br, 25crb, 25br, 29ca, 52bl; Renard Dudlei 25tr; Mihail Mihailov 112tr; Angel Nenov 115br; Yavor Popov 29br, 44c; Dimo Rogev 25cra, 45b, 53br; Nikolai V. Vassilev 24tr.

Bansko 25 Century Foundation: 39br. **Borina Publishing House:** 179cla, 179cra, 179crb. **The Bridgeman Art Library:** K. Savitsky Art Museum, Penzia Russia The Defence of the Eagle Aerie on the Shipka in 1887 (1893) Andrei Nikolaevich Popev 53bl. **Bulgaria Photos Net/ET HS-Corp:** Elena Haytova 41cra, 135tr, 138c. **BulgarianWines.com:** Festa Wines 32tr, 33br.

Canape Connection Hostel: 222bc; **Cephas Picture Library:** Mick Rock 32br, 33tr. **Checkpoint Charly Restaurant:** 223tl, 23tr. **Iliya Chernev:** 131tr. **Corbis:** Paul Almasy 27cra; Bettmann 55tr, 55bl, 56clb, 56bc, 71bl, 119br; Nicolas Bouvy 57br; Darrell Gulin 217tr; Gavin Hellier 210-11; Hulton-Deutsch Collection 51crb, 54crb, 54br; Yevgeny Khaldei 55fbr; NATO/CNP 57crb; Jose F. Poblete 53tl; Sygma/Anderson Thorne 57bc; Adam Woolfitt 39tl; zefa/Stefan Schuetz 35br.

Di Wine: 241t; **Dreamstime.com:** 2bears 15tr; Flaviu Borescu 15bc; Nikolay Dimitrov 14cl; Elenajs 12t; Delyan Gopsodinov 18; Anna Hristova 23t; Internedko 13br; Luliia Kryzhevska 14tr; Viktor Levi 82-3; Iluzia 194-5; Reich 11tr; Rutovskaya 34clb; Nickolay Stanev 102; Radoslav Stoilov 10cl; Alexey Stoyanov 252cr; Todor Todorov 198; Aleksandar Todorovic 11br, 19b; Tupungato 265bl, 268br.

EGOworld: 233b. **European Heritage Wines:** 33bc. **Evergreen Palace:** 229tl, 237br.

Hotel Forum: 225br, 237t. **Getty Images:** AFP 250-1; Images by Didenze 180; AFP/ Dimitar Dilkoff 22tl; Maya Karkalicheva 2-3, 136-7; Holger Mette 174-5; Rolf Richrdson 148. **Graffit Gallery Hotel:** 227bc. **Grand Hotel Sofia:** 220cra.

Guliver Photos Ltd: 31cla. **Hadji Nikoli Restaurant:** 228bc, 238tl, 238bc. **Hadzhidraganovite Kushti:** 232bl. **Hemingway Restaurant:** 235tr.**Hemispheres Images:** Bertrand Gardel 28tr; Christian Guy 12bc, 20bl, 21bl, 26bc. **Historical Museum of Gotse Delchev:** 128tr. **Stoyan Hristov:** 154clb.

ImagesFromBulgaria.com: 79bl. **Yassen Jekoff:** 217tl. **Jupiter Images:** Chris Sanders 28cra.

Kempinski Hotel Grand Arena Bansko: 223tr, 234b.

Litov's House: 121bl. **Lonely Planet Images:** Paul Greenway 29tr.

Peter Machkovski: 154bl, 155tl. **Martin Mitov:** 122cra. **Mary Evans Picture Library:** 8-9, 54tl, 56tl, 132bl. **Nanko Minkov:** 154tr, 155cla, 155bl.

National Museum of History Bulgaria: 89tc.

Pelican Lake Guesthouse: 226tl. **Peshev.org:** from "The Man who Stopped Hitler" By Gabriele Nissim 71cr. **Peter Petrov:** 187cl; 187bl; 228cl. **Photolibrary:** Anthony Blake Photo Libarary 33tl. **Photoshot/NHPA:** Jordi Bass Casas 31c. **Photoshot World Pictures:** 31cl. **Postbank:** 258c.

Renaissance Guesthouse: 224tl. **Rest Restaurant:** 236tl. **Reuters:** Stoyan Nenov 26br. **Rose Restaurant:** 240bl.

Sofia City Art Gallery: 86cr; **Sofia photo agency:** 38br, 40cra, 71br, 94bl, 256tr, 257bl, 268cl. **Sofia Synagogue:** 71cr. **Standart News:** 147br. **La Strada Restaurant:** 239b. **SuperStock:** Silvio Fiore 116-7; imagebroker.net 218-9; Wojtek Buss 27crb.
Vivacom: 260c.
Zagreus Winery: 33crb.

Front Endpapers:
Alamy Images: johnrochaphoto Lbl. **Dreamstime.com:** Nickolay Stanev Rbr, Todor Todorov Rtr. **Getty Images:** Images by Didenze Ltr; Rolf Richrdson Rcr.

Jacket: Front and spine - **Dimitar Atanassov Photography.**

All other images © Dorling Kindersley.
For further information see: w dkimages.com

Special Editions of DK Travel Guides

Phrase Book

In the Phrase Book, the English is given in the left-hand column, with the Bulgarian in the middle column. The right-hand column provides a transliteration. The exception is in the Menu Decoder section, where the Bulgarian is given in the left-hand column and the English translation in the right-hand column, for ease of use. Because of the existence of genders in Bulgarian, in a few cases both masculine and feminine forms of a phrase are given. The Phrase Book gives a phonetic guide to the pronunciation of words and phrases used in everyday situations, such as when eating out or shopping.

Guidelines For Pronunciation

The Bulgarian Cyrillic alphabet has 30 letters. The right-hand column of the alphabet, below, demonstrates how Cyrillic letters are pronounced so sounds in English words. However, some letters vary in how they are pronounced according to their position in a word. Several consonants have no equivalent in English.

The Cyrillic Alphabet

А а	a	alimony
Б б	b	bed
В в	v	vet
Г г	g	get
Д д	d	debt
Е е	e	egg
Ж ж	zh	leisure
		(but a little harder)
З з	z	zither
И и	i	see
Й й	y	boy (see note 1)
К к	k	king
Л л	l	loot
М м	m	match
Н н	n	never
О о	o	rob
П п	p	pea
Р р	r	rat (rolling, as in Italian)
С с	s	stop
Т т	t	toffee
У у	u	boot
Ф ф	f	fellow
Х х	h	hello
Ц ц	ts	lets
Ч ч	ch	chair
Ш ш	sh	shove
Щ щ	sht	smashed
		(with a slight roll)
ъ ъ	a or u	(see note 2)
ь		soft sign
		(no sound, but see note 3)
Ю ю	yu	youth
Я я	ya	yak

Notes

1) Й This letter has no distinct sound of its own. It usually softens the preceding vowel.

2) ъ It is pronounced like a in across or u in cut.

3) The soft sign (ь, marked in the pronunciation guide as ') softens the preceding consonant and adds a slight y sound: for instance, n' would sound like ny in 'canyon'.

In Emergency

Help!	Помощ!	Pomosht!
Stop!	Спрете!	Sprete!
Look out!	Внимавайте!	Vnimavayte!
Call a doctor!	Извикайте лекар!	Izvikayte lekar!
Call an ambulance!	Извикайте линейка!	Izvikayte lineyka!
Call the police!	Обадете се на полицията!	Obadete se na politziyata!

Call the fire department!	Извикайте пожарната!	Izvikayte pozharnata!
Where is the nearest telephone?	Къде е най-близкият телефон?	Kade e nay blizkiyat telefon?
Where is the nearest hospital?	Къде е най-близката болница?	Kade e nay blizkata bolnitza?

Communications Essentials

Yes/No	Да/Не	Da/Ne
Please (offering)	Заповядайте	Zapovyadayte
Please (asking)	Моля	Molya
Thank you	Благодаря	Blagodarya
No, thank you	Не, благодаря	Ne, blagodarya
Excuse me, please	Извинете	Izvinete
Hello	Здравейте	Zdraveyte
Good morning	Добро утро	Dobro utro
Good day/hello	Добър ден	Dobar den
(useful general greeting when meeting anyone)		
Good night	Лека нощ	Leka nosht
Goodbye	Довиждане	Dovizhdane
morning	утро	utro
afternoon	следобед	sledobed
evening	вечер	vecher
yesterday	вчера	vchera
today	днес	dnes
tomorrow	утре	utre
here	тук	tuk
there	там	tam
What?	Какво?	Kakvo?
When?	Кога?	Koga?
Why?	Защо?	Zashto?
Where?	Къде?	Kade?

Useful Phrases

How are you?	Как сте?	Kak ste?
Very well, thank you (only I am very well)	Благодаря, добре съм	Blagodarya, dobre sam
Pleased to meet you	Приятно ми е	Priyatno mi e
See you soon!	До скоро!	Do skoro!
Excellent!	Чудесно!	Chudesno!
Is there … here?	Има ли … тук?	Ima li … tuk?
Where can I get …?	Къде мога да намеря …?	Kade moga da namerya …?
How do you get to?	Как се стига до?	Kak se stiga do?
How far is …?	Колко далеч е …?	Kolko dalech e …?
Do you speak English?	Говорите ли английски?	Govorite li angliski?
I can't speak Bulgarian	Не говоря български	Ne govorya balgarski
I don't understand	Не разбирам	Ne razbiram
Can you help me? (Could you help me?)	Бихте ли ми помогнали?	Bihte li mi pomognali?
Please speak slowly	Моля, говорете бавно	Molya, govorete bavno
Sorry!	Извинете!	Izvinete!
Do you have …?	Имате ли …?	Imate li …?

Useful Words

big	голям	golyam
small	малък	malak
hot	горещ	goresht
cold	студен	studen
good	добър	dobar
bad	лош	losh
enough	достатъчно	dostatachno
well	добре	dobre
open	отворен	otvoren
closed	затворен	zatvoren
left	ляво	lyavo

right	**дясно**	*dyasno*
straight on	**направо**	*napravo*
near	**близо**	*blizo*
far	**далеч**	*dalech*
up	**горе**	*gore*
down	**долу**	*dolu*
early	**рано**	*rano*
late	**късно**	*kasno*
entrance	**вход**	*chod*
exit	**изход**	*iz-hod*
toilet WC	**тоалетна**	*toaletna*
free/unoccupied	**свободна**	*svobodna*
free/no charge	**безплатна**	*bezplatna*

Making a Telephone Call

Can I call abroad from here?	**Мога ли да се обадя в чужбина от тук?**	*Moga li da se obadya v chuzhbina ot tuk?*
I would like to call collect	**Искам да се обадя за сметка на търсения абонат**	*Iskam da se obadya za smetka na tarseniya abonat*
Local call	**градски разговор**	*gradski razgovor*
I'll ring back later	**Ще се обадя отново по-късно**	*Shte se obadya otnovo po kasno*
Could I leave a message for him/her …?	**Бихте ли му/ й предали …?**	*Bichte li mu/ i predali …*
Hold on!	**Не затваряйте!**	*Ne zatvaryayte!*
Could you speak up a little, please?	**Моля, бихте ли говорили по-високо?**	*Molya bihte li goborili po visoko?*

Shopping

How much is this?	**Колко струва? това**	*Kolko struva tova?*
I would like …	**Бих искал/ искала …**	*Bih iskal (for a man)/ iskala (for a woman) …*
Do you have …?	**Имате ли …?**	*Imate li …?*
I'm just looking	**Само гледам**	*Samo gledam*
Do you take credit cards?	**Мога ли до платя с кредитна карта?**	*Moga li da platya s kreditna karta?*
What time do you open?	**В колко часа отваряте?**	*V kolko chasa otvaryate?*
What time do you close?	**В колко часа затваряте?**	*V kolko chasa zatvaryate?*
this one	**този**	*tozi*
that one	**онзи**	*onzi*
expensive	**скъп**	*skup*
cheap	**евтин**	*evtin*
size	**размер**	*razmer*
white	**бял**	*byal*
black	**черен**	*cheren*
red	**червен**	*cherven*
yellow	**жълт**	*zhalt*
green	**зелен**	*zelen*
blue	**син**	*sin*
brown	**кафяв**	*kafyav*

Types of Shop

antique dealer *magazin*	**антикварен магазин**	*antikvaren*
baker's	**хлебарница**	*hlebarnitza*
bank	**банка**	*banka*
bar	**бар**	*bar*
bookshop	**книжарница**	*knizharnitza*
café	**кафене**	*kafene*
cake shop	**сладкарница**	*sladkarnitza*
chemist	**аптека**	*apteka*
department store	**универсален магазин**	*universalen magazin*
florist	**цветарски магазин**	*tzvetarski magazin*
greengrocer	**плод-зеленчук**	*plod zelenchuk*
market	**пазар**	*pazar*
newspapers kiosk (and magazines)	**будка за вестници (и списания)**	*budka za vestnitzi (i spisaniya)*
post office	**поща**	*poshta*
shoe shop	**магазин за обувки**	*magazin za obuvki*
souvenir shop	**магазин за сувенири**	*magazin za suveniri*
supermarket	**супермаркет**	*supermarket*
travel agent	**пътническа агенция**	*patnicheska aghentziya*

Staying in a Hotel

Have you any vacancies?	**Имате ли свободни стаи?**	*Imate li svobodni stai?*
Double room with double bed	**двойна стая с двойно легло**	*dvoyna staya s dvoyno leglo*
twin room	**двойна стая с две легла**	*dvoyna staya s dve legla*
single room	**единична стая**	*edinichna staya*
non-smoking	**за непушачи**	*za nepushachi*
room with a bath/shower	**стая с вана/душ**	*staya s vana/dush*
porter	**портиер-пиколо**	*portier pikolo*
key	**ключ**	*klyuch*
I have a reservation	**Имам резервация**	*Imam rezervatziya*

Sightseeing

Bus	**автобус**	*avtobus*
Tram	**трамвай**	*tramvye*
trolley bus	**тролейбус**	*troleybus*
train	**влак**	*vlak*
underground	**метро**	*metro*
bus stop	**автобусна спирка**	*avtobusna spirka*
tram stop	**трамвайна спирка**	*tramviner spirka*
art gallery	**картинна галерия**	*kartinna galeria*
palace	**дворец**	*dvoretz*
cathedral	**катедрала**	*katedrala*
church	**църква**	*tzarkva*
monastery	**манастир**	*manastir*
garden	**градина**	*gradina*
library	**библиотека**	*biblioteka*
museum	**музей**	*muzey*
tourist information	**туристическа информация**	*turisticheska informatziya*
closed for public holiday	**затворено поради официален празник**	*zatvoreno poradi ofitzialen praznik*

Eating Out

A table for … please	**Моля, маса за …**	*Molya, masa za …*
I want to reserve a table	**Искам да резервирам маса**	*Iskam da rezerviram masa*
The bill, please	**Моля, сметката**	*Molya, smetkata*
I am a vegetarian *veghetarianetz/*	**Аз съм вегетарианец**	*Az sam*
	вегетарианка	*veghetarianka*
I'd like … waiter/waitress	**Искам … сервитьор/ сервитьорка**	*Iskam … servityor/ servityorka*
menu	**меню**	*menyu*
wine list	**селекция от вина**	*selektziya ot vina*
chef's special	**специалитет на готвача**	*spetzialitet na gotvacha*
tip	**бакшиш**	*bakshish*
glass	**чаша**	*chasha*
bottle	**бутилка**	*butilka*
knife	**нож**	*nozh*
fork	**вилица**	*vilitza*
spoon	**лъжица**	*lazhitza*
breakfast	**закуска**	*zakuska*
barbecue	**барбекю**	*barbekyu*
lunch	**обяд**	*obyad*
dinner	**вечеря**	*vecherya*
main courses	**основни ястия**	*osnovni yastiya*
starters	**предястия, ордьоври**	*predyastiya, ordyovri*
vegetables	**зеленчуци**	*zelenchutzi*
desserts	**десерти**	*deserti*
rare	**алангле**	*alangle*
well done	**добре опечен**	*dobre opechen*

Menu Decoder

apple	**ябълка**	*yabalka*
mineral water	**минерална вода**	*mineralna voda*
beans	**фасул/боб**	*fasul/bob*
banana	**банан**	*banan*
cherries	**череши**	*chereshi*
lamb	**агнешко**	*agneshko*
peppers	**чушки**	*chushki*
chicken	**пилешко**	*pileshko*
chocolate	**шоколад**	*shokolad*
sugar	**захар**	*zahar*
vinegar	**оцет**	*otzet*

ice cream	сладолед	sladoled
white wine	бяло вино	byalo vino
garlic	чесън	chessan
boiled	варен	varen
mushrooms	гъби	gabi
goulash	гулаш	gulash
fruit	плодове	plodove
fruit juice	плодов сок	plodov sok
onions	лук	luk
fish	риба	riba
meat	месо	meso
coffee	кафе	kafe
bread	хляб	hlyab
potatoes	картофи	kartofi
sausage	наденица	nadenitza
bacon	бекон	bekon
soup	супа	supa
liver	дроб	drob
beef	телешко	teleshko
mustard	горчица	gorchitza
orange	портокал	portokal
oil	олио	olio
tomatoes	домати	domati
steamed	задушен на пара	zadushen na para
pie	пай	pay
(in Bulgarian this refers to sweet pies only)		
pork	свинско	svinsko
fried in batter	паниран	paniran
rice	ориз	oriz
steak	бифтек	biftek
grilled	на скара	na skara
cheese	кашкавал	kashkaval
feta/white cheese	сирене	sirene
salad	салата	salata
salt	сол	sol
ham	шунка	shunka
beer	бира	bira
fried/roasted	пържен/печен	parzhen/pechen
fried potatoes /chips	пържени каргофи	parzheni kartofi
cake, pastry	торта/паста	torta/pasta
sandwich	сандвич	sandvich
sauce	сос	sos
tea	чай	chai
milk	мляко	mlyako
cream	сметана	smetana
seafood	ястия от риба, раци, миди	yastiya ot riba ratzi midi
egg	яйце	yaytze
stuffed	пълнен	palnen
red wine	червено вино	cherveno vino
roll	кифла	kifla
dumplings	кнедли	knedli
watermelon	диня	dinya
melon	пъпеш	papesh
meatballs	кюфтета	kyufteta

Numbers

0	нула	nula
1	едно	edno
2	две	dve
3	три	tri
4	четири	chetiri
5	пет	pet
6	шест	shest
7	седем	sedem
8	осем	osem
9	девет	devet
10	десет	deset
11	единадесет	edinayset
12	дванадесет	dvanayset
13	тринадесет	trinayset
14	четиринадесет	chetirinayset
15	петнадесет	petnayset
16	шестнадесет	shestnayset
17	седемнадесет	sedemnayset
18	осемнадесет	osemnayset
19	деветнадесет	devetnayset
20	двадесет	dvayset
21	двадесет и едно	dvayset i edno
22	двадесет и две	dvayset i dve
30	тридесет	triyset
31	тридесет и едно	triyset i edno
32	тридесет и две	triyset i dve
40	четиридесет	chetirset
50	петдесет	petdeset
60	шестдесет	shestdeset
70	седемдесет	sedemdeset
80	осемдесет	osemdeset
90	деветдесет	devetdeset
100	сто	sto
110	сто и десет	sto i deset
200	двеста	dvesta
300	триста	trista
1000	хиляда	hilyada
10,000	десет хиляди	deset hilyadi
1,000,000	един милион	edin milion

Time

one minute	една минута	edna minuta
hour	час	chas
half an hour	половин час	polovin chas
Sunday	неделя	nedelya
Monday	понеделник	ponedelnik
Tuesday	вторник	vtornik
Wednesday	сряда	sryada
Thursday	четвъртък	chetvartak
Friday	петък	petak
Saturday	събота	sabota